D1610519

Beyond Seven Years
In Tibet

By the same author

Seven Years in Tibet

The White Spider

Tibet is My Country

I Come from the Stone Age

Ladakh

Return to Tibet

Lost Lhasa

Beyond Seven Years in Tibet

Heinrich Harrer

Introduction by
His Holiness the Dalai Lama

Translated by
Tim Carruthers

Published by Labyrynth Press
2007

First published in Germany under the title Mein Leben by Ullstein 2002

This translation first published in Great Britain 2007 by
Labyrynth Press

1

Distributed in Great Britain by
Cordee Limited
3a de Montfort Street
Leicester LE1 7HD

Labyrynth Press
14 MacFarlan Street
South Yarra, Victoria, 3141
Australia

A copy of the British Library Cataloguing in Publication
Data is available from the British Library.

ISBN 978-1-921196-00-3

Editor Simon Walliss
Cover by Greg Loveder
Typeset by Raymond Sheils
Index by David Sisson
Printed and bound in Great Britain by
Mackays of Chatham Ltd, Chatham Kent

CONTENTS

LIST OF ILLUSTRATIONS

Section I

The Penker family: Aunt Marianne, my mother Johanna, grandmother Johanna, grandfather Andreas, Uncle Andreas and Uncle Johann, who died young

The house in Obergossen, above Hüttenberg, where I was born. To the left is the ladder that led to the attic

As a young boy, with sledge and woolly hat in the photographer's studio

The family in 1923. My father Josef, mother with my brother Pepperl in her arms, and my sister Lydia. Ruth had not yet been born

With my grandmother, Aunt Marianne and my brother and sisters in 1935. Ruth, the youngest, is sitting on my lap

In the mid 1930s

At the 1934 Styrian State Downhill Skiing Championships

In Sexten, South Tyrol, where I ran a ski school for hotel guests. Twice a week I held lessons for the youngsters of the village

High spirits on the Tauplitz in the Salzkammergut region of Styria, where I ran a ski school for several years. On the far right is my friend Fritz Ehrenfried.

First ascent of the West face of the Sturzhahn. Shortly before the photograph was taken I had fallen fifty metres.

During the first ascent of the North Face of the Eiger in July 1938. My anorak was badly torn and provided little warmth

The four members of the first ascent team after the successful climb: Wiggerl Vörg, Anderl Heckmair, Fritz Kasparek and Heinrich Harrer (from right to left)

On the boat to Bombay, during the 1939 Nanga Parbat Reconnaissance Expedition. Hans Lobenhoffer and I dubbin our boots.

In the POW camp at Dehra Dun in the 1940s. From left to right: Herbert Paidar, Hans Lobenhoffer, Wiggerl Schmaderer, Heinrich Harrer and Lutz Chicken

On Chomolhari, December 1950. The brother of my friend Wangdu accompanies me on an excursion to the border of Bhutan

1948 in Lhasa. I had bought the American military greatcoat in the market.

A monk wearing a "Yeti hat" that was actually made from the wool of a Tibetan mountain goat

Peter Aufschnaiter and I chat to the Tibetan Ministers Tsarong and Chekapa at Kyitchu about plans to build a dam

Coocoola, the Princess of Sikkhim, lived in Lhasa and was married to the son of Minister Punkhang

Peter Aufschnaiter with Tessla, one of Tsarong's daughters, during a visit to the holy place of Tra Yerpa

View of the Potala, the seat of the Dalai Lama, from the roof of the Medical School. Peter Aufschnaiter surveys the site

My apartment in Lhasa was open house for my friends. On the left, the Foreign Minister's youngest son, whose life I saved; on the right, Wangchuk, who later became Governor of Gyantse

1951 in the Chumbi Valley. The Dalai Lama receives a 2500 year old Buddhist relic

The American radio journalist Lowell Thomas (far right) visited Lhasa with his son in 1949. In the middle of the picture is the Monk's Foreign Minister Liuchar Dzasa

My first meeting with my son Peter in January 1952. I am giving him a pair of Tibetan boots.

Reception at Ullstein Verlag in Frankfurt am Main in 1957: Bruno Dechamps, the publisher Frederick Ullstein, Thor Heyerdahl and Heinrich Harrer (from left)

I visited Sven Hedin a few months before his death in November 1952 at his apartment in Stockholm

Addressing the committee of the Explorer's Club in New York in 1954. Shortly afterwards I was made an honorary member.

In Alaska in 1954. During the trip I made three first ascents

Breaking trail on a thirty metre overhanging cornice on Mount Deborah

With Edmund Hillary in Nepal

With Bing Crosby and friends at the Kitzbühel Golf Club

In 1964 I met the Dalai Lama at the Sarnath Deer Park, where he was attending a conference of Buddhists from all over the world

With the Dalai Lama's mother and her two sons, Geneva 1959. We ate delicious traditional momos with dinner

Section II

Homecoming, Summer 1962. After the New Guinea Expedition my wife Carina came to meet me at the airport in Frankfurt am Main

During the 1962 New Guinea Expedition. My Leica arouses great interest

Writing my journal in Suriname, with my new invention, a hammock with an integral rain cover and mosquito net, in the background

With Carina at the home of Tenzing Norgay and his wife Daku in Darjeeling. We took the Apso puppy that Carina is stroking back to Europe with us

Family adventures, mid-1980s. Irene and Birgit have pieces of fresh sugar cane and I am holding a bunch of small Indian bananas

With the Dalai Lama and Senator Günther Klinge at Lake Starnberg in 1990

Herbert Kessler presents me with the Golden Humboldt Medal in Brunswick in 1985

March 1995. The Austrian President Thomas Klestil awards me the Fellowship of the Austrian Academy of Sciences. My friend Fritz Heppner looks on

With Jetsun Pemala, the sister of the Dalai Lama, in Dharamsala in 1981

With Rinchen Drolma Taring, one of Tsarong's three wives, in Dehra Dun in 1990

Drinking millet beer with Hermann Beilhack and Alois Anwander in Sikkim in 1990

Section III

Expedition to French Guyana, 1969. The joy of adventure is something that accompanied me throughout my life.

Ruwenzori. The tent offered little protection from the damp equatorial climate

The last metres to the summit of the 5,119 m Mount Stanley in the Ruwenzori Mountains

At the source of the stone axes, New Guinea 1962. The stones are heated and broken up into smaller fragments for ease of transport

After my tumble down the waterfall I was carried by the Dani in an improvised stretcher

My Dutch companion Bert Huizenga pays off our Dani porters after our ascent of Carstenz Pyramid. To his right is our interpreter.

With the Xingu Indians in South America in 1966. The funeral pole, known as a kwarup, is prepared for a ceremony

Huka-huka wrestling. The loser is the first wrestler to touch the ground with any part of his body other than his legs

With Carina and one of the carved ancestor statues that I brought back from my 1972 Borneo expedition

After the village shaman had sacrificed a chicken to his ancestors I was allowed to remove the blood-spattered statue

1975. The Jarawa people of the Andaman Islands were astonished at the sight of us fully clothed Europeans

An Onge man shows off his nautilus shell. The shells were once used as drinking vessels

An aboriginal inhabitant of Sentinel Island strikes a threatening pose with his spear. His tribe shun all contact with the outside world

Filming in East Africa in the late 1960s

Wagenia fish traps in the Congo. The Wagenia walk along the poles like circus tightrope walkers

Many of my trips took me to Africa. With two Ugandan women

A warrior of the Hadendoa tribe, armed with a sword and a shield made of hippopotamus leather. I visited the Hadendoa during a trip to

Africa in 1971

The Karamajong in the north east of Uganda drink the blood of animals mixed with milk

A yogi demonstrates how he is able to slow, or even stop, his heartbeat

Washing in the ice cold glacier water of the Ganges in Gangotri is an important ritual for a pilgrim. The photo was taken during my 1974 trip to the sources of the Ganges.

The traditional Nepalese "farewell" gesture, at the foot of Annapurna, Western Nepal

A Tibetan trashi gomang cabinet, traditionally used to store religious artefacts

On the golf course in Lhasa at 4000 metres. The thin air means that even complete novices can hit long tee shots!

In 1987 my friend Helmut Kreuzer and I visited the semi-nomadic Sakteng tribe in the north east of Bhutan

With Tuksey Rinpoche, the highest incarnation of Samdenling Monastery, during a visit to Darjeeling in 1994

I returned to Tibet in 1982 and met several old acquaintances

With the Dalai Lama at our holiday home in Hüttenberg on my 80th birthday, July 6th 1992

Tibet 1982. The cliff with the Blue Buddha is all that remains of the eight kilometre pilgrims' path around Lhasa

With the artist Balthus in May 1999. Here I am presenting him with the traditional Tibetan good luck scarf

Helmut Newton came to Hüttenberg in August 1997 to take my photograph for Vanity Fair

With David Thewlis and Brad Pitt, who played the roles of Peter Aufschnaiter and I in the film "Seven Years in Tibet", at our house in Hüttenberg in September 1996

The film director Jean-Jacques Annaud visited us on three occasions. Here, I show him the Heinrich Harrer Museum

At my desk with my wife Carina

Sketches of Tibet   127

MAPS

FOREWORD

THE DALAI LAMA

When he left Europe in the Spring of 1939, setting off to reconnoitre the great Himalayan peak Nanga Parbat, Heinrich Harrer probably had no inkling of how much further he would travel nor how long he would be away. Not long after, the Second World War broke out and he was interned in British India as an enemy alien. Eventually, a characteristic and restless urge for freedom drove him to break out of his prison and take his chances in Tibet. Of course, this story is by now well-known because Harrer's account of it, *Seven Years in Tibet*, not only became an international best-seller, but has also since been made into a film. Nevertheless, these were events of significance to us both, for without them he and I would not have become good friends.

Despite the epoch making changes that were going on in the world beyond Tibet's borders, I was growing up in a sheltered environment remote from it all. Heinrich Harrer helped me form my first ideas of the world at large. He taught me the rudiments of science and other modern ideas. All of this later served me well and I remain grateful to this day for what I learnt from him then.

We Tibetans generally attribute such propitious meetings to the positive result of past connections. Be that as it may, Heinrich Harrer made firm friends with many Tibetans and developed a strong and enduring affection for Tibet during the years he lived among us. His was an affection and friendship that remained strong until he died. We Tibetans will always be grateful for the way his books and the many lectures he gave throughout his life, created a tremendous awareness of Tibet and our people. His experience was unique, but he shared it widely.

It gives me great pleasure to know that before he passed away, Harrer completed this account of his life so that readers can learn something of his childhood and background in Austria and how his Tibetan experiences shaped his subsequent life. Even in his old age, our good friend continued to be active in the struggle for Tibet's right to freedom and I personally remain grateful to him for it. We will not forget him.

THE DALAI LAMA

March 1, 2007

PREFACE

My life began in a little village in the mountains of Carinthia. Nurtured in the rich soil of a large family, my boyhood dreams flourished, dreams which were to be fulfilled over the course of many years. During my globetrotting expedition years I had many companions with whom I still have contact today. I would like to say to these contemporaries that on several occasions here I have taken the liberty of summarising experiences and events and that these do not always appear in strictly chronological order in the text. Nor has it been possible, unfortunately, to mention each of my companions by name or to list all of our mutual adventures – there have simply been too many.

In my active years, although I never thought about writing an autobiography, I recorded each expedition in minute detail in my diaries. Now that I am physically not quite so fully operational as a result of my age, I would like to tell the younger generations about my most important expeditions and journeys and look back on my long life with all its successful, and not so successful, endeavours. The good events are easy to describe. The unpleasant ones, caused largely by my own mistakes, I at first repressed, but after thinking long and hard, and with the benefit of hindsight, I decided to record those, too, since they have valuable lessons to teach. I seldom use the word "luck" – and never expect it in games of chance – so when I say I have had a lucky life, what I mean is that I have been fortunate with my role models and my climbing partners. Nor do I feel able to ascribe certain events to bad luck. Whenever I have experienced "bad luck" or misfortune it has always been me that made the mistake that caused it.

This, then, is the chronicle of my long life. It contains my memories of many great adventures and interesting encounters. My life has developed logically, as a direct result of the things I have learned and the disposition I inherited – no more, no less.

When elderly people are asked what it is they have done in order to reach such an advanced age, they mostly reply that they have lived a sensible life. That is something that I can not claim and anyway, I would have found that too boring. It is all about joy and quality of life and even if one were to forgo all pleasure there would still be no guarantee of a long life. In the end it all comes down to one thing: "Everything lies in the hands of God, who knows all the world," as a shaman of the Ruwenzori once told me.

In this book I have tried to pass on several pieces of advice to young people, not because I am a know-it-all but in order to warn them of the possible pitfalls and perhaps inspire them to greater things. My expedition reports always tend to be written in an understated style. This can be confirmed by my friends and companions. Perhaps it was my determination that contributed to the fact that many of my youthful dreams were to become fulfilled. In my experience, the words of the poet Angelus Silesius, "In times of danger and hardship, the middle way spells death", have often proved true and I know from experience that a half-hearted and indecisive approach on the part of an expedition leader will transfer itself to the participants, the porters and any potentially hostile locals, whereas decisiveness will have the opposite effect, defusing the dangerous situation and turning it to good advantage.

In an autobiography one can not avoid writing about commendable experiences, even if this may leave an aftertaste of smugness. Nor do I wish to draw a veil over the depressing and often hurtful experiences. They, too, are a part of life and they contribute to the transformation and purification of the soul.

If I am successful in communicating all of this to the reader, this description of my life will have fulfilled its aim.

BOYHOOD DREAMS

I was born into the world of mountains and valleys that is Carinthia. The little windows of our house opened onto an expansive view of the Julian Alps. To explore these mountains alone, one lifetime would not be sufficient – or so I thought as a child. My birth certificate is kept at the church of the market town of Hüttenberg in the Görtschitztal. Five hundred metres above the narrow confines of the valley lies the scattered community of Knappenberg and higher up the hillside, in Obergossen, is where you will find the house in which I was born, on 6th July 1912. It was a simple home, one of the many miners' cottages that stand on that hillside. It had no running water and no electricity and in the evenings we sat in the meagre light of an old petroleum lamp.

The only living room in the house was the room next to the kitchen. It was here that our whole family life took place. There was the narrow bed in which grandmother had given birth to her children and had died peacefully, cared for by her family. My mother brought us into the world in the same bed. Against the wall stood the only cupboard, with my grandfather's initials carved between the colourful, rustic-style flowers. It came from the village of Penk in Carinthia's Mölltal. For us children, the temptation to open this cupboard was great. The inside of the door panels depicted a fairytale little world. They were adorned with amusing little emblems of church-goers and colourful images of the fire brigade and the May Day Festival. Old bunches of dried flowers hung there, too, and still gave off their soft, sweet scent. I can only dimly recall the inside of the cupboard but I can still picture the Heferl, the pretty beakers with their painted-on flowers, decorated with the names of places of pilgrimage or family members, and the small, crude wooden boxes next to them, with bituminous rocks and ointments made of red elderberries and fragrant balsam or marigolds, which were used to soften the cows' udders when milking. High up on the cupboard, too high for us children to reach, the glittering crystals and coloured rocks that grandfather had brought back from the mine were kept. Even today, you will find these modest collections of pyrites, calcites, calcedonites, amethysts and garnets from the surrounding mines in almost every house in our mining community. The cupboard also housed our home apothecary. We had collected many of the herbs ourselves: arnica, eyebright, centaury, balsamic ointment, valerian drops, red elderberry oil and caraway, together with dressings and bandages made from strips of old linen, which were "sterilised" with the hot flat iron before being applied to large wounds.

Right next to the cupboard there was a small table. On this stood a gramophone with a huge horn, a picture of a dog and the words "His Masters' Voice". We only had two records. One was a scratchy recording of a woman's voice singing 'Who We Trusted'; the other was 'The Snow Waltz' by Thomas Koschart, probably the best-known melody by a Carinthian composer.

The pantry was in a lean-to built onto the side of the house nearest the hill. Fat chunks of pork hung from the ceiling and there was a basket in which loaves of bread were stored. We only baked once a month and would only then start on the previous month's supply. We would have preferred to eat the fresh, aromatic bread right away and would have certainly devoured a whole loaf at one sitting but each had to last several days.

The barn lay a short distance from the main house. I often used to prefer to sleep in the straw rather than inside the crowded house. A steep wooden ladder led up to a platform, where there was a contraption like a wind machine that was used to separate the wheat from the chaff or the leaves from the cranberries. On the ground floor there was a stable with a cow, a goat and a pig. Next door there was a cellar dug into the hillside by my grandfather, the walls supported by pit props, rounded wooden staves of the type used down the mine. My grandfather was particularly skilful in fashioning these props and had turned the decorative carving of them into something of an art form. We stored little barrels of pear juice and strong blackcurrant wine in the cellar.

We did not enjoy the questionable good fortune of prosperity, but we did have the security and harmony of a large family. Grandfather Penker, my mother's father, had left Penk for Hüttenberg in 1880, since only one of his many brothers and sisters could take over the big family farm at Penk. He found work in the mine. "Die Alpine", the local industrial concern, ran the two-thousand-year-old Ferrum Norikum mine and iron ore had been extracted from the mine since Roman times. Huge areas of woodland were planted to meet the demand for charcoal to smelt the iron. The hillsides are still covered in trees today and many can not be built on as they hide big mine shafts. Everyone who lived in the area was employed by Die Alpine and worked shifts down the mine. I will never forget the nightly spectacle when the shift changed and the miners made their way home or set off to work. The rhythmic swinging of the carbide lamps and the mysterious way they lit up the dark edges of the woods was a fairytale sight. Once the carbide in the lamp was used up, the remainder was tipped out into the ditch at the side of the road. No one gave much thought to pollution in those days.

My grandmother Maria was almost one hundred years old and was treated with due reverence by everybody. Most of the time she sat in the corner by the warm oven. Everyone used the formal "Sie" form when addressing her, as a mark of respect. When I was at home during the holidays we would drink a glass of blackcurrant wine together and she would tell me over and over again "You should live to be a hundred!" She always used to nod off. She died just a few days before her hundredth birthday.

Aunty Marianne, a tiny woman but quick as a weasel, was also part of the family. From time to time I was allowed to accompany her down to the Forestry Office to get our wood collecting permit. We had to pay fifty groschen to the landowner, Count Henkel von Donnersmark and in return we could scour the forest floor for odd bits of firewood and take them home to burn. The Master Forester seemed unapproachable and quite scary to me, like the Director of the Hüttenberg Mining Authority, and we were glad to leave his office once we had acquired the necessary authorisation for our little venture.

Aunty Marianne was not married. A sign on her door read: "Master Seamstress". As a child she would often take me with her when she went to work for the wealthy farmers at the neighbouring estates. We had to set off when it was still dark, since it was a long way from our little house in Obergossen to Sankt Johann am Zirbitzkogel, where the farmers lived. It was during these early morning walks that I first learned what it felt like to be frightened – a feeling that was to befall me on several occasions in later years in trackless jungle or when coming face to face with an unknown tribe. I was frightened when the branches creaked or an owl screeched in the dark woods and how happy I was when my aunt would gather up her dark woollen skirt and I could stumble along behind, guided by the bright white of her long petticoats. Later, as an adult, I sometimes wished for such a guiding light to show me the way.

And then there was Uncle Andreas, who played the violin and the clarinet and who introduced me to the big, wide world. I listened to music with him and he also taught me to draw, but the most exciting thing for me was the collection of newspapers that he kept up in the loft. We used to rummage around in the piles of paper and I would gaze in rapt fascination at pictures of faraway lands, dark-skinned people and Ice Mountains at the Equator. When the circus came to town and set up camp on a field in Gutaring about eight kilometres away, there was no holding me back. It was not the clowns or the performing poodles that held such a magical attraction for me but the mysterious foreign people in the circus director's so-called "human show". The Indian with a large plate in his lower lip caused a little shiver of fear and there was an Eskimo with narrow eyes and jewellery made of ivory that did not come from an elephant but from one of the large mammals that lived up in the cold oceans of the far north. I was irresistibly drawn to the two Papuans (perhaps it was the name, or their splendid shocks of frizzy hair) but I felt sad at the lot of these people, trapped in a world that could never be theirs. I imagined how differently these proud hunters must have behaved in their home country, following the tracks of some wild animal in the jungle. Now they stood, stiff and unmoving, by the caravans until the circus director dismissed them to get on with their work and we visitors moved on from the human show to the animal show. I was starting to get an idea of the big, wide world even before I was able to read and write.

Uncle Andreas died when I was eight years old. He had been ill for a long time. This was the first time I had encountered death. I came home from school one day and there was a feeling that something unusual had happened. "Uncle Andreas has died," they said. Death – that was something deeply disturbing, even though this was not a particularly tragic event for me. I can still see the coffin as it was carried from the house and I remember someone putting a black armband around my right arm. The armband was the thing that impressed me most about this new experience and the whole time I wore it I would twist and turn so that everyone could see it.

My parents, Josef and Johanna Harrer, had met in Semmering, where my mother worked as a maid. My father was from a small farm in Styria and had a job with the Post Office in Bruck an der Mur. He was a kindly, dutiful and reserved man and had little understanding for my dreams and yearnings, unlike my mother, who was understanding, hungry for knowledge and epitomised the feeling of warmth and togetherness of a rural family. She always understood and supported me. Her caring nature and her wealth of stories were much loved constants throughout my childhood.

Father was away a lot, as his job entailed riding in the post carriage of the train, sorting the letters and passing them out at each station on the line. Since there were also valuables and cash amongst the post and he was on his own in the carriage, they chose him for his reliability and his powerful build. The nature of his trips meant that he often had to sleep away from home and so I spent a lot of time alone with my mother, particularly during the war, when father was called up, wounded in action and spent a long time in hospital.

There was no heating in our apartment in Bruck and my mother and I would often sit on the still warm stove in the evenings. We peeled apples to make apple sauce and dried the peel for tea. We used to compete with each other to see who could make the longest strip of peel. We would sometimes do one a metre long and as a rule it was me that ended up the smiling winner. It only later became clear to me that Mother generally lost on purpose. She was a clever teacher.

I remember with affection the long hours of bible study with Mother. She was a devout woman and had joined the Church of the Seventh-day Adventists at an early age. Back then, this was a small religious community with no more than twenty or thirty members in Austria. She cooked wholly vegetarian meals and observed the Sabbath as a day of rest. Once a month, the Adventists would come to our house for a prayer meeting. Mother would use the occasion to make a contribution to her chosen religious fellowship – a not inconsiderable ten per cent of my father's monthly take home pay. Although he used to moan about the "useless Brothers in their fancy black clothes", Father tolerated what Mother did. He got a bonus payment for the trips he made on the mail train, which he kept as pocket money and used to pay for the occasional social Virginia cigarette, rum for his tea and family days out.

I was the oldest of four brothers and sisters; the oldest by far, in fact, since the war intervened between me and my sister Lydia. She was born nine years after me, followed by Josef, in 1924, and Ruth, in 1931. It seemed perfectly natural that I should have to look after my three lively young brothers and sisters when my parents were busy, but I was really frightened of dropping baby Ruth when I had to carry her up the smooth stone steps, since whenever I did something wrong, punishment was always forthcoming. This usually fell to my father to administer but afterwards he was always sorry and would ask me if I fancied going out for a walk with him. When we stopped for a rest, he would pull a whole ring of cured sausage out of his rucksack, which I really loved. The Emmentaler cheese I would eat with salt and pepper but without bread.

I remember Bruck with particular affection as we had a small allotment there. Father used to do the heavy digging work, while Mother would plant the vegetables. There was a summer house where we kept the garden tools and a little peach tree. The fruit was so juicy you had to hold it away from you when you were eating it.

My favourite apples were the Norfolk pippins and Blenheim pippins, varieties that you only rarely see nowadays and only on private orchards or small holdings. The apple schnapps I later bought in Vaduz smelled of Holstein cox and ever since then these have been my favourite type, but unfortunately they are only in season for a few weeks a year. We got damson plums from the parish priest at the little pilgrimage church about ten kilometres walk away along a dusty country road lined with apple trees. I used to pull a little cart and Mother always knew exactly where the trees with the best varieties were. We were allowed to collect windfalls for our own personal use. Mother also knew where to pick the nicest wild flowers at any given time of the year. If it was a mild start to the winter we could see the red buds of the Christmas rose poking through the thin cover of snow as early as Christmas time itself.

We spent the holidays in Obergossen. I used to look after all the cows while I was there. Since each family only had one cow we took it in turns to do the job. Sometimes there would be two or three lads looking after them. Each cow had a name and a bell. I could tell by the sound of the bells whether all the cows were close by. Early one morning, when I was herding the cows up to the grazing pasture, I found a deserted beehive in the woods. I could tell by the colourful flowers on the front that it was one of ours, painted by my uncle. I ran back and excitedly reported my find. Father reacted immediately and was just about to walk the twenty kilometres to the police station but Mother stopped him. She reckoned that it must have been someone who was worse off than we were and that since it was only petty theft of food it was not a punishable offence anyway.

Whenever our parents had a difference of opinion or an argument that the children were not supposed to hear, Mother would send me to fetch water. We did not have a gushing spring but Grandfather had dug a ten metre shaft into the hillside about a hundred metres from the house, lined it with pit props to prevent it collapsing and made a gate to stop animals getting in. The water dripped from the walls and formed a puddle of clear water and I used to kneel down and fill a bucket using a ladle. As a young boy I found the noises in there a bit eerie and I was always glad to shut the creaking gate behind me again.

I liked going off with Father and our neighbours to fell trees. They used a long logcutter's saw with a wooden handle at each end. They worked on their knees, two to a saw, and when the top of the tree started to sway, Father would chop a notch in the trunk and the tree would fall with a crash in the right direction. What I really enjoyed was snack time, when I was allowed to cut off a piece of yellowish-white bacon with my own pocket knife. Since Mother only cooked vegetarian food I felt the need to eat meat now and then, even if it was a chunk of rancid old bacon. This was a dietary deficiency I had noticed back in Bruck.

It was the post-war period and we received aid parcels full of useful foodstuffs from America, which we gratefully accepted. I will never forget one of the parcels, which, apart from to the various groceries, also contained a piece of bright green velvet. Unfortunately, it was only large enough to make one child's suit but Auntie Marianne set to work straight away with great diligence. The product of her labours was a pair of short trousers and a jacket with a belt. You can imagine what I looked like with my red hair in that green suit! Thus attired, I marched off in despair to kindergarten, where I had to endure the scorn and mockery of the other children.

Since my father was a member of the Socialist Party, I was sent at the age of eleven to the *Children's Friends Association*, a children's organisation that was run in accordance with the ideals of Friedrich Engels. Here, you could learn a trade and at weekends we would go hiking in the woods with a red banner. One day, a young lad who was learning book binding played a stupid trick on me and blew the dust from the book he was working on straight into my eyes. I staggered out of the community centre in great pain and, much to the displeasure of my father, changed to the German Gymnastics Club, where I remained a junior member until we moved to Graz in 1927.

During a trip with the new club to a gymnastics festival up in the hills, I got caught in a heavy thunderstorm. I sprinted across the last meadow before the hut but the pressure wave caused by a bolt of lightning lifted me bodily into the air and flung me to the ground. The others had seen it all happen and carried me, unconscious, into the sanctuary of the hut, where I soon recovered from the shock.

At the age of six, I started at primary school in Bruck. My memories of the time I spent there are all good ones. They held a ceremony there in 1999, when they unveiled a brass plaque that commemorated the five years I had attended the school and I received a copy of an old class register that showed I had got top marks in most of my subjects. I had forgotten that I was such a model pupil, but the only person from my old class still alive, an old man like myself, confirmed that I always sat in the first row.

Primary school was followed by four years of secondary schooling at the Realschule. My favourite teacher was Franz Musger. He was an athletic young man, who taught us sport and gymnastics, subjects that I enjoyed immensely. One Monday, he did not appear for our lesson and a colleague of his informed us that he had drowned in the new reservoir. We could not believe it; such a strong swimmer – drowned! He had severed an artery on a concrete post under the water and had bled to death.

All of the pupils attended the funeral of this teacher, whom we greatly admired. I wanted to lay some roses on his grave, but where on earth was I to get roses without even a schilling in my pockets? I took a deep breath and trotted off bravely to one of the big houses near the College of Forestry that had the most beautiful flowers growing in the garden. Timidly, I begged for a few roses for my dead teacher. The owner of the house was happy to grant a young boy's request and I thanked him and set off for the cemetery clutching a big bunch of dog roses.

I walked past the College of Forestry every day on my way to school. You could hardly see the building for the trees around it. As a young child, I had dreamed of becoming a forester, rather than a train driver or a station master with a bright red cap. I fell in love with a girl in my class with blond pigtails whose father was a forester. It was a fairytale romance and I finally made up my mind to become a forester. In my dreams, I imagined risking my life to defend the forester's daughter against poachers and bears. She, of course, had no idea of my feelings for her or the pain I felt when I saw her on the way to the station in the company of a young man. Every day she took the train to Mixnitz nineteen kilometres away, where her father worked. On my eighty-fifth birthday I received a card from an elderly lady with a note that said I would probably not remember her but that she had gone to school with me and still lived in Mixnitz; whereupon, after more than seventy years, I finally plucked up the courage to write back and admit to her that she had been my first love.

My dreams of becoming a forester also faded with time and in 1924 I decided to become a teacher. I had a female teacher who really brought the subject of geography alive and it became my favourite subject. She used to accompany my class on walks and would tell us over and over again that if we wanted to see the world we first had to learn about our local area. Even then, I wanted to study something to do with nature, so what better thing to learn than geography, a subject that covers so much and contains elements of biology, zoology, botany, geology, climatology and everything from glaciology to ethnology?

My love of nature was something that was to stay with me throughout my life and was also due, in part, to my early mountaineering experiences. The things I discovered on my first climbing trip! My desire to experience new and unusual things was nourished by these trips and I longed to explore all of those areas that were blank on the map.

At fifteen I took my first trip into the mountains and made an ascent of the steep limestone peak of Mangart in the Julian Alps, an incredible climb that opened up a whole new world to me. At first, the route followed a trail through a beautiful old forest and up through marshland to the twin Weissenfels Lakes. I trudged on, skirting an Alpine pasture, and climbed a heap of rubble that stretched up for a kilometre to a pass at two thousand metres. The reality of the situation seemed unreal to me; fear and joy overwhelmed me. I had to cope with the "butterflies", too, of course – that fear in the pit of your stomach that makes itself felt in dangerous situations. The feeling was particularly intense on Mangart, since I was climbing without a partner and had to deal with my fear alone.

I saw my first eagles circling above the steep scree slope and soon came across the dead chamois they were eyeing as carrion. As I reached the narrow ridge between the Greater and Lesser Mangart, another world lay spread out before me and I marvelled at the eagle as it soared over the ridge into the next valley, taking just seconds to fly over the valleys and ridges that would have taken me days of walking. On one side of the narrow path was a vertical wall of rock; on the other, the abyss. Even today I can still remember the spine-chilling votive plaque dedicated to the huntsman who had met his end here. It was here, too, that I discovered and picked my first edelweiss.

After climbing the Greater Mangart, and then the rather more difficult Lesser Mangart, the descent route led down the long rubble slope and past the cadaver of the dead chamois, losing a thousand metres in vertical height before reaching a little Alpine pasture with a freshwater spring. I stuck my head under the cold water but was rudely awakened from my daydreams by a heavy blow to the head from behind. It was the herdsman. "You don't want to be drinking all that cold water, son. The hut is full of sour milk, buttermilk and other delicious stuff," he said. He had thumped me because he wanted to do me a favour. Eighty years old and with pure white hair, the herdsman was a very interesting chap. He told me he spoke eight languages, had travelled the world as a ship's cook and had then retired to work as an Alpine herdsman. The stories that wise, well-travelled old man told me were something I will never forget.

Even as a young lad, I was interested in international sporting events and in order to keep myself informed I built myself a crystal radio receiver. There was a First World War shooting range near the school and on the hill behind the targets there were still lots of lead bullets lying around, which I cashed in at the local ironmonger's to raise the necessary funds to buy the parts for the radio set. Working to the instructions in a handicraft magazine, I wound a length of thin wire around a cardboard tube, secured it with a piece of antenna wire and went and bought the most important, and most expensive, component – a pyrite crystal. I searched for a radio station with a thin, pointed strip of metal and could receive broadcasts through a set of headphones via the crystal detector.

I had taken the poker from the kitchen stove to forage about for the lead bullets and when I returned home that evening, instead of at midday, I got a frosty reception. Remorsefully, I replaced the poker but father punished me, the same way he had been chastised as a child.

Many years later, I was still listening to sports broadcasts on my crystal radio set. On 22nd July, 1938, Max Schmeling, the World Heavyweight Champion, was fighting Joe Louis. It was four o' clock in the morning by the time I had tuned the set in to the right station, only to hear the reporter's voice saying over and over again "It's over!". Schmeling lost his rematch with Louis in the first round.

In 1927, Father was transferred from Bruck to Graz and that lovely town again opened up a whole new world for me. I became a junior member of the Austrian Alpine Club. The Club library was a fascinating place, since it contained expedition and travel reports, which I devoured hungrily. It was also the place I discovered the Asian travel books and expedition accounts written by the great Swedish explorer Sven Hedin, which were to mean so much to me in later years. I made many trips to the mountains with the Alpine Club and mountaineering and skiing soon became my favourite sports and ones in which I was soon to have some measure of success.

My old skis, made from the curved slats of a wine barrel and with leather strap bindings, soon proved unsuitable for my abilities and I saved hard to buy a new pair. The princely sum of thirty-five schillings was hard earned. I picked snowdrops and daffodils, which I sold for a few pennies. From Uncle Andreas, I learned the art of writing Gothic script and I patiently recarved the inscriptions on old, faded grave crosses and decorated them with angels and wreaths of flowers. I got one schilling per person per month for cleaning the family's shoes and a schilling a day from the local publican for setting up the pins in the bowling alley. The pile of coins in my old savings tin grew gradually, until I was able to buy my very first pair of real skis. In the house in Obergossen, where I spent all of the long school holidays, there was a colourful catalogue from the mail order company Kastner & Öhler with a pair of wonderful ash skis for thirty-five schillings, complete with Huitfeld bindings and hazelnut poles and a very attractive one-year guarantee against breakage. The first time I used them, the tips snapped off and by the time they came back from the repair shop the winter was long gone.

At sixteen, I joined a skiing and climbing club, got my hands on a good pair of skis and took part in a few small, local competitions. Getting to the competition venue was a tough physical challenge in itself. I had to set off at daybreak and walk for hours to get to the start on time as there were no ski lifts. I frequently returned home the winner and although my parents did not always display what I felt to be the appropriate enthusiasm, they were proud nonetheless when my name appeared in the newspaper and my father's workmates mentioned it to him. The prize was often a green laurel wreath, which we kept in the kitchen. Only once did Mother show a slight lack of sympathy with the cause, when I returned home with what I thought was a particularly nice garland of oak leaves tied with a white and green ribbon, the colours of the province of Styria. My acquisition was greeted with a look of disappointment and the comment that she could not use the leaves to season her potato goulash. She was a practically-minded woman, my mother.

Since my Mangart trip, the magic word for me had been Geography. Luckily, there were some clever and understanding teachers at the grammar school in Graz, and my mother persuaded them to let me study. The first priority was Sport Studies, they thought, and since you had to enrol for a second subject at the Faculty of Philosophy at the University there was no doubt for me that this could only be Geography. Thus it was that, in addition to keeping myself physically fit, I was encouraged to study natural history and ethnology, which were to prove very useful on my later expeditions.

I had a happy time studying in Graz and it afforded me the ideal opportunity to combine my cultural and sporting interests. I often visited the theatre and the opera and was always the first in the queue for the cheap standing area tickets. I usually managed to get the only spot in the upper tier where you could lean against the balcony rail but I could only dream of the raspberry schnapps and the delicious looking ham rolls they served during the interval. I trained in all weathers on the Schlossberg and used to take a shower afterwards in the gymnasium. I swam in the military swimming pool or in the River Mur, even though the water temperature was only twelve degrees. I never really joined in the other students' weekend festivities; I preferred to get out into the countryside and lose myself in my own thoughts up in the mountains. I loved the solitude and the way it stimulated my plans and dreams.

When I went climbing in the Styrian Gesäuse, I visited the Benedictine Monastery at Admont, which has a unique, nine-hundred-year-old Baroque reading room that houses the world's largest monastic library. The fat monk librarian already knew me and opened the display cabinets with the old maps. I also remember that the librarian used to explain to every tour party how, during a huge blaze that engulfed the monastery, this precious building was miraculously spared. He added, with a roguish wink, that the miracle was due to the heavy wrought iron bars that had been placed at the huge windows for security reasons and had acted like a Faraday cage in the fire.

Every year, I went to Kitzbühel for a week. I stayed for a schilling in an unheated room at the local chimney sweep's and walked to the start of the Hahnenkamm run for training. In middle of the week we did the German Universities' Race and at the weekend a hundred participants competed in the Austrian Universities' Championships. To win the title, we had to compete in the downhill, the slalom, cross country and ski jump events. In 1937 I won the downhill at the World University Ski Championships in Zell am See. I was the only competitor to schuss down the steep Ebenbergalm and crossed the finishing line eight seconds faster than the second-placed man. I was also a member of the Austrian national squad for the downhill and the slalom and trained on the Grossglockner for the 1936 Winter Olympic Games in Garmisch-Partenkirchen but I never got to compete as our squad was recalled to Austria the evening before Games were due to start. Like the Swiss, our government decided to take this step as a protest at the politics of the National Socialists. We respected the decision and went home, a little disappointed, since we had been the favourites. The tension was really between the politicians; as skiers, we just wanted to race. After all, the trainer of the German national team was an Austrian, Toni Seelos, who had invented the parallel turn and was the reigning world champion.

I did my ski instructor's diploma and the mountain guide's exam and financed the rest of my studies by running skiing and climbing courses. In Geography, I specialised in ethnology and glaciology. During the Physical Education course we had to attend two compulsory camps in summer and two in winter. In the summer, we would set off with great enthusiasm – about 15 participants of both sexes – to camp by a lake or up in the mountains. We were self-sufficient and in the winter we had to carry heavy rucksacks up to the mountain huts. I vividly recall the first time I got caught in an avalanche, on an ascent of the 3,360 metre Geiger in the Venediger Range of the Hohe Tauern. I was disorientated at first but managed to keep "swimming" on the surface and survived the incident unharmed, having learned a valuable lesson.

The skiing course in the Lower Tauern run by the downhill World Champion Inge Lantschner did not go quite so smoothly. During a spell of bad weather I went with my friend Fredl Rössner from the Triebental Hut to his parent's house in nearby Sankt Johann am Tauern. I wanted to make myself useful and started splitting some logs. The axe rebounded off the frozen chunk of wood and severed the artery on my left wrist. I stopped the flow of blood with my other hand and Fredl took me straight away to the nearest doctor, who discharged me with sixteen stitches and the comment that I should rest the hand.

We both returned to the course, where two days later we had a final downhill run, which was assessed. Ambitious as ever, I wanted to beat our instructor and worked the poles hard on the flat sections. That evening my hand did not just swell up, my whole arm was numb and the gland in my armpit hurt. The following day, I hurriedly packed my rucksack and set off on skis to the doctor's. With my left arm strapped to my chest with a cloth, the only way I could do it was by poling along between my legs with both sticks clutched in one hand. When the doctor saw the state I was in he refused me treatment on the grounds of my stupidity, so I decided on the spur of the moment to continue down the ever-widening country road to the railway station at Judenburg. By the time I got there, I had done forty-two kilometres.

I caught the train to Graz, where one of the very first sport doctors, Professor Pauluzzi; had his practice, a true idealist, who was well known in the area. I had helped him build a hut on our local hill, where he provided first aid to the many ski accident victims, spending several weekends carrying roofing slates a thousand metres uphill. Professor Pauluzzi began treating the gaping wound by bathing and massaging it so that the scar would not become too big. Two years later, he treated my frostbitten toes after the North Face of the Eiger.

Around this time, I founded a ski school for students on the Tauplitz. My mother managed to save a brochure, which survived the war. A week's course cost fifty schillings, including third class rail travel, hut fees, a hearty breakfast with hot chocolate and cornmeal polenta, soup for lunch, evening meals and my fee as a ski instructor. The work was so lucrative that I was able to save up for a motorbike, a Puch 250, which proved very useful for my summer climbing trips. In the winter of 1937/38 I took over the running of a larger ski school in Sexten in the Dolomites.

At the beginning of March, the start of the best time for the Dolomites, I got seriously ill. The local doctor was at a loss to explain the bad pains I was having and prescribed me belladonna drops. Ignoring the prescribed dosage, I drank the stuff straight from the bottle. On my last legs, I took the train to Graz, where I was diagnosed as having severe dysentery. I received a course of Shiga-Kruse injections, which immediately took the pain away. Mother helped, with her cold compresses, wrapping me up in wet sheets like an Egyptian mummy, which also seemed to ease the pain. Someone mentioned in passing that German troops had marched into Austria. [On 11 March 1938 German troops marched into Austria on the orders of Adolf Hitler. Little resistance was met. On 13 March 1938 the Anschluss (joining) was declared and Austria became part of Nazi Germany]. During my convalescence, I walked the three kilometres to the University, played tennis and attended gymnastics classes at the Institute for Physical Education.

One day, Else Wegener enrolled at my ski school on the Tauplitz with her two daughters Lotte and Käthe. The family of the famous Polar explorer Alfred Wegener had been living in Graz since 1924, where he had held a professorship at the University. In 1930, Wegener went missing on a Greenland expedition and his wife Else, an educated and energetic East Prussian, was now both father and mother to the children. She wanted to teach the girls some life skills and also brought them along to my climbing course. Lotte was a pretty seventeen-year-old girl and very athletic. She played the cello and I gave her a lift to her lessons on my motorbike. When I picked her up outside school and she took her seat on the pillion with that huge case under her arm, we drew the envious looks of her girlfriends. Lotte and I did a lot of mountaineering and hard rock climbing together and, under the well-meaning supervision of Frau Professor Wegener, we fell in love. It was not long before my future mother-in-law was urging us to get engaged.

The double study load of Sport and Geography at the Faculty of Philosophy presented me with no difficulties. On the contrary, I was full of enthusiasm and dedicated myself to my studies. I also had the great good fortune of having some quite outstanding lecturers. I will never forget the famous German geographer, Otto Maul, who taught me for ten semesters. Back then, the universities were not as crowded with students as they are now and the contact with the staff was far more personal; it is hard to believe that there were only about a dozen of us that attended this highly respected lecturer's amusing lectures. But my pleasant days as a student were drawing to an end. I wrote my final dissertation on "The creation of blue ice veins in glaciers". My close relationship with the Wegener family meant that I had all kinds of useful documents at my disposal, which were, of course, very helpful and gave me a big advantage over my compatriots. We had to do four semesters of medicine as part of the Physical Education course. The world renowned Professor Anton von Eiselberg was a visiting lecturer and if you wanted to attend one of his lectures you had to make sure you were in the auditorium hours before the start in order to get a seat. His grandson, Christoph von Minutillo, recently gave me a copy of his grandfather's biography.

On my trips to the Dolomites during the university vacations I did several first ascents and all of the classic routes. It was there that I also met Fritz Kasparek, who was soon to become one of my most important climbing partners. I had just been climbing on the Sella Towers and was having a rest on the narrow ledge at the top when a shock of blond hair suddenly appeared at my feet, closely followed by a sharp and alert looking young man. He had been watching me from below and wanted to see who it was that had climbed the route so quickly. I had heard of Fritz; he was known to be a good climber and had done many of the hardest faces in the Eastern Alps, training for them by bivouacking on a window ledge. Just one day after we met, we went to the Civetta and did the famous 1,100 metre North West Face in a day.

By now I had achieved a few things as a climber and sportsman and these achievements gave me a great deal of satisfaction. But I was always looking for new challenges. As soon as one goal had been achieved, I would set myself a new one, which I then pursued with all my energy and ambition. In those days, the place everybody was talking about was the Himalaya. The pioneering age of alpinism was over and the attention of mountaineers the world over was focused on the Himalaya and the eight-thousanders. The English had been active on Mount Everest back in the 1920s and had experienced the tragic death of George Mallory in 1924. They measured their mountains in feet and were relatively unaware of the magic 8,000 metre barrier that represented the benchmark for continental European climbers. However, the tragedy that befell the 1934 German Nanga Parbat expedition, during which nine lives were lost, was an event that preoccupied the English, too – in particular the renowned climber and writer Frank Smythe, who planned an expedition for 1935. Nanga Parbat had become the "mountain of destiny" of the Germans and news of Smythe's intentions was greeted with alarm in Munich, the seat of the newly-founded German Himalayan Foundation.

I, too, dreamed of the Himalaya but my desire to go there was fuelled by different reasons. I first learned about the faraway mountain ranges of Tibet and Nepal through the books of Sven Hedin. Since the end of the 19th century, Hedin had undertaken several big expeditions to Asia and had also been in the Transhimalaya region. On his famous 1904 trip, he set off with a hundred yaks and twenty helpers. He was the first to explore the wilderness of Western Tibet. When he returned two years later, as ragged as a beggar and with only ten of his yaks remaining, he returned happy, as the expedition had been a success. Hedin was my great role model and once, when he gave a lecture in a nearby town, I asked him for an autograph, the only time I ever did this.

So how was I going to get to the Himalaya? I hadn't the money and I was an unknown young climber. Then I recalled the words of an English explorer, which gave me courage and hope: "Have a plan and stick to it". It became one of my mottos for life. I had to do something that would make the climbing world sit up and take notice.

Almost all of the last great problems in the Alps had meanwhile been done, all the big, steep faces climbed. Only the biggest and most difficult remained – the North Face of the Eiger. Small wonder, then, that all the really good climbers were concentrating on this face. There had been many accidents and the Eiger had claimed more than its share of victims, yet thus far no one had succeeded in climbing the North Face. My climbing partner Fritz Kasparek and I felt strong enough and we decided to give it a try. In July 1938 I hurried through my final teaching exam and rode my motorbike over to Grindelwald on the northern edge of the Bernese Alps.

MIRACLE ON THE WHITE SPIDER

At two o'clock in the morning on 21st July 1938, Fritz Kasparek and I set off up the Eiger North Face. Darkness enveloped us. We did not speak. We each went our own way, each of us lost in his own thoughts. Fritz led safely to just below the Rote Fluh, where a hundred metre cliff of smooth, steep rock towered above us. Alpine faces usually sleep in their blanket of frost in the mornings but the Eigerwand does not play by the rules and that morning there were rocks coming down. We could see them taking to the air above the uppermost rim of the cliff and flying down in a huge arc. We moved quickly, trying to get to the foot of the Face as fast as possible, since we would be safer there. We scrambled up the easy terrain to the Hinterstoisser Traverse. The rock was glazed with ice. Fritz fought his way up, inch by inch, clearing snow and ice from the holds with his ice axe as he climbed. Carefully, he felt his way out leftwards, leaning right back on the rope as he looked for the next stance, and finally reached the other end of the traverse. I clipped Fritz's rucksack to the fixed rope and followed suit, pushing the rucksack across the Traverse in front of me as I went.

We stopped for breakfast and a rest at the Swallow's Nest, Wiggerl Vörg and Hias Rebitsch's famous bivouac ledge. The weather had remained good and morning gave way to a splendid day. We felt in top form and had no doubts that we would succeed. But we knew, of course, that some of the very best had been forced to turn back.

Fritz strapped his crampons to his boots and started up the First Icefield. After much serious deliberation, we had decided that Fritz alone should take his ten-point crampons with him. I did not have any. In any case, we thought the North Face of the Eiger would be a rock route with occasional sections of ice and neve and the extra weight of a second pair of crampons (lightweight alloy crampons were not available then) was, we reasoned, something we could do without. My boots were clinker nailed in the traditional Graz style and provided good purchase on both snow and rock. Our plan was for Fritz to lead the ice sections and for me to do the rock pitches. As it turned out, we came across a lot more ice than we had anticipated.

There was no neve on the First Icefield, just brittle water ice. It was here that we realised that leaving the second pair of crampons behind had been a miscalculation. I had to compensate for the missing kit by using more muscle power, although my training in different sports paid dividends here. Fritz climbed masterfully but it still took us hours to get to the start of the Second Icefield and the point from which we could see the snow slides, stonefall and waterfalls coming down from the Spider a hundred metres above. By then, it was early afternoon.

Under no circumstances did we intend to traverse across the Icefield in the afternoon, so even though it was still broad daylight we moved right to a small knob of rock and hammered in a couple of pegs for safety before spending hours hacking out a place to sit out the night. We clipped into the pegs, spread our ropes out to sit on and started cooking a meal. We were protected from stonefall by the cliff above us. The night was cold, long and uncomfortable but even the worst night has to end sometime.

Anderl Heckmair and Wiggerl Vörg joined us the next day and a spirit of companionship immediately made itself felt. That day, we made it as far as the Ramp, where we set up camp and spent our second night on the Face. By seven the following morning we were climbing again, a difficult job with muscles still stiff from the previous two days' exertions. Anderl and Wiggerl had made quick work of the groove on the Ramp – a skilful lead by the wily Heckmair. Not to be outdone, Fritz led me up it in fine style, as if he were on home ground in the Dolomites. The ten metre bulge above was very strenuous but looked as if it would go. I had never seen anything like it before but Anderl just attacked it direct while we waited for the signal to follow. Finally, the magic words "climb when ready" came and the pitch was in the bag.

Shortly before the Spider, a sudden storm blew in, which encouraged us to speed up a bit. Climbing fast, we made it across the Traverse of the Gods with no great difficulties. By now, the sky was a bluish black. Tatters of mist blew across the mountain and soon enveloped us. It started to hail, then snow, as we headed up into the Spider, that steep patch of ice, perched in the middle of the summit headwall, from which white lines radiated outwards like the legs or pincers of some huge insect. What we did not know then was that when hail and snow avalanche off the steep summit snowfield and are funnelled under great pressure through the Spider's legs, the Spider itself can become a death trap.

I was standing on the ice of the Spider. I had chopped out a tolerable stance and was belayed to a piton, holding Fritz's rope as he went to work twenty metres above me. The snow fell more thickly. At first I could just about see him, and then I could not see him at all. The eerie howling of the wind grew louder and took on a strange, swelling sound. Avalanche! I dragged my rucksack over my head and pressed myself flat against the ice, clutching the rope with one hand. I heard stones rattling down onto my rucksack before the raging, roaring snow mass swallowed everything else around. It pulled and grabbed at me with incredible force. I was gasping for air as I desperately tried to prevent the stream of snow building up between me and the ice.

And what about Fritz? He was standing up there, exposed to the full force of the avalanche and unable to defend himself. If he fell, I would have a real job holding him. Gradually, the pressure of the snow diminished but before I had time to breathe, let alone shout, the next avalanche came down, even more powerful than the first. This one, I was sure, would spell the end for us. But then, after what seemed an age, deliverance came. The snow and ice granules trickled off into the void. Even the raging noise of the storm seemed to get softer. We were still alive. A miracle had happened on the Eigerwand. The White Spider had not claimed any victims.

At the last moment, Fritz had driven a long piton into the ice and it was this that had saved him. His hand, however, which he had been holding protectively over the loose piton to stop it being wrenched out of its placement by the mass of snow, was badly grazed and bleeding. Anderl and Wiggerl had been higher up when they were surprised by the avalanche. They had not had time to hammer in a peg and anyway I had been lumbered with most of them so all Anderl could do was hang on tight to his ice axe and grab hold of Wiggerl's collar with his free hand.

We were reunited at the upper rim of the Spider, feeling incredibly lucky to be alive. As a mark of friendship we decided to rope up together and continue to climb as one party as far as the summit ridge. On 24th July, after a further bivouac, we reached the summit of the

Eiger. It was 3 o' clock in the afternoon. We had made the first ascent of the Eigerwand.

Our rope of four had accomplished something that no one else had ever managed to do. We had started out as competitors and ended up as friends, as Anderl later commented.

Fritz Kasparek is no longer alive. In 1957 he fell to his death in the Andes when a cornice collapsed, a similar fate to the one that befell Hermann Buhl. Wiggerl Vörg died in action on the first day of the Russian campaign, the victim of a so-called "suicide order", or so I was later told. My contact with Anderl Heckmair continued uninterrupted until his death in February 2005 at the age of ninety-eight. Every year I used to give him a box of his favourite Swiss black cigarillos – Toscanellis, they were called – for his birthday. On one occasion he thanked me and then added "Just imagine – your cigars arrived at the same time as a case full of *schnapps* from my doctor in Oberstdorf and a note that read 'To neutralise the effect of the nicotine from your friend Harrer, here is the *schnapps* to go with it'". "You see," he added with his customary dry wit, "that's a proper doctor for you!"

Were we just thrill-seeking adventurers, then? Perhaps all those who set off up the Eiger North Face are, to a certain extent, adventurers. To be sure, the climb itself provides adventure but it does not necessarily follow that the climbers are mere adventurers; after all, they come well-prepared and well aware of the dangers involved. Adventurers are those who ride their luck, take stupid risks and, when it all goes wrong, think they are heroes, when in actual fact the real heroes are the men from the rescue service.

The Eiger has a unique and special life of its own and this must be respected at all costs. One should never "hurt" the mountain, by climbing in the afternoon in summer, for example. That time belongs to the mountain; it is the time it needs to rid itself of the loose rocks, ice and snow that it hurls down the Face constantly. The North Face of the Eiger would not, in any case, allow itself to become overrun by climbers. The weather regulates things perfectly well, to the extent that climbing bans are superfluous.

A child seeing a salamander for the first time experiences the thrill of adventure, while an explorer does not necessarily need to discover a Palaeolithic cave painting or be the first to stand on a summit to experience a similar feeling. The second or even the tenth person to come along can still discover something new and interesting. Young people should not give up trying; there are still enough new things waiting to be discovered. One day, perhaps, when speed records are no longer considered important, young adventurers will take a leaf out of the Tibetan Buddhists' or Indian Hindus' book and regard the mountain tops as the "throne rooms of the Gods" and therefore taboo and the ritual circumambulation of the mountain will become their objective. At this point, the hopeless idea of victory, of conquering and somehow beating the mountains into submission, will finally be a thing of the past.

As we stood on the summit of the Eiger, we were too exhausted, our senses too dulled, to realise what we had accomplished. It was only later, when we were mobbed by journalists, that we sensed what was coming. We were young lads and had lived our lives anonymously until then and suddenly we had to learn what it meant to be famous. After a celebratory meal in Grindelwald as guests of the local mountain guides, we were driven to Sonthofen by the Bavarian section of the *Bergfreunde* Club. Kasparek and I had left our little tent at the foot of the North Face and in all the excitement I even forgot to fetch my motorbike, which I had parked in a farmer's hay loft. We were met in Sonthofen by the man responsible for all political educational establishments and the Chief of Organisation of the Nazi Party, Robert Ley, who greeted us with the words that, in these heroic times, we were both a symbol of, and an example to, the Führer's new recruits. In truth, all four of us were passionate mountaineers and had climbed the North Face for nobody other than ourselves. We were acting on no one's orders and received no financial help for the climb. Now, however, the politicians began to bask in our reflected glory.

That was just the start. After being treated by a doctor for frostbite and various other injuries, we travelled by train to the German Gymnastics and Sport Festival in Breslau and were led straightaway into the full stadium by the Reich Sports Minister Hans von Tschammer und Osten. The meeting was interrupted and we were introduced to some of the famous athletes, who had won Olympic gold at the Summer Games in Berlin. I considered it a special mark of recognition that they wished to applaud our ascent of the Face in such a way; but after all, I thought, we had done our climb in a snow storm, while they received their medals and titles in the safe environment of the athletics stadium. We were then called upon to do a lap of honour around the stadium, during which spectators kept jumping over the barriers onto the cinder track to touch us or take photographs. In our clumpy curling boots that we had been given in Grindelwald because of our frostbitten feet and the summer heat, we were only able to complete our lap of honour slowly. With our baggy trousers and various injuries, we did not really leave much of an athletic impression but it was obvious that the applause of the crowd of sports fans was in recognition of our mountaineering achievement rather than a political demonstration.

The subsequent meeting with Adolf Hitler at the Hotel Monopol was a sober and businesslike affair. The Reich Sports Minister introduced us and briefly explained our ascent of the Eigerwand. "Boys, boys, what an achievement!" was Hitler's reaction. Each of us received a silver framed picture with a written dedication and Hitler then gave the waiting photographer, Hofman, the sign to proceed with the group photograph. In reply to Hitler's question about what had been planned for our recuperation, the Reich Sport Minister said that we were to be driven to Bremerhaven the very next day, from where a KDF trip to the fjords on the west coast of Norway had been arranged on our behalf. *(translator's note: through the "Strength-through-Joy" (KDF) programme, Ley ordered the building of two new cruise-liners that were used to take German workers on foreign holidays. In 1938 an estimated 180,000 people went on cruises to places such as Madeira and the Norwegian fjords. Others were given free holidays in Germany.)*

And with that, the audience was ended. The Reich Minister for Internal Affairs Frick joined us for the group photograph but he was obviously waiting impatiently for the chance to discuss more pressing political matters with Hitler. Just a few weeks later, the Munich Agreement granted Hitler's demand that the Sudetenland be ceded to Germany – with the agreement of both France and Great Britain.

Many years later I was accused of having used the words "We have climbed the North Face of the Eiger to the summit and beyond for our Führer!" in a commentary about our achievement that appeared in a book about the Eiger. However, this text does not originate from me. While we were still in Breslau, I was approached by a man who said he had been given the job of ghost-writing my story for Eher Verlag, the central Nazi Party publishing house based in Munich. He legitimized his credentials with the remark that he had also written *Flight into Hell* for Hans Bertram. The text that he wrote, under my name, was not written in the language I would have used and I neither received a copy of the manuscript to correct, nor did I ever authorise publication of the text. Later, when those wretched words were being repeatedly quoted, I went to Munich and tried to search the archives on the Nazi Party publishers for any records of authors' fees paid that might enable me to determine the name of the ghost writer but unfortunately my research was unsuccessful.

It is absurd to think that anyone would risk his life to impress others, to grant a favour or in order to prove something. It is only through passion for one's own objectives that one can summon the strength to survive such hardship. The ridiculous idea that I had climbed the North Face of the Eiger for Hitler could only have been penned by a ghost writer or author with little or no idea of climbing, a person who had not had the opportunity to measure himself against the forces of nature and thereby learn something about his own feelings.

In 1997, the question of whether or not I had carried a swastika flag with me on the Eiger Nordwand ascent also surfaced and caused quite a stir in the press. A Salzburg journalist working for the Austrian television company ORF claimed that I had carried such a flag in my rucksack with the intention of planting it on the summit of the Eiger. According to the journalist, this claim was "based" on an alleged report made by my companion, Anderl Heckmair. It is significant that a letter written by Heckmair, in which he categorically rejects this version of events stating: "In view of the prevailing weather conditions on the Face, we had more important things to do", was never published in the press.

After the Norway cruise, the four of us went our separate ways. I travelled to Graz and visited my parents, who had learned of our Eigerwand climb from newspaper and radio reports. They were delighted that I was back safe and sound and told me about a journalist that had visited them on 20th or 21st July and had asked about my whereabouts. My mother showed him a card with a Grindelwald postmark. "He must be on the North Face then!", the journalist said, before rushing off to compose a suitably lurid news item to that effect.

My next visit was to my wife's grandfather, Wladimir Köppen. Professor Köppen, the father of Else Wegener, was ninety-four years old and with his shock of snow-white hair, his neatly trimmed beard and his bright, enquiring eyes he cut an impressive figure. He was a climatologist, had studied Natural Sciences at Heidelberg and worked with Alfred Wegener on a climatological history of the world. I will never forget the moment I entered his study and he rose laboriously from a sofa that was both too low and too soft for an old gentleman. There was no greeting; he just looked at me and quoted the words of Schiller: "Yes, yes .....and do not put your lives at risk."
(*translator's note*: "und setzet Ihr nicht das Leben ein" from the poem "*Wohlauf, Kameraden, aufs Pferd*", by Friedrich von Schiller, 1797).

I am in my nineties myself now and I sometimes think about the old man's words to me. On all of my expeditions, I have never consciously placed my life at risk; nor have I ever had to overcome real fear in order to accomplish my goals. Maybe I was courageous in the face of danger, or maybe not. When we are young it is often external events that encourage our daredevil stunts. We simply want to be the best and need no other justification than that. The question why we are prepared to try something extraordinary never arises and it is only when others demand an answer that we begin to think about the reasons why we do it. It may be that the best reason is, quite simply, the thrill of the big adventure.

For me, the first priority was always to be free to realise my mountaineering dreams and not be constrained by my professional life.

As a result, I was unable to accept many of the offers of employment I received on completion of my final examinations in Geography and Physical education, as to do so would have compromised that freedom. It was only when the Gauleiter of Styria offered me a teaching post at my old grammar school in Graz, with the assurance that I would be free at any time to pursue my plans, that I agreed. The condition was that I would become a member of the National Socialist Teaching Staff and thus of the Nazi Party itself. I duly composed my application, signed it and sent it off. The reply never reached me, as shortly afterwards I went on an expedition to Nanga Parbat.

In 1952, a man came to see me who claimed to be an old school friend of mine and to be in possession of my National Socialist Party book, which he offered to destroy for ten thousand *schillings*. Without hesitating, I recommended that he should take the document to the police headquarters at the Paulustor in Graz. It seemed entirely possible that such a book might exist but, I had never made a secret of my application for party membership. I never heard from the man again.

At the same time as I was adding my signature to the party membership application, the Munich Agreement was also being signed. I remember the *Wochenschau* newsreel pictures of the British Prime Minister Neville Chamberlain returning to London and holding the Agreement aloft triumphantly with the comment "Peace in our time!" The French signatory to the Pact, premier Edouard Daladier, was also cheered in Paris. Even Patrick Joe Kennedy, the father of the future US President John F. Kennedy, supported the British Prime Minister's political stance and spoke of Hitler as being "harmless". Meanwhile, the British MP and back-bencher, Winston Churchill, denounced what he regarded as his Prime Minister's attempts to curry favour with Hitler. Although there were many who were sceptical of the Agreement, after the experience of the First World War, most of them seemed to prefer a flawed agreement to a new war. At the time I, too, believed that ratification of the Pact spelled peace for us. The great scholar and humanist, Viktor Frankl, later explained it to me thus: In contrast to animals, he said, humans do not have instincts that tell them what they ought to do, so they want the same things that others want and do the same things that others do.

In 1937, I had taken on the job of trainer of the national women's team for the Austrian Ski Federation. I was now asked to work as a sport and ski instructor for the Styrian SS. I agreed and suddenly found myself as a Squad Leader with a uniform and two stars, even though my participation in the Nanga-Parbat-Expedition prevented me from attending even a single hour of training.

I was also offered the contract to play the leading role in Ludwig Lantscher's film *Osterskifahrt*, which was scheduled to be shot during our honeymoon. Lotte Wegener and I married at the beginning of December 1938, I in the uniform of an SS Squad Leader. It was a hurried wedding, since I expected to be going to the Himalaya soon. As a freshly baked SS man this required a special permit, which took a very long time to acquire. To speed up the procedure, the clerk suggested that we simply say I was an old party member. We thought this was a splendid idea, since it saved us having to wait, and so I agreed, although I had actually only applied for Nazi Party membership in 1938 in order to be able to take up my teaching post. If I had indeed been an "old" party member there would have been no sense in applying for membership again in 1938. Nor is it true that I was in the SA, as it was later claimed. If that had been the case, I would not have had to apply for party membership in 1938.

Maybe it was youthful opportunism or maybe it was blind determination to subordinate everything in order to achieve my sporting objectives. Whatever it was, it was a mistake. I have since thought long and hard about my behaviour in 1938. The mixture of political recklessness, *zeitgeist* and my passion for mountaineering is difficult for the detached observer to comprehend nowadays. For me, it was just a brief interlude, but accusations have been levelled at me as an old man by people who were not even alive then that I lacked a clear stance on the matter and that this was combined with, and compounded by, a failure, perhaps, to distance myself appropriately from the events of that time, at least from a modern day point of view.

Now, over sixty years later, when I reflect on what motivated my actions, I do so in the certain knowledge that one acts differently when one is a young man. Back then, being a free agent was the greater good – I wanted the freedom to pursue my mountaineering dreams, and in particular the chance to go on that Himalayan expedition, without being constrained by my future professional life.

On the evening of our wedding day, Lotte and I set off on our honeymoon. We drove up to the mountain refuge on the Gerlosplatte, where Ludwig Lantscher and the film team were waiting. The SS uniform had been mothballed back in Graz. During the filming I received the long-awaited telegram from the Himalaya Foundation in Munich, asking if I was prepared to join the Nanga Parbat Expedition. I had to decide quickly, as the ship to India was leaving Antwerp in a week. There was nothing to think about as far as I was concerned. I cancelled the film contract and forgot about the teaching job and the honeymoon.

Not even a year had passed since German troops had invaded Austria. I now received the reward for my efforts to keep myself free and available for the Himalaya trip. That invitation was worth more to me than any medal or decoration I received for the Eiger North Face but I was as yet unaware of the fateful significance that this expedition would have for me. It was to change my life completely and through it I was to acquire new values – values that would continue to shape me to this day.

TO THE HIMALAYA

My first meeting with Peter Aufschnaiter took place at the office of the notary public Paul Bauer at number 4 Weinstrasse in Munich. Bauer was the chairman of the German Himalayan Foundation (DHS) and Aufschnaiter his general manager. The meeting with these two men was a happy and exciting event for me as it meant that my dreams of going to the Himalaya were one step closer to being realised. Bauer and Aufschnaiter seemed not to share my fiery enthusiasm. They both wore serious looks as they confirmed that the five thousand marks from the Styrian local government, the financial prerequisite for my participation in the expedition, had been received. Throughout the conversation we addressed each other using the formal "*Sie*" and it was only after the appearance of the other two participants, Lutz Chicken and Hans Lobenhoffer, with whom we used the informal "*Du*" form of address, a common convention amongst climbers, that the tension eased somewhat.

Born in 1899, Peter Aufschnaiter was thirteen years older than me. He asked me if I thought that a forty year "old" man could be capable of leading an expedition to a mountain that had already claimed twenty-six victims. I knew that Aufschnaiter had been there in 1929 and 1931, when Bauer had led an exemplary expedition to Kangchenjunga. Typically enough for a young man, I thought only about the climbing and the new twelve-point crampons and short ice axes used for climbing steep terrain. I had no idea that success depended on a number of other factors and that the time actually spent on the mountain represented only a fraction of the whole expedition. I had no way of knowing then that Peter Aufschnaiter and I would be firm friends through thick and thin for three whole decades until his death in 1973 and would experience situations together that one man alone would not have survived.

The aim of the expedition was to reconnoitre a route up the Diamir Face of Nanga Parbat and thus pave the way for a large scale expedition planned for 1940 under the leadership of Willi Luft, one

47

of the survivors of the catastrophe of 1934 on the Rakhiot side of the mountain. At first, I did not fully understand how the expedition team had been put together. The choice of Peter Aufschnaiter as leader was plausible, due to his Himalayan experience and his knowledge of languages, but I was at a loss to explain why no one from the Eigerwand first ascent team had been included, apart from me. Amongst those selected, Hans Lobenhoffer was a lieutenant in a Bavarian mountain paratroopers' regiment and Lutz Chicken was a medical student from Bozen and a young member of the famous German mountaineering club the Academic Alpine Club of Munich (AAVM). Eleven men from this club alone had lost their lives on Nanga Parbat. There must have been tactical reasons for the inclusion of two internationally acclaimed mountaineers in the team, although it is of course possible that the DHS had been influenced politically and been forced to take this step.

After a thorough medical conducted in a pressure chamber by the physiologist and high altitude expert Willi Luft, we travelled by train from Munich to Antwerp and on 6th April 1939 we left Europe on board the German freighter, the *Lindenfels*. Ten days into the trip, Peter Aufschnaiter had planned a welcome break for us. We berthed at Port Said and went ashore, visiting the famous museum in Cairo and the Cheops Pyramid. We were the only tourists far and wide and several camel drivers were grateful for the business. We looked for the way up to the top of the pyramid but they reckoned the climb was too dangerous and that we would go the wrong way without a guide. With all our experience of the Dolomites we had already discovered the polished bits on the blocks of rock and reckoned that we would only need ten minutes or less for the hundred and forty metre climb to the apex of the pyramid. One of the guides bet his camel against us. After eight and a half minutes we had climbed the numerous metre and a half high steps to the top and yodelled to the Egyptians below as they rode off into the distance.

We took the train for the next stage of the journey, while the *Lindenfels* navigated the 164 kilometre canal to Suez, where we rejoined her. There was little to do on board, so we passed the time cleaning our boots. Peter Aufschnaiter handed out camera films and everyone got a Rolex wristwatch. The film material and the watches remained the property of the DHS. All the crates and sacks of supplies were numbered and still bore the stamps of previous Nanga Parbat expeditions – "D.H.E", which stood for "Deutsche Himalaja Expedition". As the expedition doctor, it fell to Lutz to check the crate with the medical supplies. The smallest of the boxes was particularly heavy; no wonder, since it contained all the books and maps. We were allowed to borrow the reading material but Peter Aufschnaiter kept the box in his cabin.

We reached Bombay on the last day of April and berthed at the Gate of India, where we were received by friends of the DHS. At the Bombay German Club we were astonished to experience the lifestyle of the European in a colonial land. Despite the heat (May is the hottest month in India) we played tennis before quenching our thirst with magnum bottles of Beck's Beer and several "gimlets".

The train ride through Karachi and Lahore took four days and was a throwback to the early days of rail travel. Although the distances covered on the Indian subcontinent are huge, there were only single track rail links and they had adopted a remarkable safe working system to avoid head-on collisions. On entering the station, the locomotive driver would throw a big metal ring to the waiting driver, who caught it with one arm and was only then allowed to proceed in the opposite direction. There was plenty to eat and drink. White uniformed waiters in turbans leapt on board the train as it slowed to travel through the station and took our requests and two stations down the line the dishes would appear, prepared with fewer spices to suit our European tastes. It was all perfectly organised and the system obviously catered mainly to the prosperous Indians and sahibs on board. The passengers sitting in the cooling breeze on the roofs of the carriages were offered a more reasonable priced, and tastier, curry served on the green leaves of rubber or teak trees with freshly baked chapattis on the side.

Peter Aufschnaiter took our health seriously. All the fruit had to be washed before being eaten and the water was sterilized first with potassium permanganate crystals. Our train bore the name "Express", but the journey through the hot Sind Desert still took ages. Whenever there was a longer wait in a station for the train coming the other way to pass, we would proudly don our lightweight tropical helmets and get out to stretch our legs. We three youngsters decided to imitate the locals and left our shirt tails hanging out of our trousers until Peter

Aufschnaiter reprimanded us with the comment that we should behave like sahibs and not like Indians.

To cool us down they brought us a tin box containing a block of ice that must have weighed around forty kilos, which we placed between us on the floor of the compartment – a wonderful method of combating the heat and probably far healthier than a modern air conditioning system. Aufschnaiter voiced all of his requests to the Indians in their mother tongue and our respect for him changed to amazement. The Indians addressed him as "Bara Sahib", or "Big Boss". Although Chicken was modified to "Lutz", Lobenhoffer became "Hans" and I was called "Heini", we maintained a respectful distance to our leader, whom we continued to address as "Herr Aufschnaiter".

In the evening of 6ᵗʰ May, we arrived at Rawalpindi, the terminus of the railway and the provisional capital of Pakistan. Here there was only one place for Europeans to stay: Kuhn's Park Hotel. The Swiss hotelier and his army of servants took charge of our expedition luggage and welcomed us with an Engadine nut gateau. Although we had only been away from home for two months, we really appreciated the Swiss hospitality. On the cool veranda, we weighed out the loads for the porters. The prescribed weight was twenty-three kilos but the volume of the load also played a big role. We were helped by three high altitude Sherpa porters who had made the journey from Darjeeling. In Rawalpindi we also met up with our cook from Kashmir, who was called Ramona – a nice name, we all thought. He had already been on a number of other German expeditions and was renowned amongst climbers for his powdered sugar and raisin pancakes.

The approach march with the column of porters through the Kaghan Valley was unforgettable. To begin with, we were enthralled by the forests of mighty cedars and then the villages grew smaller and after a week or so we got our first view of the snow covered peaks of the Himalayas. Ramona hurried on ahead of us every day and would be there waiting for us with hot tea. In one of the villages he bought a chicken and hard boiled some eggs for the next day's march – a good idea in regions where the standards of hygiene do not always match our own.

We had to break trail through deep snow across the 4,145 metre high Babusar Pass for our barefoot porters and to our great surprise, a European man was waiting for us at the top of the pass with fresh fruit.

It was Lieutenant Strower, a young Englishman who was stationed at Chilas in the Indus Valley. He looked just like the archetypal Englishman described in books and seemed to me to have an enviable life: a young man out and about in the world, with a responsible job and time to pursue his hobbies. Strower lived in a fortress where the doors were locked and bolted every evening. He was an officer, a judge, a hunter and, above all, an explorer and he collected minerals and flower seeds. He made sketches, owned a small but select library of books and kept in contact with the nearest hill station by Morse code. He had known for a while that four Germans were coming and that they had permission for the Diamir Valley, which was part of his administrative district. The lieutenant also commanded a small troop of Gurkha soldiers.

Peter Aufschnaiter had given me the job of going ahead and reconnoitring the best route for the porters. After four days, we reached Base Camp, where a stone hut was built to house the equipment and the food supplies. Aufschnaiter impressed us with his knowledge, particularly the fact that he spoke Tibetan with our high altitude porters.

We gazed in wonder through the binoculars at the mighty North West Face as we searched for a possible safe route to the 8,126 metre summit. Later, at one of the higher camps, we got an idea of the vast natural forces at work up there as we observed a huge avalanche coming down off the Mazeno Ridge a little further to the west, watching in awestruck fascination as clouds filled with ice crashed down onto the flat Diamir Glacier where it abutted the steep face. A short time later, the pressure wave flattened our tents and the entire camp was sprinkled in a sugary coating of snow, even though we must have been a good kilometre away from the avalanche itself.

Exploring the steep ice gullies between the various rock ribs was great fun with our twelve-point crampons. On one occasion, Aufschnaiter and I took our porters up to establish a higher camp and during the descent it was all we could do to stop them sliding back down the thousand metres on the seats of their pants. Our probings on the face went only a little higher than six thousand metres and were concentrated on finding a route that led to the North Summit. Lutz and Hans also reconnoitred the historic route that the British mountaineer Alexander Mummery had attempted in 1895 with two

Gurkhas and made an interesting find: a small piece of wood that could only have come from Mummery. Mummery was a courageous man but had obviously been forced to concede that his proposed route was too hard. Searching for another possibility, he went across to the Rakhiot Face, where he lost his life in an avalanche.

The DHS had applied in London for permission to attempt the 7,780 metre peak Rakaposchi. However, Lieutenant Strower brought the news that this would not now be possible, so we climbed two other minor peaks in order to take photographs of the whole of the Diamir Face. One of my last tasks was to take measurements of the glacier. When we arrived I had fixed markers on both sides of the moraine and had even built cairns from rocks and lengths of wood at three other points on the glacier. Now, two months later, I was able to measure the change in the distance between the markers and thus calculate the speed at which the glacier was moving. Long after the war was over I received a letter from the well known glaciologist Wolfgang Pillewitzer informing me that my humble survey had been of use to him in his work.

Although we had now completed our reconnaissance tasks we also investigated the classic Rakhiot Face in order to reach a final verdict on the best possible route of ascent. It was while doing so that we were able to experience the famous view of the vast, gleaming white Nanga Parbat massif with the Silver Saddle perched four thousand metres above the dark cedar trees and the lush green of the "Fairy Meadow" – an appropriate name for one of the most beautiful places on earth.

We also paid a visit to the memorial to the eleven climbers and fifteen porters, who had perished on German expeditions to Nanga Parbat. Aufschnaiter considered that he could now go back to Munich and recommend the Diamir Face route for the big 1940 expedition with a clear conscience, since, at five kilometres, the distance to the summit on this route was just a third of that of the fifteen kilometre route up the Rakhiot Face that had previously been used.

The 1940 expedition never happened, however, as the outbreak of the Second World War intervened, and it was not until 1962 that the Diamir Face was first climbed, by Toni Kinshofer and Anderl Mannhardt, who both agreed that the route had demanded far more from them than they had anticipated. Nine years previously, Hermann Buhl had made the first ever ascent of Nanga Parbat via the Rakhiot Face. Buhl had been one of the few climbers to survive the 1934 tragedy on Nanga Parbat and had climbed the North Face of the Eiger in dramatic circumstances in 1952. On my return to Europe the same year, Nanga Parbat was again the big talking point amongst climbers in Germany and Austria and I was asked by the expedition leader, Karl Herrligkoffer, if I wanted to accompany Buhl to Nanga Parbat and lead the summit push from base camp. Buhl suggested a route on the Grubreissen Towers north of Innsbruck as a training climb but I found it hard to second the climb and had to have a tight rope on the bits that he simply strolled up with his customary elegance. I had to concede that my climbing skills had long been surpassed. In fact, it turned out to be the last hard rock climb I did. So I decided to give up my place on the expedition and this was then taken by Peter Aschenbrenner.

Thanks to Hermann Buhl and his extraordinary talents as a mountaineer, the 1953 expedition was a resounding success. Climbing solo, Buhl reached the summit of the ninth highest mountain in the world and the photograph taken of him after the ascent bears shocking testimony to the hardships he endured. The British team that had climbed Mount Everest a few weeks previously reckoned that the climb had earned Buhl a place in the list of the greatest mountaineers of all time.

Although Hermann Buhl was the first to summit Nanga Parbat and Kinshofer the first to climb the Diamir Face, their success was due in no small measure to their predecessors, on whose shoulders it all rested. The geographer Adolf Schlagintweit, the brave Alexander Mummery (in all probability the first climber to visit the Himalaya), the reconnaissance trips and the twenty-six victims from other expeditions that the mountain had claimed – all of these formed the basis for the eventual success.

After months of snow and ice we returned to Gilgit, where we enjoyed the fresh fruit and vegetables on offer. There were enormous quantities of orange coloured apricots lying on the flat roofs of the houses. Later, during my escape and in Lhasa, I really appreciated this windfall. Peter Aufschnaiter had planned a new route for the walk out. It was late summer and the flowers were in full splendour. We were well acclimatized and reached Srinagar, summer capital of the state of Jammu and Kashmir , all too quickly.

When I look back now I remember the approach marches and the walks out being far livelier and nicer than the actual days on the mountain. The glaciers and avalanches seemed huger, the air thinner, the variety of people, animals and vegetation somehow more impressive. In Srinagar we stayed on a houseboat moored on Wular Lake. Major Hadow, a member of the Himalayan Club, helped us buy souvenirs. He told us we should get some saffron – "but please don't buy it from a Kashmiri" – and that he would handle the purchase of this expensive spice personally. He drove us in his car up to the Gulmarg hill station at two thousand five hundred feet, from where we had another long look at "our" Nanga Parbat.

We arrived back in Karachi in mid-August, where we were due to board the freighter that would take us back to Europe. We went down to the harbour every day but there were no ships arriving any more. We read in the newspapers that all "aliens" were now obliged to register with the authorities. Furthermore, it was forbidden for foreigners to leave the main arterial routes. The penalty for any failure to comply was up to ten years imprisonment.

We three youngsters told Peter Aufschnaiter that it was looking like war and suggested getting out of India by the land route but Aufschnaiter became agitated and argued that there was no nation that would wish to wage war again. He had been a young soldier himself and had fought against the Italians in the Dolomites campaign.

We learned from the taxi driver that drove us down to the harbour every day that the ruling family of the little princely state of Las Bela, which lay on the route to Afghanistan, were allegedly anti-British in their outlook. Las Bela belonged to the province of Baluchistan, an arid and remote region and an area through which Alexander the Great had passed on his legendary campaign to the mouth of Indus in the fourth century BC. Aufschnaiter dismissed the idea as senseless and refused to come with us but we considered it an attractive prospect to head for Las Bela and find a route back west along the Gulf to Persia or via Kandahar to Afghanistan. Our idea was pretty naïve at the time but later, with the benefit of experience, I realised that it had been a good plan.

Although our every step was being shadowed, we managed to give our watchers the slip and travelled in an ancient car through the steppes and the desert to Las Belas, where we found accommodation at the Dak Bungalow, or colonial rest house, and learned from messengers that "His Highness" would grant us an audience. The "Palace" turned out to be a castle-like building on a hill and the guards welcomed us with fixed bayonets. The Maharaja, more boy than man, could obviously speak no English and his interpreter informed us politely that there was a car waiting to take us back to Karachi. We were not arrested but several soldiers sat with us in the car. It was the last few days of August.

Our escape attempt had been brief and painless but it left all of us with an unpleasant feeling. During the return journey we mostly kept silent and could come up with no strategy to talk ourselves out of the situation. Soon we were standing before the Chief of Police, who was built like a bull, but before we could utter a word of apology he said "Well, gentlemen, so you lost your way while hunting, did you?" Our reply was not exactly quick-witted but at least it was timely. "Yes, Sir!" we answered in unison. And with the parting remark that he would pay us a visit at our hotel after work, that was the end both of our interrogation and our stomach aches. Back at the hotel, we were greeted with silence by Peter Aufschnaiter but we could guess what was going on behind that high forehead of his. He considered our escape attempt to be just a juvenile prank.

A few days later we were sitting under the huge mango trees in the hotel garden drinking chilled English beer with the friendly Chief of Police when suddenly twenty-five soldiers marched up to the low garden wall, where they took up positions. An Indian officer entered the garden and it was all we could do to stop the Chief of Police from reprimanding him. We shook hands as we took our leave. That brief encounter with a true gentleman was something that I will always remember. It was the third of September 1939 and the Second World War had just begun.

BEHIND BARBED WIRE

Our first prison camp was situated outside Karachi on the edge of the Sind Desert. The military censor seized all our expedition baggage and gave Peter Aufschnaiter a receipt. It was a provisional camp with just a few inmates. Later they transferred us to the Central Internment Camp (CIC) at Ahmednagar, two hundred kilometres to the east of the hot and humid city of Bombay in the hills of the western Ghat. Ahmednagar served as a garrison town for the colonial power; part of the town had been sectioned off as an internment camp and was surrounded by a double fence of barbed wire.

The sixteen barracks had high rooms and an electric motor that worked a complicated system of iron rods and suspended mats that fanned the hot air. Fifteen hundred Germans and about thirty Austrians were interned here. All the big German companies were represented in India – AEG, Siemens, I.G. Farben – and they employed a number of engineers, many of whom were interned at the camp, who worked on the construction of paper and chemical factories. Amongst the Austrians there were a few professors, with the rest made up of musicians, chefs and yoga students. There was even a snake catcher, who used to sell cobra venom to pharmaceutical companies.

Two Bavarians also shared our fate. Wiggerl Schmaderer and Herbert Paidar were imprisoned after their first ascent of the 7,363 metre Tent Peak in Sikkim, while their expedition leader Ernst Grob, a Swiss national, was allowed to return to Europe. I made friends with Wiggerl and we discussed the climbs we were going to do together after the war was over. A happy addition to our community came in the shape of thirty or more sailors, whose songs ensured a good atmosphere in the canteen. Since we were not regular soldiers, we were classed as civilian internees and were treated in accordance with the Geneva Convention for Prisoners of War.

The many Germans from Bombay had long since established themselves at the CIC and had elected one Oswald Urchs as their camp leader to represent their interests. He had worked as a doctor for Bayer Leverkusen in India. He assigned us to the free bunks in his barracks. Urchs had specialised in malaria and had had great success with the drug Atibrin, which was made by his company. He, and all the others, encouraged us to collect the Anopheles mosquitoes that were the carriers of malaria and could be identified by the black stripes on their legs. At night, when the ramshackle wind machine was turned off, each of us had his own mosquito net. At ten o' clock in the evening all the lights went off – only the barbed wire was still brightly illuminated – and the quiet of the big room was disturbed by another kind of pest: bed bugs. Although these nasty little insects were easily caught, you only made the mistake of crushing them between your fingers once, as the resultant stench was overpowering. In the mornings it was easy to determine whose blood they liked and who the lucky ones were that they avoided. The camp leaders gave us blowlamps of the type that plumbers use and we used to burn the little beasts in the joints of the metal beds.

The German camp leaders organised the necessary "chores" with great efficiency. Peeling potatoes and chopping onions were popular jobs as large quantities were needed for the five hundred internees and when the twenty men sat in a circle to do the work they could chat away and swap experiences. I also had the opportunity to practise my profession as a PE teacher. Morning exercises were very popular and there was a football pitch and a tennis court but the most common physical activity was vigorous walking. The longest route was a kilometre long stretch alongside the barbed wire enclosure. The elderly internees preferred to walk in the cool of the evening and chat to their compatriots as they went.

The bunk opposite mine was occupied by a man from Berlin called Ede Krämer. He showed me various newspaper cuttings, from which I learned that he was the European champion in a style of wrestling known as "catch-as-catch-can". He had lived in India as the guest of a Maharaja, who loved to surround himself with strong men. "Von Krämer", as he was known in India, had even beaten the local champion, a deaf and dumb colossus by the name of Gunga. Krämer had made a wrestling mat filled with coconut fibres with the help of another Berliner, Hanne Kopp, who was known to all and sundry as "Chest and Legs" due to his heavily muscled upper body. The training bouts always drew a big crowd of prisoners and even some of the British guards were curious to see what was going on, but it was the sailors that showed the greatest interest in this unusual sport. There was a famous story about Ede's most brilliant performance, when Ede took on, and killed, a thousand kilo Brahma bull. Ede faced the bull head on, grabbed the tips of its huge horns and kicked its legs from under it while twisting the horns to one side. The bull fell, Ede won and the Maharaja scooped the big pot of bets. Ede's training partners were treated just as roughly.

We had been in Ahmednagar just a few months when I had a tragic accident that involved Ede, of all people. In addition to the irregular, unannounced checks conducted by the Major, every Saturday morning saw the Camp Commandant's general inspection, which was personally conducted by the commanding officer himself. The Commandant would arrive with his entourage like a hospital consultant making his rounds. Everything had to be folded and arranged with military precision, as is customary with soldiers. There was an expectant silence in the barracks as I glimpsed something moving beneath my tightly made bed covers.

I immediately realised that it could only be Mungo, Ede Krämer's tame mongoose. I threw my sandals at the lump, hoping to scare it away, and the movement stopped abruptly. I can not describe the feelings I had during that inspection. This cute little animal was not only Ede's pet; everyone else in the barracks loved the funny little fellow, who only ever wanted to be stroked. It was typical of Ede, the big, tough wrestler whose evil grimaces struck fear into his opponents, that he should act like a big softy with his little pet mongoose. When I pulled back the bed covers, my worst fears were confirmed. A few drops of blood dripped out of Mungo's ear onto my bed sheets, leaving me in no doubt that Ede's little pet was dead. Ede did not seem to register my apology; he was too wrapped up in his own thoughts and was obviously struggling to keep his feelings under control. For me, it was a close brush with fear and misfortune.

Later, in Lhasa, I owned a statue that played a big role in Asian mythology. It represented the God of Wealth, known in Tibet as Tseten and in India as Kubera. On his lap, he held a mongoose that was spitting gold coins. Ceremonies were held where one could beg for the god's help, but the petitioner's wishes were only granted if they were both sincere and reasonable. If ulterior motives were suspected, the petitioner would be plagued by fleas and bed bugs.

Since the very first day of my internment, I had become increasingly annoyed at my sudden loss of freedom and by the fact that I was being forced to spend time behind barbed wire simply because some maniac had decided to start a war. I had done nothing wrong, yet I was being punished nonetheless. I had not broken any laws and had nothing to repent; on the contrary, I felt as if it was my right to do everything I could to escape. As the months passed, my initial wishful thinking that the war would soon be over gradually evaporated. When a criminal is sentenced to a year's imprisonment, he makes 365 marks on the wall of his cell and knows when he has served his time. The uncertainty of our situation meant that we were constantly hatching escape plans. We had no complaints about our treatment in the camp; we had plenty to eat, we could do sports, there were books to read and the standards of hygiene – so important in the tropics – were the same for us as they were for the English soldiers. There was no reason to escape because conditions were bad or the situation unbearable. I just wanted out. But that was easier said than done.

By the beginning of the New Year, 1940, hopes of being free again any time soon were fading fast. Long-term projects like the building of a bakery had begun, while the professional musicians amongst us rehearsed in the camp chapel under the baton of Herr Hertrampf, a former teacher at a conservatory of music. Hertrampf owned a large concert harmonica, on which he gave a very professional rendition of Gershwin's 'Rhapsody in Blue'. He even managed to persuade the Camp Commandant to get a piano for the orchestra.

By now, the bunks in the barracks were all taken and new arrivals were accommodated in tents. I was on friendly terms with a number of the internees from IG Farben, amongst them a man called Rolf Magener, who had been on a study trip in Bombay, organised by the

accounts department of his company, when war broke out and had
ended up here. One day, we were sitting with a few of his colleagues
when our Sudeten baker, a former confectioner at the Grand Hotel
in Calcutta, passed us a note informing us that he was intending
to make some chocolate marshmallows and asking us how many
we wanted so that he could order the necessary ingredients. As an
expedition internee, I received less than twenty rupees spending
money a month, which was just about enough for toothpaste and
soap, so I only ordered two. My IG Farben companions, on the other
hand, had eighty rupees a month at their disposal. Although the
assets of employees of large companies had been frozen, they were still
allowed to draw this princely sum each month. When Rolf Magener
saw my modest order he remarked that I could surely eat more than
that. "How many do you think I could handle?" I asked him. "A
dozen, easily!" he replied. And when Doctor Urchs objected on the
grounds that my stomach would be unable to handle it, Magener
asked him if he was prepared to finance the bet. Urchs agreed. I ate
the lot with no difficulty and Urchs had to pay for them.

The Camp Commandant seemed concerned for our welfare. We
got the daily newspapers and whenever something had been clipped
out by the censor it was only ever a matter of a few hours before
the content of the forbidden lines was spread around the camp. The
rumour mill produced the most incredible tales of German success
on the war front.

By the beginning of the autumn 1940 we were receiving regular
news from Germany. Until then, the postal service had been a big
problem and it was a relief for all concerned when the service slowly
began to function. All the letters and parcels came via the Red Cross
and were checked by the censor. We kept getting parcels of stuff sent
from Europe and the internees repeatedly tried to stop them coming,
since they were completely superfluous to our needs. In view of the
circumstances, we could have wished for nothing more really. At the
beginning of 1941 I received the news from the Swiss Consulate
General in Bombay, our 'protecting power', that my son Peter had
been born in December 1939. It had taken them a year to inform me

that I had become a father.

The German Clubs in India sent us a whole library full of books, all of which were carefully sifted by the censors, and even our heavy box of expedition books eventually found its way to the camp. Aufschnaiter received a list of the books and maps that the censor had retained, including various documents relating to the Nanga Parbat region. It later transpired that the censor, like us, was in Ahmednagar, which was almost on the Indian Ocean, and had no way of knowing that we would soon find ourselves in a camp in the foothills of the Himalaya, so he saw no reason to confiscate our maps and books like Sir Charles Bell's *Colloquial Tibetan*. Aufschnaiter was reunited with his books, which meant so much to him.

On New Year's Day 1941 the news came that we were to be transferred to another camp in four weeks' time. Sergeant Whitacker told us that the major talking point for the British soldiers stationed in the big garrison was the fact that the "bloody Germans" had a far "nicer" camp than they did, a complaint that the British military leaders had obviously decided to address.

Compared to Ahmednagar, conditions the new camp at Deolali could only be described as catastrophic. The report from the Swiss protecting power, dated 4th March 1941 had this to say:

"Accommodation totally inadequate, no sports facilities, unhygienic sewage systems, inadequate catering standards…"

The hot pre-monsoon season had now begun, yet the showers produced only a feeble dribble of water. The sand storms blew in at midday and since the walls of the barracks consisted of bamboo and reeds, our beds and other personal items like toothbrushes were soon covered in sand.

Urchs called a hunger strike. We sewed several sheets together and every time a train went past the camp (the tracks were only about two hundred metres away) we held up a banner with the words "German POWs' on Hunger Strike due to Inhuman Treatment". We were soon to feel the effects of our protest as one General after another arrived with their entourages to assess the situation. To begin with, the British did not really believe that we were serious about our hunger strike and checked the rubbish bins for empty tins of food. They needn't have bothered. We really were starving and by day three of the strike the camp hospital was full of internees too weak to move. At first, I kept up with my exercises but by the fourth day I just lay sweating under my mosquito net. The sole topic for discussion amongst the inmates was food and drink. I was so plagued by hunger that I swore an oath that in future I would be satisfied with one portion of fried potatoes a day. On the fifth day of the strike a General arrived from Army Headquarters, who was authorised to take decisions. One of the camp internees, an architect who had previously built for the wealthy Maharaja of Darbhanga, was given the task of designing a completely new camp according to our wishes in a place called Dehra Dun, where the new Central Internment Camp was to be built.

Dehra Dun – it sounded like a magic word after the misery of the old Deolali Camp. Aufschnaiter knew that Dehra Dun was a small town in northern India, about two hundred kilometres north east of Delhi, and served as the departure point for expeditions to the Gharwal Himalaya. There was a botanical garden that housed the Institutes for Forestry and Cartography. Dehra Dun lay up in the hills at eight hundred metres and was an ideal place for Europeans. The hot Indian climate at Ahmednagar made us lethargic but the cooler weather in the north would certainly improve our spirits.

We were housed in the old barracks at a military camp until the new CIC was ready and in October, eight months later, we left Deolali. The journey via Delhi in a specially commissioned train took four days. Although we were closely guarded, there would have been plenty of opportunities to escape but the prospect of a comfortable trip back to the foothills of the Himalaya kept us quiet.

In Dehra Dun, we were greeted by the sight of red brick barracks with thatched roofs that called to mind a vision of a village in Lower Saxony. The only things missing were the carved horses' heads on the gable ends of the buildings. Each of the long, narrow huts contained forty beds and verandas ran the full length of the walls, providing both shade and protection from the rain. There were even enough sports pitches.

We could not see the tops of the highest mountains on Earth, clad in their permanent covering of snow and ice, as the view was blocked by a chain of two to three thousand metre mountains to the north of the camp but in the evenings we saw the lights of Mussoorie, a hill station where the English and wealthy Indians spent the hot summer months. The few of us who were still contemplating escape were now faced with a completely new situation. The old destinations like Persia, Afghanistan or the Portuguese enclaves were out of the question but only two hundred kilometres away lay the five to six thousand metre high mountain passes of the Himalaya and, beyond, the mysterious kingdom of Tibet. I remembered the fascinating expedition reports written by Sven Hedin. When we left Europe for Nanga Parbat, no one, not even Peter Aufschnaiter, had the slightest idea that circumstances might conspire to put us so close to the little state at the roof of the world but now the location of the camp invited us to investigate every possible way of reaching the "forbidden land" of Tibet, a place that even the English people stationed in India required special permission to visit.

Over the winter months the temperature fell to two degrees and I kept myself busy improving the sports facilities at the camp. We levelled the running track around the football pitch using a hand pulled stone roller. We dug a high jump and long jump pit and filled it with wood shavings, while the keen hockey players even got their own special pitch. A team of tradesmen from Heidenheim built a bakery to professional standards under the master craftsman Wiggerl Schmaderer and the fresh bread rolls were enjoyed by internees and British alike. In a big hut next to the kitchens, dubbed the "*Falscher Friese*", we installed a canteen that served both alcoholic and non-alcoholic drinks. Between the barracks were flower beds with bougainvillaea and hibiscus and a plot with various vegetables. I planted some papaya seeds as I loved the fruit and had heard that the plants bore their pumpkin-like fruit after just nine months. Beneath a huge, broad-leaved tree, one of the tradesmen constructed a proper blacksmith's shop with a block of stone that served as an anvil. The library was well stocked with classic literature and there was a lending list of rare books that we could borrow from private collections and a second list of records with classical music.

The best of the CIC institutions, however, was without doubt the "Parole Trip" Permit. The internee signed a piece of paper giving his word of honour that he would not go into town (Mussoorie or Dehra Dun) or use any form of transport and promising to be back at camp at the prescribed time. Of course, we also had to sign a pledge that we would not use this temporary freedom to escape. Some of the really fit inmates went to the top of the three thousand metre high Nag Tibba, from where they were able to see the seven-thousander Nanda Devi.

While most of the camp inmates felt quite safe and secure at the CIC and rejected the risks involved in an escape bid, Peter Aufschnaiter was constantly occupied with the thought of escaping. The commonly held opinion was that there was little chance of success and that breaking out would just cause problems, since parole outings and cinema visits were temporarily suspended after every escape attempt. Furthermore, they said, as a white man in India one would be discovered immediately and sent back. The season for escape attempts across the Himalaya was in April and May, as the little monsoon was over then and there was a window of a few weeks before the big monsoon began that gave ideal weather for a traverse of the high mountain passes. In spite of the favourable snow and weather conditions, finding a route over the mountains in the thin air, with a heavy rucksack and rudimentary navigation aids, required a considerable effort. We were undeterred, however; after all, as mountaineers we had more experience than most and considered that we were better able to cope with any problems we might encounter. All we needed was an escape plan and a suitable opportunity to present itself.

Meanwhile, the war continued. Photographs of wives and girlfriends started to disappear from the bedside tables. This latest development was noticed but rarely discussed. My wife had also filed for divorce and remarried. A letter arrived one day with the request that I allow Lotte to divorce me. She had met a German officer who wanted to marry her but according to German law she could only have our existing marriage annulled with my agreement. I was not aggrieved at this, since I realised that the past few years had been hard for her, too. We had married young and our marriage had only really existed for a few months before I went away. She now had a child, our son, whom I had never even seen, and the longer I was away the more Lotte's hope faded that I might return any time soon, if ever. Nevertheless, the divorce increased the distance between me and my home by a little bit more.

We had by now made ourselves at home at the POW camp. I lived in Barrack 23, which had five rooms, the first of which was occupied almost exclusively by internees from IG Farben. My room, which I shared with Lobenhoffer and a few of the engineers, was right next door. We had our problems, of course. Two snorers moved out voluntarily. If anyone was ever inconsiderate enough to encroach on the other occupants' space at the table, a line was drawn down the middle of the disputed area. If a pencil rolled across this "demarcation line" it was replaced with a reproachful look.

Tempers became particularly frayed at the start of the "big rain", as the monsoon was called, when the thermometer rose to over forty degrees in the shade. The sky turned to grey, the air filled with dust and you could not even see the hills nearby. At night, we carried our beds out onto the football pitch but even there the heat was oppressive and sleeping without a mosquito net was not an option.

However, all in all, things were fairly harmonious and we lived a busy and productive life. An interior designer decorated the walls of the "*Falscher Friesen*" and constructed a stage. The theatre group had to perform *Hokuspokus* by Kurt Goetz several times, so great was the interest in the piece. The professional musicians gave concerts and a string quartet played Haydn, Mozart and Schubert. The English collaborated in exemplary fashion. By "gentleman's agreement" we were allowed to walk without an armed guard beyond the barbed wire fence to the cinema, where we watched *They Shall Have Music* with the virtuoso violinist Sascha Heifetz and later *Gone with the Wind*.

In order to get a little more peace and quiet I decided to build myself a bunk on the veranda on the north side of the barracks. With raffia mats and a horse blanket as a curtain, a bed and a small table,

I created my own little world. Here I learned Hindi and Tibetan, and later Japanese. Aufschnaiter lent me some maps and I made two copies of each, one for the escape and another that I hid in the straw on the roof. Von Magener gave me some German and English books. I had plenty of time to read them now, whereas as a student every free moment had been dedicated to sport. My bunk was my place of refuge and others soon followed suit. After a while, most of the verandas were full of similar constructions.

Dehra Dun was more than twice as big as our previous camp and after Japan entered the war, Germans from the Dutch East Indies were also brought here. The camp had seven wings, all enclosed in double barbed wire that was illuminated at night. During my third year as a POW I lived in Wing One; the new arrivals from Java, Sumatra and Bali were assigned to Six and Seven. Between the wings there was a kind of no man's land. This was only occasionally patrolled and the barbed wire was left unguarded. I had made a couple of hooks with which I could pull the wire apart and slip through into the night.

In the area between our wing and the two that housed the Dutch East Indies internees, the English guards allowed us to play football and handball. We even organised a decathlon competition. The favourites to win were two lads from Java who were six foot five and won the high jump easily. Although I did not come first in any of the individual events, I did take the title in the "Open Class" and the next age group, the over-32s, was won by Rolf Magener. Since we both lived in the same barracks, there were a lot of thirsty people in our canteen for the "post-match celebrations".

Through my involvement in sport, I made many new friends and acquaintances at the camp, amongst them Heins von Have, whose story we all knew from newspaper reports. He had experienced some terrible things. An Allied ship convoy carrying POWs had been shot at by Japanese fighters. One of the ships had been sunk and over five hundred Germans and the entire crew had lost their lives, amongst them some of Heins von Have's friends. After arriving in India, he had made two escape attempts with his friend Peter Hülsen, both of which had failed. After being recaptured during their second attempt at escape, they were being driven back to their camp in a police bus when Have jumped out. As Hülsen tried to follow, he was hit by the swinging door and killed. The sober tone that Heins used to tell us about the accident could not hide his inner turmoil.

During my "parole outings" I had started equipping a gear depot in the jungle, about ten kilometres away from the camp, and it was here that I hid a set of my maps. Gear dumps were not allowed but, then again they were not expressly forbidden, either. I still had to be careful, however, since when leaving the camp you could be searched at any time. Every year in June there were jungle fires, most of them lit on purpose by the locals to produce fresh green shoots for their goats out of the ashes. One night, I was watching with concern as one such fire spread to the area where I had my depot. I asked a friend to let me have his place on the Parole Trip list so I could visit my secret hiding place. Unfortunately, my fears were confirmed. I ran like mad through the jungle but even from far away I could see that the tree, under whose roots my treasured cache lay, was blazing fiercely. When I got there, the tin of fat had exploded, the sugar had melted and the valuable maps and Tibetan grammar were charred and useless. All that remained were the silver coins, strewn around the slope, and the valuable gold sovereign that the camp cobbler had hidden in the heel of one of my mountain boots. The boot was on fire but I just managed to save the coin. Dripping with sweat and black as a chimney sweep, I bathed in a puddle in a dried up river on the way back and arrived at the camp fence punctually at five o'clock. I was a broken man, but Rolf Magener consoled me with the news that there was a General in the Italian camp who was also entertaining thoughts of escape and might perhaps be able to supply me with a replacement compass and a pair of army boots.

By now, Hans Lobenhoffer had left. One day, he was simply told to pack his things ready to leave Dehra Dun for an unspecified destination. After the war he told me about his odyssey. He was taken first to Bombay, then by ship via Durban and Cape Town to Halifax in Canada, where he was instructed to report for work at the carpentry shop in the POW camp. He then pretended to be mad and was redeployed.

The war showed no signs of ending and some of the internees now had to accept certain cutbacks. There were some smokers who swore they would give up if American cigarettes like Camels were no longer available and others who said the same things about English tobacco like Black & White. There were similar opinions about beer. By 1942, however, all of the smokers had switched to Indian *bidis* and in the canteen we drank beer from an Indian brewery.

Better, and stronger, alcoholic drinks were available and we made these ourselves. I became a "bootlegger" and produced illegal wine. I would buy a cheap forty kilo sack of Kashmiri raisins, put them through the mincer and after just a few hours in that warm climate the resulting brew would start to ferment. Hanging on every veranda were the round, porous clay vessels, known as *chatne* jars, that kept our drinking water pleasantly cool. I bought ten of these *chatnes*, with a total capacity of about twenty-five litres, and used beeswax to seal the inside of each jar. Before sealing the top of the jar, I inserted a pipe with a double U-bend into the narrow neck to allow the gas to escape, and to stop air getting into the raisin mash, the end of each tube ran into a container filled with water, usually a large, empty cigarette tin.

The bubbling of the escaping gas was music to my ears. After three weeks I used a rubber pipe to siphon off about twenty bottles of wine. The sweet raisins produced a wine similar to a Trockenbeerenauslese *(translator's note: the German term for "dry selected berries," used to describe wines made from specially selected, overripe grapes that are left on the vine until nearly dry)*. Business was brisk. Since I had no tax to pay and my labour costs were nil, I made a two hundred percent return on my investment and my escape fund profited accordingly. Once a year, the climbers got the contents of a whole *chatne* all to themselves. When Lutz Chicken and Wiggerl Schmaderer performed their breakneck balancing act on the roof beams of the *"Falscher Friese"* half drunk on the sweet wine, there was always a big crowd of spectators at the windows. I suppose you might say it was an eagerly-awaited annual event at the camp.

The were several chemists amongst the internees and they were the ones that produced the real moonshine. They would buy a sack of sugar cane molasses and distil the fermented mash through a system of pipes hidden in the walls of the barracks. The clear spirit was sold as gin, white rum or arrack, or coloured with burnt sugar and offered as whisky or cognac. Since the English were also feeling the pinch, even they bought gin and whisky from the illicit distillers.

Good quality alcohol had never been so cheap; a 0.7 litre bottle cost one rupee. The Commandant was clever and allowed practically anything as long as the camp was quiet and the Germans did not cause any problems.

ESCAPE

One night, Magener and I crawled through the barbed wire fence to the neighbouring wing in which the forty Italian Generals were housed, who had been taken prisoner in North Africa. We visited Marchese, the man who was to be my escape companion. Although Marchese was not an Italian noble, his agreeable manners, his clothes and his elegant air were certainly aristocratic. He seemed to be in good physical shape, the most important prerequisite for a strenuous escape across the high passes of the Himalaya. Marchese drew the pay of a British general, so money was not a problem for him. He was able to procure things for our escape that I could not even have dreamed of obtaining. What he needed was a partner who was familiar with the Himalaya. Several times a week I used to clamber through the wire to discuss details with Marchese. In May 1943 we had completed all our preparations. We were equipped with money, provisions, compass, boots and a small mountaineer's tent.

On the night of 20ᵗʰ June we decided to make our attempt. We leant a ladder, which we had grabbed and hidden after a small fire in the camp, against the wall of a hut and waited in the shadows. It was nearly midnight and in ten minutes the guard would change. The sentries on duty were obviously ready for a break and wandered up and down lethargically. Several minutes passed until they reached the point where we wanted them. Just then, the moon came up over the tea plantation. The big electric searchlights cast short, double shadows. It was now or never.

Both the sentries had reached their furthest point from us as I got up from my crouching position and ran to the wire with the ladder. I leant it against the overhanging top of the fence, climbed up and parted the wires that had been put there to prevent anyone climbing onto the thatch. Then I slipped through onto the roof.

We had agreed that Marchese should follow me immediately, while I held the wire apart for him, but he did not come. He hesitated for a few dreadful seconds, thinking that it was too late and that the guards were approaching – and indeed, I heard their steps. I left him no time for further deliberation, as I grabbed him by the collar and dragged him unceremoniously onto the roof. We crept across the ridge and dropped heavily down into freedom.

The whole thing had only taken about ten or fifteen seconds but in the still of the night the humming of the wire did not pass unnoticed. The sentries were alarmed but as their first wild shots whipped through the night we were swallowed up by the dense jungle. Signal flares went up and whistles sounded near us. They were coming after us already. We ran for our lives and made rapid progress, using short cuts that I had got to know very well during my reconnaissance trips from the camp.

We hardly noticed our rucksacks at first, but later on the heavy loads made themselves felt. In Asia, the "sahib" invariably travels with an escort of servants and never carries even the smallest item of luggage himself, so two heavily laden Europeans walking in haste through the countryside were bound to attract attention. So we decided to walk only at night, knowing that the Indians are afraid to enter the jungle in darkness on account of the wild animals. We did not feel entirely happy about it ourselves, since we had often read reports of man-eating tigers and panthers in the newspapers available in the camp.

The first night passed and in the grey light of morning we hid ourselves, exhausted, in a hollow in the ground and spent the whole day there, sleeping and eating the endless, searing hot day away. The worst thing was that each of us had only one water bottle, which had to last the whole day. It was no wonder that when evening came, after sitting quietly all day, we could hardly control our nerves. The nights seemed far too short to make good progress. We wanted to find the shortest way across the Himalayas to Tibet and that would mean weeks of strenuous marching before we could feel safe.

At any rate, we crossed the first ridge just a few hours after going over the wire but we had to press on now and get down into the Jumna Valley. In one of the side valleys we came across a narrow gorge which halted our progress and we had to wait until morning. The place was so remote that I was even able to take the time to dye my blonde hair and beard black without fear of discovery. I also stained my face and hands with a mixture of permanganate, brown paint and grease to produce a dark complexion. By this means, I acquired some resemblance to an Indian; this was important since, if we were challenged, we intended to pass ourselves off as pilgrims making their way to the sacred Ganges. As for my companion, he looked enough like a light-skinned Indian not to stand out at a distance.

Thus far, the greater part of our route had avoided tracks; only occasionally along the river courses were we able to use fishermen's paths. On this morning, after several days in the field, Marchese was very much exhausted. Towards evening my companion's spirit of enterprise returned. However, soon after midnight, his energy deserted him; he was simply not up to the enormous physical effort required. My hard training now proved a godsend to us both and I carried his pack strapped on top of my own.

During the next two nights we wandered further upstream, frequently having to wade through the Aglar, a small tributary of the river Jumna, when our way along the bank was blocked by jungle or cliffs. At last, the valley broadened out and our path led us through rice paddies and cornfields, but it became more and more difficult to find a good hiding place for the daytime. During the following nights we marched through less populated country. We learned soon enough, to our sorrow, why there were so few people. There was practically no water. We suffered terribly from thirst, yet the next three days and nights brought little relief, as our path went through dry fir woods. Fortunately, the area was so remote that we seldom met any Indians.

On the twelfth day of our escape, the great moment finally came – we found ourselves on the banks of the Ganges! The most pious Hindu pilgrim could not have been more deeply moved by the sight of that sacred river than we were. Admittedly, its significance for us was practical rather than religious but reaching the river meant that we could now follow the Pilgrim's Road up the Ganges to its source and that would surely lessen the hardships of our journey considerably.

I had managed to buy some provisions in a shop on the Pilgrims' Road. My disguise had worked well enough but what really convinced them were the bank notes. We spent a happy day. At last we had enough to eat. But our contentment was short-lived. The days spent in hiding were frequently more strenuous than the nights as we were in a state of constant nervous tension. By midday our water bottles were generally empty and the remainder of the day seemed never-ending. Every evening Marchese marched heroically onward and would carry on until midnight in spite of his exhaustion. After that he had to have two hours' sleep before he was able to go any further. Towards morning we bivouacked, and from our hidden campsites we could look down on the big road with its almost unbroken stream of pilgrims.

I knew from the many expedition books I had read that we would soon have to cross the so-called "Inner Line". This line runs parallel to the true frontier at a distance of about 200 kilometres. With the exception of local residents, everyone crossing this area between the two lines must be in possession of a pass. Since we had none we had to take particular care to avoid the police posts and patrols.

The Ganges Valley became more and more sparsely populated the higher we went. In the daytime we had no trouble finding suitable places to camp and I could usually leave our hiding place to go and fetch water without fear of discovery. Once I even made a small fire and cooked some porridge – the first hot meal for a fortnight.

We had now reached a height of about two thousand metres and during the night we often passed camps of the Bhutia, the Tibetan traders who in the summer carry on their business in southern Tibet and in the cold winter months go across into India. Many of them spend the summer in little villages situated at three to four thousand metres, where they grow barley.

It was then that the accident happened. Attempting to cross a stream, Marchese slipped and fell in the water. Soaked to the skin and completely exhausted, he could not be induced to go on. In spite of my insistence that he take cover in the woods, he just spread out his things to dry. For the first time I began to regret that I had not granted his repeated requests to leave him behind and carry on alone. Suddenly, an Indian stood before us, who after a glance at the various objects of obviously European origin lying on the ground began to ask us questions. Only then did Marchese grasp how dangerous our situation was. He quickly packed up his things, but we had hardly gone a couple of steps when we were approached by a second Indian, an imposing fellow leading a group of about ten tough looking men. In perfect English he asked for our passes. We pretended not to understand and said we were pilgrims from Kashmir. He thought this over for a while and then made the decision that would spell the end for us. There were, he said, two Kashmiris in the neighbouring house. If we could make ourselves understood we could go on our way. What devilish coincidence had brought two Kashmiris into this region at that very moment? I had only used this excuse because I knew it was extremely unusual to find Muslim Kashmiris in this Hindu region of the Ganges.

The two men of whom he spoke were flood damage experts who had been called in from Kashmir. As soon as we faced them we realised that the moment of our unmasking had come. As we had agreed to do in such a case, I began to speak to Marchese in French. The Indian immediately interrupted us in the same language, ordering us to open our packs. When he saw my English-Tibetan grammar he said we might just as well admit who we were. We then admitted that we were escaped prisoners but did not reveal our nationality and continued to speak English to him. Soon after we were sitting in a comfortable room at the Forestry Office drinking tea, but I could not hide my disappointment. This was the eighteenth day of our escape and it now seemed as if all the privations and hardships we had endured had been for nothing.

Today when I think about the peculiar set of coincidences that led to our capture, I cannot help feeling that we were the victims of something worse than ill-luck; that we were powerless over our fate. All the same, I did not doubt for one minute that I would escape again. Marchese, however, was far too exhausted to come with me. In a spirit of comradeship, he handed over some of his money to me. I ate all day long and tucked away half of what the forestry officer's cook brought me in my rucksack. Early in the evening we said we were tired and wanted to sleep. The door to our room was locked behind us and the forest officer had his bed put on the veranda in front of our window. However, as soon as he went away for a short while, we took the opportunity to stage an argument. Marchese took both parts and stomped around the room screaming abuse in a high-pitched voice and then a low key as if we were quarrelling violently. Meanwhile, I swung myself through the window, rucksack and all, onto the forest officer's bed and ran to the end of the veranda. I waited a few seconds until the sentries on patrol had vanished round the corner of the house then I dropped down the four metres to the ground below clutching the heavy pack. The ground was not very hard and the impact was not too severe. I recovered quickly and disappeared over the garden wall into the dark forest.

In my excitement I ran head-first into a flock of sheep. Before I could get back a sheepdog fastened on to the seat of my trousers and did not let go until he had bitten a piece out. I ran away in terror but I soon realised that the path I was on was far too steep and so I had to go back and creep around the sheep until I found another way. Soon after midnight I had to admit that I had gone the wrong way again. So once more I had to go back a few kilometres in breathless haste. My aimless wanderings had lost me four hours and the day was already dawning, so I hid again, although the region showed no trace of human habitation. I knew that there must be a village before the Tibetan border, beyond which lay freedom. I marched through the whole of the following night and reached an altitude of about three thousand metres – but there was no village. According to my sketch maps it ought to be on the far bank of the river and somewhere there should be a bridge across. So I trudged on in a carefree mood, even after daylight had come.

That was my undoing. As I came round a heap of boulders I found myself standing right in front of a group of houses and a whole horde of gesticulating people. The village was wrongly indicated on my map and my aimless nocturnal wanderings had allowed my pursuers to catch up with me. I was ordered to surrender, after which I was led into a house and offered refreshment.

Here I met for the first time with the real Tibetan nomads, who wander into India with their flocks of sheep and loads of salt and return laden with barley. I was served Tibetan butter tea mixed with tsampa, the staple food of the Tibetans. My stomach protested rather energetically against these unaccustomed delicacies, however.

I spent two nights in this village, which was called Nelang, toying with the idea of another escape attempt, but I was far too tired and dispirited to translate my thoughts into action.

The return journey was like a pleasure trip compared to my previous exertions. I did not have to carry anything and I was very well looked after. On the way I met Marchese, who was still staying as a guest of the forest officer. I was invited to join them. It is hard to describe my astonishment when a few days later two other escapees from the camp were brought in – one of whom was my former expedition leader Peter Aufschnaiter. Together, we set off on the march back to the camp.

One of the forestry workers who accompanied us was particularly obliging. He carried my rucksack, made tea for us and helped when we had to wade through the mountain streams. His name was Padam Chand and he told me that, years ago, when he was working as a porter for a "blonde German sahib", he had dropped the man's camera on a rock. "He didn't hit me; he didn't even scold me. You look just like him and I just want to say thank you," he said. He told me he had a small farm near Harsil and said he would run ahead and tell his wife to cook some potatoes for me to eat when we caught him up. Potatoes, like apples, had been introduced to the Upper Ganges Valley by the English to see if they would flourish and were something of a novelty and a delicacy in these parts.

I did not want to be suspicious of this good man but I was still a little cautious. The rucksack that he carried for me contained several things that meant a lot to me and I asked him if he would keep them safe for me. At the farm, which lay directly on the Pilgrim's Road, I took out my maps, the book by Charles Bell, the compass and about a hundred silver rupees – things that the guard would confiscate at the entrance to the camp.

"I will come and get my things at the beginning of May next year. I will come on the stroke of midnight and call out your name twice," I said.

"Yes, but I might be away for days cutting wood."

"Can you not take leave? What is your monthly wage?" I asked.

"Twenty rupees."

I gave him the twenty, and an extra month's pay on top. He promised to look after my things and to wait for me.

So now we had to go back to the camp. It was a bitter experience and was only made bearable by the thought that I would be making another escape attempt soon. This was now my fourth failed attempt at escape. First there was the attempt to reach Afghanistan in 1939, then I tried to jump off the convoy of trucks when we were being transferred to Deolali and now, in 1943, I had twice been recaptured.

Marchese was still sick and could not walk so they gave him a horse to ride.

This latest episode had left me with visible marks, which appeared when on the way back I bathed in a hot spring and found my hair coming out in handfuls. It appeared that the dye I had used to disguise myself as an Indian had had damaging consequences. As a result of this involuntary depilation and the traces left on my face by the hardships I had endured, some of my comrades in the camp found it hard to recognise me when I arrived.

"You made a daring escape and I admire you. However, the Geneva Convention stipulates that you now spend twenty-eight days in solitary confinement", said the Camp Commandant, Colonel Williams, by way of a welcome. His words of "admiration" for my "daring escape" were still ringing in my ears as I was taken to my cell. My bunk, the only piece of furniture in there, consisted of several raised planks with no bed linen. The cell was right next to the "chicken run", where the guards patrolled constantly. Food was brought by a fellow internee from my wing. The portions were generous and I soon regained my strength.

I did not really think of the four weeks in solitary as a punishment; they were more like a period of physical and mental recuperation. I had plenty of time to think, plan and consider the mistakes I had made. Occasionally I was able to engage the bored sentries outside my window in conversation and thus improve my spoken Hindi. Books and newspapers were not allowed but my comrades managed to smuggle a few in with my food and the security lights of the perimeter fence provided me with enough light to read by at night. I fashioned a hiding place under the bunk for my reading material which I could use in the event of a search.

Every morning, Sergeant Major Whitacker would arrive with a

spade, which I shouldered like a rifle, and he would then march me out of the camp to a place where I was told to dig a trench. He would sit in the shade of a large mango tree and, after a while, would order me to fill in the trench again. He tried to curb my enthusiasm for the job with the remark "Mr. Harrer, don't slog away like that – it's only a formality," to which I replied "I'm training for my next escape attempt!" Whitacker had a crooked front tooth, which earned him the nickname "Nutcracker". He was nothing like the archetypal strict Sergeant Major. He was fed up with the war and freely admitted it.

Back in the camp, I retrieved my maps from their hiding place under the straw roof and made new copies. I also copied out the little booklet *Colloquial Tibetan* again. I could not rely on getting the things back that I had deposited with Padam Chand.

Searches at the camp, whether announced or otherwise, were conducted by the deputy commandant, Major Taylor. In order to nurture the impression that I posed no risk to security, I started taking violin lessons with Hertrampf. As a boy, I had had a few lessons at the request of my mother and could just about play 'A Little Night Music'. By now, Heins von Have had also moved into our wing and provided valuable reinforcements for the team competitions.

Life at the camp continued, although the uncertainty about how long it was all going to last was hard to bear at times. During roll call one morning, when the Sergeant Major called out, or rather droned through, the names and numbers of the internees and each answered in turn with a shout of "here!", he stopped at number 1084 – my number – and said " I heard shots in the night and thought to myself 'that's got to be Harrer'"! We could talk openly with the guards about our intention to escape, since once an escape route became known it was, of course, made secure again. We had been studying the layout of the camp day and night, however, and had now discovered another possible way out.

I felt convinced that my next escape attempt would succeed and was determined to go it alone this time. Marchese promised to help in any way he could but said he would not entertain the possibility of joining me. "You are super-human," he commented ruefully. Busy with my preparations, I found the winter passing quickly and by the time the next "escape season" came around I was well-prepared. This time I wanted to start earlier, so as to get through the village of Nelang while it was still uninhabited.

I was not the only one who wanted to break out. My two best friends, Rolf Magener and Heins von Have, were also preparing their escape. Both spoke fluent English and they aimed to work their way through India to the Burma front. I prepared a little booklet of useful phrases for them in case they should meet any Japanese soldiers. Some of the other internees also had escape plans: Peter Aufschnaiter, who this time had as his partner Bruno Treipel from Salzburg, and the two fellows from Berlin, Hans Kopp and Kurt Sattler, who, like me, wished to escape to Tibet. There were seven of us in all and we decided to make a simultaneous break-out on the grounds that successive individual attempts merely increased the vigilance of the guards and made it more difficult for the rest to escape later. If the mass escape succeeded, each of us could then follow his own route.

The break-out was scheduled for the afternoon of April 29th, 1944. Our plan was to breach the fence by disguising ourselves as a barbed wire repair squad. Such working parties were a common sight, since the white ants were always gnawing away at the numerous posts that supported the wire and these had to be continually repaired. Working parties consisted of several Indians with an English overseer.

At the appointed time we met in a little hut near one of the least closely watched barbed wire corridors, where make-up experts from the camp transformed us in an instant into dark-skinned Indians. Have and Magener dressed in the English officer's uniforms that had been made in secret by some of the internees, while we "Indians" had our heads shaved and put on turbans. As serious as the situation was, we could not help laughing when we looked at one another. We looked like masqueraders on the way to a carnival. Two of us carried a ladder, which had been conveyed the night before to an unguarded spot near the fence. We had also managed to misappropriate a long section of barbed wire and rolled it round a post. Our belongings were stowed away under our baggy robes and in bundles, which did not look out of place as the Indians were always carrying something around with them.

Escape

Our two "English officers" behaved remarkably realistically. They carried rolls of building plans under their arms and played arrogantly with their swagger sticks. We had already made a hole in the fence through which we now slipped one after another into the unguarded passage between the barracks. From here it was about another 300 metres to the main gate. We attracted no attention and only stopped once, when the staff sergeant rode past the main gate on his bicycle. Our "officers" chose that moment to conduct a diligent inspection of the wire. After that we passed through the gate without being challenged. The sentries saluted our "officers" smartly and did not even give us "coolies" a second glance. Kurt Sattler had left his hut rather late and arrived after us at a run, swinging a tar pot energetically, his face smeared with black make-up. He caught up with us outside the gate. As soon as we were out of sight of the guards we vanished into the bushes and got rid of our disguises. Beneath our robes we wore khaki, our usual dress on outings. We bade each other a swift goodbye. Have, Magener and I ran for a few miles together and then went our separate ways.

We all found it hard to part company like that; after all, we did not know whether we would ever see each other again. Rolf and the others were also worried that I might have bitten off more than I could chew with my plan to work my way through to Tibet, but I believed in myself and in my physical fitness. In fact, I was far fitter than my friends. I had also gathered valuable experience on my first escape attempt and was attracted by the possibility of acquainting myself with that legendary land at the roof of the world that suddenly seemed so close. If necessary, I could always pass myself off as a medicine man with my travel apothecary or even court and marry a native woman if the opportunity presented itself. I felt well-prepared and ready to handle whatever lay in store for me.

I intended to follow my old route through the Aglar Valley but this time I was determined to stick to my original plan and travel only at night. My four comrades, for whom Tibet was also the objective, had the nerve to use the main road which led via Mussoorie into the Ganges Valley. During the first night I must have waded through the Aglar at least forty times. I made such rapid progress that when morning came I lay up in exactly the same place which it had taken me four days to reach the previous year. I was happy to be free and felt satisfied with my performance, even though I was covered with scratches and bruises.

The next few days passed without any significant incidents and I was able to draw on my previous year's experience to negotiate the few difficulties I encountered en route. At length I came to the farmhouse of my Indian friend Padam Chand. The timing was perfect; it was now the beginning of May, which was exactly the time we had agreed that he was to expect me. To be on the safe side, I hid my rucksack before approaching the farm, which was bathed in bright moonlight.

What I needed most were fresh provisions, since I had everything else with me. At the stroke of midnight I approached the farmhouse, hid myself in the shadows of an outbuilding and called his name out twice very softly. The door was flung open and out rushed Padam Chand. He threw himself at my feet as tears of joy flowed down his cheeks. Then he led me through the creaking stable door and into the hay loft. From a wooden chest secured with an enormous padlock he retrieved a carefully sewn canvas bag which he handed to me. He then left me with the remark that his wife would cook a big pot of potatoes. I opened my parcel in the light of a pine-wood torch, and to my delight and surprise there were all the things that I had entrusted to Padam spread out before me. Of the valuable silver rupees, not a single coin was missing.

I ate the potatoes with plenty of salt and then asked Padam Chand to get me some provisions. He thought that five kilos each of flour, sugar and fat was an impossible task, since everything was rationed. "Offer them double the price," I suggested. I gave him the money and arranged with him to pick up the things the following night. Deeply touched by his loyalty and trustworthiness, I went back to my hiding place in the hills feeling elated. I slept for ten hours and woke well rested and ready to make a return trip to Padam Chand's smallholding, where he proudly showed off the things he had managed to procure for me. He also made me a present of a pashmina shawl that his wife had made. I then took my leave. Meeting this man had been one of the most profound and moving experiences of my life. Many years later, whilst on expeditions in the Gharwal Himalaya, I never missed the opportunity to call at the farm with presents for my friend.

In spite of the thirty kilo load I was carrying, I made rapid progress. My route took me through the deep valley of the Ganges and the walls of the gorge narrowed and steepened as I went. I felt liberated. I was alone, I had no companion to worry about, I could walk or rest when I wanted, and even hum a little tune or two as I trudged along. I felt strong and enjoyed the feeling and the adventure. It felt as if I was finally living the way I had always wanted to. To experience this feeling for just one brief moment should really have been enough for me but I was aware that in my situation it was crucial to hold onto it for as long as I could.

I had now reached an altitude of over three thousand metres and the air was getting thinner. I forced myself to take a minimum of fifty steps before taking my pack off and resting. Fixing my gaze on the next objective and estimating the number of paces it would take to reach it was a mental trick I had learned in the Alps. As a rule, it always turned out to be further than I thought. The canopy of cedar trees made it impossible to navigate by the stars but I remembered the route from the previous year and this saved me from going off on the wrong track.

I had been on the march for ten days when I reached the village of Nelang, where last year destiny had wrecked my plans. This time I was a month earlier and the village was still uninhabited. But words cannot describe my delight at bumping into my four comrades from the camp there! They had overtaken me when I was staying with my Indian friend. Sattler had an attack of mountain sickness; he felt wretched and declared himself unequal to further efforts. He decided to turn back, but promised not to surrender to the English until two days were up, so as not to endanger our escape. Kopp, who had penetrated into Tibet by this route the previous year with Krämer the wrestler, joined me as my partner and we continued as a group of four. But it was to take us a further seven long days' hard marching before we finally reached the frontier between India and Tibet.

On 17th May, 1944 we stood at the top of the Tsangchokla Pass. We knew from our maps that the pass lay at a height of 5,300 metres. It was an auspicious day.

So here we were on the frontier between India and Tibet. For the first time we enjoyed an unaccustomed sense of security, for we knew that the English military could not arrest us here. We did not know how the Tibetan government would treat us but as our country was not at war with Tibet we hoped confidently for a hospitable welcome.

The top of the pass was marked with piles of stones and prayer flags dedicated to their gods by pious Buddhists. Although it was very cold, we took a long rest and considered our situation. We had almost no knowledge of the Tibetan language and very little money. Worst of all, we were near starvation so we had to find human habitation as soon as possible. But as far as the eye could see there was nothing but desolate wilderness and mountains.

After an icy-cold bivouac without a fire we reached our first Tibetan village, Kasapuling. The doors were all shut; nothing stirred. We then discovered that all the villagers were busy sowing barley in the surrounding fields. Bent double, they put each individual grain of seed into the ground with the speed and precision of machines. We looked at them with the same kind of feelings that Columbus might once have had when meeting his first American Indians. Would they be friendly or aggressive towards us? For the moment they took no notice of us at all. The shouts of an old woman, who looked like a witch, were the only sounds we heard. They were not directed at us, but at the countless wild pigeons that swooped down on the newly planted grain. Until evening the villagers hardly bestowed a glance on us, so we four established our camp near one of the houses and when at nightfall the people came in from the fields we tried to trade with them. We offered them money for one of their sheep or goats but they rejected our advances and made it clear that they did not wish to sell us anything. As Tibet has no frontier posts, the whole population is brought up to be hostile to strangers and there are severe penalties for any Tibetan who sells anything to a foreigner. We were starving and had no choice but to intimidate them. We threatened to take one of their animals by force if they would not voluntarily sell us one and as none of us looked like a weakling exactly, this method of persuasion eventually succeeded. It was pitch dark before they handed us the oldest billy-goat they could find – and for a shamelessly high price.

The Tibetans in the next villages were just as dismissive of our approaches, as we had been led to believe they would be in the books we had read. We tried to find an official who might understand our requests for leave to reside or travel, but with no success. Even Peter Aufschnaiter's extensive knowledge of Tibet was unable to help us. In fact, the officials were actually on their way to find us. One day we heard the tinkling of bells and two armed men on ponies rode up and demanded of us in the local dialect that we return to India by the same way as we had come. We knew that we would not achieve much with mere words alone and so to their great surprise we just pushed them aside. Luckily they made no use of their weapons, thinking no doubt that we too were armed. After a few feeble attempts to delay us, they rode away and without further hindrance we reached the next settlement, where the local governor had his offices.

We learned that the governor was packing his things for the move to Schangtse, his summer residence. We were more than a little astonished to find that he was one of the two armed men who had ordered us to retrace our steps. Accordingly, his attitude was not exactly obliging and it was all we could do to persuade him to give us a little flour in exchange for medicines. The little medicine pouch I carried proved to be our salvation.

At length the governor showed us a cave where we could spend the night and told us once more that we must leave Tibet using the same route by which we had come. If we agreed, he said, he would provide us with provisions and transport at no cost. We refused to accept his proposal and tried to explain to him that Tibet was a neutral state and should at the very least grant us freedom of passage. But he was not intelligent enough to grasp this concept, nor was he competent enough to take a decision even if he had understood it. So we proposed that we should leave the decision to a high-ranking official, a monk whose official residence was in Thuling, only eight miles away.

Here, too, we were told angrily to return the way we had come. Eventually we managed to persuade the official to allow us to return to India by a different route to the one we had used. Having agreed terms, they provided donkeys to carry our baggage and as much meat, flour and butter as we wanted. All the same we felt dejected at the unappealing prospect of ending up behind barbed wire again. Bruno

Treipel, who had grown to dislike the country, decided to give up and return to the Dehra Dun camp. Of the seven escapees, only three now remained – Peter Aufschnaiter, Hanne Kopp and me. We were determined not to return to the wire-fenced prison camp.

Although we left an inhospitable Tibet, at least we had had three weeks to experience one of the most important historical regions of the country and had seen the Red Temple of Tsaparang and other monastic ruins of the ancient kingdom of Guge, which had played such a large part in Buddhist legends. The Shipki Pass formed the frontier but there were no border posts, Tibetan or Indian. Nothing but the usual prayer flags and a milestone which said
"SIMLA 200 MILES".
We were on British sovereign territory once more and within striking distance of Dehra Dun. The Tibetan soldier who had accompanied us bade us farewell. "Perhaps we shall meet again in Lhasa. There are many pretty girls and good beer," he said with a smile.

In the first Indian village we came to, we passed ourselves off as American soldiers on leave, slept in the official resthouse and bought fresh supplies without arousing suspicion. Our plan was to slip back over the border into Tibet again. We followed the Spiti Valley and passed through the sparsely populated region that a year later was to prove fateful for our friend Wiggerl Schmaderer. When Aufschnaiter and I failed to return to Dehra Dun in 1944, Wiggerl and Paidar decided to follow our example and escape themselves. They followed our tracks into the Spiti Valley and managed to buy fresh supplies in a village there. While resting up a little later, however, they realised that they did not have sufficient provisions for the next stage of the journey. Encouraged by the ease with which they had been purchasing supplies, Schmaderer went back for more while Paidar stayed with their baggage. That was their fatal mistake. They had not considered the fact that there were travel bans in force on both sides of the frontier for those who did not have the required permit. After their first shopping trip, the locals would have been able to use the excuse that they had not recognised them as foreigners but a second visit could not be explained away quite as plausibly. Schmaderer and Paidar had probably underestimated the danger. The sad fact is that Schmaderer was murdered and his body abandoned in a riverbed.

We followed the Spiti River upstream, past several Tibetan monasteries, and then veered north-east and crossed two 5,600 metre high passes to avoid British sovereign territory. A friendly family of nomads explained to us that we were already in Tibet. We reached the upper Indus Valley at Trashigang. The caravan route was busy and we attracted little attention as we made our way to the collection of mud-brick huts that was Gartok, the "capital city" of Western Tibet. Our negotiations with the senior official, known as the Garpon, were friendly. He held the rank of nobility in Tibet and had already held discussions with the English. After a few days the Garpon informed us that he could only give us travel passes and transport for his province, Ngari, and that we would in no circumstances be allowed to enter the inner provinces of Tibet. We conferred and suggested that he should give us a travel permit to the Nepalese frontier. After some hesitation he promised to send a letter outlining our request to the Central Government in Lhasa, but he explained that we might have to wait several months for a reply. We had not given up the idea of pushing on to the east and were anxious to continue our journey at all costs. As Nepal was a neutral country situated in the direction which we wished to go, we felt that we could be satisfied with the result of the negotiations.

The Garpon then kindly asked us to remain for a few days as his guests, as pack animals and a guide had to be found for us. After three days our travel pass was delivered to us. It stipulated that our route should pass through the following places: Ngakhyu, Sersok, Montse, Barka, Tokchen, Lholung, Shamtsang, Truksum and Gyabnak. It also stated that we had the right to requisition two yaks. Of particular importance was the clause that required the inhabitants to sell us provisions at local prices, and to provide us with free food and servants for the evenings.

We set off on July 13th and our proud little caravan consisted of our two yaks with their nomad driver, followed by my small donkey carrying nothing but a tea-kettle. Then came our guide, a young Tibetan called Norbu, on horseback, while we three Europeans brought up the rear rather more modestly on foot.

The next few weeks passed uneventfully and we had time to enjoy the colours and the wide expanses of the Tibetan countryside. A gentle pass brought us to the source of the Brahmaputra, known as the Tsangpo in Tibet, a region known in the western world through the explorations of Sven Hedin. The 6,714 metre high Mount Kailash, the Sacred Mountain, is a coveted objective for Buddhist and Hindu pilgrims alike. Herbert Tichy had circumambulated the mountain via the 5,636 metre Drolma-La in 1936 and had returned with photographs depicting pilgrims prostrating themselves and making the entire circuit on their hands and knees. The faithful hope to be rewarded with a higher incarnation in the next life for the hardships endured in making such a pilgrimage over stony ground and in the thin air. This circumambulation, or *kora,* is a perfect example of the old adage that the journey is more important than the destination.

We would have loved to walk around the mountain as the pilgrims do but our letter from the Garpon did not provide for such a detour, so we contented ourselves with a chilly swim in Lake Manasarovar instead. The landscape to the north was dominated by the peak of Mount Kailash and to the south by the glaciers of the 7,100 metre Gurla Mandhata. Then there were the wide plains interspersed with low passes and fast flowing rivers, through which we often had to wade, while our local companions stayed dry on horseback – an unusual reversal of roles for Asian circumstances.

On the road to Tokchen we met a large caravan with the new district governor. We halted by the roadside and our Tibetan guide performed a deep bow, hat in hand, he extended his tongue in greeting – the picture of total subservience. He explained our presence, weapons that had been readied were put away and we were graciously offered dried fruit and nuts from their saddle bags.

We lived like nomads; for the past three months we had been sleeping mainly in the open air, and our standards of comfort were lower than those of the native population. All the same we were happy and contented. Very few Europeans had set foot in these regions and we knew that everything we observed might be of value at a later date. At the time we still thought that we would be returning to civilisation within the foreseeable future. The shared dangers and hardships had formed a strong bond of companionship; each knew the others' virtues and failings and so we were able to help one another in times of difficulty.

Meanwhile, Magener and Have's escape was over. In thirty-five days, they had managed to get through India and cross the Allied battle lines. At first they had been arrested as spies by the Japanese in Rangoon but four months after our mass break-out they ended up at the German Embassy in Tokyo.

We were now approaching Gyabnak, the last name on the list of places mentioned on our travel permit and the place where the authority of our friend from Gartok ended. The decision about what to do next was taken out of our hands, for on the third day of our stay at Gyabnak a messenger arrived from Tradun and summoned us to go at once to that place, where two high ranking officials from Lhasa wished to speak with us.

THE VILLAGE OF HAPPINESS

I will always remember the next day as one of the best experiences of my life. After a short march, we caught sight of the tiny golden towers of a monastery in the far distance. Above them, tremendous walls of ice glistened in the morning sun. It slowly dawned on us that we must be looking at the eight-thousanders Dhaulagiri, Annapurna and Manaslu. The view was overwhelming; even Kopp, who was not a climber, shared our enthusiasm. Tradun and the filigree towers of its monastery, lay at the far end of the plain and we had many hours in which to enjoy the view of these giant mountains. Not even a wade through the icy waters of the Tsachu River could dampen our spirits.

It was evening when we reached Tradun. The red monastery with its golden roof lay on a hill and shone like a fairy-tale palace in the last rays of the setting sun. The houses, the usual air-dried mud-brick dwellings, were hidden away on the lee side of the monastery, protected from the wind, and here we found the whole population of the town waiting for us in silence. We were taken immediately into a house which had been made ready for us. Hardly had we unloaded our baggage when several servants arrived and invited us most courteously to accompany them to their masters.

We walked through a whispering crowd of servants into a larger room where the highest seats were occupied by a smiling monk and a secular official of equal rank. A little lower down, an abbot, the monastery official from Gyabnak and a Nepalese merchant had taken their places. The merchant spoke a few words of English and was to act as interpreter. They had prepared a bench seat made out of cushions for us, so we did not have to sit cross-legged on the floor like the Tibetans. Tea and biscuits were pressed upon us and all questions politely postponed. Finally, they asked to see our travel pass. This did the rounds and everyone studied it carefully. There was an oppressive silence. Hesitantly, the two officials voiced their misgivings. Were we really Germans? They simply could not believe that we had escaped from British custody and presumed that we must be Russians or British. We were made to fetch our luggage, which was thoroughly searched.

Their chief worry was that we might have a radio set or weapons and it was hard to persuade them that we possessed nothing of the sort. The only thing that caught their attention was our Tibetan grammar book.

Since our travel permit stated that we wished to go to Nepal, they promised to help us in any way they could. They said we could set off the next morning and reach Nepal over the Korela Pass in just two days, but we were determined to remain in Tibet at all costs. We begged for the right of asylum, hammered on about Tibet's neutrality and compared the position of Tibet with that of Switzerland. The officials insisted stubbornly, if politely, that we adhere to the conditions laid down in our travel pass. We argued our case with equal stubbornness. During the months we had spent in Tibet we had become better acquainted with the Asiatic mentality and knew that one should not give up one's position too easily. The remainder of our discussion passed off in an atmosphere of the greatest calm. Over countless cups of tea, our hosts informed us modestly that they were there on a tax gathering trip and that in Lhasa they did not have quite the same high rank that they seemed to enjoy here in Tradun. They were travelling with twenty servants and numerous pack animals and one got the impression that they must be government ministers at the very least. With the remark that we wished to remain for a few days more, we finally took our leave.

Next day a servant brought an invitation to lunch from the Bonpos, as all high-ranking persons are called in Tibet. A splendid meal of noodles awaited us. We must have given the impression that we were hungry, judging by the huge quantities of food they set in front of us. Even when, with the best will in the world, we could eat no more, they kept pressing us to do so, until finally we learned that it was the custom to thank one's hosts before one was full. We were greatly impressed by the skill with which they handled their chopsticks, even managing to pick up individual grains of rice with them. The mutual astonishment contributed greatly to the friendly atmosphere and there was much hearty laughter on both sides. At the end of the meal Tibetan beer was served and the atmosphere became even more cheerful.

Gradually the talk turned to our problem and we heard that the authorities had decided to communicate our request for permission to stay in Tibet to the Central Government in Lhasa. We were instructed to compose a petition in English to that effect, which the two officials would append to their letter. We drafted our request and it was attached there and then to the officials' letter, which had already been prepared. This was then sealed with due ceremony and handed to a courier, who immediately set off for Lhasa.

We could hardly believe the friendly reception, nor the fact that we would be allowed to stay in Tradun until an answer came from Lhasa. Our experiences with junior officials had not been the best, so we asked for written confirmation of the permission to stay. This we obtained. Happy with the outcome, we returned to our quarters. Hardly had we arrived when a procession of heavily laden servants trooped in, carrying sacks of flour and rice and four freshly slaughtered sheep. At first we had no idea what this meant until the mayor explained to us that the food was a present from the two officials. As we parted, the easy-going Tibetan offered a few words of wisdom that were to serve me well during my time in this land. He said that the haste of Europeans had no place here and that we must learn patience and to bide our time if we were to achieve our aims.

We had more than enough time on our hands and hoped to use some of it to learn the art of patience. It was summer and there were plenty of distractions in Tradun. Caravans large and small called here; high ranking district officials with their entire families used the warm weather to travel. After taking up residence in the quarters prepared for them by the servants they would invite us over, as curious to see us as we were to meet them. We all found the cultured young women with their red lacquered finger nails and heavy make up rather pretty and were sad to lose their charming company when the party moved on the next day.

One day a rather more unusual convoy arrived. The happy sound of bells that often accompanied such visitors was absent and the weapons they carried were modern carbines. It was a government official from Nepal who had come to Tradun to visit us in the guise of a pilgrim. We had the feeling he wished to persuade us to accompany him to Nepal. He said we would be well received in the capital Kathmandu and that we would find work there. Our journey would be organised by the government and three hundred rupees had already been allocated for our travel expenses. It all sounded very attractive – perhaps too attractive.

After three months in Tradun we were starting to lose our patience and our friendship suffered as a result. Kopp kept indicating that he wished to accept the invitation to go to Nepal. Aufschnaiter went his own way. He purchased four sheep as pack animals and announced his intention to set off for Changtang, an inhospitable region that lay between the two main trade routes. This was contrary to our plan to await the letter from Lhasa but we were now beginning to doubt that we would receive a positive answer.

Aufschnaiter marched out one afternoon with his sheep. Kopp, too, began to pack and the local authorities promised to provide him with transport, as they were pleased at his decision to go to Nepal. They were less pleased with Aufschnaiters behaviour and from that day onwards guards slept in front of our door. The next day, to our astonishment, Aufschnaiter returned. During the night his sheep had been attacked by wolves, which had devoured two of them. This forced him to return and so we three spent one more evening together.

The next day Kopp took his leave. The whole village turned out to see him off. So now, of the seven original escapees, only Aufschnaiter and I remained. As mountaineers, we were probably better suited physically and mentally to cope with the lonely and strenuous life in this harsh country. It was now late November and the caravan routes were no longer very busy. The official from the monastery in Gyabnak sent us some sheep and twelve loads of yak's dung for fuel. We were glad of it, too, for by now the temperature had dropped to minus twelve.

In spite of the winter temperatures we were more determined than ever to leave Tradun, with or without the letter. We started hoarding provisions and bought a second yak. Then we received the news that a letter had arrived for us. What we had feared had, in fact, transpired – we were forbidden to travel into Inner Tibet. We were informed that we could travel to Kyirong, only eight miles from the Nepalese frontier and seven days' march to the capital, Kathmandu, and that we would be given transport and servants for the journey. We agreed at once, as our route would take us a little bit further into Tibet and the longer we remained on the right side of the law the fewer difficulties we would have, we reasoned.

On 17th December we left Tradun, the place which had granted us shelter for more than four months. We bore the Tibetans no ill feeling for their refusal to allow us to go to Lhasa; indeed, we were grateful to them for the eight months we had spent outside the barbed wire. The road to Kyirong took us again over the main Himalayan watershed. It was bitterly cold, and the Tsangpo was frozen solid. After a week we reached Dzongkar, a settlement of about a hundred mud brick houses and scattered ruins hidden behind a thick, fortified wall. A monastery and adjacent larger building comprised the regional seat of government of a Dzongpon, or high ranking district official.

Although we had not planned to stay here long, heavy snowfalls kept us in Dzongkar for almost a month. All day thick snowflakes fell and communications were interrupted. We enjoyed our time here and observed some of the ceremonies at the monastery and the performances of a company of dancers. A number of aristocratic officials lived here and we soon made friends with them. By now we spoke good Tibetan and could hold long conversations with them. New Year's Eve 1944 passed quietly, but our thoughts dwelt more than ever on home. We wondered how our parents, brothers and sisters might be faring with no news at all from us.

On 19th January, 1945 the roads were sufficiently passable to allow us to set off again, this time in the company of a huge yak caravan. At the head of the column, unladen yaks stamped through the snow like snow ploughs and seemed to enjoy themselves tremendously. The valley soon narrowed to a gorge and in the first two days we counted no fewer than seventeen bridges. My yak, which came from the desolate region of Changtang, was spooked by the bridges and protested vigorously whenever he had to cross one. He behaved like a stubborn ox and it was only when the yak drivers helped out by pushing from behind and pulling in front that we managed to get him across. I had already been warned not to bring him to Kyirong as he would not be able to stand the warm summer climate, but I had not wanted to leave him behind as we were still determined that we would not leave Tibet and would mount a renewed escape attempt if necessary, for which the yak might prove very useful.

We were deeply impressed by a cliff-top monastery near the village of Longda. Two hundred metres above the valley floor red temples and cloisters clung to the rocks. Despite the danger of avalanches, Aufschnaiter and I could not resist climbing up for a closer look. We met some of the monks and nuns and learned from them that this was the monastery founded by Milarepa, the famous Tibetan saint and poet, who lived here in the eleventh century. The monastery bore the name Drakar Taso. We could easily understand that the glorious surroundings and the unique location were ideally suited to the sensitive soul intent on meditation and poetry. The snow was becoming more sparse each day now and after reaching the tree line we found our winter clothing too warm.

Kyirong literally means "the village of happiness" and it certainly deserves that name. I will never stop yearning for this place and if I could choose anywhere to spend my twilight years, I would choose Kyirong. I would build myself a house of red cedar-wood and have one of the rushing mountain streams running through my garden, in which every kind of fruit would flourish and grow, for though the place is at an altitude of 2,770 metres it also lies on the twenty-eighth parallel, at the same latitude as North Africa.

Since there were no hotels or guest houses in Tibet, we were again accommodated in a small farmhouse. The house was built of wood on stone foundations and was roofed with shingles weighed down with heavy rocks. It reminded us of our Tyrolean houses back home. In fact, the whole of the village could have been in the Alps, except that instead of chimneys the roofs of the houses were decorated with prayer flags.

On the ground floor were the stables for the cows and horses. A thick wooden ceiling separated the stalls from the first floor, where the family lived. The living quarters were only accessible by a steep wooden ladder leading up from the courtyard. An open fire illuminated the house altar, with seven butter-lamps at the back of the room.

The room that we were assigned to was very small – two straw filled mattresses served as beds and easy chairs and a tiny window provided just enough light to write by – so I decided to sleep in the hay barn next door. We cooked and ate with the family by the open fire. Although we had new hosts, we continued our unceasing battle with mice, bugs and fleas and never quite managed to get the better of these pests, although the view of the nearby glaciers and seven thousand metre peaks more than compensated for our discomfort. Aufschnaiter, normally the taciturn Tyrolean, was of the opinion that we could happily stay here for the rest of our lives.

In the event, we stayed for just nine months but we could easily have filled an entire book with our experiences. Right at the beginning of our stay we paid a visit to the district authorities and informed the officials that we would like to stay for a while in Kyirong. They took this very calmly and promised, at our request, to inform Lhasa of our wishes. We also visited the representative of Nepal, but were careful to remain unswayed by his advances, since we had learned in the meantime that Kopp, after just a few days in the Nepalese capital, Kathmandu, had been deported to an internment camp in India. Accordingly we decided to remain in this fairy-tale village until we had formulated a new plan of escape.

We were not in the least bored. We filled thick diaries with our observations on the manner and customs of our hosts and rarely did a day go by without a trip out to explore the neighbourhood. Of course it was the mountains that attracted us most; that and the hot springs around Kyirong. There were several of these, the hottest of which was in a bamboo forest on the bank of the ice-cold River Kosi. The water bubbled out of the ground nearly at boiling point and was diverted into an artificial basin, where it still had a temperature of about forty degrees Centigrade. Spring was the bathing season. Swarms of Tibetans came along to the pool and bamboo huts sprang up everywhere. Men and women tumbled naked into the pool and any signs of prudishness provoked roars of laughter. The local aristocrats would also travel to the hot springs with their servants. But the whole circus lasts only a short time as the snow melts in summer and the springs disappear beneath the raging torrent of the river.

The Tibetans celebrate New Year in the middle of February, as unlike ours, their year is based on the lunar calendar. There are many customs associated with this festival. This was our first Tibetan New Year and we followed the preparations with great anticipation. The son of our host family attached a small, freshly cut pine tree decked out with colourful prayer flags to the roof of our house. After placating the gods with offerings of food we all went to the temple of the Phawa Monastery to top up the butter-lamps. They were already full to the brim but we learned that they had to be overflowing in order to please the gods. The pagoda-like style of the Phawa Monastery-Kloster reminded me of similar buildings in the neighbouring country of Nepal. The monastery had maintained close links with Lhasa since the seventh century and it was for this reason that Kyirong was a holy village and an important place of pilgrimage.

The celebrations included a sports festival with horse racing, archery and a rock lifting competition. I joined in the fun, to the general astonishment of the spectators. In fact I almost won the running event. I was in the lead right from the start but on the last, and steepest, section I was caught by another runner, who grabbed me by the seat of my trousers. I was so surprised by this tactic that I stopped dead in my tracks. This was the chance that the rascal had been waiting for. He overtook me to touch the finishing marker stone just ahead of me. I had not reckoned on such trickery and, to gales of laughter from all those present, I received a consolation prize of a white ribbon instead of a sheep.

Unfortunately the festive spirit was clouded by tragedy in our house. One day I was called into the room of our hostess's youngest sister. The room was in darkness and only when a pair of hot hands gripped mine did I realise that I was standing next to her bed. Once my eyes had grown accustomed to the dark, I recoiled in barely concealed horror. There in the bed lay someone who only two days before had been a pretty, healthy young girl. Though only a layman, I instantly saw that she had smallpox. Her larynx and tongue had already been affected and she slurred her words as she complained that she was dying. She was beyond help and I could only hope that an epidemic would not break out. Two days later she died.

The days grew warmer, and the spring snow conditions gave us the idea of making skis. We cut planks of wood from a couple of birch trunks, shaped them on the charcoal fire and devised a kind of strap binding system. Our enthusiasm was dampened somewhat when the

Ponpo issued an order forbidding us from trying them out in the mountains on the grounds that "riding the snow" would displease the gods and thus affect the harvest. During the next few weeks we obeyed orders but one moonlit night we slipped out and headed for the mountain-side. The next day we enjoyed ourselves on splendid neve right in the middle of the Himalayas. We were both surprised that we were able to ski so well after such a long break from it. We broke the skis eventually, and hid the remains of these implements that the Tibetans found so strange. The people of Kyirong never found out that we had been "snow riding".

As the weather grew warmer my yak fell sick. He had fever and the local veterinary, Traba Ongdi, reckoned that only the gall of a bear would help him. I purchased the expensive gall, more out of a desire to appease the vet than from a belief in its healing properties, and was not surprised at the lack of success. Finally, I had to have the trusty yak slaughtered, as I wanted at least to save the meat. With the loss of the yak our escape options were now significantly more limited.

Our relationship with the Dzongpon of Kyirong was good but we were asked to refrain from making longer excursions, as there were many bears, leopards and even dangerous wild dogs. His worries were justified; we had often seen deep footprints in the snow that could only have been made by bears. People with more imagination than I possess might have attributed them to the legendary Abominable Snowman. The Tibetans tell of a mythical creature called the Migo, a friendly beast that occasionally pays them a visit, but they know nothing of the Yeti story, which originates from the tribes of northern Nepal, who, like the Sherpas, migrated to Tibet many hundreds of years ago. A hat reputed to have been made from Yeti fur caused a sensation for a while until zoologists identified the fur as having come from a rare breed of wild goat. Later, in Lhasa, I met a monk with a hat just like it. As a precaution against bears we always used to carry a tin full of powdered red pepper. Two of the farmers in Kyirong had badly scarred faces and one had been blinded by a blow from a bear's paw.

In the middle of the summer, when we were helping with the buckwheat harvest, the Ponpos summoned us to the fortress. This time they called upon us energetically to limit our stay in Kyirong. They even asked us to swear an oath to this effect. We duly promised to leave in the autumn; after all, they had not specified in which direction we were to go. The war had ended, this much we had learned from Nepalese merchants, and we certainly did not intend to head south back to the internment camp. Once we had made our decision we no longer felt obliged to limit our excursions and began a systematic exploration of the long valleys. We often stayed out for several days, taking provisions, drawing materials and a compass with us. We camped on the high pastures alongside the herdsmen who, just as they do in the Alps, spent the summer months grazing their cattle on the luxuriant mountain meadows. There were hundreds of cows and female yaks grazing on the green pastures in the middle of a world of glaciers. I often helped with the butter churning and it was a pleasure to receive a slab of fresh golden butter for my work. To speed up the process we fetched chunks of ice from the nearby glacier and threw them into the huge butter churns.

There were fierce, vicious dogs at the herdsmen's huts: mastiffs, known as "*dokyi*" in Tibet. They were tied up with leashes made of woven goat's hair and by their barking at night protected, the herd of cattle from panthers, wolves and wild dogs. Very powerfully built, their usual diet of milk and raw calves' meat gave them enormous strength and made them particularly dangerous. I had several disagreeable encounters with them. On one occasion one of these *dokyis* broke loose as I approached and sprang at my throat. I parried his attack but he bit me on the arm and did not let go till I had wrestled him to the ground. My clothes hung in tatters but the dog lay motionless on the ground. I bound up my wounds with what remained of my shirt. To this day, I still bear the scars. My wounds healed very quickly as a result of repeated baths in one of the hot springs, which at this time of the year were more frequented by snakes than Tibetans. The herdsmen told me later that I was not the only one to have come off badly from the battle. The dog had lain in his corner and refused to eat for a week.

Our excursions resulted in a wealth of useful material, maps and sketches but we found no pass which would have provided us with a route of escape. Twenty kilometres from Kyirong, on the road to Dzonga, we established a supply depot. The countdown had begun. It was now autumn and the permitted term of our residence was coming to an end. If we had decided to head for Nepal there would have been no need for secrecy, but since the Ponpos were afraid of being punished by the authorities in Lhasa if we were successful in our attempt to penetrate further into Tibet, they had ordered the inhabitants of the village, who lived in constant fear of their local rulers, to turn us in if we should disobey their orders.

On November 6th, 1945, Peter Aufschnaiter brazenly left the village with his pack on his back. For tactical reasons it was agreed that he should leave first on the pretext of an excursion. With him went Kartru, my long-haired Tibetan dog – a present from an aristocrat in Lhasa. We had become rather attached to the creature.

A feverish search for Aufschnaiter ensued and I was repeatedly cross-examined about his whereabouts. The authorities were not convinced by my feeble attempts to persuade them that he had gone on one of his harmless excursions. On the evening of November 8th I had resolved to leave – by force if need be. There were spies stationed both inside and outside the house who did not let me out of their sight. I waited until ten o' clock at night but they showed no signs of disappearing, so I made a bit of a scene, pretending to be very angry and complaining loudly that their behaviour made it impossible for me to stay there and that I must go and sleep in the forest. As they watched I started packing. My hostess and her mother came in, horrified, and when they saw what was happening threw themselves to their knees before me and entreated me with tears not to go. They said that if I did they would be whipped out of the village and would lose their house and possessions. The old mother handed me a white veil as a token of respect for me and when she saw that my heart was not softened by her appeals, offered me money. The offer was not meant as an insult, since bribery is common enough in all circles in Tibet and the usual way of getting things done. I tried to persuade them that nothing would happen to them if I went away but their cries and screams had aroused the whole village and I had to act quickly, if it was not already too late.

I can still see the butter-smeared Mongol faces staring up at my window with the light of the pine torches shining upon them. And now the two mayors arrived panting with a message from the Ponpos to say that if I would stay until morning, I could then go wherever I wished. I knew this was only a ruse and said nothing. My hostess clung to me weeping and saying that she had always treated me like one of her own children and that I ought not to cause her such pain and grief.

By now my nerves were stretched to breaking point. Something had to happen. I resolutely shouldered my pack and walked out of the house. I was surprised that the crowd assembled around the door did not offer me any resistance. Like a mournful choir they chanted "He's going, he's going," but no one touched me. They must have noticed that I really meant business. A couple of young lads shouted to one another to stop me but that was as far as they got. I walked untouched through the crowd, which gave way before me.

But I was glad when I had passed out of the torchlight into the dark. I ran along the Nepal road for a bit in order to deceive possible pursuers, then I made a wide detour round the village and by morning had reached our agreed meeting point twenty kilometres away. Aufschnaiter was waiting for me on the side of the road, and my dog jumped up to greet me. We walked on for a while in search of a good hiding place for the day.

For the last time for many years we camped in a wood. We had found a good hiding place and spent the first day of our escape in comfort. We had spent nine pleasant months in the Village of Happiness – it really had been the land of milk and honey for us – but now it was time to move on. The deep valley of the River Kosi stretched before us and beyond this lay Dzonga. We intended to walk this section at night, since we knew that the Tibetans were just as frightened of ghosts and demons as the Indians. The bridges over the Kosi were glazed with a film of frozen spume from the river and we had to cross on all fours, pushing our packs in front of us, which cost us valuable time. Before reaching Dzonga we hid once more.

The following night we got lost several times. Earth and stones froze to our feet as we removed our shoes to cross several small streams. It was unimaginably hard going, as my diary at the time attests. We stumbled over ice-glazed scree and slid down steep slopes in the dark, our heavy packs a constant burden. We were plagued by blisters and frostbite but somehow managed to keep going. Since we had emptied our depot of provisions, our packs each weighed at least forty kilos. It was impossible to lift and carry them by their narrow straps alone but the herdsmen had given us some additional carry straps which we fastened around the pack and our foreheads.

After two more night marches we slipped quietly past Dzonga and found shelter in a cave that had obviously once been inhabited by a hermit, judging by the many devotional objects that had been left there. The path led steeply upwards and we had to rest often. To keep up our strength we ate frozen knobs of butter and cloves of garlic. The heavy packs and the thin air were beginning to make themselves felt. Little wonder – after all, we were at an altitude of 5,180 metres, more than two thousand five hundred metres above Kyirong. At the top of the Chakhyungla Pass were the usual stone cairns adorned with wind-tattered prayer flags. Like a grim reminder, a *stupa* appeared – a spiritual monument to a revered holy man, or *lama*.

In this snowy, barren wasteland, an area seldom visited by people, we ventured to travel by day. We made good progress, and after our next camp, which we spent freezing horribly, we were rewarded the next morning by a splendid view of the deep-blue Lake Pelgu lying below us. The plateau on which we were camped was ringed by a gleaming chain of peaks, two of which we knew by name: the 8,012 metre high Gosainthan, or Shisha Pangma, and the slightly lower Laptschi Kang. Both were still awaiting their conquerors, in common with most of the other Himalayan giants. Our fingers were stiff and cold but we still managed to make an outline sketch of the mountains. Aufschnaiter took the bearings of the most important peaks with a shaky compass and noted down the figures.

We went down through this winter landscape to the shore of the lake, where we found a ruined caravanserai and had to spend another night in the snow. We were actually quite surprised at how well we had adjusted to the altitude and the progress we were making, considering our heavy loads. But our poor dog was miserable. He kept pace with us bravely, even though his only food was our excrement and he was half-starved. At night he lay across our feet and helped keep them warm. It was a comfort for both us and the dog, for the thermometer showed minus twenty-two degrees.

How happy we were to find a trace of life next day! A flock of sheep came slowly towards us, followed by some shepherds muffled in thick furs. They pointed out the direction we should take to reach the next habitation and the same evening we reached the village of Trakchen. It was high time for us to see some human beings again. Aufschnaiter reckoned that, at four thousand six hundred metres, it might well be the highest settlement in the world. The natives took us for Indians, so buying provisions was no problem. We had pooled our cash resources in Kyirong and after extensive haggling we acquired a yak and a sheepskin coat.

One day Mount Everest appeared. The mountain had certainly never been viewed by a European from this perspective, and we made a few sketches. On December 2nd, 1945, we reached the great Tsangpo, or Brahmaputra, River. We had been worrying for days about how to cross it. In Chung Rivoche, the village on the far bank of the river, there was an immense *stupa*, as big as those we had seen in pictures of Gyantse. The Tsangpo was full of huge blocks of ice and there was a fierce current running, so swimming across was unthinkable. A passing nomad, having noticed our perplexity, pointed upstream, where we found a hanging bridge spanning the torrent. It was one – perhaps the last – of one hundred and eight bridges that had been built by Thangtong Gyalpo five hundred years ago. Gyalpo was a Tibetan *mahasiddha*, or great adept, and is known in the western world as the Leonardo da Vinci of Asia. We unloaded our kit, and the yak walked dutifully into the freezing water. He was almost submerged by the torrent, leaving only his head above water, poking up between the thick chunks of ice, and was caught by the current and swept some way downstream but he was an excellent swimmer and after about a kilometre he reached the opposite bank.

We had no time to marvel at the brilliant construction of the bridge. As we scrambled onto the first bridge support, our dog immediately got his legs stuck in the criss-cross network of cables and webbing. Only then did we notice that there was no proper walkway. We had to place our feet very carefully and try not to look down at the dizzying drop. I waited till Aufschnaiter had reached the next support before I started my balancing act. I carried the shivering dog under one arm and held tight with the other in order to counteract the swinging action of the narrow bridge. It was all highly adventurous and the prospect of having to make the crossing twice was a little daunting. To prevent our fingers freezing to the metal we wore socks over our hands but the bitter cold made it a real ordeal. We had been on the move for hours and the day was drawing to an end. But we had now overcome the biggest obstacle on our journey north.

Chung Rivoche had several caravanserais and we had no difficulty finding somewhere warm to spend the night. We were joined at the fire by a Tibetan pilgrim, who had lived for several years in India. He sold us a writing pad and two pencils, so that we could continue writing up our diaries. In the morning a man asked us if it was our yak down there beyond the village. And there he was: our yak, standing stoically on the river bank festooned with icicles. He seemed just as pleased as we were about the reunion; so much so that he let us saddle him up without any of his customary stubbornness.

Lhasa was only a few weeks away by the normal caravan route, but for us this was out of the question. One of the locals was of the opinion that the direct route, heading due north and crossing the Changtang plains, was impossible in winter. We would not meet a soul for days on end and, later, only robbers, he said. But we paid no heed to his warnings, as we knew that the route across the Transhimalaya was our best chance of avoiding the authorities.

IN THE NO-MAN'S LAND
OF THE CHANGTANG

We knew that we were about to embark on an adventure, the outcome of which was highly uncertain, and we had a nervous feeling in the pits of our stomachs. Had we overestimated our strengths? What if one of us was unable to carry on? But as we crossed the watershed of the Transhimalaya in light snowfall, the feeling of apprehension vanished with the wind. This was usually the way with me; once I got going, the doubts disappeared.

We were now at an altitude of five thousand four hundred metres. Before us, the unending high plateau stretched away in the distance. Apart from the two of us, the yak and the dog, there was no sign of any living creature far and wide. Even the snow leopards and wolves seemed to avoid these endless, barren wastes. We only realised we had crossed another pass when we noticed that the rivulet of water beneath the blanket of snow was running with us rather than against our direction of travel. In this no-man's land, even encountering a rough stone wall built by nomads to provide shelter in summer, was a happy event. Here we found enough dry yak dung to make a fire.

One day a small black shape appeared on the horizon, which we at first took to be some kind of mirage. Since one could see a long way ahead in the clear, thin air it was several hours before we were able to identify it as a nomad tent. The approach of several large long-haired mastiffs was greeted in heroic fashion by our dog, Kartru, who cowered pathetically with his tail between his legs until the nomads appeared from the tent and called their dogs off. As we warmed ourselves by the fire they told us they had been snowed in for weeks and had already lost some of their herd of animals. We got the impression that our friendly hosts were as glad as we were to see human faces again. We were taken for Indians and served with huge portions of meat. The crowning glory of the meal came when one of the men took a deep-frozen sheep's liver and roasted it on the open fire. He then held one end in his teeth and cut it into small pieces with a dagger before sharing it out. We bought a leg of yak, some of which we cooked immediately. Even Kartru was able to eat his fill that night.

Our kind hosts were horrified to hear of the route we proposed to take and strongly advised us to reconsider. We failed to understand the reason; the word "khampa" meant nothing to us. Fortified by the meal we set out next day and soon ran into thick, driving snow. Walking became a torture in our inadequate footwear. The upper crust of snow was treacherous and we and our yak often broke through. In some places there were streams running under the snow, which meant wet feet and shoes and trouser legs frozen stiff. Progress was painfully slow and we covered only a few kilometres that day.

We stopped for the day earlier than usual and as we removed our shoes from painful feet we noticed the first signs of frostbite, which was a cause for concern. That evening Aufschnaiter and I had a long and earnest talk. We could still turn back. We massaged our feet, rubbing some life back into our blue toes, and my mind went back to the Eiger, when my feet had become swollen with the cold. Peter Aufschnaiter recalled the time, back in 1929, when at seven thousand metres on Kangchenjunga his climbing partner Ernst Beigel had slipped when traversing a ridge and had fallen some way down the face. Always the quick-witted climber, Aufschnaiter had saved the day by leaping down the opposite side of the ridge. Beigel suffered frostbitten feet and medical help came too late to save his toes. The expedition was over.

That evening we agreed to give up. Christmas was coming and common sense prevailed over our resolve and our willingness to endure further hardships. The next day, however, things looked different. Without a word, we packed our few possessions and headed north-east, to Lhasa. The North Star and Orion showed us the way.

Now, more than fifty years later, I can perhaps explain our decision. The previous evening, it had seemed pointless to carry on; we were afraid of losing our feet to frostbite and grew despondent. By morning our spiritual balance had been restored; we had regained our composure, our equanimity and our self-confidence. For someone who has never been in such a situation, this may be difficult to understand. Perhaps our unspoken decision to continue resulted from our matter of fact attitude to the situation in which we found ourselves.

With Peter Aufschnaiter there was never any conflict of opinion. We were friends, and the more difficult the situation, the firmer the bond between us. After the war, certain critics suggested that there might have been some disagreement between us. I can only confirm their suspicions, but I would also add that these people quite obviously do not have the slightest idea of the emotions that one has to contend with in situations of such extreme hardship. There was cursing and swearing, certainly, but not once did either of us complain to a third party about any problems we might have had.

It was still tough going but Aufschnaiter, undeterred, continued to take compass bearings on the unknown peaks and make sketches of the route. We crossed a snowy pass at about five thousand seven hundred metres and to our astonishment the softly undulating mountains that lay ahead were totally free of snow. Our silent decision to carry on that morning had been correct. Or, as my diary entry for December 11th, 1945, attests: "Providence had decided for us."

We were now covering between twenty and thirty kilometres each day, depending on whether we came across nomads' tents or not. Often enough, we had to bivouac in the open. At those times it took us all our energy to collect yak dung, and even talking was too much effort. We suffered badly with our hands, which were always stiff with frost, since we had no gloves and used socks instead, which we had to remove when doing jobs. Once a day we cooked meat, if we had any, and spooned the gravy straight out of the simmering saucepan. The boiling point was so low at this altitude, and the spoon soon cooled in the chill air, so we were able to eat straight from the pot without ever scalding our tongues.

I will never forget the misery of those long, cold nights as we lay awake for hours, pressed tightly together to stop us from freezing, the dog curled up at our feet. The yak seemed unconcerned by the cold and grazed placidly near our campsite. But there was another problem. Hardly had we got warm when we were mercilessly plagued by the countless blood-sucking lice that had infested us and whose number had multiplied alarmingly. It was absolute torture. It was halfway through the night by the time they had had their fill of our blood and given us some respite, whereupon we fell into an exhausted sleep for a few hours. Back to back in the chill cold of morning, we waited for the first rays of sun.

We walked for more than two weeks through the inhospitable Changtang. At one point we crossed the route taken by Sven Hedin on his failed attempt to reach Lhasa at the beginning of the twentieth century. Hedin wrote that he had had to endure temperatures of minus forty degrees. It was probably just as cold for us, but since we were up on the arid high plateau at a fairly constant five thousand metres altitude we found the cold bearable with suitable clothing. Apart from the nights, that is. We were mighty glad when from time to time we came across nomads who let us sleep in their warm tent. On one such occasion, once we had survived the usual onslaught of the big black dogs, we were invited by a nomad family to share their fire. After trading a sewing kit for two legs of mutton, our friendly host told us that there were many Khampas on the route we intended to take and asked us if we were carried any weapons. There it was again – that undertone of fear and warning. We still did not understand why we kept hearing it, since in all the books we had read, the Khampas, the inhabitants of the eastern province of Tibet known as Kham, were described as brave warriors, industrious merchants and great artists, skilled in the making of religious artefacts. When the nomad told us that he had had to give the Khampas a yak and two sheep before they would leave him in peace, we had our answer. We were told that, many hundreds of kilometres from their home territory, certain rogue groups of the Khampa clan conducted campaigns of robbery and violence, extorting goods rather than money from their unfortunate victims. For the nomads of this region, the word "Khampa" thus had a special, and sinister, meaning.

Before my book *Seven Years in Tibet* was published in the Tibetan language I asked my friend Rakra Rinpotsche, the former rector of the highest order of Tibetan monks' to pay particular attention to the correct translation of the term "Khampa". Several highly honourable and well respected Khampas complained to me that I had written, that throughout the Changtang, the word Khampa was synonymous with "robber". There must be several hundred Tibetologists in the world and the robber Khampas would make an interesting research project, since they differ significantly, both in appearance and in character, from the people of Kham.

We set off next morning with some misgivings. We had our doubts about continuing but after a brief consultation, decided to stick to our plan. We both had the feeling that we had now passed the point of no return. Later that day we came across a tent where, instead of the usual mastiffs, Kartru was mobbed by a pack of small, hairless dogs, who ran up to him, tails wagging. We were no less surprised to receive a friendly welcome from the people at the tents. Everyone, young and old, came out and started unloading our yak – something which no nomads had ever done. The children fingered our things, the men unpacked our meagre possessions and one of the women ran off with our only kettle. Suddenly it dawned on us that they were Khampas and we had walked into a trap. We put on a brave face and tried to make the best of a bad situation. At least we were on our guard and hoped that politeness, foresight and diplomacy would help us find a way out of the mess.

We had hardly sat down by the fire when the tent began to fill with visitors from the neighbouring tents, who had come to see the strangers – men, women, children and dogs. We had our hands full trying to keep our baggage together, as these people were both inquisitive and insistent. When they heard that we were pilgrims they urgently recommended us to take one of the men, a particularly good guide, with us to Lhasa. He said he would show us a road somewhat to the south of our route that, according to him, was far more suitable. The man was short and powerful and carried a huge sword in his belt. Not a type to inspire confidence. However, we accepted his offer and agreed on his pay. There was nothing else to do, for out here we were completely at the mercy of the Khampas.

The inquisitive visitors gradually drifted off to their own tents. As we prepared to go to bed I told Aufschnaiter, loudly, to use the rucksack with the pistol in it as a pillow. It was meant as a bluff, since we did not actually have a gun. During the night one of the men repeatedly tried to prise the rucksack away from Aufschnaiter, but we remained on our guard and stayed awake all night. That was not very difficult, although we were very tired, since the woman muttered prayers constantly. It occurred to me that she was praying in advance for forgiveness for the crime the men intended to commit against us. At any rate, we were glad when day broke.

At first everything seemed peaceful. We exchanged a pocket mirror for some yak's brains, which we cooked for breakfast. Then we began to get ready to go. Our hosts followed our every move with glowering faces and almost became aggressive when I handed our packs out of the tent to Aufschnaiter. But we shook them off and loaded our yak. We looked out for our "guide" but to our relief he was nowhere to be seen. The Khampa family urged us to opt for the southern route, as that way we would meet nomads who were also making a pilgrimage to Lhasa. We promised to do so and set off without further ado.

We had gone a few hundred metres when I noticed that my dog was missing. He usually came running after us. As we looked around, we saw three men following us. They soon caught us up and told us that they too were on the way to the tents of the nomad pilgrims and pointed to a distant plume of smoke. It all looked very suspicious, as we had never seen such plumes of smoke over the nomad tents. When we asked about Kartru they said that he had stayed behind in the tent; one of us could go and fetch him. Now their plan was clear. Our lives were at stake. They had kept the dog back in order to separate Aufschnaiter and me, since they lacked the courage to attack us both together. And they probably had companions waiting where the smoke was rising. If we went there we would be heavily outnumbered and they could easily do away with us. No one would ever learn anything about our disappearance. We now regretted that we had not taken the nomads' warnings more seriously.

We went a short way in the same direction as though we suspected nothing, and discussed what we should do. The two men were now on either side of us while the adolescent boy walked behind. As is the custom for robbers, they wore double sheepskin coats, to protect them against knife thrusts, and long swords stuck in their belts, while affecting an air of lamb-like innocence.

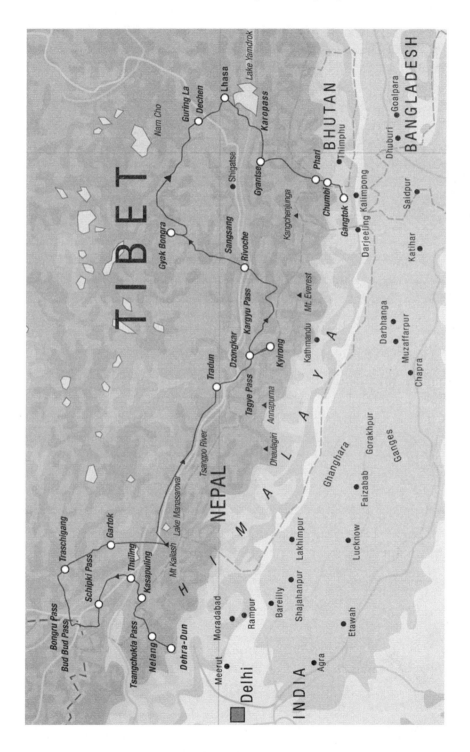

Something had to happen. Aufschnaiter thought we ought first to change direction, so as not to walk blindly into the trap. No sooner said than done. Still speaking, we turned on our heels. The Khampas stopped in surprise; but in a moment rejoined us and barred our way, asking us, in none too friendly tones, where we were going. "To fetch the dog," we answered curtly. This seemed to confuse them. After standing and staring after us for a while they went on their way, presumably to inform their accomplices.

As we got near the tents, the woman came towards us leading the dog on a rope. After a friendly greeting we went on, but this time we went back the way we had come to the camp. Unarmed as we were, to continue along our proposed route would have meant certain death. After a forced march we arrived that evening at the home of the friendly family with whom we had stayed two days before. They were not surprised to hear about our experiences and told us that the region in which the Khampas got up to their tricks was called Gyak Bongra and was avoided by the caravans. After our adventure, it was a blessing to be able to spend a peaceful, undisturbed night. Our decision to turn back had probably saved our lives.

Next morning, we bought more meat and headed east into a totally unpopulated region. We matched our pace to the slow, plodding gait of our trusty yak and halfway up a steep slope we had to rest. There was no doubt about it. The Khampas were back. Aufschnaiter and I were of the same opinion: we should sell our lives as dearly as possible. We looked for a place with cover from the rear where we could stand and fight. I was armed with two tent poles, while Aufschnaiter had a handful of stones – not much against the razor-sharp two-edged swords of our pursuers, but it would have to do. Then we saw that the two men had stopped. They seemed to be discussing something. Then they turned and went. We breathed a sign of relief and drove our yak on up the hill.

When we reached the crest of the ridge we understood why the men had turned back. Before us lay the loneliest landscape I had ever seen. A sea of snow-covered mountains stretched endlessly before us; wave after wave of peaks and valleys.

Had the Khampas really given up the pursuit? To be on the safe side we carried on marching even after nightfall. The snow gleamed in the moonlight; it was so light that we could even see the summits of the Transhimalaya in the distance.

I shall never forget that night march. It was the sternest challenge for mind and body that I have ever had to endure. But the very fact that the region was so inhospitable would prove to be our salvation. We trotted on for hours through the virgin snow, while our imaginations went their own way. I was tormented by visions of a warm, comfortable room, hot food and steaming hot drinks – memories of my student days in Graz, when the first self-service buffet was opened. Aufschnaiter's thoughts wandered different paths to mine. He muttered dark curses and swore that he would return armed to the teeth and exact a terrible revenge against the Khampas.

It was after midnight by the time we stopped. We slumped down in the snow, exhausted. Apart from a snow leopard slinking slowly through the white winter landscape in the distance, we had seen no signs of life on the long march. Finding dry yak dung to make a fire was hopeless; we had no energy left for such tasks. Ravenously hungry by now, we unloaded our yak and tried to eat some tsampa and a raw leg of mutton, but it was so cold that as soon as we put a spoonful of dry flour into our mouths the metal stuck to our tongue and lips and would not come away. We had to tear it loose, cursing loudly, our mouths cut to ribbons. With appetites blunted by the pain, we huddled together and, despite the piercing cold, fell into the leaden sleep of exhaustion.

We set off next morning in slightly better spirits. Our yak had spent the whole night vainly searching for grass and now, in desperation, was eating snow to slake his thirst. We had not found any water at all during the previous day. The springs we came across had all frozen solid into bizarrely shaped cascades of ice.

Day after day we toiled on, trudging along in the footprints of our brave yak, hardly raising our heads. Then we saw some tents. At first we thought it was a mirage. The nomads must have been on their guard, for as we walked towards the first of the tents we were approached by a pair of wild looking men, heavily armed, who told us curtly to go to the devil. This was no mirage. We stopped in our tracks, raised our hands to show we carried no weapons and explained to them that we were harmless pilgrims. We must have looked as if we were in a pitiful state, for after a brief consultation the owner of the largest tent invited us in to stay the night. We warmed ourselves by the fire and were given a bowl of steaming hot butter tea. It was December 24th, 1945. The nomads gave both of us a small bread roll. It was almost as if they knew it was Christmas Eve. In the wilds of the Changtang, this rare delicacy meant more to us than Christmas cake. We packed our presents away and thought about these good people as we ate the hard bread a few days later.

After several more days of hardship and deprivation, we finally reached the great northern caravan route. The no-man's land of the Changtang was finally behind us.

We now dropped the Indian pilgrim disguise and slowly reverted to being Europeans, bluffing our way past the road officers on the caravan route with the old travel permit which the Garpon had issued us with in Gartok a year and a half earlier. At the time, we had drawn lots to decide who should keep it and Kopp had won. But when he left us, I bought it back from him. And now its hour had come.

The northern caravan route was not a regular road, but there were staging posts at intervals, so-called *tasams*, where one could spend the night in houses or tents, change yaks and horses and buy fuel and provisions. The *tasams* were administered by low-ranking officials, or *ponpos*, and a local government permit, a *lamyig*, was required to use them. Although our permit showed a different route, the seal of the Garpon was sufficiently impressive for the *ponpos* to let us spend the night at the *tasams*.

We followed the tracks of the caravans through hills and steppe country. We no longer needed to navigate by the stars as the way ahead was clear – east instead of north. The wind and the cold were our constant companions, however. It seemed as if our whole world consisted of hurricane force winds and temperatures of minus thirty. We were again reminded of the books of Sven Hedin and the temperatures he had recorded on his Tibetan journeys. We suffered greatly from being insufficiently clothed and I was fortunate to acquire an old sheepskin coat from one of the tent-dwellers. It was too small for me and had half a sleeve missing, but it only cost me two rupees. Our footwear was also in a wretched state. Aufschnaiter had frostbitten hands and I was still having trouble with my feet. Most of all, we worried about our animals. My faithful dog was reduced to skin and bones. We had hardly enough food for ourselves and could spare very little for him. His paws were raw from walking and he moved so slowly that we often had to wait for hours in our camp before he finally caught up with us. The yak was little better off. He had not had enough grass to eat for weeks and was terribly emaciated. Even though we were now well below the snowline, the grass was scarce and dry and there was little time for grazing.

We spent our second New Year's Eve in Tibet in a *tasam*, where we reviewed our situation. What had we achieved so far? We were still travelling illegally – two down-at-heel, half-starved vagabonds, forced to dodge every petty official – and the "Forbidden City" of Lhasa still seemed like an illusory goal. It would have been easy to lose faith. As it was, our thoughts turned instead to home and family.

At first we had intended to have a rest day on New Year's Day, in order to top up our energy reserves, so it was all the more difficult to accept the offer of a friendly caravan driver to travel with his convoy. He shook his head as he looked at poor, emaciated Armin and suggested that he load what little baggage we had on one of his animals and let our yak run along free with the rest of the herd for the next twenty kilometres. It sounded good, so we decided to forgo our day of rest and contemplation. Kartru was too exhausted to go on. I called and whistled but he just wagged his tail feebly and refused to get up. It was simply too much for him. His paws were sore and bleeding from all the walking and he was half-starved. There was nothing else for it; we would have to leave him. I would have liked to have given him to someone who would treat him well and it was small consolation to leave him behind at the settlement. He would find it hard to assert himself with the other dogs there but the fact was, he would not have survived another forced march.

There was more unpleasantness to come. At the next *tasam* there was no house but there were a lot of tents. Suspicious-looking characters gathered around and eyed our belongings with interest. We were too tired to worry about them; in any case, we had nothing worth stealing. Next morning, to our horror, we noticed that our yak was missing. The scoundrels who had been there the night before had also vanished without a trace and it was not hard to guess what had happened. The loss of our yak was a serious blow but our protests to the *ponpo* fell on deaf ears. In the *tasam*, he said, everyone was responsible for his own belongings.

We had little time to mourn the loss of our trusty companion. We had already been marching for some days towards a huge chain of mountains. We knew this was the Nyentchenthangla Range and that several of the peaks were more than seven thousand metres high. We also knew that there was only one pass, the Guring La, and that this led direct to Lhasa. The ascent began at a staging post called Tokar; the next *tasam* was five days' walk away. We did not dare to think how we would manage to keep going that long.

The days that followed seemed endless and the nights even longer. We travelled through a typical Tibetan landscape and passed by the highest lake in the world – Nam Cho or Tengri Nor, a lake so large that it takes eleven days to circumnavigate it. The climb in the rarefied air had left us completely drained, and the altitude dulled our senses. From time to time we looked with wonder at the still higher peaks that surrounded us. At last we reached the top of the Guring La pass at 5,972 metres. Before us, the first and only European to have crossed this pass had been the Englishman Littledale in 1895. Sven Hedin mapped it as the highest of the passes in the Transhimalaya. I think I am right in saying that it the highest pass in the world that is traversable the whole year round.

Pilgrims arrived at the Guring La from Lhasa, flew colourful prayer flags, chanted "lha gye lo" – "may the Gods be victorious" – and hurried off back to their homeland, the Changtang. While we were resting at the top of the pass, a young man and a pretty young girl with red cheeks and thick, black pigtails caught us up. Their happy faces were like the Tibetan version of *Romeo and Juliet*. The young girl had previously lived a happy and contented life with her husbands – three brothers – for whom she kept house in a nomad tent in the Changtang. Polygamy and polyandry are both quite common in Tibetan society. One evening a young stranger had arrived and asked for lodgings for the night. From that moment on, everything changed. It must have been a case of love at first sight. The youngsters understood each other without saying anything and next morning they left the tent together, seemingly oblivious to the perils of an escape across the wintry mountains. Now they were happy to have arrived here, and wanted to begin a new life in Lhasa.

I remember this young woman as a ray of sunshine that lit up those difficult days. As we were resting she reached inside her purse and smilingly handed each of us a dried apricot. This modest little gift was as precious to us as the wheat-bread the nomad had given us on Christmas Eve. We had sampled this golden yellow fruit in 1939 in Gilgit. It was now January 1946. Much time had passed since Gilgit and we had travelled a long way. Again the memories came flooding back.

We marched on for three successive days without coming across any tents. Far below, we kept seeing the weather-bleached skeletons of fallen caravan animals, which bore mute testimony to the dangers of the pass, and we heard from the nomads that every year pilgrims died here in the winter snowstorms. We thanked God for the fine weather, which allowed us to descend two thousand metres in the first few days.

In the distance we saw a huge column of smoke rising into the sky. We wondered if it came from some kind of settlement, but when we got nearer we saw it was the steam rising from hot springs. We were soon gazing at a scene of unexpected natural beauty. A number of springs bubbled out of the ground, and in the middle of the cloud of steam that enveloped them, a geyser shot up four metres into the air. We were overwhelmed by the sight and our next thought was to have a bath. The water was boiling when it came out of the ground, but in the cold air it was quickly cooled to a bearable temperature. We enlarged one of the natural pools to make a comfortable bath-tub. How we enjoyed it! Since the hot springs at Kyirong we had not been able to take a bath. The air temperature was fifteen below zero and our hair and beards froze stiff in an instant. I placed the piece of soap we had brought from Kyirong on the raised edge of the pool, but before I was able to wash myself, a crow swooped down and made off with our treasure.

At the next bivouac I had my first bad attack of sciatica. I had always regarded this painful complaint as a disorder of old age but there was a plausible reason for it. For weeks we had been sleeping on the frozen ground, back to back and always on the same side, pressing hard on the exact spot where the nerve is located.

Only a few days walking now separated us from Lhasa. The temperature grew more pleasant and my thick sheepskin cloak became too warm to wear. We were walking into springtime. Freshly ploughed fields were interspersed with specks of green with winter seedlings and we were accompanied by the twittering sounds of birdsong. We had made it thus far by a mixture of cunning and trickery and now, as day gave way to evening, we stood at the edge of the city of Lhasa. We spent a restless night trying to assess our situation. We had only one and a half Indian rupees left and looked like beggars or brigands. The best we could come up with was a huge, barefaced lie: we decided to pass ourselves off as emissaries from a powerful British ambassador and immediately demanded that the *ponpo* provide us with transport for our baggage. We decided that if the ruse did not work we would take our diaries with us and leave the rest of our stuff behind. Incredibly, the bluff worked and we were given a donkey and a driver. Even many days after our arrival in Lhasa, the high-ranking Tibetan officials were still greatly amused by this story, and laughed out loud at the way we had tricked the unfortunate *ponpo* into helping us.

It was January 15th, 1946, when we set off on the last stage of our march. We walked round a mountain spur and saw in the distance the gleaming golden roofs of the Potala, the winter residence of the Dalai Lama and the most famous landmark of Lhasa. We were almost moved to kneel before it and touch the ground with our foreheads like the pilgrims. Since leaving Kyirong we had covered almost a thousand kilometres. We had marched for seventy days, forty-five of which had been spent crossing the Changtang – days of hardship and struggle against hunger, cold and danger. We had met many good people, who had helped us, and encountered bad people, who had robbed us and put our lives in danger. Now, as we gazed at the golden pinnacles of the temple, all the fear and hardship was forgotten – just ten kilometres more and we would reach our goal.

We sat down near the stone cairns which the pilgrims put up to mark their first sight of the Holy City. Our driver performed his devotions. On the last few kilometres to Lhasa we mixed with a stream of pilgrims and caravans. From time to time we passed roadside stalls displaying all sorts of delicacies – sweets, white bread rolls baked in butter and the like – which almost brought tears to our eyes. But we had no money. Our last one and a half rupees belonged to the donkey driver.

We soon began to recognise all the other landmarks of the city, which we had read so often about, without ever daring to dream that one day we would be here to see them for ourselves. Over there must be Chagpo Ri, the hill on which one of the two famous Schools of Medicine stands. And here in front of us was Drepung, the greatest monastery in the world, home to ten thousand monks – a city in itself, with its many stone houses and temples. A little lower down lay the terraces of the Nechung Monastery, which has for centuries housed the greatest mystery of Tibet. It is here that one finds the manifestation of a protective Buddhist Deity, whose secret oracle guides the destiny of the state of Tibet and is consulted by the Government before any important decision is taken. We still had eight kilometres to go and with every step we took there was something new to look at. Before us lay the broad meadows ringed by willows where the horses of the Dalai Lama are pastured. A long stone wall flanked our route and we were told that the famous summer palace of the God-King Norbulingka lay behind it. Next we passed the British Trade Mission, situated just outside the city, half-hidden by tall poplar trees. Our driver turned into the grounds, thinking it obvious that this was where we wanted to be, and we had some trouble in persuading him to go straight on. For a moment we considered presenting ourselves to the English authorities, as we longed for civilisation and the company of Europeans, but the memory of the internment camp was still fresh in our minds and we thought that, since we were in Tibet, it would be prudent to ask the Tibetans for hospitality.

Nobody stopped us; nobody seemed in the least bothered about us. We could scarcely believe it, but later we learned that no one, not even a European, was regarded with suspicion, because no one had ever come to Lhasa without a pass.

Suddenly we saw a great gate crowned with three *chorten*. It was the only opening in the city walls, the gateway to the "Forbidden City". Our excitement was intense. This was the decisive moment. Almost every book about Lhasa says that this gate is guarded by powerfully built monks. We approached with beating hearts. But there was nothing. No soldiers, no control post, only a few beggars holding out their hands for alms. We mingled with a group of pilgrims and walked unhindered through the gateway into the city.

THE "FORBIDDEN CITY" OF LHASA

We stood and stared, hardly able to believe that we were actually in Lhasa. To this day I can find no words to express what we saw and how we felt at that moment. We were simply overwhelmed. Our emotions had become over-sensitive, our minds exhausted by the hardships we had endured, we were no longer able to absorb and process the impressions that now assaulted our senses.

We were shivering with cold and had to find lodgings for the night, but in Lhasa one can not simply walk into a house as one would walk into a tent in the Changtang. When we tried, the people living there either begged us to go elsewhere, or screamed at us until we left. Finally we came to a house that was much larger and more distinguished-looking than any we had yet seen; it even had stables in the courtyard. But yet again we were confronted, this time by the servants, who swore and shouted at us and tried to drive us away. This time, however, we refused to be moved and unloaded our donkey. Our driver had been pressing us to let him go home; he had long since realised that everything was not in order. We gave him his money and he went off with a sigh of relief.

Dead-tired and half-starved we sat on the ground by our pitiful bundle of things, indifferent to what might now befall us. We only wanted to sit, to rest, to sleep. When the crowd that had gathered around us saw our swollen and blistered feet, the angry shouts subsided and these good-natured, open-hearted people took pity on us. A woman was the first to react with kindness, bringing us an earthenware pot of butter tea. Then they all brought us things: tsampa, dried cheese, even yak dung to make a fire with. Appetites aflame, we forgot everything else and fell greedily on the food.

Suddenly we heard ourselves being addressed in perfect English. We looked up and saw a richly attired Tibetan, who must have been a person of the highest standing. We told him our story, said that we were Germans and asked him to take us in. He considered this for a moment and then said that he could not accommodate us at his house without the approval of the town magistrate, but added that he would

123

go there at once and seek the necessary permission.

The others, who had been standing around in a circle whispering amongst themselves and had treated the master of the house with the utmost reverence, then explained that his name was Thangme and that he was a high-ranking *ponpo*. We learned later that he was usually addressed as Kungo, or Your Highness, as a mark of respect. We noted the correct form of address and adopted it forthwith.

Thangme returned and explained that the magistrate had permitted him to take us in for one night, but that any future arrangements would have to be brought before the Cabinet. A room was prepared for us – a proper, clean, comfortable room. We hardly dared to sit on the clean, carpet-covered beds in our filthy old rags and felt ugly and shabby in such civilised surroundings. Our humble possessions, for years our most precious items, suddenly became worthless and we felt we would be glad to get rid of them. A delicious supper was brought in and, slightly dazed by now, we tucked in, our hosts continually urging us to eat more. They could hardly believe that we had crossed the Changtang in winter and walked over the Nyenchenthangla. We were embarrassed at our appearance and tried to hide our rough, unkempt hands. The contrast could not have been starker or more ironic – there we were, two down-at-heel Europeans in tattered, lice-infested sheepskin cloaks, given lodgings in a fine house by a noble Tibetan family. It was a meeting of two worlds, but under totally juxtaposed conditions.

Dead-tired and confused we finally fell into bed, but we could not fall asleep. We had spent too many nights on the hard, frozen ground with nothing but our sheepskins to protect us from the ravages of the cold. Now we had soft beds and a well-heated room, but our bodies could not adjust so quickly to the unaccustomed comforts and our thoughts revolved like mill wheels in our heads.

The next morning, before we were properly awake, we found a servant standing by our beds with sweet tea and biscuits. Then he brought us warm water and we patiently set about the grim task of removing our long beards. Finally we looked a little more respectable.

We did not see Thangme again until midday, when he returned from the Foreign Ministry. He brought us good news; we would not be handed over to the English. For the time being we would be allowed to remain in Lhasa, but we were politely requested not to leave the home of our host until the Regent had made an official statement about our future. Later that day we received a visit from an official sent by the town magistrate. He was very polite and asked permission to inspect our baggage. We ventured to ask him if all the officials, through whose districts we had passed, would be punished. His reply was well-considered. "The whole matter will come before the Cabinet," he said, "and the *ponpos* must expect some form of punishment." We were terribly upset by this and to his amusement we told him how we had bluffed and dodged our way past the district officials. It was our turn to laugh when he then announced that the evening before he had been expecting a German invasion of Lhasa! It seemed that everyone we had spoken to and asked for lodgings had rushed off to report to the magistrate that there were two "Germans" roaming the city. Austria was relatively unknown in Tibet, so we were thought of as Germans here, as we had been in Dehra Dun. The term "German" was a familiar one, at least for educated Tibetans, as German products were highly regarded here due to their quality.

During the next few days we were the talk of the town. Many people came to visit us, and not just out of curiosity – some of them took pity on us and brought us useful gifts. They seemed to be astonished at our fluency in Tibetan, but would often exchange puzzled glances when we spoke. At first we did not understand this, but later our friends told us that Peter Aufschnaiter and I spoke the rough dialect of the Himalayan peasant, sprinkled with nomad words and phrases, whilst the people of Lhasa expressed themselves in pure High Tibetan and used many polite forms. Fun-loving as they were, our friends continued to use our common, rural slang just to tease us, even after we had long since learned to speak the variety of Tibetan used in Lhasa.

Our period of "house arrest" was anything but tedious. Visitors kept trooping in and were served the customary butter-tea or Darjeeling by Thangme's wife. Thangme himself was a noble of the fifth rank and it was a great honour for his household to receive visits from the more highly placed officials and revered monks who wished to see us, whereupon Mrs Thangme would withdraw from the room with a subservient bow. The visitors brought us English newspapers and although they were months old they still gave us a good picture of post-war Europe, and of the hard times being endured by our countrymen in POW camps in England and France, which only served to strengthen our resolve to remain in Tibet.

Eight days passed, during which we dutifully followed orders and stayed indoors, so it was a great surprise when, one day, servants arrived, bringing an invitation to visit the home of the Dalai Lama's parents, and telling us to come at once. We dressed in the clothes and shoes that the government had given us. Thangme gave each of us a *kata*, a white silk scarf offered by the Tibetans in greeting, and told us that we should present them, as etiquette prescribed, when we were granted our audience.

The house of the parents of the Dalai Lama, Yabschi Sarpa, was barely a kilometre away, and was guarded by a huge gateway. The gatekeeper was waiting, and bowed respectfully as we approached. We followed him through a large garden, full of vegetable plots and groups of willow trees to the palace. We were shown up to the second floor; a door slowly opened and we found ourselves standing before the mother of the God-King. She looked the picture of aristocratic dignity. She was sitting on a small throne, in a large, bright room surrounded by her personal servants. The Gya-yum Chenmo, the Great Mother, smiled at us and was visibly pleased when we handed her the scarves with deep obeisances. Her face lit up with a benevolent smile as she shook our hands in greeting, contrary to Tibetan custom.

A short time later in came the father of the Dalai Lama, a dignified, elderly man with a friendly smile. We bowed low again and handed him our scarves with due ceremony, surprised at the unaffected way in which he, too, greeted us. Servants came and went, poured tea – first the father, then the mother and finally us. The aroma of the tea and the way it was made surprised us. They told us that it was prepared the way they used to drink it in their home town in Amdo, not as the Tibetans do with butter, but adding milk and salt. They had brought something else from their old home – the dialect they spoke. They spoke only a little of the Tibetan tongue used here in the central province and the fourteen year-old brother of the Dalai Lama, Lobsang Samten,

The Trakar Taso Monastery in Kyirong

Lhasa's famous city gate with the Potala Palace in the background

The Potala Palace where the Dalai Lama lived during the winter months

interpreted for them. He had come as a child to Lhasa and spoke pure Tibetan fluently.

Lobsang Samten was a bright, lively boy and quickly took over the conversation. He was full of curiosity about us and asked us all manner of questions about our experiences. He told us that his younger brother, the Dalai Lama, had entrusted him with the task of reporting everything about us in detail. We asked a few modest questions of our own and learned that the name Dalai Lama is a Mongolian expression meaning "Wide Ocean" and is not used in Tibet at all, where the Dalai Lama is more properly referred to as the "Gyalpo Rinpotsche", which means "Precious King". His parents and brothers use a more intimate form of address. They call him "Kundun", which simply means "Presence".

As we rose to leave, a line of servants appeared with sacks of flour and rice, a large pat of butter and two soft woollen blankets. "On the personal request of the Kundun," said the Great Mother with a smile, and pressed into our hands a hundred-sang note, the highest denomination note in Tibet.

On the way back to Thangme's house we both had the feeling that we had been granted a great honour. Confirmation of the success of our audience was not long coming; in fact the very next morning the news came from the Foreign Ministry that we were to be granted freedom of movement in Lhasa. Thus began our legitimate stay in the Forbidden City, which was only to come to an end years later, with the invasion of the Red Army troops from China.

We spent the next few days making courtesy calls, first to the four Cabinet Ministers and the powerful Chikyab Khenpo, the highest-ranking of the monastic officials. After visiting the Tibetan dignitaries we went to the British Trade Mission, which was situated in a beautiful park just outside town. Servants in red livery showed us first into the "Happy Garden", the Dekyi Lingka, and then conducted us into the Mission House. The Head of the British Mission, Arthur Hopkinson, greeted us cordially. It seemed a long time since we had last sat on comfortable chairs and seen table cloths, vases of flowers and books in a nice, welcoming room furnished in the European style. Our host understood what we were thinking and smiled as our eyes wandered

The Penker family: Aunt Marianne, my mother Johanna, grandmother Johanna, grandfather Andreas, Uncle Andreas and Uncle Johann, who died young

The house in Obergossen, above Hüttenberg, where I was born. To the left is the ladder that led to the attic

As a young boy, with sledge and woolly hat in the photographer's studio

The family in 1923. My father Josef, mother with my brother Pepperl in her arms, and my sister Lydia. Ruth had not yet been born

With my grandmother, Aunt Marianne and my brother and sisters in 1935. Ruth, the youngest, is sitting on my lap

In the mid 1930s

At the 1934 Styrian State
Downhill Skiing Championships

In Sexten, South Tyrol, where I ran a ski school for hotel guests. Twice a week I held
lessons for the youngsters of the village.

High spirits on the Tauplitz in the Salzkammergut region of Styria, where I ran a ski school for several years. On the far right is my friend Fritz Ehrenfried.

First ascent of the West face of the Sturzhahn. Shortly before the photograph was taken I had fallen fifty metres.

Every summer I climbed in the Dolomites and slept in haylofts or bivouacked outdoors. This photo was taken in 1934

During the first ascent of the North Face of the Eiger in July 1938. My anorak was badly torn and provided little warmth

The four members of the first ascent team after the successful climb: Wiggerl Vörg, Anderl Heckmair, Fritz Kasparek and Heinrich Harrer (from right to left)

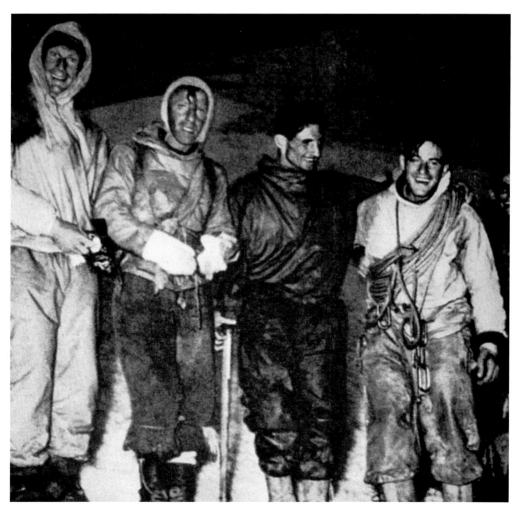

On the boat to Bombay, during the 1939 Nanga Parbat Reconnaissance Expedition. Hans Lobenhoffer and I dubbin our boots.

In the POW camp at Dehra Dun in the 1940s. From left to right: Herbert Paidar, Hans Lobenhoffer, Wiggerl Schmaderer, Heinrich Harrer and Lutz Chicken

On Chomolhari, December 1950. The brother of my friend Wangdu accompanies me on an excursion to the border of Bhutan

1948 in Lhasa. I had bought the American military greatcoat in the market.

A monk wearing a "Yeti hat" that was actually made from the wool of a Tibetan mountain goat

Peter Aufschnaiter and I chat to the Tibetan Ministers Tsarong and Chekapa at Kyitchu about plans to build a dam

Coocoola, the Princess of Sikkhim, lived in Lhasa and was married to the son of Minister Punkhang

Peter Aufschnaiter with Tessla, one of Tsarong's daughters, during a visit to the holy place of Tra Yerpa

View of the Potala, the seat of the Dalai Lama, from the roof of the Medical School. Peter Aufschnaiter surveys the site.

My apartment in Lhasa was open house for my friends. On the left, the Foreign Minister's youngest son, whose life I saved; on the right, Wangchuk, who later became Governor of Gyantse

1951 in the Chumbi Valley. The Dalai Lama receives a 2500 year old Buddhist relic

The American radio journalist Lowell Thomas (far right) visited Lhasa with his son in 1949. In the middle of the picture is the Monk's Foreign Minister Liuchar Dzasa

My first meeting with my son Peter in January 1952. I am giving him a pair of Tibetan boots.

Reception at Ullstein Verlag in Frankfurt am Main in 1957: Bruno Dechamps, the publisher Frederick Ullstein, Thor Heyerdahl and Heinrich Harrer (from left)

I visited Sven Hedin a few months before his death in November 1952 at his apartment in Stockholm

Addressing the committee of the Explorer's Club in New York in 1954. Shortly afterwards I was made an honorary member.

In Alaska in 1954. During the trip I made three first ascents

Breaking trail on a thirty metre overhanging cornice on Mount Deborah

With Edmund Hillary in Nepal

With Bing Crosby and friends at the Kitzbühel Golf Club

In 1964 I met the Dalai Lama at the Sarnath Deer Park, where he was attending a conference of Buddhists from all over the world

With the Dalai Lama's mother and her two sons, Geneva 1959. We ate delicious traditional *momos* with dinner

around the room. When he saw us looking at his books he kindly offered to let us use his library. He told us that he had been informed in detail of our escape from the camp and that he, like the Tibetans, was full of admiration for us.

Tea was served, accompanied by warm almond horn cakes, and we forgot our manners and devoured the lot straight away. Tea was followed by drinks and chocolates and again we were powerless to resist. Hopkinson smiled and refilled our glasses, after which we submitted our request to be allowed to contact our relatives, since they had received no news from us for several years. Hopkinson promised to arrange for a message to be sent through the Red Cross in India. We asked him if we were still regarded as prisoners of war and if the Dehra Dun camp still existed but he told us he did not know.

This was the start of many happy years living in a free and happy land, with cheerful and likeable people. Now, more than half a century later, as I look back on those times it is like replaying a favourite film. It would seem that my long term memory is still intact, for in spite of my advanced age, I can still vividly recall events, even those which I did not enter in my diaries at the time. As my life in Lhasa settled into a routine, I stopped making detailed notes on all the little daily occurrences. At the time, I also dismissed many of the thoughts and encounters I had as unimportant, which was a pity, really, since they are important now, as we were the last witnesses to a great culture that ended in catastrophic destruction.

As we grew more accustomed to our life in Lhasa we gradually became part of the community. What made our stay in Lhasa so unproblematic was the fact that we lived like the Tibetans and respected their customs. The Tibetans' attitude towards us was completely different to the behaviour described in books written by the few visitors to the country. One explanation for this was the fact that, unlike them, we had arrived in Lhasa destitute and unannounced, in the middle of a cold winter, with fewer possessions than even the poorest Tibetan. We were not conspicuous, we had no weapons and we did not come as the representatives of a foreign government, so we were not in any way suspicious. To put it simply, we did not behave like the kind of foreigners the Tibetans had come to mistrust. The fact that we had endured months of cold and hardship meant that, in their eyes, we were something akin to their yogic mystics or Lung Gompas, the running monks of Tibet renowned for their ability to cover vast distances in a trancelike state. If our behaviour had been conspicuously European it would have been viewed with disapproval, particularly by the all-powerful Regent, who was known to despise all things foreign.

There were many reasons for the Tibetans' scepticism with regard to foreigners. With the notable exceptions of the reports written by Englishmen like Charles Bell and Hugh Richardson, most of the foreign books on Tibet had caused great distress in Lhasa. "Tibetans do not wash, they are polygamous and they feed their dead to the vultures" were just some of the allegedly typical Tibetan characteristics highlighted in these books, which also contained interesting observations on the widespread superstitions and the ability to levitate or to see with the third eye – all very mysterious and surreal for the Western reader – yet made hardly any mention of Tibet's two-thousand-year-old culture, her medicine and age-old knowledge of herbal remedies, or the fact that block printing was also practised here in the Middle Ages, as it was in Europe. At the foot of the Potala there is a building that contains more than a hundred thousand printing blocks carved from magnolia and birch wood.

During my seven years in Tibet, I never witnessed any supernatural feats performed by hermits or monks; nor did I ever seek to prove, or disprove, whether a Tibetan was really able to separate his spirit from his body. I never doubted the power of amulets or denied the possibility that they might ward off an enemy bullet, but neither did I feel moved to experiment. My common sense prevented me from experiencing such miracles, yet again and again things happened in Tibet that were beyond any rational explanation. I believe that this is all part of the mystery of this fascinating land.

I have often tried to put into words the colours and the beauty of the landscape of Tibet, but I am bound to say that mere words can not convey such splendour. As a geographer, I am naturally keen to give an accurate picture of the country which, although known as the Roof of the World, does not consist entirely of ice-clad mountains, steppes and uninhabited country roamed by nomads. For example, it is a little-known fact that to the south of the main range of the Himalaya, at a similar latitude to the Sahara or Florida, lies the Tibetan province of Pemako, where tribes still live who have no form of writing and where a rich variety of tropical fruits grow and flourish. The annual rainfall here is almost equivalent to the world record amounts recorded in nearby Cherrapunji. The climatic differences between the arid north and the south, which has ten to sixteen metres of rain, are extraordinary.

The Kingdom of Sikkim was also once a part of Tibet. The Tibetans call this region Drejong, which means "Rice Land". Mention should also be made of the steep hillsides around Darjeeling, the Anglicised phonetic form of the Tibetan word Dorjeling, or "thunderstone garden", where the finest and most costly tea in the world grows.

Whilst on the subject of the diversity of this land, I would like to make a little personal observation – a hymn of praise for the home of the Dalai Lama. When the Earth was created, Tibet was presented with many great privileges. I believe that this rich diversity of beauty and natural treasures was given to the humble people of Tibet because the Creator knew that they would use their gifts with care and caution and would try to ensure that the relationships between all living things were kept in harmony. They do not prospect for iron ore, nor mine for coal or gold, and thus the air and the water remain clean. They have respected the miracle of creation for thousands of years and their stewardship of the land has been benevolent. The Tibetans have always been the greatest of animal protectionists; hunting is simply forbidden. The extensive forests with their high grade timber are only sparingly felled and provide a clean water supply and a benign climate. Although unfamiliar with the term, an ecologically responsible lifestyle is something the Tibetans pursue as a matter of course.

We could now move about freely in the city and we were surprised at the consideration shown to us, two poor refugees, by the Tibetans. One of our visitors was the son of the renowned Minister, Tsarong, who brought us some useful Western gifts and an invitation from his father to stay at his house. We had enjoyed Thangme's hospitality and his comfortable house, and we will forever be indebted to him and his family for making us feel so welcome in Lhasa.

We now moved into a large, comfortable bungalow with a small inner courtyard, set in the gardens of the Tsarong residence, where we each had our own room. We shared the bungalow with the younger sister of our host, a lively and fun-loving woman. Her first marriage had been to the King of Kongpo and as a mark of respect everyone still addressed her as "Queen". As her neighbours, we were allowed to call her by her maiden name, Drolma-la. Her new husband was Kuscho Tsenam-la, and one day he invited us to see the estates that his wife had inherited.

It was our first big excursion from Lhasa and it took us into a region that was one and a half day's journey from the city. We travelled in comfort with horses and servants, like the *ponpos*, whom we had so often envied during our escape. The estate was like a *dzong*, or fortress, and was surrounded by a moat. There were extensive fields all around and Peter Aufschnaiter, who was an agricultural engineer by profession, was able to provide some helpful suggestions for the cultivation of crops. News of our excursion spread quickly and presently Aufschnaiter was summoned by a high monastic official and commissioned to advise on suitable improvements for Lhasa.

In the meantime I had also found work. I had often been the guest of Surkhang, one of the four cabinet ministers, and he and his father, Surkhang Dzasa, soon became my most important employers. Surkhang Dzasa was a secular representative who worked alongside the monastic Minister for External Affairs, Liuschar Dzasa, and one of my first jobs was to translate several English travel books at the Ministry. While I was there I also discovered a number of map cards made by pilgrims. These simple colourful drawings had a graphic style and were easy to read, since all the mountains were faithfully represented, the passes were marked with colourful prayer flags and the ferries indicated with the symbol of a boat. There was no scale, but I assumed that the Tibetan pilgrim was interested only in where the passes were and where he might find a ferry to take him across to the opposite river bank – how far that might be and how long it might take him to get there was largely immaterial, as the pilgrim has a different concept of time and distance. One of the maps was particularly fascinating. It showed the region where the mighty Brahmaputra river breaks through the Himalayan range. Notched tree trunks served as ladders up steep cliffs perched above the raging torrent and the drawing awakened the desire in me to go and explore this gorge. I set about making a true-to-scale copy of this unique map that could be read by Western visitors.

Aufschnaiter and I soon became employees of the government and received regular fixed salaries. We also assumed our place in the rigid hierarchy of Tibetan society. We were classified as Letsempa, nobles of the fifth rank. During official receptions we wore Tibetan robes and sat with the many other Letsempas. On such occasions the secular representatives of the Letsempas were also obliged to wear round caps of yellow wool.

Meanwhile, Aufschnaiter had found somewhere to stay outside Lhasa that was nearer his place of work. He had also bought a horse and now only used his room at Tsarong's house when he came into Lhasa on special occasions.

We had been in Lhasa for almost a year now, and Christmas was drawing near. I had received so much kindness and hospitality that I wanted to give my friends some pleasure in return for once, so I decided to throw a real Christmas party with a tree and presents. My friend Trethong, whose late father had been a Minister, lent me his house for a few days. I hired trained servants and cooks and bought small presents for my guests, such as pocket torches, penknives, table-tennis bats and board games, which I wrapped in festive fashion. The main attraction was the Christmas tree. Mrs. Tsarong lent me a juniper tree in a beautiful pot and I decorated it with candles, apples, nuts and sweets.

The party began in the morning, as is usual in Lhasa. Wangdu-la, my closest friend, supported me as Master of Ceremonies as I was still afraid of committing some kind of social gaffe. My guests arrived full of curiosity, examined the tree from all sides and stared at the presents arranged beneath it. Everyone was full of excitement and anticipation. We spent the day eating, drinking and playing games and when it grew dark, I invited my guests to go into another room. Wangdu-la put on his fur coat inside out and played the part of Santa Claus, while I lit the candles on the Christmas tree. The old gramophone played "Silent Night, Holy Night", the door opened and with eyes wide with astonishment my guests gathered around the tree. It was a strange scene – a medley of races in the heart of Asia singing the dear old Christmas hymn of our homeland. I had become pretty good at controlling my emotions, but I could not hold back the tears and I longed for my family and my home in Austria. The cheerfulness of my guests and their pleasure at seeing their presents – helped by a little alcohol – helped me over my homesickness. When my guests left they told me repeatedly how much they had enjoyed our "German New Year". A year ago in the desolate wastes of the Changtang a couple of white bread rolls had been an exquisite Christmas present. Today we sat around a richly laden table in the company of kind and friendly people. We were very fortunate.

It was always a great pleasure to see Peter Aufschnaiter on the rare occasions that we now met. It was only now that we were apart that we realised how the difficulties and dangers we had endured during our escape had deepened and strengthened our friendship. I had prepared a special surprise for Peter that Christmas. One day as I was strolling through the bazaar I was approached by an elderly man. "Henrig-la," he said, "you can repair everything. Will you give me fifty sang for this?" He opened his hand and I straight away I could see that the broken object he held had once been a valuable Rolex expedition wristwatch similar to the one that Peter had sold when we were in western Tibet. A pocket torch cost fifty sang, so it was a lot of money for a broken watch, even a high quality broken watch. But I paid the price without hesitation and took the wristwatch to one of the Kashmiri merchants, who really could repair anything. He left the mechanism to soak in petroleum for several weeks and managed to get the cogs turning again. A new watch glass, face and bracelet were added and the Christmas present for my friend was ready. Peter was speechless as he slowly unwrapped the little parcel and examined his gift, a valuable little reminder of our epic journey.

The same Mohammedan craftsman who had repaired Peter's watch also lent me his camera and sold me some film and magnesium for the flash, so I was able to capture our first Christmas in Lhasa on film.

He later offered me two German-made petroleum lamps. They had metal filaments inside and lighting them took a little bit of practice. Peter and I both found them very useful and we were soon approached by several well-to-do Tibetans who enquired where they might find similar lamps for their games of chess, mahjong and cards. With a certain amount of pride I told them that I came from the same place as the inventor of the metal filament light bulb, Carl Baron Auer von Welsbach, and had been privileged to attend the memorial service held after his death in 1929.

We now had bright lights, courtesy of von Welsbach, but the petroleum we needed to power the lamps was difficult to obtain and outrageously expensive. I knew a few merchants who regularly traded between Lhasa and Kalimpong, in the Indian province of Bengal, but an order took months to arrive. You could only really be sure of receiving your goods in the winter months, as the heavy monsoon rains generally made the caravan routes impassable during the summer. Furthermore, the metal petroleum canisters could only be transported by mule, as the stubborn yaks would not carry loads that sloshed around and would buck and rear in protest, sending the containers flying down the steep hillsides. Due to the great differences in temperature and air pressure between 1,600 and 5,600 metres on the trade route, it was crucial that the petroleum canisters were not filled to the brim. This meant that the contents would slop around noisily, which was not a problem for the stoical mules. For me, the camera I had borrowed from the Mohammedan trader was more important than the lamps, since I could now capture some of the rich impressions of Tibet in photographic images, whereas previously I had only been able to sketch them.

Peter Aufschnaiter and I had been living happily in Lhasa for over a year when we were summoned to the Foreign Ministry. Since the POW camp in Dehra Dun still existed and the Tibetans had never made a final decision about allowing us to stay, we presumed that our visit to the Ministry might have something to do with this. In the event, even our worst fears were overshadowed by the pictures they showed us there. Two sepia print issues of the *Illustrated London News* contained gruesome photographs of the concentration camps discovered by the allies after the end of the war. Far away from our homes we were now confronted by the full extent of the Nazi crimes against humanity. We were speechless. How could such a thing happen in the 20th century, in spite of the International Red Cross and the Geneva Convention? The shock was great and I was depressed to think that I had applied for membership of Nazi Party before I left Europe. Aufschnaiter and I were adamant – and said as much to the Ministers – that no one amongst our circle of friends could have had anything to do with such terrible events. In fact, the pictures had no influence on the behaviour of the Tibetans towards us, since they were all witnesses to the fact that we had been living amongst them, far away from Germany at the other end of the world, during the time that these crimes were committed.

My philosophy on life had changed during my years in the peaceful country of Tibet. My materialistic European attitudes and values were no longer valid here. I had learned that all of God's creatures, even the humble earth worm, should be respected and protected from harm. I had developed a sensitivity that had been completely absent ten years ago in that fateful year of 1938. Back then I had had no presentiment of the dreadful events to come; I had pushed everything else to the back of my mind and thought only of my expedition to the Himalaya. Now, however, I began to ask myself whether I might have seen it all coming if I had been blessed with a "Tibetan soul". In my later years my intuition was a great help in estimating possible dangers and on some of my expeditions it saved porters and participants from potentially fatal situations.

In spite of the warning signs that things were not as they should have been, in 1938 I still obviously lacked the sound common sense and awareness needed to react in an enlightened and sensitive way to the events of the time. Now, in 1948, I recalled amongst other things the death of Frau Köppen, the mother of Else Wegener. At her cremation service the string quartet had been forbidden from playing Mendelssohn Bartholdy. I did not know at the time that the composer was a Jew and I did not understand why his music could not be played as requested.

Those photographs in the newspaper left an indelible impression on Peter and I and once more our resolve not to return home was strengthened. My passionate love of the mountains and the success of the Eiger climb had brought me into close contact with this disastrous political system, yet this passion was finally to prove a blessing to me, since it had taken me far away from that terrible war to the Himalaya – to the Roof of the World.

The people of Lhasa, whether noble officials or humble shopkeepers, now treated us as Tibetans. We were no longer referred to as "the Germans", since everyone, at the Foreign Ministry at least, now knew that we were keeping in touch with the Austrian Embassy in New Delhi. It was from there that we eventually received our long-awaited documents, in the shape of Austrian passports that gave Lhasa as our place of residence. Ten years had now passed since I received my visa for India from the English authorities in Vienna that allowed me to travel to Nanga Parbat.

One day, when I was walking through the centre of town, in the Barkhor district where most of the shops were concentrated, I bumped into the young couple we had met at the Guring Pass during our escape. They were in a pitiful state. They complained bitterly about the conditions in the big city and said they wished to return home. When they had been with the nomads there had been meat, cheese and milk in abundance; here in Lhasa they had to work hard to earn the money to buy food. It was nice to be able to thank them for the delicious dried apricots and to help make their return home a little easier.

There was another little reminder of our long trek from the POW camp to Lhasa. The unfriendly official from Tsaparang, who had made us sleep in a cold cave instead of letting us stay in his house, came to us one day with his tongue outstretched in the subservient manner, a lucky silk scarf and a large pat of butter. He said he wished to apologise for his behaviour. As I gave him the scarf and an envelope containing the usual bank note I remarked that he had only been doing his duty and recalled the tax collector in Tradun, who said that he was only an important *ponpo* outside the city of Lhasa.

On one occasion I was sampling the barley beer served in a pub that had a reputation for brewing really good *chang*, when a well-dressed man approached me. He turned out to be an old acquaintance – the soldier from western Tibet who had escorted us to the Indian border and whose parting remark had been " perhaps we'll see each other in Lhasa again; there are lots of pretty girls there." As a government messenger he had naturally heard that we were in Lhasa but had not dared to enter the house of the famous Minister Tsarong to pay us a visit.

At least once a year Peter and I used to climb the six thousand metre mountain Mindrutsari, for a view of the snow-covered peaks of the Himalaya and the Nyenchenthanglha Mountains. We were so well-acclimatised that we could do the climb and make it back to Lhasa the same day. Our Tibetan friends could not understand why anyone would want to climb a mountain, with all the hardship that this entails, just to see another mountain. I think they doubted whether we had actually been up there at all. In order to help the Tibetans make sense of the pleasure we derived from these trips, the next time we went we lit a sweet-smelling ceremonial bonfire on top with the azaleas that grow up there.

The parents of the Dalai Lama often invited me to their house. They had had fourteen children, of whom only seven were still alive. With Peter Aufschnaiter I attended the birthday celebrations of their youngest son. The Dalai Lama had given him the name Tendzin Choegyal, but at the age of four he was recognised as the 15th Ngari Rinpoche, a title that is conferred through reincarnation, and several important monasteries in Zanskar and Ladakh came into his possession. The Great Mother had given birth to three "Reincarnations" – Tagtser Rinpoche, the older brother of the Dalai Lama, known to his family and friends as Norbu, the Dalai Lama himself and Ngari Rinpoche – which was extraordinary. I took some nice photographs of the children on the roof of the palace with the Potala in the background, which pleased the family greatly.

There was also cause for celebration in the Tsarong house. Tsarong Junior, known as "George" to his friends, a nickname he had acquired at Saint Joseph's College in Darjeeling, had married the pretty daughter of the Cabinet Minister Cheka-pa and she had given him five children. George's father, the venerable old Tsarong, was proud and pleased to learn that the youngest child had been recognised as a very high-ranking Reincarnation. At the age of three, His Holiness

Drikung Kyabgon Chetsang Rinpoche was taken from his parent's house to be educated at a monastery one hundred and sixty kilometres east of Lhasa. I followed Chetsang Rinpoche's adventurous life from his birth in 1946 right up to his visit to the Heinrich Harrer Museum in Hüttenberg in July 2000. His was not the reclusive existence of a monk but a life full of excitement that took him all over the world. His parents George and Yangchen-la viewed being parted from their child with mixed emotions. On the one hand it was a great honour to have a Rinpoche in the family, but saying goodbye to their beloved child was obviously a painful experience for them.

Peter Aufschnaiter had now moved to Changdab Risur, five kilometres to the east of Lhasa, where he was building a small dam and an irrigation channel. In the course of his excavations he made some valuable archaeological finds, which I later took to Kalimpong, as Peter wanted to make a detour to Kyirong before he left Tibet.

I kept myself busy with a variety of jobs. I built a house for the family of the Cabinet Minister Kabcho, which incorporated the innovative feature of a large room that dispensed with the customary four supporting pillars. I got the long timbers I needed for the job from a province south of the Tsangpo, where Kabcho owned extensive areas of woodland. I also took on a supervisory role on Peter Aufschnaiter's dam building project. I even managed to find time for sport, and was accompanied by several enthusiastic Tibetan friends. We went "knife skating", as they called it, on a frozen tributary of the Kyitchu River, which was all very amusing, especially when one of us fell over. In summer the cold river was a popular place to swim and the open parkland by the river was a nice spot for a picnic. On one occasion Jigme, the son of the Foreign Minister Surkhang Dzasa, was caught in a whirlpool and dragged under. I managed to get hold of the unconscious lad and haul him back to the bank where, to the astonishment of those present, I gave him mouth-to-mouth resuscitation and got him breathing again, to the great joy and gratitude of his father, who on impulse offered me the use of his empty house, Polingka, where I had worked as a gardener.

So I moved from the Tsarong's bungalow to Polingka, where I had so much room that my servant Nyima was able to bring his family

139

from the country. He moved happily into a small utility building next to the stable. I had room to spread out and for the first time in years I was able to furnish the place the way I wanted. My writing desk stood in front of a large, bright window and I was even able to install a long-coveted shower. Nyima would fill an old US army petrol canister with warm water and hang it upside down from the ceiling. All I had to do was open the top halfway, and the twenty litres of water would slowly flow out. The "shower" was a new attraction for my friends and it was nice to be able to have a good wash in warm water after a day in the mountains. Nyima loved it when I brought guests home. He was in his element. He would prepare delicious meat loaves for any number of guests and fetch water for the shower, for which he received both praise and payment. The vegetable garden provided celery, spring onions and tomatoes of record-breaking size. The good water supply, the high quality manure and the sunshine produced some exceptional successes. I love eating vegetables and once remarked to my friends that I thought I might possibly be the reincarnation of a cow. They could not stop laughing at this.

The interest that the Tibetans showed in sports and their endurance gave me an idea. Between Shigatse and Gyantse lies the monastery of Schalu Gompa, which houses a school for the famous *lung gompa* "trance runners". Admission to the school is restricted for outsiders and the *lung gompa* train in total isolation, building up their leg muscles by running on a pile of grain, while strict teachers provide the mental training. During important religious festivals the monastery nominates a man who has the mental and physical abilities to run the hundred or more kilometres to Lhasa without food, drink or rest. On reaching the holy city, the runner is received with due reverence by a guard of honour. He then runs up the many stone steps of the Potala where the Dalai Lama presents him with a white silk scarf in recognition of his feat. The *lung gompa* is then invited into the great houses of the Tibetan nobility, where he is richly rewarded and honoured as a yogi, a man who is able to free his soul from material things.

With exceptional skills such as these, the Tibetan trance runners would have achieved great success at the Olympic Games and their country would have received widespread recognition. Even without their supersensory talents, living and training at altitudes between four and six thousand metres alone would have given them a huge advantage over athletes from other nations. I was only able to discuss my ideas with my closest friends, of course, since the trance runs of the Lung Gompa were regarded by the Tibetans solely as a religious ceremony and any profane exploitation of the runners' almost supernatural abilities would have attracted the severe displeasure of the all-powerful Regent. He had already stripped my friend Cholkhang Wangdi of his rank because he posed for a photograph "kneeling like a foreigner", which was considered undignified for an official dressed in a monk's robes.

One day Tagtser Rinpoche, whom I also now called Norbu, surprised me with the news that the *dobdob* from his monastery wanted to compete against me in a sporting event. Norbu lived in Drepung, the largest monastery in the world, which was situated eight kilometres to the west of Lhasa. The *dobdob* were employed at large ceremonies in Lhasa, where they policed crowds of up to twenty thousand monks. They were huge, powerfully built men and their white monks' robes lent them a fearsome appearance, an effect that was enhanced by the decorative symbols they painted on their faces with soot and the strip of red cloth they tied around their right arms to make their biceps stand out more prominently. They controlled the crowds at large events and would shout and brandish their whips at anyone who failed to make way for a high-ranking monastic official. The *dobdob* were completely ignorant of holy scriptures and dedicated themselves solely to the pursuit of physical fitness.

I had already had a bad experience with competitive sports during the New Year race in Kyirong. One of the other events had involved lifting heavy rocks and carrying them to a predetermined place. This was out of the question for me, since the rocks were round and smooth and weighed at least a hundred kilos apiece. So it was agreed that I would compete against the *dobdob* in a long jump competition. They had heard that the world record stood at around eight metres and they bet me that they could jump much further than that. Below the monastery there was an easy-angled sandy slope covered in little thorny plants. Here the *dobdob* had constructed a firm take-off area and when

I saw it I knew right away that I was going to lose my bet. The *dobdob* jumped barefoot and their robes ballooned out like sails as they flew through the air. Jumping downhill, they easily achieved distances of ten to twelve metres. Although I had the technique, I was no match for them in my heavy army boots. Hundreds of monks, who had come from the monastery to watch the show, cheered wildly as they watched my pitiful attempts. After I had tipped the sand out of my boots we went back up to the monastery in a cheerful mood and celebrated the monks' victory in Norbu's two tiny rooms. Later that evening we ate Tibetan *momos*. These are dumplings filled with meat, not unlike large ravioli parcels, and are steamed in a special pan. A perfectly cooked *momo,* like the ones we ate at Drepung, should be held aloft and eaten like a ripe peach so the meaty juice drips into one's mouth. I stayed with Norbu at the monastery for several more days and we have been firm friends ever since.

I also enjoyed very friendly relations with Arthur Hopkinson's successor at the British Mission, Hugh Edward Richardson. We played bridge together every week and often met at various social functions. Unfortunately, when India gained independence in 1947 he was replaced and had to return to Britain. In addition to his duties as an ambassador he found the time to compile a Tibetan grammar book, and his wonderful garden bore testimony to his love of flowers. He used to bemoan the fact that there was no opportunity to indulge in his favourite sports, golf and tennis, so I suggested to him that I build a tennis court in his garden, which he happily agreed to. He immediately ordered the tools and materials I needed and I began the job of levelling the ground. A small caravan bringing dried yak dung from the nomads to the north of Lhasa was summarily diverted to Dekyi Lingka and I bought the whole load there and then. Two sacks, or one yak load, cost the same as a bottle of mustard oil used for roasting. Fresh pats of wet dung were very much cheaper and easier to find than the dried variety. We mixed them to a paste in an old tin bathtub and smeared the sticky mess on the levelled ground. The dung dried quickly in the arid air and the next layer was then applied. In this way, I managed to create a playable surface.

The tennis court was an instant success and every week a happy and colourful mixture of people met to play. There was an Englishman, a Nepali, a Chinaman, an Indian, a Tibetan and an Austrian, all fully paid-up members of the cheapest tennis club in the world.

One day Richardson asked me if I would like a puppy from the litter of his German Shepherd bitch. I could have first choice, he said, and added that the mother was a pedigree animal and the father was unknown, but the puppies were so handsome that he thought the father might have been a Tibetan wolf. It was certainly possible. You could hear the wolves howling at night and it was well known that hungry leopards had once killed and eaten one of the many street dogs in Lhasa. I accepted Richardson's kind offer and from that moment on the little mongrel accompanied me on all my excursions. Sometimes he would go off on his own and return the following day, when he would lie on my doorstep, exhausted by his attempts to hunt antelope.

Twice a year I used to walk up to the I-Tso, a lake at five thousand metres that was reached in just a few hours via the Doti valley. The Government had given me the job of checking the water level from time to time, as the I-Tso was directly connected to the lake in Lhasa on which the great Tsuglagkhang Temple stood and the officials were convinced that the water was the same. I told them that we had something similar back home in Austria. There is a lake at two thousand metres on the Zirbitzkogel, our local mountain, and my grandmother, who knew all the local legends, used to tell us children that the "Wildsee" was directly connected to the larger Wörthersee, which was sixty kilometres away and much lower down. The theory had been proved a long time ago when an ox, which had fallen into the Wildsee, was later found floating on the surface of the Wörthersee.

I had to set off very early to walk up to the I-Tso and back to Lhasa in a day. As dawn broke I approached the Sera Monastery. Nearby, to the east, was the Durtro, a massive chunk of rock that centuries ago had broken off from the mountain and had been worn to a smooth finish by the weather. Sera Durtro was an unusual place. It was here that the daily "sky burial" ceremonies took place. A monk sat on a cushion reciting holy scriptures, while the *dobden* dismembered the corpses with swords and knives and smashed the skulls and bones on the burial rock. Common vultures, ravens and bearded lammergeier circled overhead, while the dogs waited at a respectful distance for their scraps. The *dobden* hurled the bones and chunks of flesh into the air and they were caught by the birds in flight. One could hear the rushing of the birds' wings and the monotonous drone of the lama as he recited his litany. The air was full of the screeches of the birds as they fought over the best bits, yet one could still feel the stillness of death that hung over the place. I maintained a discreet distance from the burial rock out of respect for the ceremony and never took photographs. Even when the *dobden* stopped what they were doing and gave me a friendly wave, I merely returned their greeting and carried on walking. The task the *dobden* performed was passed down from generation to generation and there were well known dynasties of *dobden* in Lhasa. They had a good knowledge of anatomy and illnesses, which they shared with the medical schools in Tibet.

This kind of burial ceremony, which has often been described as strange and unusual, is actually not only common in Tibet. I remember a visit to Bombay in 1939 when we were shown the tourist attraction known as the "Tower of Silence". There was a feeling of awe and a slight shudder of horror as we gazed at the high, red towers and walls behind which the Parsi sect, a breakaway religious community with its own traditions and customs, celebrated its own "sky burials" in a similar manner to the Tibetans. The Parsi did not dismember the corpses but placed them in the middle of the towers, where they were eagerly devoured by the circling vultures. Here, too, we maintained a respectful distance. We only heard and saw the large birds as the skies grew dark with their beating wings. The Parsi in Bombay left everything to the birds but from time to time someone would come and shovel the stripped bones into a hole in the middle of the arena.

Shortly before our second Tibetan New Year we received our first letters from home in three years. They had taken twelve months to get here. It was a good feeling to know that at last there was a line of communication between us and Europe, albeit a very slender one. In fact, the poor postal service did not improve during all the years we spent in Tibet. Nonetheless, we were still able to send regular reports from Tibet, some of which were published in the *Himalayan Journal*, whose editor Peter Aufschnaiter knew from earlier expeditions. I maintained a lively correspondence with Sven Hedin, who wrote that he was happy that I had turned his dreams into reality. Above all, we had contact with our families at long last. Life in post-war Austria sounded troublesome compared to the life we had in Lhasa. I corresponded with my parents and my brother and sisters and toward the end of my stay in Lhasa my sister Lydia even tried to visit me, but this was thwarted by the Chinese invasion of Tibet. From time to time Else Wegener sent me news of my son Peter, who was now living with her. Lotte had been unlucky with her new husband, the army officer. Shortly after she had given birth to his child he had been killed in action. Alone now and with two young sons to care for, she had turned to her mother for help.

Sometimes when I thought of home I longed to have a woman, a companion for life, at my side; someone who was suitable for a man like me. The Tibetans kept telling us that Aufschnaiter and I should look for a Tibetan wife, but even in Lhasa I still felt like a European and thought I would feel closer to someone from my own culture. Also, sexually transmitted diseases were widespread in Tibet so it paid to be cautious.

Yet I was to find love in Lhasa. The object of my affections was Coocoola, the Princess of Sikkim. Today, when I look back on the affection we had for each other it is the Tibetan words that most readily come to mind to describe my feelings. To fall in love is "sem schor wa" and means "to lose one's soul"; to describe a woman as one's darling the term "Nying dug" is used, which translates as "to strike the heart". In the case of Coocoola, both were accurate. She was very different to the other Tibetan girls. She had a delightfully attractive face and a lovely slim figure that was not hidden by several layers of thick clothing in traditional Tibetan style, but draped in close-fitting garments of colourful silk. On social occasions we would gaze at each other but rarely had the opportunity to speak and during the English lessons she gave me, there were always servants present. She had received a Western education and for me she provided a bridge to Europe. But Coocoola was also the wife of a high-ranking Tibetan nobleman and any liaison was therefore unthinkable. For her younger sister Kula, who lived in Gangtok, I acted as a kind of *postillion d'amour*, or go-between, composing love letters in English to her for my friend Wangdu-la. Kula was such a pretty girl that she had already come to the attention of visiting European Tibetologists and there was even talk of her becoming the future wife of the King of Bhutan.

The house in Polingka soon became a real home and it was also a popular and welcoming place for my Tibetan friends to spend time. It often happened that a messenger would arrive unexpectedly with the news that a *kutra*, a member of the Tibetan nobility, wished to visit that afternoon. They would often bring a sheep as a gift. The value of a sheep was determined by the amount of fat it had on it and a two-finger thick layer of fat was considered a highly prized gift by my servant. My friends did not only come to eat, of course. I also had other things to offer. They could relax and listen to the radio the Foreign Minister had given me to keep him informed of political events. Because of the increasingly threatening stance adopted by China, the BBC and the Australian news programmes often ran reports about Tibet, which my friends used to listen to with interest. They often misheard the word "debate" as "Tibet" and were consistently surprised at the amount of news coverage their country seemed to be receiving! My servant Nyima would bring us hot tea and eventually the steaming pot of mutton pieces would appear. We would all eat with our hands, dipping the tasty morsels into a little bowl of *sibin*, a spicy mixture made from chopped hot peppers. Occasionally a servant on horseback would come by in the evening to take me to the home of the parents of the Dalai Lama. I often cooked for them, as the following extract from *Tibet: My Story*, the autobiography of the sister of the Dalai Lama, Jetsun Pema, explains:

"I think that this is now the right moment to describe my first encounter with the Western world. It took place in 1947, when I was just over seven. Two Austrian prisoners had escaped from an Indian POW camp and taken refuge in Tibet. Lhasa was in a state of great excitement, with everybody wanting to see them.
My brother, Lobsang Samten, became friends with them, especially with the one called Heinrich Harrer. Heinrich was the first European I ever saw. On his visits, which became more and

more regular, he would lift me up onto his shoulders and carry me around. He loved nature and even planted poplars and fruit trees in our garden. Perched high up on his shoulders, I found it hard to hide my amazement – I had never seen a man like this, so tall and thin, dressed in canvas trousers and a shirt. Clinging to him, I was fascinated by his silky hair, which I was allowed to touch as much as I wanted.

Heinrich Harrer often ate with us. One day, he surprised us with a Western recipe. I remember vividly the moment when he entered the room where we used to eat, bearing a steaming dish which he laid on the stove exclaiming: 'Try it. Tell me what it's like.' After a long moment of hesitation, my mother and sister tasted this strange delicacy. Visibly appreciating it, they gave a piece to each of the children, who, up until then, had been awaiting Amala's opinion with curiosity. From that day on, roast chicken has been one of my favourite foods."

Lobsang Samten was the closest confidant of the Dalai Lama and about three years older than his brother. He lived with his parents in Lhasa and was a coveted guest, since people hoped that he might mention their name in the presence of his brother. Lobsang was an enthusiastic participator in my various sporting enterprises. He was a talented ice skater and the first Tibetan to master the difficult Axel-Paulsen jump.

The Dalai Lama would watch with interest from the roof of the Potala and instructed Lobsang Samten to ask me if I would build him a cinema at his Summer Palace, the Norbulingka. Life in Lhasa had taught me never to say no, even when asked to do things with which I was completely unfamiliar. I spent the winter of 1949-50 building the cinema and in the spring, when the great procession took place to mark the Dalai Lama's move from the Potala to his summer residence at Norbulingka, it was ready.

This procession, which took place twice a year, was a magnificent spectacle. All of the inhabitants of Lhasa came in droves and lined the route, their hands clasped in reverence. At the head of the procession came the monk servants and a mounted band, followed by the highest nobles of the country, the teachers of the Dalai Lama and all the other dignitaries of rank and status. At the end of the procession came the young Dalai Lama himself, clad in yellow silk and carried by thirty-six bearers wearing green silk robes.

The next day Lobsang told me "Tomorrow at ten o' clock sharp you must be at the Norbulingka. Wait there with my mother until you are summoned. The Dalai Lama wishes to see you."

AN AUDIENCE WITH THE DALAI LAMA

About fifty metres away from the gate in the Yellow Wall was the bungalow where the family of the Dalai Lama spent the summer months. I arrived at the gate on time, as instructed, and a servant was there waiting for me. The Great Mother offered me some Amdo tea and said that we had to wait until the Kundun came out of the gate in the Yellow Wall and returned to his own palace, by order of the Regent. Until the Dalai Lama reached the age of majority, the Regent Tadrag Rinpoche was his representative in all matters. His authority was absolute, he was widely feared, and even the Great Mother, who was usually so free and open with her opinions, particularly in matters concerning her sons, spoke about him in a hushed whisper. She kept watch, peeping through a gap in the curtains. Presently she said "The door is opening now. He's coming out. He's turning into his palace."

I had to wait a few more minutes. I looked over the Great Mother's shoulder and saw the most powerful man in Tibet disappearing from view with his aides. "Go now!" she said. With beating heart, I approached the huge gate in the Yellow Wall. There were kennels for the guard dogs on either side of the gate but only one was occupied. A large Tibetan *dokhyi* snarled ferociously. He had a white yak's tail stained with blood tied around his neck, which made him look even more intimidating, and he strained at the thick goat's hair leash as he jumped up and down, barking hoarsely. The gate opened silently and I walked through, happy to be standing in the familiar surroundings of the garden.

I made straight towards the cinema, but before I could enter, the door opened from the inside and I was standing before the Living Buddha. Conquering my surprise I bowed deeply and handed him my scarf. He took it with both hands and laid a hand on my head in a blessing.

I had built a dividing wall between the theatre and the projector, thinking that His Holiness could sit at the front while I operated the projector, but he immediately ordered the three abbots, his guardians, to sit in the viewing area and act as spectators and led me by the hand to the projection room. He beamed all over his face and poured out a flood of questions. He seemed to me like a person who had for years brooded in solitude over different problems, and now that he at last had someone to talk to, wanted to know all the answers at once. He gave me no time to think over my answers, but pressed me to go to the projector and put on a film which he had long been wanting to see. It was a documentary film about the capitulation of Japan. The main character was the US General Douglas McArthur, a man the Dalai Lama greatly respected.

I must have seemed quite slow and clumsy in handling the projector, as he impatiently pushed me to one side and, taking hold of the film, showed me that he was a much more capable projectionist than I was. He told me that he had been busy the whole winter learning how to work the apparatus and had even taken a projector to pieces and put it together again. I realised then, for the first time, that he liked to get to the bottom of things instead of taking them for granted. And so, later on, like many a good father who wished to earn the respect of his son, I spent many an evening reviving my knowledge of half-forgotten things or studying new ones. I took the utmost trouble to treat every question seriously and to answer them all to the best of my ability.

For the next film we selected the reel containing my footage of the New Year Festival. Even the stiffly formal abbots forgot their dignity when they recognised themselves on the flickering screen. There was a burst of laughter when a close-up appeared on the screen of a Minister who had nodded off during the ceremony. But there was no malice in their laughter, for each of the abbots had sometimes had to struggle to keep awake during these festivities. All the same, the word must have got around amongst the officials that the Dalai Lama had witnessed his Minister's moment of weakness, for afterwards whenever I appeared with my camera, everyone sat up and posed.

The Dalai Lama himself took more pleasure than anyone in the cinema, of course. His usually slow movements, deemed by his tutors as dignified and practised over the years, became youthful and lively and he commented enthusiastically on every picture. When the film had finished he got me to announce through the microphone that the show was over. He then opened the door leading into the theatre, told the abbots that he did not need them any more and dismissed them with a wave of the hand. It was again clear to me that here was no trained puppet but a clear-cut individual will capable of imposing itself on others.

When we were alone, we sat down in the theatre with the sun streaming through the open windows onto the magnificent carpet. It was fortunate that I had long since acquired the habit of sitting cross-legged on the floor, as there were no chairs or cushions in the Dalai Lama's household. To begin with I declined his invitation to sit down, knowing that even Ministers were not supposed to sit in his presence, but he just grabbed my sleeve and pulled me down next to him.

He told me that he had long been planning this meeting as he had not been able to think of any other way of becoming acquainted with the outside world. He expected the Regent to raise objections but he was determined to have his own way and had already prepared a rejoinder in case of opposition. He was resolved to extend his knowledge beyond purely religious subjects, and it obviously seemed to him that I was a suitable person to help him do this.

He then asked me my age and was surprised to learn that I was only thirty-seven. Like many Tibetans he thought that my "yellow" hair was a sign of age. He studied my features with childish curiosity and teased me about my large nose. By European standards, it is quite a normal sized nose, but it had frequently attracted undue attention from those with snub-nosed Mongolian features. Finally he noticed the hair growing on the back of my hands and said with a broad grin: "Henrig, you are as hairy as a monkey!" I had an appropriate answer to this, as I was familiar with the legend that the Tibetan race is derived from the union of their god Chenrezi with a female demon. Before coupling with his demon-lover, Chenrezi had assumed the shape of a monkey, and since the Dalai Lama is one of the Incarnations of this god, the comparison was in no way meant to be insulting.

Time passed swiftly. It seemed as if a dam had burst, and the boy's questions came flooding out. He suggested that I should visit his family the next day, who lived in the Norbulingka during the summer. He told me to wait in their house until he had finished his duties and he would then send for me.

As I rose to leave I asked him to grant me one last request and instruct the handler of the big guard dog to keep his beast under control when I passed. The Kundun seemed a little disappointed at my cowardice until I showed him the scars on my arm and told him about my fight with the *dokhyi* in the Himalaya. He kept repeating the words "nying jey". It was a phrase I had heard old Tsarong use while we were walking along the sacred path of Lingkhor in Lhasa, where we came across two beggars, ex-criminals who had removed their shackles. As we walked past them, Tsarong kept repeating "nying jey", " I am sorry; you have my sympathy."

I made my way slowly to the main gate of the Norbulingka, where I mounted my horse. The guards had changed while I had been in the Palace and now presented arms. I rode back to Lhasa deep in thought. Had it not been for the bag of cakes hanging from my saddle, a present from the Great Mother, I might easily have dismissed the whole thing as a dream. It was hard to believe that I had just spent five hours with the Living Buddha, the Dalai Lama. In the middle of the twentieth century, at the Roof of the World, it was like a fairy-tale come true.

This meeting in the Summer Palace marked the beginning of a new phase of my life in Lhasa. My existence now had a deeper significance. I no longer felt unsatisfied or incomplete, as I had done on occasion. I did not abandon my former duties. I still collected news for the Minister, I still drew maps, but now the days were all too short and I often worked till late into the night. I had little time for pleasures and hobbies, for I had to be available when the Dalai Lama summoned me. But it was no great sacrifice; indeed, I was happy in the knowledge that I had now found a really worthwhile task. The hours I spent with my pupil were as instructive for me as they were for him. I learned a great deal about the history of Tibet and the teachings of Buddha. We often had long discussions about religion and he was convinced that he would succeed in converting me to Buddhism.

Our hours together were always lively and exciting and the time passed far too quickly. The Dalai Lama kept finding new subjects to discuss with me, and the flood of questions continued unabated. Once, after a heavy storm, he wanted to know how thunder and lightning were caused. I explained the process to him and the next day Lobsang handed me a letter with a drawing of two clouds meeting and a lightning bolt striking 'the enemies' on the ground below. I was unsure whether he meant the enemies of Tibet or those people who envied us our friendship, both of which certainly existed. There were enough people in Lhasa who wondered why it was that they were obliged to bow before the throne of the Dalai Lama while I, a mere foreigner, was treated like a member of his family and allowed to visit him in the Summer Palace. The fact that I had gained the favour of both the Great Mother and one of his two tutors, Trichang Rinpoche, was significant. Both of them viewed my friendship with the Dalai Lama as beneficial for his education, yet in spite of this I never felt as if I were a tutor to His Holiness, nor did I ever describe myself as such. It was other people who referred to me thus. It was more like a father-son relationship that developed and matured into lasting friendship.

I maintained a kind of secret correspondence with the Dalai Lama. We wrote letters to each other in Tibetan, but to ensure that the contents really did remain 'secret' I taught him the Gothic script I had learned in school. During an interview recorded on 10th July 1998 in Vienna the Dalai Lama said, "During this time there was secret correspondence and we were good friends, Henrig and I. It was my brother, Lobsang Samten, who first brought Harrer to me. The court officials, all of them old monks, were naturally opposed to my friendship with Harrer, and to the fact that he was teaching me English. They were happy when he left Tibet in 1950."

Around this time, Giuseppe Tucci, the renowned Italian tibetologist, came to Lhasa for a few days. His guide was none other than Sherpa Tenzing Norgay, who had already achieved recognition as the travelling companion of the famous English author and mountaineer Frank Smythe and had been to over eight thousand metres on Himalayan expeditions. During his first meeting with the Cabinet Ministers, Tucci also found out that, in addition to Tibetan, Norgay also spoke a further twenty languages. Unfortunately, during one such meeting, Tucci embarrassed me badly. We were discussing the formation of the Earth, which the Tibetans believe is a flat disc. I, quite naturally, vigorously defended the theory that it is spherical in shape. The Tibetans seemed to find my arguments quite convincing and I called upon Professor Tucci to support my case. To my great surprise, Tucci sided with the doubters. In his opinion, all scientists must constantly revise their theories and one day, he said, the Tibetan theory might indeed prove to be correct. His comments caused general consternation, as it was well-known that I also taught geography. Professor Tucci stayed in Lhasa for eight days and left with a rich haul of scientific data and several valuable books from the National Library.

I told the Dalai Lama about the embarrassing situation that Tucci had put me in and that I was doubly aggrieved since Geography was a subject that I had studied.

In 1948 the Tibetan government dispatched a trade delegation with the object of establishing international political and economic contacts. The four high officials began their long journey in India and then visited Japan, followed by the USA and Europe, before returning home. They brought back several crates of advertising material and I was given the job of sorting it by country of origin and type of industry. The delegation had also been charged with the task of seeking help from large and powerful nations, since China's threats to 'liberate' Tibet had been growing more and more explicit. The news on the radio, which I noted and brought to the attention of the Foreign Minister on a daily basis now, was worrying. The Maoist troops had taken the province of Sinkiang and were now close to Amdo, the birthplace of the Dalai Lama.

When the Chinese occupied Sinkiang, the American consul stationed in the capital city of Urumchi, Douglas Mackiernan, fled to Tibet with a young student called Frank Bessac and three White Russians, having first requested the US Embassy in India to ask the Tibetan government for permission to travel through Tibet. Lhasa immediately dispatched messengers north to instruct the frontier posts and patrols to make no difficulties for the fugitives. Their three thousand kilometre journey took them through the remote Takla Makan Desert and the Nun Kun mountains to the Changtang Plateau in North West Tibet. Both humans and animals withstood the journey well. Then, after seven months, on 9th May 1950, a terrible tragedy brought their odyssey to an abrupt end. Fate decreed that the Government messenger with the travel permit was late in arriving at the frontier post where the party was to cross into Tibet. Before the caravan was even within shouting distance of the frontier post, the soldiers, tempted perhaps by the sight of a dozen heavily laden camels, opened fire without warning, killing on the spot the American consul and two of the Russians. The third Russian was wounded and only Bessac escaped unhurt. He was taken prisoner and brought with the wounded man to the nearest District Governor. Bessac was badly treated by the soldiers, who insulted and threatened him. They shared the spoils and were overjoyed to find such valuable objects as field-glasses and cameras. Before they reached the next *ponpo* they were met by the messenger carrying a red flag and orders to treat the Americans and their companions as guests of the Government. This caused a change of attitude. The soldiers were sheepish and outdid one another in politeness but the damage could not be undone. Their behaviour had cost three people their lives. The Governor sent a report to Lhasa and the authorities, horrified by the news, were at great pains to express the regret of the Government in every possible way. A hospital orderly who had trained in India was sent with presents to meet Bessac and his wounded companion. They were invited to come to Lhasa and asked to appear as witnesses for the prosecution against the soldiers, who had already been arrested. A high-ranking official who spoke a little English rode out to meet the approaching travellers, as custom dictated. I attached myself to him thinking that it might be some comfort to the young American to have a European to talk to about his unfortunate adventure. I also hoped to convince him that the Government could not be blamed for the incident, which it deeply regretted. We met the young man in pouring rain. He was a lanky fellow and completely dwarfed his little Tibetan pony. I could well imagine how he felt. The little caravan had been on the road for months, always on the run and exposed to dangers, and their first meeting with the people of the country in which they sought asylum had caused the deaths of three members of their party.

New clothes and shoes were waiting for them in a tent by the roadside and in Lhasa they were put up in a garden-house with a cook and a servant to look after them. Fortunately the injuries the Russian, Vassilieff, had incurred were not life-threatening and he was soon able to hobble about the garden on his crutches. The two men stayed in Lhasa for a month, during which time I made friends with Bessac. He bore no grudge against the country which had at first received him so inhospitably. He asked only that the soldiers who had mistreated him be punished. He was requested to be present when the punishment was carried out, to make sure there was no deception. When he saw the floggings, however, he asked that the number of lashes be reduced. He took photographs of the scene, which later appeared in *Life* magazine. Bessac was received by the Dalai Lama and left Lhasa shortly afterwards. I was asked to accompany him for a few days on his journey to India.

It was a convivial and relaxing trip. We glided down the Kyichu in a yak-skin boat to the junction with the Tsangpo and followed this great river downstream to Samye. I showed Bessac the ancient Samye Gompa monastery and the cave in which the Indian guru, Padmasambhava, had lived in the year 775, and explained that Padmasambhava had founded the Tibetan, or Tantric, school of Buddhism. We had plenty of time to enjoy the journey. Bessac asked me if there was anything he could send me from the USA. I told him that I needed some more film, as all the rolls my friends had brought me from India were now old and useless. Frank Bessac had an old Leica that he had rescued from Mackiernan. Strictly speaking it was US government property but in spite of Bessac's misgivings I managed to persuade him to part with it and the Dalai Lama received a gift of a nice camera. Bessac's government had horses waiting for him when we arrived in Samye. We bade each other farewell and he rode off for Sikkim and India. I took the route over the pass to Lhasa and arrived home the same day.

While the Tibetan trade delegation was staying in New York, the well-known American radio news broadcaster Lowell Thomas was granted permission to visit Tibet with his son. They arrived in Lhasa in the summer of 1949 after a long journey. This is the best time of the year for the Tibetans, as this is when the Summer Palace of the Dalai Lama, or "Jewelled Garden" to give the Norbulingka its direct translation, hosts day-long mystery plays in the grounds. Beneath a huge ceremonial canopy decorated with good luck symbols stood a shrine to Thangtong Gyalpo, who was not only known as a builder of bridges but was also revered as the founding father of Tibetan theatre. During these performances the Dalai Lama would sit behind a yellow silk curtain on the first floor of his palace. He once remarked to me that, for him, this was the most wonderful time of the year before adding, in typically tongue-in-cheek fashion, "There were no tutors there".

The two Foreign Ministers had arranged a reception for the American guests in the Cabinet's own bungalow and one of the monk Ministers, Liuschar Dzasa, took me along as his interpreter. The three secular Cabinet Ministers, Liuschar Dzasa and I sat cross-legged on the floor, while the guests took their places on comfortable upholstered seats that had been brought in especially for them. They were rather surprised that I was interpreting and said that they wanted to meet Peter Aufschnaiter and me the next day. Thomas recorded the interview for his evening radio show back in New York and explained that he wanted to write a book about our adventures. We told him we did not wish to court publicity and preferred to live a quiet life amongst our Tibetan friends.

I went on a photo and film shoot with Lowell Thomas. During the time that I had no decent quality film, I had compiled a list of the times and seasons when one would get the best shots of various subjects. The correct lighting was crucial, especially for photographs of the facades of the buildings with their windows, corners and niches and the bas-reliefs and colourful murals adorning the rock walls around the city. We clambered down the stony ridge from the School of Medicine to Liuschar Dzasa's apartment. He was expecting us. His little home had the finest aspect in the whole of Lhasa, with the golden tipped stupas of the Western Gate directly below and the mighty frontage of the Potala forming the backdrop. As Thomas Junior was changing films, I noticed that he had a case full to the brim with 35 millimetre colour films. After taking a shot of his father with the Minister and the Potala in the background he gave me two rolls. I now had my decent film but I still lacked a flashgun for interior shots. When we visited the Potala to see the holy *stupa* that contained the remains of the thirteenth

Dalai Lama, I held my camera steady against one of the pillars, set the aperture and managed to get my shot just as Lowell Thomas operated his flashgun. Several of the photographs I obtained in this way were later reproduced in books and glossy magazines and during the year 2000 one of them was even included in a photography magazine's shortlist of the photographs of the century.

During the days that the Thomas' spent in Lhasa we had plenty of time to chat. I still vividly recall one of Lowell Thomas' remarks: "You know, Henry, I shouldn't really tell you this, but my job is a gold mine. Forty million dollars I've made." The extent to which their visit might have helped the Tibetan's cause is beyond my knowledge, however. The head of the British Mission, Hugh Richardson, who was by far the most experienced foreign politician in matters concerning the situation in which Tibet found herself, was of the opinion that the Americans' ideas about the "Land at the Roof of the World" were far too optimistic and were largely based on James Hilton's famous novel "Lost Horizon", which was published in 1933 and made into a film by Frank Capra in 1939. Although Hilton had never described his story as a factual documentary, this was how it was perceived and the general public had been particularly impressed by the Capra's fascinating scenes of "Shangri-la", which had become a synonym for all things mysterious and other-worldly. This romantic notion of Tibet was a false representation of the country. In truth, little was known about the very real problems that isolation brought.

In 1948 the process of repatriation of the German prisoners interned in the Indian POW camps had begun. I would have loved to have visited Europe myself but the expense of such a trip was prohibitive. However, a visit by the Englishman Robert Ford in the same year brought a little European flair to Lhasa. Ford, or Bob as he was known, was a young man and his visit certainly enlivened the social life of the city. Bob had brought his record collection with him and the new music and dances proved very popular with the young wives of the Tibetan nobility, particularly those who had learned English. My own contribution to the festivities was to translate several of the English songs, amongst them "Ten Green Bottles", into Tibetan. My greatest success was teaching the Tibetans the words to "My Hat It Has Three Corners". At the end of the song, when the words have to be mimed rather than sung, they laughed out loud as only Tibetans can.

Ford had worked for two years for a radio station in Sikkim and was now employed by the Tibetan government. After setting up the first Tibetan radio station in Lhasa, as the Chinese threat grew ever more serious he was commissioned to establish a second station in Chamdo in eastern Tibet in 1949, from where he used to send daily reports to Lhasa. In October 1950 he was arrested by the Chinese Communists and sentenced to five years in prison. In later years he travelled the world as a supporter of the Dalai Lama and the Tibetan cause. Ford and I were the last European witnesses to a free Tibet.

Meanwhile, in Lhasa, wild rumours were circulating about the aggressive plans of the Chinese, whereupon the Tibetan government issued two seemingly contradictory decrees. The first concerned the placement of prayer flags, prayer wheels and shrines on the mountains to protect the country against the enemy. Now, more than ever, the holy scriptures were being read and recited in the monasteries and private homes of Lhasa. At the time, friends of mine began training with outdated machine guns, soldiers were recruited and new regiments formed. Some of these left Lhasa for eastern Tibet and the border with China; others went to Gyantse, where it was said that modern weapons had arrived from India.

I walked up to about five and a half thousand metres on Mindrutsari and cached a few items under a boulder, including a revolver that I had bought on the market in Lhasa. I had never possessed a weapon before but I considered this a sensible precaution.

On 7th January 1950, I conveyed the news report to the Minister at the Foreign Office that China was preparing to "liberate" Tibet. Of course, no one in Lhasa quite knew what it was that the Tibetans ought to be liberated from.

At about the same time I went to pick up some English films from Hugh Richardson at the British Mission. He advised me to try to find out if the books that had been earmarked for an English school in Lhasa at the time of the thirteenth Dalai Lama were still in existence. This I duly did, and the very next day I picked up two heavy boxes of books from the Foreign Ministry. Unfortunately, my treasure trove came to light a little too late.

For the time being, my visits to the Dalai Lama continued undisturbed. I managed to borrow the film *Henry V*, with Laurence Olivier in the leading role, from the Indian Embassy in Dekyi Lingka. I thought that it would provide an easier introduction for the Dalai Lama than the Complete Works of Shakespeare that lay amongst the books in the box. I replayed the impressive scene with the line, "Uneasy lies the head that wears the crown", several times. (*translator's note*: the line was lifted from *Henry IV Part II*). The Dalai Lama immediately understood the relevance of Shakespeare's words to the difficult times that lay ahead.

The evil omens became more frequent, culminating on the 15th of August, when a serious earthquake shook the city of Lhasa. It began at eight o' clock in the evening and lasted just four minutes, but it seemed like an eternity to us. A rumbling and crashing filled the air and some people thought they saw flashes of light in the skies to the south. After the earthquake, a religious sculpture that had adorned a stone column at the foot of the Potala was found lying on the ground in fragments, but there was a feeling of relief the following morning when we established that there had been no serious damage to any of the houses or to the Potala Palace itself. It was an evil portent, nonetheless.

I was able to explain to the Dalai Lama that this had been a tectonic earthquake and could be explained by the theory of continental drift first proposed in 1912 by Professor Alfred Wegener. A little while ago I had shown him a crayon drawing made by my son Peter when he was four, and I now told him that the famous Professor was Peter's grandfather. The Dalai Lama considered the theory that plate tectonics was still causing the Himalaya to rise but dismissed the explanation as insufficient and added that, in his opinion, there was still something mysterious about the earthquake that was beyond scientific explanation.

When the Dalai Lama left the Norbulingka and returned to the Potala Palace that was the end of the happy hours we spent together. It also marked the end of many of my ideas and dreams.

FAREWELL TO TIBET

On October 7th, 1950, the Chinese army marched across the Tibetan frontier. Since the breach occurred several hundred kilometres to the east of Lhasa, there was no outbreak of panic in the city, but I accelerated my preparations to leave. I asked at the Foreign Ministry for permission to take a holiday and for a letter that confirmed my status as a government employee. I also addressed a note "To whom it may concern" requesting a permit to return to Tibet. This was important, since I knew that the Indian government was in the habit of issuing transit visas only to those who had permission to enter Tibet.

I left Lhasa in the middle of November. I had acquired a number of cheap tin packing crates, which were filled with generous gifts from friends and several standard reference works from the English school library collection. Transport was not a problem, since Minister Surkhang had placed an unlimited number of pack-animals at my disposal after I had agreed to accompany his wife and child and their nurse to India. Several well-to-do businessmen and nobles had already arranged for their families to be evacuated to a place of safety. Many of the families also took personal valuables and religious treasures with them.

Finally it was time to go. The caravan with our baggage had already left Lhasa when we embarked in our yak-skin boat, which was to take us, a little more comfortably and swiftly than by road, down the Kyichu as far as its junction with the Yarlung Tsangpo. My friends stood on the bank waving and throwing silk ribbons while I took photographs of them. Then the current caught the boat and they were soon out of sight. I had several white *katas* draped around my neck – leaving presents from my friends that were meant to bring me luck in the future. As we floated down the river I could not keep my eyes off the Potala, which still dominated the view long after we had left. I knew the Dalai Lama would be on the roof of the palace looking at me through his telescope. During the previous few weeks we had often talked about the future and my young friend had finally pressed me to leave. I consoled myself with the thought that we might meet again in the south of the country. Preparations had also been made for his escape, albeit under a strict veil of secrecy.

On the same day I caught up with my caravan, which consisted of fourteen pack-animals and two horses for me and my servant, the faithful Nyima, who had insisted on accompanying me. At Yamdrok Yumcho, a large, crystal clear lake, we found lodgings with a farmer. I knew I had to part company with Nyima here, as he had to return to his family, but it was as hard to convince him of this as it had been back in Lhasa when I had been invited out by friends and did not want him to come with me. Every time I left the home of our host at Yamdrok Yumcho, the figure of Nyima would emerge from the shadows and follow me protectively. When the time came for us to part company he was inconsolable. I suggested that he might be able to sell vegetables from my large garden in the Polingka to the Chinese to make a living. It was seven years to the day since I had said goodbye to our faithful Indian friend, Padam Chand, shortly before reaching Tibet. Now, as I was about to leave Tibet, I again had to bid farewell to a devoted companion with whom I had developed a real friendship and empathy.

Our journey continued in the comfortable style that is customary when travelling with Tibetans. The pack-animals would set off at dawn with two of the servants and by the time we caught up with the caravan at the end of the day's ride, hot butter tea and biscuits would be waiting for us. In Gyantse we stayed with Surkhang Wagchuk, who had been one of my best friends during my time in Lhasa before he left to take up his appointment as Governor of Gyantse. As the younger brother of the Cabinet Minister Surkhang, he was also the uncle of the little baby in our party. We were now seven days' march from Lhasa and thus felt safe from surprise attacks by the Chinese, so I decided to wait for a few days in Gyantse in the hope that some country might come to the aid of Tibet against her aggressors.

I made profitable use of my time and took an excursion to Shigatse, the second largest town in Tibet, in the province of Tsang. The fortress in Shigatse was built in the shape of a small Potala, and the post of Governor, was the most sought-after in the whole of Tibet. Although Shigatse lies at a higher altitude than Lhasa, it is here that the best quality wheat grows. During my time in Lhasa I had repeatedly made suggestions to the Government for economic development of the country, including a plan to start producing safety matches and another idea to use some of the wheat grown in the province of Tsang to manufacture biscuits for export. My suggestions received a rather arrogant reply from one of the government officials, who remarked that "We can afford to import both!" This was indeed possible, as Tibet exported hundreds of thousands of bales of sheep's wool which financed the purchase of all the luxury items they required. Economically speaking, the country was totally self-sufficient.

The people of Shigatse seemed less afraid of the Chinese. Next to the Governor's fortress lay the great monastery of Trashilhunpo, one of the largest in Tibet and home to several thousand monks. Trashilhunpo was also the seat of the Panchen Lama, the second highest religious figure in Tibet after the Dalai Lama. This high incarnation had for generations been supported by the Chinese as a rival to the Dalai Lama and proclaimed by Peking as the rightful ruler of Tibet. The present incumbent lived here in Shigatse under close Chinese supervision. The *stupas* beneath the golden roofs of Trashilhunpo commemorating the deaths of the previous Panchen Lamas were similar to the memorials to the Dalai Lamas in the Potala Palace in Lhasa. I was particularly impressed with the largest building, the Hall of Buddha Maitreya (known as Buddha Quamba in Tibet), with its twenty six metre high bronze statue of the Buddha Quamba. The head of the statue was so huge that I had to climb several steep ladders to get my photographs.

Back in Gyantse, my friend Surkhang Wagchuk was waiting excitedly for me with the news that the Dalai Lama had left Lhasa on December 19th and was on his way here. Orders had been issued to prepare all of the staging posts and rest houses along the route for his arrival and to repair the roads. His mother and his brothers and sisters had already arrived in Gyantse. I also had a happy reunion with Norbu, whom I had not seen for three years. He had already been travelling for months after tricking the Chinese into believing that he would persuade his younger brother to remain in Tibet. Norbu was happy to have got away and was now travelling southward with his family.

Surkhang Wagchuk and I rode out to meet the Dalai Lama. After three days we ran into the advance party of his caravan on the Karo Pass. A rough wind had blown up and the flapping of the many colourful prayer flags almost drowned out the chanting of "Ki Ki So So Lha Gye Lo" of the outriders. The young ruler had an escort of forty nobles and a military guard of some two hundred hand-picked soldiers with modern machine guns and howitzers. An army of servants and cooks followed, and a seemingly unending train of 1,500 pack-animals walking in single file brought up the rear.

In the middle of the column two flags were waving: the national flag of Tibet and the personal banner of the fourteenth Dalai Lama. The flags denoted the presence of the ruler. When I saw the young God-King riding slowly up the pass, I involuntarily thought of an ancient prophecy that one sometimes heard people quote under their breath in Lhasa. An oracle had long ago declared that the thirteenth Dalai Lama would be the last of his line. Several weeks ago, and two years before reaching the age of majority, my young friend had been officially proclaimed by the National Assembly as the fourteenth Dalai Lama and the ruler of his country. It seemed that the prophecy was fulfilling itself. He was the king, but he had not yet taken up the reins of power; the enemy was at the gates and the ruler was in flight. As he rode by me on his white horse, I doffed my woollen cap. It seemed to me a happy coincidence that the thick smoke from the many incense fires hid both our faces and our feelings from view.

The Dalai Lama spent the night in a small monastery. Compared to the Potala or the Norbulingka the accommodation was modest to say the least. I thought of him sitting in an unfriendly guest room with only a few dusty idols for company. He would find no stove to warm him and the paper-covered window panes were his only protection against storm and cold, while a few butter-lamps provided just enough light to see by. He was completely alone with his problems. The three abbots and his two tutors were ill, unused to the cold and the thin air. His brother and closest confidante, Lobsang Samten, had unfortunately suffered a heart attack shortly before leaving Lhasa and had had similar problems with the altitude, becoming unconscious again on the journey. The Dalai Lama's physician treated him with a primitive cure better suited to horses, applying a red-hot branding iron to various parts of his body as a rudimentary kind of cauterisation or heat therapy.

Lobsang regained consciousness and was placed in the caravan's only sedan chair to allow him to recuperate. In any case, it was so cold that the Dalai Lama preferred to ride his horse than be carried. Only when the procession passed a monastery and all the monks and nuns knelt to pray before him would he clamber into the palanquin. In many places, small whitewashed stones had been laid along the route to prevent evil spirits and demons from crossing his path. Until now, the young ruler had only ever seen the city of Lhasa and its immediate surroundings. He was now able to use the sad circumstances to appreciate for the first time how beautiful his country was. At the Kora Pass he had ridden past enormous glaciers and now, in Gyantse, he stood before the immense Chorten Temple, with the eighteen monasteries on the hill behind representing the various schools of Tibetan Buddhism.

In Gyantse I also met up with Peter Aufschnaiter, who had decided to remain in Tibet and planned to avoid the advancing Chinese army by heading into the western part of the country. He wished to spend some more time in Kyirong, the Village of Happiness, and also intended to visit the meditation cave of Milarepas. He later wrote a paper about Milarepas, the most important Tibetan yogi, for the ISMEO, the institute Tucci had founded in Rome. Aufschnaiter went on his way, free and independent, to pursue his interests. He was a man who lived life to the full. Only once did he reveal something of his inner self, when he wrote to his mother in the Tyrol: "You would have been surprised to see how tenderly Angdi's eighteen-year-old daughter treated me. If it weren't for the Communists, I would start making plans." When the Chinese then marched into Lhasa and it became apparent that they were not about to leave, Peter no longer felt safe and, on 21st January 1952, together with his friend Draba Angdi, he finally left his beloved Tibet. In Lhasa we had often talked about where we might go in the event that Tibet should no longer be a free land; we thought about Australia or the USA. Peter Aufschnaiter ended up in the Himalayan kingdom of Nepal, where he was received with friendship and hospitality.

We left Gyantse at the beginning of December, heading south. I had attached myself to the caravan of the God-King. During the journey south, the weather got even colder and every day around noon the hurricane-force sandstorms that are common at the start of the Tibetan winter swept across the high country and snatched at the banners and flags of the caravan, which had to be hurriedly packed away. In the distance we could now see the massive pyramid of the 7,328 metre Chomolhari. To the west of the mountain lay the provincial capital Phari, which was our next objective. To get there we first had to cross the vast expanse of the Tuna Plain.

To combat the cold we went on foot; even the Dalai Lama, who was flanked by two abbots. Walking was a completely new experience for all the nobles. After several hours of marching we established our camp for the night. As expected, the wind dropped in the late afternoon. The banners were unfurled and we pitched our tents in the cold shadows of the mountain. Up on the summit ridge of Chomolhari we could see a huge plume of windblown snow glowing in the evening sun.

During the long march I found time to think about the safety of the Dalai Lama. The Chinese had now been in eastern Tibet for three months and the four hundred square kilometre Tuna Plain would provide them with an ideal landing strip for their aircraft. But it would also provide a means of spiriting the Dalai Lama away to a place of safety. Both before and after the Chinese invasion, I had argued the case for voluntary exile, as I believed that this would give him a better chance of returning one day to a free Tibet. In the Second World War, many rulers had survived by fleeing their country.

Since leaving Gyantse we had all been suffering from the intense cold and the hardships of the journey and were looking forward to reaching Phari, where comfortable, warm lodgings in proper, solid houses awaited us. Phari lies several hundred metres higher than Lhasa and is the recognised as the highest town in the world with a permanent governor. The Governor was Dzongpon Targyela, the younger brother of my best friend Wangdu Sholkhang in Lhasa. The next morning, all of the Ministers were keen to press on to Phari without taking a rest day. We were all happy to come down off the cold, high plateau into the warm, wooded landscape of the Chumbi Valley.

I decided to stay a while in Phari and take up Targyela's invitation to spend a few days as his guest. I wanted to delay my inevitable departure from the land that had become my second home for as long as possible. I suppose I simply refused to face up to reality and clung to the chance of being able to prolong my stay. Here in the high country of Phari, I was surrounded by endless hills, broken only by the ice-clad peak of Chomolhari, Mountain of the Goddess, and I was pleased to be able to experience the wide expanses of snow once more. Targyela and I had a trip out to climb one of the subsidiary peaks of Chomolhari and this was the first time I had ever set foot in the Kingdom of Bhutan. Many years later, I was to make several visits to Bhutan and to get to know this jewel amongst the Himalaya states.

Now, however, it was time to follow the great caravan. The thousand metre descent from Phari was steep and rocky, so I decided to walk. I was also mindful of the Tibetan saying "a horse that will not carry a man uphill is not a real horse and a man that will not dismount and lead his horse downhill is not a real man".

I soon caught sight of the shingle-roofed houses of the Chumbi Valley, the provisional destination of the Dalai Lama's caravan. Around the monastery of Dungkar Gompa, where he was staying, new prayer flags fluttered in the breeze. I found lodgings in a cosy little farmhouse, right next door to the house where Norbu was billeted. I made several excursions with him to the frontier with Bhutan. The wives and children of the Dalai Lama's officials travelled straight to India. Some fifty crates filled with gold dust and bars of silver had already been taken to Sikkim for safe-keeping. This was the State Treasure, which the Tibetans understandably wished to preserve. The actual value of the treasure, in common with many other things relating to Tibet, was of course grossly exaggerated in foreign news reports.

Meanwhile, in Chumbi, I was getting bored and restless. Although I was still reporting the radio news to the Foreign Minister, Surkhang Dzasa, who had remained in Lhasa, I felt that my continued presence in Chumbi was superfluous. The daily rumours that came from neighbouring Sikkim and from the Indian soldiers provided little clarity. The Cabinet met each day without announcing its decisions. There was a feeling of uncertainty and disarray. The only calming influence was the Great Mother, who was more concerned about her son than with politics.

At the end of May we received the shocking news from Peking that the representatives of the Dalai Lama, under the leadership of Cabinet Minister Ngabo Ngawang Jigme, had signed the "Seventeen Point Agreement" with the Chinese, which now bore the official government seal of Tibet. It was immediately obvious that this agreement could only have been secured under duress, since the State Seal of Tibet was in the possession of the Dalai Lama at the Dungkar Monastery. The seal appearing on the document was therefore a copy forged in Peking by the Chinese authorities. Tibet's fate was now sealed, however, as the agreement left no doubt that Tibet was henceforth to be considered a part of China. What would the Dalai Lama do now? Would he accept the agreement and return to Lhasa or go into exile and take up the fight against Tibet's aggressors?

The Dalai Lama had heard the news on the radio. I tried to imagine how the young man might be feeling and how hopeless the situation must have seemed to him. Although he was still only a child, his intelligence, his sense of responsibility and his serenity made it possible for him to weather the storm of well-meant, yet often contradictory suggestions made by his many advisors and to remain steadfast in his purpose. I admired him, but even as his friend, I was powerless to help him in this situation. Nor did I have any opportunity to speak to him, since visiting him here in Chumbi was not as straightforward as it had been whilst he was living at the Norbulingka. It was obvious that in these times of crisis the old monks regarded my friendship with him with suspicion and did their best to keep me isolated. I therefore bade him farewell in a letter, in which I advised him to seek asylum in India. Meanwhile, a Chinese General by the name of Zhang Jingwu was on the way to Chumbi to speak with the Dalai Lama. I had finally made up my mind to go to India, since for me, returning to Lhasa was out of the question. In March 1951 I left the Chumbi Valley.

My Tibetan odyssey had lasted exactly seven years. Now I sat alone in the sun on the Natula Pass, on the border between Tibet and India. Like seven years before, there were no border guards or customs officers. Kangchenjunga stood close by and I had the time to deliberate at leisure what these years had meant to me and what insights they had brought. I thought mostly about the unforgettable experiences I had had, about things I could never have dreamed.

Everything I had done was overshadowed by the time I had spent with the young Dalai Lama, and the friendship that has lasted to this day. I thought about how quickly he had been confronted with the wise words of Shakespeare: "Uneasy lies the head that wears a crown". I thought, too, about his tutor Trichang Rinpoche, who had always shown understanding for my visits to his pupil. In Lhasa, I had once asked him if he would "take me under his wing", so to speak. The phrase has great significance in Tibetan as a request for both protection and patronage. During the cold days of our flight from Lhasa I had found the opportunity to thank him for his kindness in granting my request.

I had been privileged to live in a feudal state as it might once have been in the Middle Ages, but that time was now over and I deeply regretted the fact that an enemy power was now to bring about unavoidable changes. I shall never forget the hospitality of those happy people, their joyous laughter or the politeness they showed at every meeting. Instead of shaking hands, they place their palms together in front of their chest; instead of kissing, they greet those closest to them by touching foreheads. The nicest custom, and the one I came to love best, is the giving of a white silk scarf for good luck. This is offered with both hands, as is everything one takes or receives. To this day I have retained the custom of holding my tea or coffee cup to my lips with both hands. It is one of the many small gestures that I learned in Tibet that have now become a part of me.

The years I spent in Tibet were a wonderfully happy time for me. I not only felt contented living amongst the Tibetan people, I also felt useful and appreciated. As a jack of all trades, I always seemed to have something to do and every task I was asked to perform I tried to do to the best of my ability. If I was asked to build a dam, a bridge or a house I either turned to Peter Aufschnaiter for advice or consulted the books in the English library for the best way to go about it. For the Tibetans, isolated as they were, everything I did was new. But much of it was new for me, too, as I was often doing these things for the first time. I did my best never to refuse a request and took pleasure in trying. My reward was the good feeling I got from helping and the appreciation of a job well done. We became so well known in Lhasa that the Dalai Lama extended me the great honour of summoning me to him. My farewell to Tibet was also a farewell to a life that was fulfilled, and to a time that will never again exist, not even in Tibet.

KALIMPONG

By the crystal clear waters of Tsogo Lake, a few kilometres below the Natula Pass, but still above the tree line, stood a bungalow, my destination for the day. I was more than a little surprised to be greeted there by a slim man with a European appearance and an American accent. "Mr. Harrer," he said, "I am James Burke, the New Delhi correspondent of *Life* magazine. I've been expecting you."

My thoughts were still somewhere in Tibet and I regarded this first meeting with Burke as rather confrontational. He represented a world that had become alien to me. Copies of *Life* magazine had occasionally been available in Lhasa but they were always at least a year old. Burke came from a family of missionaries and had been born in China, so he understood the reasons for my rather cool attitude. In spite of my reservations, I agreed to let him accompany me and at the next rest-stop in Gangtok, the provincial capital of Sikkim, he asked me if I had taken any photographs during our escape from Lhasa. The bulk of my luggage was now safely in Kalimpong with the Surkhang caravan but I had kept hold of my valuable diaries and films. I told Burke that there must be some colour shots of the large ceremony that had been held in Chumbi, when Indian scholars had presented the Dalai Lama with a golden urn containing the remains of the Gautama Buddha. They were the last photographs of the Dalai Lama that I had been able to take and to the best of my knowledge, the last photographs ever taken of the God-King in a free Tibet. Burke suggested that we have the films professionally developed in New York and use the shots to illustrate an extensive article he was working on for *Life* about the current situation in Tibet. We travelled to New Delhi together, where I was given a room in his family's bungalow.

During the following days I learned what modern journalism was like when money is no object. We worked day and night. As soon as a page was ready it was given to a bicycle messenger, who rode straight to the post office and had the text telegraphed to New York, express rate. One morning, as we were still eating breakfast, a telegram arrived that was several pages long. Burke read it through and said, "Henry, all the photos are good. They are giving us the cover story!" He went on to say that the colour photograph of the Dalai Lama with the golden urn was to be used as the cover shot.

The seven million covers for our issue of *Life* were already at the printers when the surprise news arrived that President Truman had dismissed General Douglas MacArthur, the victorious commander of the Southwest Pacific Theatre in the war against Japan. This was sensational news in the US and had a direct bearing on the country's domestic politics. The editor decided to run my cover photograph anyway, but our ten page article was moved from the front of the magazine to the middle section. Burke was happy and proud nonetheless. He told me he had been authorised to negotiate my fee but confided to me that he would not be allowed to exceed the maximum payment of $10,000. This seemed such a huge amount of money that I jokingly replied, "Well, what about 9,900 then?"

The fee made it possible for me to stay in India and also allowed me to entertain the idea of organising an expedition to climb one of the Himalayan peaks; perhaps even the trip to Kanch I had discussed with Tenzing Norgay during his visit to Lhasa. First of all, however, I had appointments to keep with the representatives of the international press. Interest in Tibet was great and there were daily news reports in the Indian newspapers. I found the interest shown in me surprising; it reminded me of the media frenzy after the first ascent of the North Face of the Eiger in 1938. I had no idea that my life in remote Lhasa had been so closely observed, or that I would be called as a witness to events in Tibet.

Meanwhile, the US Ambassador, Loy Henderson, had asked Jim Burke if I would agree to pay him a visit. He was well informed about the political situation in Tibet and I was happy to provide him with additional information. I told him that the Dalai Lama was more intelligent than his advisors, that he admired MacArthur, trusted the United States and expected them to come to his aid. I explained that the problem he had in deciding whether to remain in Tibet or go into exile, was compounded by the fact that he had to listen to so many differing opinions. Everyone had their own suggestions – his elder brother, who had married a Chinese girl, another brother who was fleeing the Chinese occupation, the two Cabinet Ministers, the highest ranking abbot in the land, his two tutors, his mother, the English, the Indians and the Americans. I tried to explain to Henderson that the present 14th Dalai Lama might be subconsciously aware of his previous Incarnation, the 13th Dalai Lama Thubten Gyatso, who had fled Tibet and then returned to rule the country with great success, and that this might prove instrumental in persuading the Kundun to leave Tibet.

While I was voicing these thoughts to Henderson, the Chinese General had arrived in India *en route* to Tibet. Time was now of the essence; something had to be done quickly, before the General met the Dalai Lama in Chumbi. Fifty years after the event, the details of their negotiations, which were kept secret at the time, are a matter of public knowledge. It is the custom in Washington for documents of this kind to be opened for public inspection after forty years have elapsed. On 6th July 1992, on the occasion of our joint birthday celebration held in my holiday home in Carinthia, I showed the Dalai Lama a copy of the Swiss daily newspaper *Der Bund*, which carried a front page report on my 1951 meeting with Henderson and documented his promise to provide help and support. In 2000, former CIA officer Kenneth Knaus's four hundred page book *Orphans of the Cold War: America and the Tibetan Struggle for Survival* was published in America. In it, Knaus refers to the message I sent to the Dalai Lama on 24th June 1951 outlining Henderson's promise to support the Dalai Lama in exile.

As I was saying goodbye to Ambassador Henderson, he said, "Oh, Mr. Harrer, there's a parcel here for you." It was from Frank Bessac and contained, amongst other things, twenty rolls of colour film.

In order to be closer to political events as they unfolded, I returned from New Delhi to Kalimpong, which is only a day's ride away from the Tibetan frontier. I had difficulty getting a room at the Himalaya Hotel, as the place was swarming with journalists. On opening my caravan loads, which had arrived from Lhasa, there was a nasty surprise. Packed at the top of one of the crates was the silk robe I had worn at official state occasions. It was now mildewed and rotten. Worse was to follow, and I now recalled how, when the luggage was being loaded onto the Tsangpo ferry, one of the pack-animals had shied and fallen into the water with two of the Indian tin cases. We had managed to save them, but now, months later, the extent of the water damage was all too apparent.

The servants at the hotel were all from the Lepcha community, the aboriginal inhabitants of the present day province of Sikkim. They were Buddhists of the old school and groaned in dismay as they unrolled my *thangka* paintings depicting gods and holy men, as some of the pictures had been totally destroyed by the soaking they had received. As they spread them out on the green lawn of the hotel garden they chanted "Om mani padme hum" like Tibetans. All Tibetan *thangkas* are antique pieces painted using natural colours, so of the pictures contained in that load, not a single one remained undamaged. Unfortunately, there was an even greater loss, which I noticed when I opened the bundle of letters containing my entire correspondence with Sven Hedin. Some of the letters that the great explorer had written on a typewriter were still legible, but those written in ink could barely be deciphered.

After a few days the hotel moved me to Room 7 on the first floor, where I could spread my belongings out. I stayed there for several months. There was no running water, but early each morning one of the Lepcha would clamber up an almost vertical ladder propped up against the outer wall of the hotel carrying two buckets of water for the bathroom, which had its own separate entrance. Ensconced in my hotel room, I began to jot down the experiences I had had in Tibet. I wrote in English, firstly because English was the language spoken here and secondly because my vocabulary for Tibetan religion and geography was derived almost entirely from English books.

The work progressed only slowly, since I was invited out almost every day, either for drinks in the hotel or for dinner in one or other of the many beautiful houses in the town. The invitations came from various sources: hotel guests from all over the world, scientists, linguists and Tibetologists. I was particularly pleased to receive a visit from Prince Peter of Greece and Denmark. He had rented the former house of George Sheriff, who was an enthusiastic botanist and had turned the garden of the British Mission in Lhasa into an absolute jewel. The garden in Kalimpong, to which I was invited by the Prince, had been laid out just as beautifully. I learned that the Prince and his wife were planning an anthropological expedition for the museum in Copenhagen and were waiting in Kalimpong for their permits to enter Tibet to materialise. They never did. It seemed as if China's grip on Tibet was tightening.

The Princess was of Russian extraction and had strikingly red hair. I had never even seen caviar before, let alone eaten it, but she asked me so many questions about the fabled sorceresses of Tibet that I hardly had time to swallow. "I am writing a book about witches", she said, which explained her thirst for knowledge.

I related the story of Kyirong and the skis I had carved from birch wood. Before Aufschnaiter and I had even had the chance to use them, I was summoned by the Dzongpon. "Please do not ride on the wooden planks on the snow," he implored us, "There have already been complaints from the farmers. They are saying that the Tumo, the witches, will destroy the harvest if you do, since flying is the sole privilege of the Tumo." We had plenty of interesting things to chat about that evening and resolved to meet again soon. As things turned out, our next meeting was a year later in Denmark.

The influential Rani Dorje invited me to a gala evening held at Bhutan House. I had met her before in Lhasa. It was common knowledge that the King of Bhutan was going to marry her daughter Kesang. It was the first time that I had seen the colourful fabrics, wood carvings and cultural artefacts of Bhutan.

I kept in touch with Jim Burke. He telephoned me one day to tell me he had landed a big "assignment" as he called it. *Life* wanted to do a special issue on the monsoon and Burke wondered if I might like to take it on. I had to travel to Cherrapunji, the wettest place in the world. Cherrapunji once recorded a total yearly rainfall of 26,461 mm – a world record, and an incredible figure when one compares it to European statistics. At the beginning of July Cherrapunji usually has around 400 mm of rainfall within a very short space of time. By comparison, the Salzburg region in Austria receives an annual average rainfall of about 1,000 mm.

The assignment for *Life* was a welcome opportunity, since I had wanted to take a trip to Shillong, the famous hill town and capital of the province of Meghalaya. From here, Cherrapunji is only about forty kilometres away to the south. I took the bus from Kalimpong to Siliguri, where I boarded a train on the narrow gauge railway that runs for a thousand kilometres to the east through the famous tea plantations of Assam. There was no hotel at my final destination, but I had reserved a room at the "Post Bungalow". In India, you always take your bedding with you – mattress, sheet and blanket – and all of the guest bungalows have staff on hand to cook and look after you. The straw roof, a common feature of buildings in these parts, had recently been replaced with rainproof corrugated iron sheets and during my first night there it rained so hard I thought the roof was going to collapse. In the first light of dawn, when there was just enough light to take photographs, it unfortunately stopped raining and I could only get shots of the swollen streams rushing down the hillsides and the landslides the rain had caused. Fortunately I had brought my tennis racket with me and the concrete tennis court dried quickly, so I managed to play a few sets in the sun with the owner of the tea plantation to while away the time. Eight days passed, during which the predicted rainfall did indeed arrive, but it was only later, in Calcutta, when 600 mm of rain fell within a single hour, that I was able to get some really good photographs of the monsoonal downpour.

Meanwhile, in Chumbi, a decision had been made. The Regent Tadrag Rinpoche had arrived from Lhasa and sided with the Dalai Lama's two tutors and the old monks in pleading the case for his return. They largely ignored the efforts of the other advisors, and the promises made by the USA, for although they were masters at applying their own Buddhist beliefs to the situation, they had a rather narrow view of world events and little understanding of Western ideals. They seemed to have forgotten the fact that the thirteenth Dalai Lama had for years enjoyed the hospitality extended to him by their southern neighbour India during his exile and had thereafter returned to rule Tibet in a time of great prosperity and freedom. The naïve political wrangling was eventually concluded and on 16th July 1951, General Zhang Jingwu arrived in Chumbi to find that all the remaining members of the Dalai

Lama's entourage, with the exception of his closest confidante Lobsang Samten, had already left Tibet.

I continued to use my room in the Himalaya Hotel as a base; it even became a home of sorts. The guests were a colourful mixture of international travellers. An author would have found ample material here for a novel, with exotic princesses, secret agents, globetrotting scientists and academics and much talk of the yeti, the oracle and yogi mystics. Fine examples of Tibetan *thangkas* adorned the walls of the dimly lit dining room of the hotel, but I noticed that there always seemed to be one missing. David MacDonald, the former British Trade Agent to Tibet, confessed to me that he had acquired a number of *thangkas* when serving as an officer during the British invasion of Tibet in 1904 and had sold several of the paintings. He was not the only one to profit from the sale of Tibetan works of art.

Through Burke I got to know Jim Lassiter, a pilot who had been decorated many times for the courageous missions he had flown during the Korean War. He was now employed by the wealthy Maharaja of Darbhanga. In 1947, India was granted independence and the Maharaja lost his absolute power, but he could still afford the luxury of purchasing a DC3 aeroplane and having it equipped with a drawing room and bedroom. Lassiter was a daredevil pilot, but he had one very sound piece of advice about flying. "Never board an aircraft in bad weather," he said, "the pilot has no control when it is foggy." Jim Lassiter said that he would remain on permanent standby to fly the Dalai Lama to freedom anywhere he wished and would even fly him out of Tibet if necessary. Meeting Lassiter was an experience, and an adventurous one at that. The flights we made along the southern side of the huge Himalayan Mountains were breathtaking. I had never flown before and now I found myself occupying the co-pilots seat next to Jim. We did not have supplementary oxygen on board and Jim would only drop below six thousand metres when he noticed my face turning blue!

Darbhanga was not far west of Kalimpong on the Ganges plain to the south of the border with Nepal. One day Jim sent me a message asking me if I would like to fly to Kathmandu. The Maharaja had been invited there by the King of Nepal. When I boarded the plane, he was sitting in the salon sipping tea with his family, so Jim put me in the radio operator's seat. Thus it was that I managed to visit Nepal in 1951, long before the country started issuing tourist visas.

Kalimpong lay at an altitude of 1,400 metres, which made the climate there very pleasant. Darjeeling was better known, however. Situated at 2,000 metres above sea level, the town served as a summer retreat for British dignitaries and boasted several good hotels. The social hub of the town was the Planters Club, where the owners of the world famous Darjeeling tea plantations met. The journey from Kalimpong to Darjeeling was made in one of the numerous original Jeeps left by the Americans at the end of the war. As many as ten passengers would grab tight hold of the framework of the vehicle as it negotiated the tortuous bends, and one generally arrived totally exhausted by the experience. There was precious little opportunity to admire the teak and tea plantations, but mercifully the trip usually included a long break at the Tista River crossing, where exhaustive checks were made on passports and travel documents. On subsequent trips, I learned that the waiting time could be significantly shortened by the payment of baksheesh.

My first duty call in Darjeeling was to the wife of Gyalo Thondub, Lobsang's elder brother, who was now in Hong Kong on a diplomatic mission on behalf of the Dalai Lama. Mrs. Gyalo Thondub had founded the Tibetan Refugee Handicraft Centre in Darjeeling, which employed craftsmen like carpenters, painters and tailors, and sold their products with great success to the many tourists.

I now had more time to pursue my personal interests and one of the most important jobs on my list was a visit to Sherpa Tenzing Norgay. As I mounted the steep stone steps to his house I was mobbed by a pack of barking dogs. These white Lhasa Apsos were a popular Tibetan breed and Tenzing made a little extra money from breeding them, which was useful as living in Darjeeling was very much more expensive than in his home at the foot of Mount Everest. Tenzing also had a store of second hand, high quality mountaineering equipment. I acquired a few items, including a down sleeping bag that had once belonged to the Canadian climber Earl Denman, with whom Tenzing had made a secret attempt to climb Mount Everest from the Tibetan side in 1947. Denman was a tall man and his sleeping bag and down jacket were correspondingly large. I envisaged myself going on an expedition with Tenzing, with all this luxury kit.

Since we were still planning to attempt Kangchenjunga, my next visit was to the Royal Family in Sikkim, whom I had already met through Princess Coocoola. During a meal at the modest palace in Gangtok, I broached the subject of Kanch. At first there was no reaction, just an embarrassed silence, before I was reprimanded by the young King. "You, of all people, ought to understand, after so many years living with us, that the idea of climbing our most sacred mountain is completely out of the question," he said, and added that the peak stood on the border with Nepal and that both governments had agreed to refuse all such requests. I excused myself and asked them to reconsider my request and grant me first option on the peak, in the event that permission to climb it was ever granted.

The name "Kangchenjunga" is often translated as "The Five Treasures of the Great Snow" and to the people of Sikkim and Nepal, who live in its shadow, the mountain is revered as the symbolic throne of their god and protector, whose death mask is said to be kept under lock and key in the "Chamber of Ghosts" of the Bon Monastery at Puntsoling, west of Gangtok. If you stay the night in Puntsoling, you literally share a room with a view of Kangchenjunga. At the time of my visit in 1951, Kanch was thought to be the second highest mountain in the world at 8,586 metres, but in 1987 more exact measurements concluded that K2, or Mount Godwin Austen, in the Karakorum, was actually 24 metres higher. Early in 1950 the newspapers ran the sensational story of the first ascent of the 8,091 metre peak of Annapurna in Nepal, the first 'eight-thousander' to be climbed. The expedition leader and summiteer Maurice Herzog later told me that he had read an article in the *Himalayan Journal* by Peter Aufschnaiter illustrated with panoramic sketches that I had made in Tradun. At that time, none of the eight-thousanders had ever been climbed. Our description of the mountain had induced Maurice Herzog to opt for Annapurna and, on June 3rd 1950 he and his partner, Louis Lachenal, summitted the peak. During their epic climb Herzog was severely frostbitten and ended up losing all his fingers and toes.

In the summer of 1955, Kangchenjunga also received its first ascent. I was bitterly disappointed on hearing the news and was quite open about my feelings on a later visit to the Royal Family in Gangtok. What had happened? I was informed that an English expedition had been granted permission for Kanch after their leader George Band had promised the Nepalese Government that none of the climbers would set foot on the actual summit, the throne of the God of Kanch, out of respect for the local religion. Nepal had not informed the Sikkim authorities of this agreement and they were naturally surprised. Needless to say, Tenzing and I would have been happy to have made a similar promise. George Band had stopped short of the summit, stuck an ice axe in the snow, attached the British and Nepali flags to it and photographed it.

During one of my later expeditions I had the opportunity to meet the key holder of Puntsoling Monastery. At my request, he fetched the precious death mask from the Chamber and I photographed the God with his "throne" in the background. I sent George Band a copy of the photograph.

Tenzing was just as disappointed as I to be refused a permit to climb Kangchenjunga in 1951, but his fame as a high altitude Sherpa and his ability as a climber meant that he had little difficulty in securing a place on another expedition. I, too, was keen for a chance to use the top quality climbing equipment I had received from Tenzing. When Jim Lassiter flew me to the source of the Ganges for an aerial view of my escape route and we passed a range of peaks in the Garhwal Himalaya that bordered Tibet to the north and Nepal to the west, an idea began to take shape. I had already found some information about the remote peaks of the Garhwal at the Himalaya Club, of which I was a member. There were five prominent peaks in the massif of Panch Chuli. In the local dialect, the name literally means "Five Chimneys" or "Five Hearths" and it was the highest of these, the 6,904 metre Panch Chuli II, that I wanted to climb. (*translator's note: according to Hindu legend, these were the five hearths on which the Pandavas cooked their last meal before ascending to heaven.*) The eastern approach had already been explored by the British climber Hugh Ruttledge and friends in 1927. It was my intention to reconnoitre the glaciers on the western side and to attempt the summit via the West Ridge. As luck would have it, a chance meeting in a New Delhi hotel with the Australian climber Frank Thomas provided me with a partner for the venture.

Finding a route through the crevasses and séracs that guarded the western side was laborious work. We bivouacked at a little over six thousand metres on a small flat area that later became known as the Balati Plateau. From there, the line took an ice field that was about the same angle as those on the Eiger, but twice as high. It seemed the ideal type of terrain for my twelve-point crampons. In the morning I soon found myself three pitches, or about a hundred metres, up the ice field. I belayed to pegs and an axe and started to bring Frank up. As things got a little steeper, Frank elected to move off the direct line and traverse right to an outcrop of rock, which he thought looked easier. He was about twenty metres from my stance when he lost his footing and fell, swinging helplessly like a pendulum with his back to the ice slope. He had been having trouble with the climb anyway, but it now became clear that we should abandon our attempt. In the heat of midday, as we were descending through the labyrinth of the glacier, I was caught by an avalanche. The feeling of dizziness and disorientation when everything around me started moving reminded me of my experience in the Hohe Tauern and this time, too, I managed to keep myself on the surface. With the benefit of hindsight, I realise that the attempt on Panch Chuli ran contrary to my usual attitude towards climbing, and in particular Himalayan expeditions. Twelve years after the Eigerwand and Nanga Parbat, I still had the desire, the hidden urge, to explore new territory, but I had lost touch with climbing during those happy days in Lhasa and was now having to re-learn the process, at a cost.

Panch Chuli had been a far too ambitious an objective. This was later confirmed by the Indo-British Panch Chuli Expedition in 1992, which included some of Britain's best climbers, amongst them Chris Bonington and Stephen Venables. The team followed my route to the Balati Plateau, from where four of the members made the first ascent of Panch Chuli V. During the descent, Venables' abseil anchor pulled out of the ice and he was lucky to escape with just two broken legs.

He survived the tortuous descent, fighting unconsciousness and pain, because of his will to live and because his partners were all competent climbers and close friends.

In March 1951 I had been issued with a six month residence permit for India. This had been extended in the summer by a further six months, and the due date was fast approaching. The Austrian Ambassador in New Delhi managed to get me an appointment at the Ministry of Home Affairs, where I was received by an extremely friendly young civil servant, a Sikh by the name of Harmanda Singh, who had once worked in Gangtok for the Minister responsible for Sikkim, Tibet and Bhutan. On the table between us lay a pile of files held together by a jute string. Harmanda Singh opened the files to reveal various hand-written reports with additional comments attached with paper clips. "All of these documents relate to you, Mr. Harrer," he said. The files started in 1939 and contained reports about the Nanga Parbat expedition, my various escape attempts and my stay in Tibet. Even my activities during recent months, and my attempts to help the Tibetans, had not escaped the attention of the Ministry. In view of this, Mr. Singh thought that it would be difficult to grant another extension to my residence permit. He advised me to leave India before the end of the year; that way, he said, when I applied for permission for future visits and was asked if I had ever been refused a visa, I could truthfully answer no. The advice was well meant. I decided to take it.

During my final two months in India, Jim Burke came up with another interesting assignment for me. Jawaharlal "Pandit" Nehru was due to give a speech in Madras before an audience that was expected to number an incredible one million people and *Time* magazine wanted photographs. My knowledge of Hindi was sufficient to get me past the secret police and onto the podium and during the lengthy speech I climbed onto the scaffolding behind Nehru, a precarious balancing act, to get my shots. Unfortunately, a little imagination was required to sense the one million spectators as the photo only captured the front section of the half lit stage, but *Time* ran a close up anyway and noted in the accompanying text that Nehru had begun his address in Hindi, before changing abruptly to English, with the remark that he had received his political education in London and could better express his emotions in that language.

In Delhi I booked a cabin on an Italian ship scheduled to leave Bombay for Europe in mid December. I spent my last few days doing a little sightseeing. I went down to Agra to see the Taj Mahal, one of the Seven Wonders of the World, and travelled on to Allahabad, at the confluence of the Jumna and the Ganges, where I had the great good fortune to witness the Kumbha Mela, a religious gathering that attracted over a million Hindu pilgrims, who came to bathe in the sacred river in order to cleanse body and soul. The festival also included a huge fair where animals were traded, yogis meditated for alms and itinerant fakirs displayed their skills.

I got my best photographs down on the banks of the river as the pilgrims emerged from the water, many of them wearing the Brahma pendant that identified them as members of the highest caste. The Rajastani women were particularly photogenic as they climbed out onto the river bank, their red and yellow saris soaking wet and accentuating their beautiful figures.

Presently, two policemen wielding batons approached me. "Come with us!" they ordered, and led me away. The officer in the police tent spoke good English. "You have been taking photographs of naked women!" he accused me. After I had hurriedly explained that they had all been fully clothed, we drank tea and he then placed a uniformed constable at my disposal for the rest of the day. The big Indian newspaper *Illustrated Weekly* had also published my *Time Life* pictures, which meant that help and privileged treatment was more readily available, it seemed.

In the meantime, Chinese troops had now been stationed in Tibet. This meant that there was also a Chinese military presence on the border with Ladakh, which was part of the disputed province of Kashmir. The Indian Government was concerned. There were daily news reports from Tibet and I recall the Indian Defence Minister's furious remarks to the United Nations to the effect that the whole world was focussed on Tibet while everyone seemed to have forgotten that, after the Partition, India had accepted ten million refugees. In the north of Nepal, in the kingdom of Mustang on the Tibetan frontier, courageous

Tibetan freedom fighters had mounted several well-organised strikes against the forces that were occupying their homeland.

I could well understand the reluctance of the Indian authorities to extend my residence permit, since both the Defence Ministry and the Foreign Ministry had a say in the matter. I boarded the luxury liner in Bombay with my entire luggage from Lhasa plus a heavy box of old books that I had found in the "Oxford Library" bookshop in Darjeeling, bound for Europe. What awaited me there was anyone's guess.

RETURN TO EUROPE

As the liner docked at the port of Trieste, I saw my twelve-year-old son Peter for the first time, standing on the pier with his grandmother Else Wegener. I managed to bypass the first awkward moments by asking her if I could show Peter the big ship. From Trieste we took the train to Brenner, where the Austrian border officials were expecting me. I asked them if they would keep my arrival a secret for a little while, since I wished to spend a quiet week skiing with my son. In Innsbruck we kitted ourselves out with the latest and best skiing equipment available and headed for Kitzbühel, where I used to compete in the annual University Skiing Championships as a student. Peter had been given an extra week's holiday by his school. We skied every day and I learned much about his life with the Wegener family. He had grown up in an all-female household and I realised now that it might have been a mistake not to have asked my parents to look after him. In Kitzbühel I made the acquaintance of an officer of the French Army, and learned that after the war, the four Allied powers in Austria had split the country into four occupation zones.

Peter had to return to his boarding school, so I went to Graz to visit my parents. They had received no news from me for three years until I was able to make contact with them through the Red Cross and knew only that I had escaped from the POW camp. My father, a postman, had been transferred during the war to the old bishopric of Marburg an der Drau. At the end of the war he had to leave there in a hurry when Marburg changed its name to Maribor and became part of Slovenia. My sister Lydia was away on a business trip, Pepperl was studying in Graz, and Ruth had emigrated to Canada to work as a nurse.

While I was in Graz, newspaper interviews and reunions with old school friends and sporting acquaintances soon brought me to the attention of the local police and I was asked to report to the main police station at the Paulustor. I explained what I had been doing since leaving Graz in 1938 while the interviewing officer took notes. It was all very friendly and matter-of-fact – part of the process of 'denazification'. Everything was carefully minuted and placed in a file that contained newspaper clippings and our wedding photograph. My visit to the British authorities at the Palais Meran followed a similar format. This time, the officer who interviewed me was very much better informed than the Graz police had been. With a wry smile, he told me about the newspaper reports that had portrayed me as the Commander-in-chief of the Tibetan troops in Lhasa in the fight against the People's Liberation Army. Subsequent to my interviews, I received nothing in writing from the either the Austrian or the British authorities, but my denazification was thus complete.

I also paid a courtesy call to the Jäckel family to thank Professor Jäckel, a lecturer in architecture and the Principal of the Technical College in Graz, for the plans he had sent me, which I had used when I was building a house for Minister Kabcho and for my bungalow in Lhasa. I had often taken his daughter Hilde to local dances and in 1959 she married my brother. Their son, Florentin Harrer, now has a son and a daughter of his own.

I used some of the money I had earned from the *Time* and *Life* assignments to purchase a piece of land for my parents. They no longer had an allotment and now that my father was a pensioner they were missing the exercise and the fresh produce that my mother liked so much. There is a part of Graz called the "Kingdom of Heaven" – a lovely name, I always thought – and whilst out walking there one day I saw a sign on the side of the road that said "For Sale – Reasonable Price". The following day I acquired the plot of land for just 17,000 shillings, which really was good value. When I visited Graz again that autumn the once overgrown plot had been completely transformed and my parents were harvesting damsons, raspberries, pears and all kinds of vegetables. My father had also built a shed, where he kept the garden tools and could take shelter from the rain.

During the Ski World Championships in Bad Gastein in February 1952, I was approached by a representative of the publishing company Ullstein Verlag, who wished to acquire the rights to the book I was writing about my time in Tibet. He also told me that several magazines had shown an interest in a pre-print. I informed Ullstein that I was happy to agree to a deal and decided to move to Kitzbühel to get on with the book. It was the perfect place to write, as I could spend my free time skiing to my heart's content. I rented a room from some friends and looked forward to a pleasant combination of mental and physical activity.

It was the high season in Kitzbühel and I was constantly approached by people wanting to know all about my Tibet story, so I took the advice of a friendly hotelier and booked his dancehall for a lecture. So many people turned up that many of them had to sit on the window ledges or stand. With some difficulty, friends of mine had managed to track down a projector and a tiny screen. The poor hotel keeper did not cover his costs, however, since the crowd was so large that serving drinks was out of the question.

That same evening, Count Arthur Strachwitz, the publisher and owner of Liechtenstein Verlag, approached me about the rights to my Tibet photographs. Count Strachwitz lived in Vaduz and was married to the elder sister of the reigning Prince of Liechtenstein, Franz Josef II. We arranged to meet in Vaduz and discuss matters there. It was the start of a very successful relationship, one that was to last for half a century. We signed a contract for the worldwide rights to my book and photographs that excluded the rights for the German edition, since these had already been contracted to Ullstein Verlag. In the autumn of 1952 I moved to Liechtenstein, after first approaching the Aliens Police Department in Bern, which was a legal requirement at that time. A few months later I received my residence permit, and an additional ID card from the authorities in Liechtenstein with a stamp that confirmed my "right of abode" and granted me all the rights of citizenship apart from the right to vote. Liechtenstein Verlag obtained a plot of land for me, on which I later built a house, and the car I had bought for my lecture tours, a Mercedes 170 Diesel Roadster, was re-registered and acquired a new licence plate, FL 2710. I still have this registration number today.

While the arrangements were being made for my move, I was still living in my little room in Kitzbühel and enjoying the hustle and bustle of the place. There was so much happening that it was hard to establish a regular work routine. I went ski touring with Willy Bogner senior, whom I knew from my competition days, and his two sons. Bogner senior told me all about his successful venture into the sports clothing business, which "Junior" was later to develop into a leading worldwide brand. With my new ski equipment and the greatly improved piste preparation, I was able to ski the "Streif", the most famous downhill run of them all, faster than I had during the 1935 competition, when I had placed fifth with a time of five minutes dead.

There was a lively social scene in Kitzbühel, and the resort's many guests came from far and wide. There were emigrant Austrians who had returned to their country and many French skiers, as the Tyrol was part of the French occupation zone. Almost all of them were staying at the Grand Hotel, then the only decent hotel in town. One evening the owner of the hotel, Herr Kofler, telephoned me with an invitation to dinner. He said that one of his guests, the writer Jean Cocteau, wished to meet me and told me to be there at eight. I was to go straight through to the salon, which was where Keller kept his precious collection of Baroque Madonnas. I turned up at the appointed hour, full of anticipation and eager to meet the renowned French author.

After greeting me with a flamboyant embrace, Cocteau tuned to his young friend Jean Marais – himself a famous actor, although at the time I had never heard of him – and said "Jean, this is the man you have to meet!" This was a completely new world for me and I listened in fascination, as Cocteau spoke about making his film about Henri de Toulouse-Lautrec. The title song had become a hit and had brought fame and fortune to the composer, a hitherto unknown friend of Cocteau's. Marais was quite obviously bored by Cocteau's stories, which he had doubtless heard many times before. "Fetch me my new book from my room, then you can go," Cocteau said as he dismissed him.

Before I left, Cocteau made a sketch on the blank fly leaf of his book and added a friendly personal dedication. He enquired whether I had found a French publisher for my Tibet book and said that he would be happy to arrange this for me. I told him that B. Arthaud had already acquired the French rights and Cocteau said they were very good. As I was leaving, he added that he would be delighted to have me as his guest at the Académie Française if I was ever in Paris.

Kitzbühel was a place for serious sports, but after the long war years, it was also a place for having fun. There was always a big crowd in the hotel bar for 'afternoon tea'. From time to time, the local dentist used to invite people over to his house on the "sunny side". He had a lot of trouble repairing my teeth, as I had not seen a dentist for fourteen years. I still have vivid memories of the foot-operated drill he used. On one of these evenings I met the Austrian physicist Hans Thirring and his wife. Thirring was conducting research into nuclear power and was particularly interested in its peaceful application. During the Nazi era he had been prohibited from teaching, a burden he had borne with typically stoical good humour. After the war, many of the banned professors were reinstated and Thirring was now the Dean of Vienna University. He was a kind and considerate man and always happy to be of help. He advised me to teach Geography again on the grounds that it would provide me with some financial security and added that I would only have to give five lectures per term.

Thus it was that I found myself at the Geographical Institute of the University of Vienna, lecturing to an overcrowded auditorium on my years in Tibet. I ended the lecture with a piece of advice to the students – to study Natural Sciences, in particular Geography, in combination with Physical Education, since a fit scientist is better able to conduct the fieldwork required to observe and describe the natural world in any great depth and research trips can lead to all kinds of interesting adventures. It was the only lecture I ever gave there, however, since I wanted to be free of regular work commitments.

At the home of Harry and Pamela Rüttimann, it was always open house for anyone interested in mountaineering. One of their regular guests was Hias Rebitsch, who had studied Biology but had put aside his subject to pursue his passion for expeditions to the world's highest mountains. In 1937, Hias Rebitsch and Wiggerl Vörg were the first team to make a successful retreat from the Eigerwand during bad weather. Rebitsch had also been on Nanga Parbat and had taken part in the 1938 expedition that had attempted to airlift supplies to the high camps using a Junkers Ju 52.

Hias used to challenge every climber he met to pull-ups competitions on door lintels and cupboard frames. If there was ever a piece of door frame missing it was a safe bet that Hias was to blame. He told me about his most recent expedition to the Andes. His partner had not been equal to the task and they had had to turn back. He advised me to try the 6,384 metre peak Ausangate, since the difficulties were well within the capabilities of a fit and experienced mountaineer.

One of the genuine native Tyrolers in town was the painter Alfons Walde, who had a studio right next to the church. I used to visit him regularly. The Tyrol dialect he spoke was as thick as the signatures on his paintings and the lines on his posters. Even now, several decades after his death, his heavily stylised work is seen as symbolic of the town of his birth. He would tell stories as he applied one splash of colour after another and when the packet of cigarettes and the two litre bottle of red wine were empty, he would set the picture to one side and sleep for a few hours. Walde made multiple copies of his paintings, which did not prove popular with the art critics. Since he never had any money, he would occasionally pay the grocer and picture framer in kind. Alfons Walde shared his unfettered artist's life with the architect Clemens Holzmeister and the deaf sculptor Gustinus Ambrosi in their little log cabin on the Hahnenkamm.

Walde had studied architecture at the Technical College in Vienna and used to build houses and hotels in the traditional Tyrolean style. He had also renovated the run-down Schloss Mittersill and turned it into a posh hotel. Walde's client was Baron Hubert Von Pantz, whose American wife, the owner of the Avon cosmetics company, had acquired the dilapidated old castle. Schloss Mittersill was only twenty-five kilometres from Kitzbühel, in the American occupation zone. I received an invitation to the grand opening of the new hotel. A drawbridge led to the main building and above the ancient gate I discovered a set of large and powerful horns that had once belonged to a Tibetan wild sheep, or argali. I asked Hubert Pantz where he had come by this splendid trophy and learned that during the war, Schloss Mittersill had been the study centre for zoologist Ernst Schäfer's Nazi-sponsored 1938/9 expedition to Tibet. I knew nothing of this, even though I had been to Munich to visit one of the senior members of the Schäfer Expedition, Ernst Krause. Krause had been the expedition photographer and had promised me copies of some of his pictures. We leafed through the thick photo albums of carefully mounted images.

The forty thousand negatives had unfortunately disappeared, Krause said, and without further ado he made me copies of the photographs I wanted. It is worth mentioning that, although the members of the expedition had been obliged to sign an agreement – similar to the one used by the German Himalaya Foundation – to the effect that any publication of the expedition's reports or photographs was to be handled by the expedition leader, Ernst Schäfer, Krause did not feel obliged to seek Schäfer's permission.

Apart from the Tibetan sheep's head, there were no other traces of the Schäfer Expedition at the Hotel Schloss Mittersill. It was hoped that the Americans might have removed all the documents, including the missing negatives, in order to save them and in 2001 I learned that they had been found in Washington and were due to be returned to the Museum of Ethnology in Munich. I never met Ernst Schäfer in person, but in Lhasa I had often heard the names of the five expedition members mentioned. They had made themselves very popular with the Tibetans by giving generous gifts and leaving a large quantity of medicines from the expedition pharmacy.

Many filmmakers also converged on Kitzbühel, particularly during the winter season when the ski races took place and there was a good chance of seeing records being broken. The use of modern materials made the new skis even faster and now even moderately talented skiers were racing down the slopes. Amongst the film people, I ran into an old acquaintance from my student days in Graz, Etta Truxa, who had since married a German director. Etta was just as pretty and desirable as I remembered her and now, in Kitzbühel, she began to take an interest in me, too. We quickly became more than just friends. Etta soon filed for divorce and in the autumn of 1952, just a few months after we had met, we were married. Yet once again I had that nagging feeling that I had somehow been rushed into marriage. It lasted only a short while and just a year later, after my first big expedition, we were divorced.

When the snow melted in Kitzbühel, all the hustle and bustle died down. The cows wandered through the middle of the empty town to their summer pastures, and I finally found the peace and quiet I needed to work on my book. I had kept a regular diary, so I had plenty of material to draw upon; the only difficulty was in deciphering my notes. In Tibet, and particularly during our escape, writing paper had been hard to come by, and the school exercise books and scraps of paper containing my notes were a dense jumble of shorthand, Tibetan place names and sketches.

By the end of June, all that was missing was the conclusion. I wanted to express my thoughts about the time I had spent with my Tibetan friends, and in particular the Dalai Lama, and my hope that things would turn out well for them. My thoughts were interrupted by the arrival of a long telegram from the German magazine *Stern*, in which a Mr. Beckmann asked if he might pay me a visit. I was more than a little surprised at this request, since *Stern's* Editor in Chief, Henri Nannen, had previously rejected the idea of a pre-publication extract, on the grounds that the fee I had requested was too high. Herr Beckmann came down from Hamburg and during our first conversation he intimated to me why it was that *Stern* had had this sudden change of heart. "Nannen is on holiday," he explained, "so I am currently the Editor in Chief." Beckmann had read my manuscript overnight and he now offered me a considerably higher sum that the one that Nannen had rejected. He said that they planned to publish at least six instalments; in the end, it turned out to be twice as many.

I spent several relaxed and happy weeks in Hamburg. We worked long and hard until each issue was ready, then drove up the autobahn to the Baltic Coast, or visited my friend from the POW camp, Heins von Have, who had a house on the Outer Alster. I also found the time to go to Berlin and work on the book with the Ullstein brothers. The collaboration with these two gentlemen publishers could not have been better, but I found Berlin itself deeply distressing. In Hamburg I had seen entire districts destroyed by the bombing but most of the ruined buildings had been cleared away. In Berlin, however, the clearance work was still in progress, with usable building materials still being salvaged from the rubble. The city had been split into four Allied sectors, with a white painted line marking the boundary between them.

After reading the first excerpt in *Stern*, Sven Hedin dropped me a line to say how much he had enjoyed it and that he was eagerly awaiting the next instalment. I was a keen athlete and intended to travel to Helsinki in July to watch the Summer Olympics, so I asked Hedin if I might visit him in Stockholm on the way. He replied by return of post and invited me to his younger brother's birthday celebrations. The whole family would be there, he said, together with his assistant Gösta Mantell, who had accompanied him on several of his Asian trips.

After a long train journey, I arrived in Stockholm and went straight to the address I had been given – Mälarstrand 5, on the corner of Ehrenvärdsgatan. In the doorway to the apartment block was a sign with the inscription "Floor IV – HEDIN". Sven Hedin's sister Alma greeted me and introduced me to the people there. Seated around a large table were the five brothers and sisters, all of them advanced in years, and in the middle of the table stood a birthday cake. Sitting next to my great role model, I was tongue tied. I wanted to tell him how Aufschnaiter and I had crossed the route of his Trans Himalaya expedition several times and how helpful his scientific observations had been to us, but I was so excited that I was unable to utter a word.

The awkward silence was broken by the arrival of three young women, admirers of Hedin. What I witnessed next was to stay with me for the rest of my life as an example of how to treat people. Hedin signed each book slowly and meaningfully, looking each of the girls in the eye as he did so. There was no room for them to sit down but each of the girls was offered a piece of cake and a cup of tea. This was hardly the time for serious discussion, so after dinner we arranged to meet the following day.

Fifty years on, I still have vivid memories of my meeting with Sven Hedin, together with the photographs I took with the self-timer that captured this unforgettable event. Hedin took me out onto the balcony and showed me Lake Mälar, just as a flock of birds landed on the water. He said that now, in his old age, his greatest pleasure in life was to sit and gaze at the blue lake. Three years previously, he had had to undergo a difficult eye operation to restore his sight. Now he could watch the birds again. Hedin was eighty-seven years old, but his grip was firm as he held my hand. I was only forty and could easily have been his grandson. When I told him that many of his letters had been damaged during the crossing of the Tsangpo, he went to a huge filing cabinet, pulled out the draw marked H and showed me that he had kept my letters, too. On his desk lay several copies of *Stern* with the excerpts from my Tibet story.

In the afternoon, his sister Alma showed me some of the medals and awards that Hedin had been given, those that he particularly valued. Hedin had received just about every honour and title it is possible to confer. Statesmen and politicians, emperors and kings, academics and artists, and all the world's great universities, had honoured him. His contribution to science and learning will live forever; his immortality symbolised by the rivers and mountains that bear his name.

Later, as he was signing a few copies of his books for me, Sven Hedin told me of his genuine admiration for the German people. When working on a book about Germany, he had been given a lot of support by the German Propaganda Ministry, who had also given him the use of a villa on the Wannsee and granted him permission to visit all of the government facilities that had been such a cause for concern to the foreign powers. While researching his book he had also attended the 1936 Olympic Games in Berlin. According to Hedin, when he presented the finished manuscript to the German publishers in Berlin, they insisted on several significant changes. Hedin had described the leading figures in the Third Reich without glossing over the truth, reporting only what he had seen and heard, and refused to make the changes. The book was finally published uncensored in South America.

Before I left, Sven Hedin gave me his nine-volume work "Southern Tibet", together with some prints of his sketches of yaks and nomads. He told me that he had been quite happy that his camera had broken, as this had given him an excuse to draw.

I took the ferry from Stockholm to Helsinki, where I watched the decathlon and the long distance running events at the Olympic Games. I also met Paavo Nurmi, the Finnish runner who had set twenty-two official world records before being banned for life from international athletics competitions by the International Olympic Committee in 1932 for allegedly contravening the rules on amateur status. Nurmi was still highly regarded in Finland and carried the Olympic flame at the opening ceremony, which took place a few days before I arrived. I visited him later at his shop, a gentlemen's outfitters in Helsinki.

Immediately after my visit to Stockholm, I had sent Sven Hedin a copy of my Tibet manuscript so that he did not have to wait for each instalment to appear in *Stern*. In his letter of reply, he praised my work and told me that he had particularly liked my narrative style. He said he was pleased at the absence of sensationalism or exploitation, and noted the fact that I obviously understood my subject. During my life the book has received many positive reviews, but this one, from my great hero Sven Hedin, will always occupy a special place in my heart.

I returned to Liechtenstein, where I had another Tibet lecture booked for November 26th in the neighbouring town of Feldkirch. That same morning the papers brought the sad news that Sven Hedin had died in Stockholm. That evening, when I entered the crowded lecture hall, there was a letter addressed to me lying on the lectern. Without opening it, I realised straightaway that it was from Sven Hedin. It was the last message I ever received from the great explorer. I sent a telegram expressing my deepest sympathy to his family, to which I received the following reply. I quote it here verbatim, since it describes the final few hours that Hedin spent with his family.

"Stockholm, December 9th, 1952

My dear Mr. Harrer,
You might find it strange that we did not reply sooner to your telegram after the death of Uncle Sven, but I put it to one side with the intention of replying in full once I had finally finished answering the many thousands of telegrams and letters we received.
Uncle Sven used to speak about you often and with such enthusiasm. How strange it was that you received his last letter at the same time as the news of his death. Yes, it all happened very suddenly. On Sunday November 23rd, he worked as usual but he was very tired in the evening and went to bed at 9.30 pm. During

the night he suddenly became very ill and we called the doctor. He told us that Uncle Sven had a severe viral infection, a kind of flu, but thought that a course of vitamin injections and the new wonder drug, Chloromycethin, would soon restore him to health. But he was coughing badly and having great difficulty breathing and I was really frightened waiting for the nurse to come, since during the worst of his coughing fits he could not even sit up in bed without help. Poor Uncle Sven! We felt so helpless sitting with him, unable to do anything for him. By the Tuesday, he was semi-conscious and could not speak but several times he looked at us helplessly and held our hands. That night, a specialist came and said that there was nothing more he could do and that he only had a few more hours to live. When he passed away, half asleep, his four brothers and sisters were all with him. They simply noticed that had stopped breathing.

That same day, many relatives and professors arrived with flowers and there were lots of telegrams. Upstairs, in his bed, Uncle Sven lay quietly, as if asleep, his hands clasped, holding two flowers in the Swedish colours, a yellow rose and a blue iris. Beside his bed, two candles burned in a silver candelabra. They took him away the next morning and I followed him downstairs for the last time. The morning sun was shining on the water and on the snow on the bank of Lake Mälar, a view that Uncle Sven had always loved so much. Very slowly, the black car drove away.

The funeral was very simple and dignified. On Thursday his ashes will be placed into the grave. At the burial of one of his expedition friends, Uncle Sven once said 'His name is engraved upon the history of Asia, an obituary more lasting than one of copper'. The words also hold true for him. We will never forget him.

With best wishes from my mother and Aunt Alma,

Yours sincerely,

Ann Marie Wetterlind"

TO THE SOURCE OF THE AMAZON

In November 1952, my Tibetan memoirs were published in German by Ullstein Verlag in Berlin. It was a privilege to have Ullstein as my publisher and a happy coincidence that in the same year, both the underwater explorer Hans Hass and the ethnologist Thor Heyerdahl had books published by Ullstein. Having "The Three H's" was a useful marketing tool, to be sure, but interest in our books was trumped by the young Françoise Sagan, whose *Bonjour Tristesse* scandalised 1950s society when it was first published because of its portrayal of 'free love'. I spent two days in Berlin attending various press events with Thor Heyerdahl and while I was there I met both Hans Hass and the young Frenchwoman. They were interesting encounters, but what impressed me most was Heyerdahl's *Kon-Tiki* story – a real adventure, but one that was also of scientific interest. Heyerdahl and I got on well from the start and met again on several occasions.

My book sold surprisingly quickly and Liechtenstein Verlag was able to agree to worldwide translation rights at that year's Frankfurt Book Fair. The right to almost all the foreign language editions went to those publishers who had also taken the *Kon-Tiki* title. This was to prove a very interesting time for me, as in the following months and years I visited many of these publishers and went on lecture tours in several different countries to tell my Tibet story.

I remember several of the visits particularly well. In spring 1953 I went to London to see the publisher Rupert Hart-Davis. I eventually found their premises at Soho Square, but it was hard to imagine the inconspicuous little building housing such a famous publishing company. Back then, I knew nothing about the art of British understatement. A steep wooden staircase led up to the rather modest office occupied by the great publisher. Here, Hart-Davis introduced me to a friend of his, a fellow Englishman called Richard Graves. Graves had come to discuss a translation assignment with Hart-Davis and there on the table lay a copy of my manuscript. Graves took the manuscript, said goodbye and left.

Rupert Hart-Davis took me to dinner at Wheeler's, a well-known gourmet restaurant. The restaurant was in a typical old Soho building. On each floor there was room for only two or three tables, all of which appeared to be reserved. My host must have been a good customer, for with none of the customary arrogance on the part of the waiters, we were each served a "very dry sherry". Hart-Davis explained that Richard Graves was the older brother of Robert Graves, a famous author who lived on Majorca. Having Graves handle the translation seemed like a promising arrangement. It meant a lot to me, since I had always had a fondness for all things British. Hart-Davis said he hoped to see me in London again soon, to help with the preparations for the book launch.

In the meantime, I had been busy hatching plans for a big expedition. Unlike Germany and Austria, there were no currency restrictions in Switzerland or Liechtenstein, which made the task of financing the trip much simpler. For a while now, I had been thinking about going to Peru and attempting the first ascent of Ausangate, which Hias Rebitsch had so narrowly missed out on, and now seemed the right time to do it. However, in comparison with previous trips, it was now not just the mountain itself that motivated me, but also the idea of travelling to far-flung places and experiencing foreign life and culture. It was a change in attitude that I attributed to the time I spent in Lhasa. Subconsciously, I still could not cut the ties that bound me to that snowy kingdom; I still yearned for my lost homeland of Tibet. I wanted to visit the ancient Indian tribes of the high Andes and compare their way of life to that of the Tibetans. I had also convinced myself that the similarities and comparisons between nomadic mountain tribes would provide an interesting subject for another piece of writing. I was finally realising my ambition of studying living Geography. I had little idea at the time that this trip was to be the start of a lifetime passion for ethnological expeditions.

Before I set off for South America, however, I first had to go to Vienna, where the Ullstein brothers had another publishing house and wished to negotiate with me about a book of photographs. I began the journey with mixed feelings; with some justification as it turned out. There was a Russian checkpoint at the Enns Bridge, the border between the American and Russian occupation zones. As we approached, two of the border guards exchanged glances and one of them nodded his head to the side to indicate that I should pull over and park. We had no common language and the soldiers had obviously never seen a car with an FL registration plate; nor were they able to decipher my Liechtenstein car documents and the blue driving licence. The officer in charge took over and, after making a telephone call and establishing that I was harmless enough, he allowed me to proceed.

I hardly recognised Vienna. Before the war I had visited the city with a friend. We had cycled the two hundred kilometres from Graz to the Danube island of Lobau, where we camped out, as we did not have the money to pay for accommodation. This time it seemed that everywhere I looked there was building work going on. The war-damaged St Stephen's Cathedral was being carefully repaired and one of the stonemasons shouted a greeting from his lofty perch on the cathedral tower. It turned out that I knew him from climbing. He had obviously found his ideal job.

Business concluded, I finally boarded a turboprop aeroplane and left Europe for South America. There were five intermediate stops before we even got to New York. We had a long wait in Ireland and in the airport shop I noticed that they had an attractive offer for travellers to the US on a gallon of duty free alcohol, which I bought for the expedition "for medicinal purposes". The long flight across the Atlantic to Gander in Newfoundland was interesting and enjoyable. The sea to the south of Greenland was covered in ice floes. The sun was low in the sky and bathed the icebergs in a magnificent light. The aeroplane was practically empty and the pretty stewardesses found time to chat to the few passengers on board.

We landed at New York-Idlewild. My connecting flight to Peru was scheduled to leave the following day. The customs officer wanted me to pay tax on the alcohol and explained that the duty free allowance of one gallon only applied to US citizens. My luggage was locked in a cage and I was sent to the transit lounge, where I had to surrender my Austrian passport and have my fingerprints taken. After several hours, a non-uniformed official arrived and drove me to Manhattan, as there was no hotel for transit passengers at the airport. Impressed by the famous skyline, I asked if the tall building in front of us was the Empire State Building. My Secret Service man remained silent. He maintained the air of secrecy even after checking me into a room on the eightieth floor of a skyscraper hotel. He placed a chair outside the room, locked the door and sat down to wait. The bright lights of the building opposite illuminated my room. The window would not open and through the door leading to my bathroom I could clearly hear someone using my toilet. The waiter brought me a tray of food and explained that in this hotel, two rooms shared the same bathroom, which was why it was cheaper. That night I hardly slept a wink. This was probably due in part to the time difference, but what disturbed me the most were the sirens of the police cars and ambulances that raced through the city all night long.

The next day there was a different, somewhat friendlier, policeman sitting outside my door. He took me back to the airport. The Peru flight was very crowded, everyone spoke Spanish and after four days and various stops I was relieved when we finally landed in Lima. From here, an overcrowded bus took me up the narrow, dusty road into the Andes and the town of Cusco. I knew from my travels in India that paying extra would get me the seat next to driver. I asked him how he could dare to take the narrow, blind bends at top speed. "Today, all the buses are going uphill and you rarely meet a private car coming the other way. Tomorrow it's a one-way road downhill," was the explanation I received.

Cusco lies at 3,380 metres above sea level. I checked into a modest hotel and was immediately served a *cuba libre*, a drink mixed with coca leaves that, in my experience, is the best cure for a headache. Over the years I had adapted well to the high altitudes in Tibet, but I was no longer acclimatised and I really noticed the lack of oxygen. I did not intend to stay long in Cusco and only visited the ruins of the Inca complex of Sacsayhuaman. The walls were built with huge stones and without mortar and their origin remains a mystery to geographers and architects to this day.

Before I set off to visit the Altiplano Indians, I went up to the Hacienda Lauramarca, a remote ranch situated at four thousand metres in the highlands of southern Peru, where I had arranged to meet the Bavarian climbers Fritz März, Heinz Steinmetz and Jürgen Wellenkamp for an attempt on Ausangate in the nearby Cordillera Vilcanota. The peak was visible from as far away as Cusco and when the sun came up over the ridge it was easy to understand how the summit had been revered by the Quechua Indians as the throne of the gods. At Base Camp, we paid off the porters and spent an enjoyable few days acclimatising and reconnoitring the mountain. I found the job of breaking trail, and the climbing itself, easier than in the Alps, as we were only ten degrees south of the Equator and the high sun made the snow softer and the ice more granular in texture. Caution was still required, however, as the climate and terrain in the Cordillera can be treacherous and dangerous, even for experienced alpinists. Apart from a few sections, which we roped up for, the climb gave us few problems, and towards midday we became the first people ever to stand on the summit of Ausangate. On first ascents it is the custom all over the world to place the national flags of all of the participating climbers on the summit of the mountain, with the flag of the country in which the mountain is situated taking pride of place. Since both Peru and Austria have a red and white flag, one pennant was enough for both; we added a German one for good measure. Flags are only ever flown on the summit of a mountain when it is climbed for the first time. It is never done to mark the subsequent ascent of one of the faces, for example, as was the case with our Eiger climb.

There was a nasty surprise waiting for us when we returned to Base Camp. The porters, all of them Indians, had made off with our kit. We had already experienced difficulties with them on the walk in, when they had done their utmost to dissuade us from attempting the climb, warning us that the gods would never allow it and that we would certainly never return alive. They later explained to us why they had taken our things during our absence. They did not see it as theft; they had merely taken our spare food and equipment because they were convinced that we would not return from the mountain.

My Bavarian climbing friends went on to bag several more unclimbed peaks. I was happy with my ascent of Ausangate and my thoughts now turned to my ethnographic objectives. I had always been interested in the idea of exploring the watershed regions of the great rivers of the world. During my escape I had visited the sources of the Indus, the Ganges and the Brahmaputra, and shortly before departing for Peru I had read somewhere that yet another source of the Amazon had been discovered. It is now known that this mighty river actually has its origins in no fewer than seven South American countries, although the challenge still remains for future expeditions to determine which of the tributaries is the furthest from the outlet and which carries the greatest amount of water. At present, the Rio Carhuasanta, which rises in the Peruvian Andes, is widely considered to be the longest feeding source of the Amazon. Born as a small stream high up in the mountains, the Amazon flows six thousand kilometres through tropical rainforests to the Atlantic, a fact that I found fascinating in itself. Since I had no other pressing engagements and could occupy my time as I wished, the next few months took on less of the character of an expedition than of a pleasant journey.

Travelling alone and carrying all my equipment in a single rucksack, meant that it would be easier to get around on my visit to the Altiplano Indians. My plan was to eat with them, sleep at their camps and observe their customs. I hoped I might even find someone with whom I could travel up one of the many tributaries of the Amazon. I began my journey at Lake Titicaca, the highest navigable lake on earth, which lies at an altitude of 3,812 metres. By way of comparison, I thought about Lake Namtso in Tibet. It takes seventeen days to circumnavigate Lake Namtso on foot. Lake Titicaca is four times as large, more than 8,200 square kilometres, but ships, roads and a railway make it easier to explore.

Around two million Aymara Indians lived here. At the northern end of the lake I met some fishermen and asked them which tribe they were from. To my astonishment, they replied that they were not Aymara, but Uru. I learned that the Uru Indians, although commonly grouped with the Aymara, were the aboriginal inhabitants of Lake Titicaca and that was why they held the fishing rights. The cold, clear river that ran into the lake was alive with numerous large lake trout. The Urus had just returned from a successful fishing trip and were in high spirits. They invited me out to their island, where they said a fine meal was waiting for us.

Staying with these hospitable people was the ideal romantic prelude to my trip. It was such a pleasant experience that I could quite happily have stayed for weeks. The Urus told the time by the sun and being so close to the Equator they had little concept of the seasons of the year. The Conquistadors had introduced Christian festivities to the region and these celebrations were a welcome diversion and the perfect excuse to consume large quantities of aguardiente, or sugar cane alcohol. There was a lovely smell around the Uru camp, an indescribably heady mixture of smoke, food and aguardiente, which was accompanied by the sounds of the pigs and hens and the haunting Andean music the Indians played on their reed flutes, or zampoñas, music that managed to sound both cheerful and melancholic at one and the same time.

One of the high points of my stay was the Harvest Festival, which was very different to the church festivals I knew from my home in the Alps. There was an open market, where everything from llamas and horses to fake jewellery and fresh produce was bought and sold. The most popular product, however, was the green coca leaves. The coca plant is widely cultivated in South America. The leaves have been used as a medicine since the time of the Incas but the alkaloids in the leaves are also extracted and used to make cocaine, a dangerous and highly addictive drug. After the market, the crowd moved on to the walled churchyard next to the cemetery to join the many others already gathered there. Several musicians with trumpets joined the zampoñas players, and they all played different melodies in a similar rhythm in a kind of musical competition that was only interrupted when the bottle of aguardiente was circulated. With due respect for local tradition, every time I was offered the bottle, I poured a little drop on the ground before taking a drink. It is said that alcohol was the favourite offering of the Inca gods and even today, bus drivers will stop before every bridge and every pass and pour alcohol onto the ground as a ritual sacrifice. The Tibetans have a similar custom, but there the *chang* is sprayed towards the altar or squirted into the air.

My experiences in Tibet had also taught me that to refuse any offer of food or drink, or to refuse to participate in local rituals, might be viewed as an insult, so I drank the aguardiente, even though the thin, dry air at this altitude meant that I was soon feeling the effects. On my later expeditions, I always tried to adhere to my self-imposed rule of behaving, wherever possible, in the same way as my hosts, the only exception being on a visit I once made to a tribe in the north of Brazil, when I watched with interest as the women chewed cassava roots and spat the resultant paste into a large wooden trough, where it soon began to ferment into alcohol. I was not in the mood to join in the feast that evening and came up with the only excuse I knew would be respected. I told my hosts that, for religious reasons, I was observing a period of abstinence. In fact, there were two reasons why I did not wish to sample the brew: firstly, I was disgusted by the sight of the women chewing and spitting and secondly, I knew that the milky liquid in the cassava root contained poisonous prussic acid.

Years later, I was to pay a return visit to the Altiplano Indians at Lake Titicaca, this time in the company of a cameraman. My research trips had started as one-man expeditions; I travelled alone, with no sponsors and no commitments. I took photographs, made sketches and wrote diaries, which were later published in book form. Then the television companies started showing an interest, but they demanded film material. My equipment got heavier, but I still travelled alone and remained flexible and independent. I managed to do this for many years, and I even financed my 1962 New Guinea Expedition myself. The television company – Hessische Rundfunk, part of the ARD in Germany – bought the material that I brought back with me and produced a series called *Heinrich Harrer Reports*, which over the years was to run to forty broadcasts. I used the fee from each report to finance the next expedition.

At first, black and white images were sufficient for both photographs and films. Then colour arrived. One could not work without an exposure meter and the films required various emulsions: one for snow and ice in the high mountains and another for the damp tropical jungles. It was all becoming too much for me. I wanted to wind up the reports, but the ARD thought otherwise and in order to keep the series running they paid for a cameraman.

When I returned to Lake Titicaca with a professional cameraman,

I made some interesting observations. The idea of drawing comparisons between the Altiplano Indians and the Tibetans proved to be astonishingly productive. However, simple comparisons are often clumsy and I also noted several significant differences. Both the Indians and the Tibetans created monumental edifices. They transported huge stones, weighing many tons, with no knowledge of the wheel. Both made sacrifices to their gods and erected cairns on high mountain passes. I established that similar living conditions gave rise to similar customs and traditions. Both sets of people had an extensive knowledge of the healing powers of certain plants that stretched back thousands of years; both believed in the absolute rule of living god-kings and in both South America and Tibet, the land was the property of the state.

Unlike the Tibetans, the Indians built many thousands of kilometres of roads and because of the heavy rainfall, these were almost always paved with stones. They also mined for gold, which the Tibetans did not do, for fear of upsetting their earth gods. The Maya also had rainmakers, soothsayers and oracles, who influenced the daily lives of the people, and astrologists, who formulated calendars. Even the languages exhibit certain typological similarities. There is still plenty of research to be done. In the spring of 2000, archaeologists unearthed an ancient city in Guatemala that was estimated to be more than a thousand years old and was comparable to the discoveries of the great pre-Columbian Mayan culture. It is known that there are other sites that still await discovery in the areas to which the Indians retreated from the advance of the Conquistadors.

Both of these ancient cultures met with tragic ends, however. The South American Indians were exterminated in the name of Christianity, while the Tibetans were invaded and their culture suppressed by the Chinese. The ancient treasures of Tibet, along with those of the Incas, the Maya and the Aztecs, can now only be viewed and studied as exhibits in a museum. When visiting such exhibitions with the exiled Dalai Lama, I often saw him gazing in astonishment as he saw the precious sculptures and paintings of his people for the first time. Both the Potala Palace and the Inca fortress of Sacsayhuaman in Cusco were included in the UNESCO list of World Heritage Sites. In 2000, representatives from one hundred and forty nations attended the inaugural meeting of UNESCO's World Mountain Forum in Paris. The objective of the Forum was to discuss the draft World Charter of Mountain Populations, a group of people that comprises ten percent of the world's population.

My television broadcast about high Andean culture bore the title *The Sun Gate of Tiahuanaco*. The programme attracted high viewing figures, and this was attributable to the time at which it was aired – 8.15 on a Friday evening. Everyone involved in the production was in the studio and there was an atmosphere of eager anticipation as the programme editor studied the bank of monitors and manipulated the images to create the desired effect. During the commercial break before the programme, the screens showed a close up of Karin Tietze, the attractive blond announcer, as she rehearsed her opening lines. She was struggling with the pronunciation of the word "Tiahuanaco" and getting more and more annoyed with herself, but of course she had no idea that we were all watching her. When we went live, her delivery was word perfect. For the next programme, on the Maya in Mexico, unpronounceable words like Popocatepetl and Iztaccihuatl were deleted from the announcer's script.

After concluding my 1953 expedition I was invited by the La Paz Ski Club to spend a weekend skiing with them. We all crammed into a rather ancient bus and, after several unscheduled stops to fix the carburettor, we finally arrived at the international weather station and observatory, five thousand metres up in the mountains. It is worth describing the lift system the ski club had here, of which they were very proud. A simple hut had been tacked onto the planetarium, which had no exterior wall on the side facing down into the valley. This was the only similarity with lift stations in the Alps. One of the club members went to fetch some fuel while another coaxed the old engine into life. A long drive belt was connected to a wheel rim poached from a large truck and this operated as a cable winch. We had marvellous fun carving turns in the neve of the hundred and fifty metre long run. I tried to ski stylishly, but it was strenuous work in the high, thin air and I was soon out of breath. The "valley station" was a similarly rudimentary construction with another wheel rim cable winch contraption. I was strapped into a harness and instructed to copy what those in front of me did. They grabbed the moving cable and clipped the hook on the harness into the cable. The cable sagged alarmingly under our combined body weight, but you could then be towed uphill without having to hold on. To avoid being dragged through the winch mechanism at the top, you had to pull down on the cable and release the hook on arrival. I was relieved to see that the winch operator kept a close eye on me, ready to stop the engine if I did not disengage in time. The whole thing was a little too adventurous for my taste and after two strenuous runs I decided to take photographs of Illimani instead. This 6,485 metre peak is one of the highest mountains in Bolivia and the most famous landmark of La Paz.

One of the keenest of the skiers was a pilot, whose job it was to fly supplies in to the gold miners in the Tipuani Valley. He offered to fly me round Illimani to get some aerial photographs of the mountain. I jumped at the chance of flying across the main chain of the Andes, as this was the area where the Spanish and Portuguese Conquistador armies had met during their conquest of South America five hundred years ago. Not content with stealing the Incas' priceless gold treasures, the Conquistadors also wanted to find the actual mines, the source of the Inca gold. The Portuguese came up the Amazon, meeting the Spanish, who crossed over the Andes, in the Tipuani Valley. The ensuing battle was won by the Spanish under Francisco Pizarro. This area is now part of Spanish-speaking Bolivia, while Brazil, of course, is the only country in South America where Portuguese is the official language.

It was still dark when we drove up to the airstrip on the high mountain plain. The plane was already fully fuelled and the pilot was busy weighing the freight. Due to the altitude, weight was critical and of the many Índios waiting there, only two were allowed to board the aircraft. The co-pilot helped them buckle their safety belts and indicated that I should take the seat opposite. The metal seats had no padding and were arranged in two rows along the length of the fuselage. In the space between sacks and crates had been lashed to the floor and piled high, so all I could see of the two Índios were their heads and shoulders. As promised, the pilot flew once round Illimani, and we passed so close that I could even make out the crevasses. We had originally agreed that I should move up into the cockpit to take my shots but severe turbulence prevented me doing so. The two Índios started retching, whereupon the co-pilot unbuckled their belts and pointed to the toilet at the end of the cabin, the door of which had already sprung open. I was too late.

As we flew over the huge, dark green swathe of the Amazon rainforest, I was finally able to go up into the cockpit and take the co-pilot's seat. As he brought us in to land in the narrow Tipuani Valley, the pilot explained that he would be unloading and then flying straight back. He handled the landing with the typical skill of the bush pilot. There was no tower to radio instructions here, so he relied entirely on his knowledge of the local conditions. Like bush pilots the world over, he was an adventurous character, who accepted risk as a part of his daily life. I wanted to stay a while in the Tipuani Valley, so I thanked him for the flight and said I would see him again in La Paz.

I bought myself a mosquito net and found lodgings at a restaurant with a tin roof that provided a measure of shelter from the daily downpours of rain. The town stretched along a wide main street lined with shops, bars and restaurants. Buses and trucks honked their horns and jostled for position on the unsurfaced dirt road, spattering the many pedestrians with mud and water, although they seemed not to notice. The townspeople were a mixed bunch of Índios and a few whites who looked like outlaws, fortune hunters and dropouts from the Foreign Legion. I thought it prudent to refrain from asking why they had come to live here. In spite of their differences in background and behaviour, they formed a close-knit community and some professions even had their own workers' cooperatives. Those that did the carpentry work down the mines were particularly highly regarded. They knew exactly what type of wood to use for the pit props and after their work on the shafts was completed they received a sack of sand containing gold as payment. The prospecting methods had changed little over the centuries, the only difference being that motorised pumps were now used to drain the water out of the shafts. There were few permanent buildings in town, mainly banks, and one of them housed the "Officina de Claim", where the prospecting rights were awarded. It was here that I found out about the opening ceremony that was taking place for a new mine.

According to the religion of the mineworkers, the underground world was the realm of spirits and devils, who had to be appeased with sacrificial offerings before digging began. The ceremony of humouring the devils is called the "challa" and the ritual I witnessed was conducted by a shaman, or Jatiri. The shaman slit the chest of a llama open, tore out the still beating heart and hurled it against the wall of rock, beneath which the mine was to be dug, all the while chanting magic spells. Since the devil is always thirsty, aguardiente was then poured over the rocks. The Jatiri then called upon the devil to provide a rich vein of gold for the prospectors. The flesh of the sacrificial animal was eaten by the miners, while the carcass and entrails were later sewn into the llama skin and buried underground.

After this brief journey back in time I wanted to return to La Paz, and to the pure, natural world of the mountains, where my experiences would not be determined by the rogues and opportunists of the Tipuani Valley. I decided not to wait for the aeroplane, but to opt for public transport across the Andes. That evening I went to the control post, where there was a queue of old buses and trucks waiting at the barrier. It was forbidden to drive at night and during the day each and every vehicle was checked and registered, as there were many dangers lurking along the route. For the waiting passengers there were kiosks serving hot tea, steaming potatoes and tortillas. Even here, in the lowlands of the mighty Amazon basin, it was cold and thick swirls of mist wafted through the valley. Instead of riding up front in the driver's cabin, I found a place to sit with the Índios in the back of the truck in the fresh air. Although I had managed to rearrange the sacks to make a hollow to sit in, the journey was pure torture. Try to imagine it: five thousand metres of ascent in a series of hundreds of hairpin bends. Even the truck went on strike. A mechanic made the whole journey perched on the running board of the truck, ready to jump down and fetch buckets of cold water from the mountain streams to pour over the steaming radiator or, in the event of a total breakdown, to open the creaking bonnet and readjust the carburettor as the air grew ever thinner.

Hours later, we reached the tree line at around four thousand metres, where I noticed a proliferation of stone cairns decorated with paper flowers that marked the places where cars and buses full of people had left the road and plummeted down the mountainside. Since leaving the town we had been followed by a pack of emaciated dogs, who had kept pace with the truck by taking short-cuts through the serpentine bends. The passengers threw them some food, the local superstition being that this act would grant them a safe passage during the dangerous journey over the pass. They told me that they believed that all living creatures should be treated with kindness in order to appease the mountain spirits. Llamas grazed peacefully on the slopes of the mountains and I learned that, in former times, those that had unusual markings – pure white coats, for example – were sacrificed in the temples to honour the Sun God. Nowadays they are merely regarded by the Altiplano Indians as an important and useful animal, providing meat and fine, warm wool to make clothing.

At the rest stops one could buy drinks and spicy tortillas and at one of the parking places there was an altar where offerings of alcohol were made to Pachamama the Earth Mother. The higher we went, the more often the truck had to stop, and as if we had not suffered enough already, to cap it all, it now grew bitterly cold and started to snow. As we crested the five thousand metre Cumbro Pass, a savage wind lashed us mercilessly. One could barely make out the many crosses and cairns that had been erected in memory of the travellers who had frozen to death here and I had to abandon the idea of taking the photograph I wanted of Illimani. Instead, I crawled into my sleeping bag and resigned myself to my fate, forgetting my original intention to be ready in an instant to leap out of the truck in the event of an accident. At last we passed the checkpoint and approached the city of La Paz. I was so exhausted that I found it hard to appreciate the fact that this is said to be one of the most beautiful cities in the world. I also had difficulty in deciding which had been the lesser of two evils – flying or travelling by road. I generally have little sympathy with the notion of a "lucky life", but after my experiences over the last few weeks, even I had to admit that I was thankful that I was still alive.

After all the excitement, I was now ready to return home. The friendly pilot had to be at the airport in the morning and he drove me to the border. In addition to the old freight airplane, he also owned a newer

Cessna, which he used to transport government officials, and this work afforded him certain privileges. I was never able to determine whether the life he led was daring and adventurous or simply reckless. I thanked him for his hospitality and returned over the border to Peru without any further problems.

The last leg of my South American journey was accomplished without any mechanical contraptions and this alone was a reason to be cheerful. After climbing Ausangate I had made the acquaintance of some Índios who went on fishing expeditions in the lower reaches of the Amazon basin. When I met them they had a leaky old dugout canoe and I asked them if they would build me a new, larger boat, which I would then buy from them. Now, a month later, the new dugout was moored on the bank of a little river, bobbing happily on the water, the inside still black from the burning and hollowing out process. We soon agreed a price and four of the men offered to accompany me.

During the first three days we encountered numerous rocks and rapids and we spent more time stumbling through the jungle on portages than sitting comfortably in the boat. We then came to a stretch of fast, clear water, where the Índios controlled the dugout with two paddles. There were a few scattered huts on the river bank and I learned from the occupants that the river was called the Rio Inambari. It was never my intention to try to discover a new source of the Amazon, but the fact that I was navigating one of the many thousand tributaries of that great river pleased me greatly and I soon slipped into a timeless state dictated by my Índio companions and the river itself. Fish, freshwater crabs and fruit were plentiful, although bathing demanded considerable caution as the dangerous crocodiles were perfectly camouflaged in the mud near the banks.

The river grew wider and we drifted along nicely without having to paddle. We had covered just four hundred kilometres of the greatest river on Earth, yet my altimeter read just over one hundred metres. Even after making allowances for barometric pressure differentials caused by the prevailing weather conditions, I still found it hard to grasp the fact that there should be so little height loss on the remaining six thousand kilometres to the point where the Amazon flowed into the Atlantic. Yet that was indeed the case, and the Índios fashioned another two rudimentary paddles and worked them hard in the totally calm water, as the journey grew monotonous and uninteresting.

Shortly before the confluence with the Rio Madre de Dios, we reached a settlement. If the name of the river itself was pleasant to the ear, the place itself sounded rather less reassuring. It was called Maldonado. A little way beyond the bank I caught sight of a large bungalow, built in a similar style to the rest houses found in the British colonies. The wooden building stood on piles and was surrounded by a veranda that the owner of the property had screened with mosquito mesh as protection against mosquitoes. After so many weeks of wretched accommodation it seemed to me to be the epitome of luxury. The door stood open and the rooms were empty, so we carried my few possessions up through the bushes to the bungalow, where I paid off my friendly Índio companions and make them a present of the dugout canoe.

The large garden was overgrown and the containing fence dilapidated. There were hundreds of orange trees and banana bushes, but it was obvious that no one came to harvest them, as the ripe fruit lay rotting and neglected on the ground. I met the plantation owner when I went into town the next day. He was German by birth. He gave me a lift back to the bungalow in his old, open-top Jeep. He told me he was now sixty years old and happily married to a local woman. He owned a house in town and no longer had any appetite for hard manual work. He said he would give me the bungalow and the plantation if I wanted them. As we chatted, he showed me the best way to extract the juice from a ripe orange. He produced a penknife and cut a conical hole in the top of the fruit, held the orange to his lips and pressed with the fingers of both hands until the delicious juice ran into his mouth.

In addition to the yield from the plantation, I could make good money from the sale of crocodile skins and jaguar pelts, he said, but the biggest profits were to be made with Brazil nuts, as these were very popular in the USA. They were plentiful in the jungle and all one had to do was collect them and crack them without damaging the kernel inside. He explained that undamaged nuts would fetch ten US dollars per kilo and that there were as many people as I needed locally for the work of collecting and cracking them.

His success story can only really be understood by those who appreciate how he could be happy living in that God-forsaken place. The image of Paradise that he described failed to tempt me; Maldonado was no Eldorado – and I wanted to go home. I waited impatiently for the aeroplane from Cusco; it would come soon enough, I was informed. We shook hands on the airstrip, and the plantation owner pointed to my leaving present, which was lying on the ground next to the aircraft. Wrapped in a parcel tied with liana vines, was the skin of a crocodile that had been killed the previous day. He had already salted it and the pilot, a friend of his, had agreed to accept the additional twenty-five kilo load. He said that the skin would make two handbags for my wife and a briefcase for me. I hope that the kind German emigrant will forgive me for leaving the heavy parcel in Lima before I boarded my flight back to Europe.

ON THE LECTURE CIRCUIT

On my second visit to London, Rupert Hart-Davis arranged my accommodation. I stayed at the exclusive Saint James's Club, tucked away in a quiet side street just off Piccadilly. A butler led me silently through a room in which an elderly gentleman was sitting in a deep leather armchair reading the newspaper. He did not look up. My room could best be described as spartan. With the words "Breakfast at seven o'clock in the morning, sir," the butler handed me the key and withdrew. I hardly dared breathe; it was all very British.

At breakfast time, I sat alone in the large club room. The butler explained that, unfortunately, there was no marmalade. I was a little confused by this, as there were two varieties on the table. "Will there be anything else, sir?" he added, to which I replied "Ham and eggs, please." "Yes sir," came the reply; but the eggs did not come. The cultural attaché at the Austrian Embassy later explained to me that the German word "marmalade" translates into English as "jam" and that in English "marmalade" is used to refer to a preserve made exclusively from orange peel. He also provided a plausible theory to explain the absence of eggs. He told me that every night over a million eggs came to England by boat from Denmark and that the vessel might have been delayed by a storm en route to London. The fact that the butler had nonetheless replied in the affirmative, he attributed to his reluctance to disappoint.

Over lunch in a gourmet Greek restaurant, Hart-Davis told me that his son, who was attending Eton College as a boarder, had expressed the wish to meet me and that the Headmaster of the college had already given his permission. As a former teacher myself, the opportunity of visiting the school where the sons of the aristocracy were educated was too tempting to miss.

The size of Eton College alone bore scant comparison with the schools of my home country of Austria, and I was particularly impressed with the extensive sports facilities. The son of my publisher had his own room with a bed, a table and a bookcase, and we were soon joined there by his schoolmates from the neighbouring rooms, who had questions of their own to ask.

We had asked the taxi to wait. I love London cabs; they are, without doubt, the best in the world. You just step right inside, without having to bend double, and you can sit comfortably, with legs outstretched. The cabs can turn on a sixpence in the narrowest of streets; the turning circle is quite remarkable. Even better, there is a partition between driver and passengers, which means you can carry on your conversation in private. I slid open the partition and asked the cabbie how long the journey to Soho Square would take. In all likelihood he did not understand my English and I understood the ensuing flood of Cockney slang even less. I said "Sorry," slid the partition closed again and resolved to do without the information, but my love of all things British, and London in particular, was in no way diminished by this unsuccessful encounter with the language. For longer trips in the city it is often better to take the Underground. At rush hour, it is full to bursting with businessmen, many of whom still wear bowler hats and carry furled umbrellas. Some read the morning papers, while others stand and wait, killing time by doing the difficult crossword puzzle in *The Times*.

At midday, I took the Tube to Kew Gardens near Richmond-upon-Thames, where I met the British officer F. M. Bailey for lunch. Bailey had been in Lhasa in 1904 and loved Tibet. During an expedition in 1913 he had discovered the bright blue Himalayan poppy, which was on display in Kew Gardens. The writing on the sign said "*Meconopsis baileyi*". Bailey told me proudly that he had found many new butterflies and plants on his expeditions, but it is the blue poppy for which he is best known.

I returned to London in the late autumn of 1953, when the English version of my book was published. This time, my publisher had booked a room for me at the prestigious Savoy Hotel and arranged several appointments for me. Hart-Davis and I went first to the Royal Geographical Society in Kensington Gardens, where I was due to give a lecture. The library and map room were worth a visit in their own right.

For anyone who travels on expeditions to far-flung places, an invitation to address the Royal Geographical Society is considered a great honour. The only people who had been invited to attend my talk that evening were the members of this most traditional of clubs, amongst them one Peter Fleming, then the most famous of all expedition and travel writers and the man whom the *Times* called upon whenever they required a foreign correspondent in places that were geographically remote or in a state of political unrest. His best known book, *Brazilian Adventure* is a classic account of his quest to find the missing British colonel, P. H. Fawcett, who had disappeared in 1925 in the Matto Grosso. Fleming had also travelled widely in the Far East and the story of his journey with the Swiss traveller Ella Maillart, recounted in her book *Forbidden Journey*, makes fascinating reading, not least because of the author's unvarnished portrayal of the differences in the protagonists' characters and attitudes. Maillart dismissed Fleming's love of hunting and pipe smoking and was irritated by the affectations of his Oxford English, while there was much about Maillart that Fleming himself had just cause to find fault with. Nevertheless, after a chance meeting at the northern border of Tibet, they joined forces, and travelled for months on end through deserts and mountains, united in difficult times by common sense and a common purpose. Their journey inspired two exciting books, and I wrote a preface for the US editions. Ella Maillart later retired and lived a quiet life in a chalet high above the Swiss village of Zinal. I visited her there after climbing the Zinalrothorns (4,221 m). Many years later, when I was on a golfing trip down the valley in Crans Montana, I brought her a small Tibetan *thangka*, which depicted the great Tibetan poet and yogi Milarepa.

I was pleasantly surprised to learn that Peter Fleming himself had written the introduction to *Seven Years in Tibet*; I could think of no better person for the job. I was also pleased that Fleming had agreed to say a few words of introduction before my talk at the Royal Geographical Society later that evening. Afterwards, over dinner, I had the pleasure of Lady Ravensdale's company. She was the eldest daughter of Lord Curzon, the famous Viceroy of India, and had lived in India as a young girl, so we had plenty to chat about. She said she was very much looking forward to my lecture the following evening.

Rupert Hart-Davis had booked the huge Royal Festival Hall for my lecture. I was envious of Hart-Davis' cultured Oxford English; I had acquired my knowledge of the English language in Lhasa by listening to the BBC news, spoken at dictation speed, with the Dalai Lama and in conversation with Coocoola and felt a little unsure of myself. Hart-Davis dismissed my doubts with a smile and suggested that I begin my lecture with that story. He also told me that the Royal Festival Hall had been sold out for weeks and that Lady Ravensdale would be introducing me to the three thousand paying guests.

A busy and exciting day began with the book launch at the Savoy Hotel. *Seven Years in Tibet* had been voted "Book of the Month", so there were several other interested parties present in addition to the press. The translator, Richard Graves, explained that when he received the German manuscript, he found the first few pages so interesting that he made the decision to read only one chapter a day at the most. "To keep myself in suspense", was how he put it.

In the course of my lifetime I have given many lectures all over the world, but that evening at the Royal Festival Hall in London was certainly one of the most remarkable events I have ever experienced. There were several letters waiting for me when I arrived in the Green Room, one of which bore the name of the sender, Colonel Williams, which I opened and read there and then. When I walked onto the stage I did not know whether to bow or raise my hand in greeting, so I looked to Lady Ravensdale for reassurance. She was the only person I recognised in a sea of unfamiliar faces and I felt a little overwhelmed by the occasion. She was standing at the lectern ready to make her introductory remarks. She spoke about her childhood with her father in India and was so charming and amusing that the audience soon warmed to her. As I listened, I felt the tension ebb away. When it was my turn to speak, I forgot Hart-Davis' well-meant advice about excusing myself for my Austrian-accented English and instead I began by reading out the letter from Colonel Williams:

"As the Commandant of your POW camp in India, your escape meant that I had to endure the shame and disgrace of a reprimand from my superiors at HQ. As if that were not enough, this evening I find myself obliged to pay good money for the privilege of hearing first-hand how you accomplished it."

The ensuing standing ovation was for Williams, who was sitting somewhere in the hall, but the positive atmosphere it created also banished my stage fright once and for all.

Peter Fleming wanted to do an exclusive interview with me for the *Times*, so we arranged that he would pick me up at the Savoy the following morning and drive me to his office. As I waited out of the rain under the canopy at the hotel entrance, a vintage yellow Rolls Royce convertible pulled up. The driver waved to me; it was Peter Fleming. We drove in silence to Fleet Street, where all the big newspapers then had their premises. Once again, it was all so typically English. Fleming drove with the top down and was wearing a scarf and a stylish checked cap. I do not think for a moment that he was trying to impress; he was simply correctly attired for the weather. I liked the way that everything was so traditional, yet so matter-of-fact here in England and the live and let live attitude of the English people. It is worth mentioning here that there is something of a tradition in the Fleming family when it comes to writing good books. Peter's younger brother, Ian Fleming, achieved international fame as the author of the "James Bond" series of espionage novels. I also admired Hart-Davis' ability to run a successful publishing company whilst only visiting the office two days a week. He told me he lived out in the country and did not like driving in rush hour traffic. Another thing I admired about the English was the way they administered their Empire, and their policy of withdrawing from their territories at the appropriate time.

The invitations to present my new book came flooding in from all over the world. Since I could not possibly honour them all, I decided to concentrate on Europe. After London, I went first to France, where B. Arthaud, who had published Maurice Herzog's bestseller *Annapurna*, had acquired the rights to *Seven Years in Tibet*. I took my own car to Paris to be a bit more mobile, and arrived without any difficulties. However, whilst I was looking for the publishing house, I managed to become embroiled in the chaotic traffic at the Arc de Triomphe roundabout, where both my sense of direction and my driving abilities suddenly deserted me. I was greeted at the publishers' by the translator Henry

Daussy, who accompanied me everywhere for the next two weeks. He helped me to freshen up my school French and translated the special vocabulary I would need for my slideshows. Daussy also knew where to find the best bouillabaisse in town and in the evenings he took me to all the little theatres that do not appear in the tourist brochures. It was bitterly cold in Paris, and the pavement cafés were all shut. Daussy did not own a car, so we took the Metro to the Salle Pleyel, where my lectures took place, every one of which was sold out. Daussy also gave me a lesson on the cultural history of Austria and explained that the hall, the largest in Paris, had been built by one of my countrymen, Ignaz Joseph Pleyel. Pleyel had started as a Kapellmeister for his patron Count Erdödy and had gone on to found a piano making business. The firm had provided pianos used by Frédéric Chopin.

Claude Arthaud, the daughter of my publisher, had designed the cover for the French edition of the book, *Sept Ans d'Aventures au Tibet*, and invited us to her apartment one evening for what proved to be a pleasantly relaxed soirée. She introduced me to her young artist friends and we all sat on the carpet and chatted. It was a far cry from the formalities of England, but I soon got used to the bohemian ways of these young French people. A bookish looking man with thick spectacles passed me a glass of red wine and placed a bowl of walnuts next to me on the carpet. He informed me that the best nuts in the world came from his home town of Grenoble. Then he went over to an old confessional that had been adapted to serve a rather more profane purpose as a telephone box. A young woman who had just arrived showed us all a weathered old board into which a number of carpentry nails had been hammered to form a crucifix. It was her interpretation of Passiontide, she explained. Her idea of representing the Crucifixion in this way met with loud applause.

I spent several interesting hours in the company of these young artists, although this was not, and could never really be, my world. I then made contact with the French Alpine Club who, together with *Exploration du Monde*, an organisation that provided support for explorers, were organising my lectures. After the war, French mountaineering had experienced something of a boom period, spawning a new generation of top-class climbers. I had heard about some of their achievements at the British Trade Mission in Lhasa, where we had had a discussion about the increase in popularity of mountaineering. The North Face of the Eiger was criticised as a typical example of the trend, and I could not refrain from mentioning that I had been one of the four climbers that had made the first ascent. I had the impression that they did not quite believe me at first, but in the spirit of fairness that is so typical of the English, the head of the Mission later sent me a newspaper clipping that described the second ascent of the Eigerwand by the French team of Lionel Terray and Louis Lachenal in July 1947 and mentioned the names of the four men who had first accomplished the climb.

Lachenal and Terray had also accompanied Maurice Herzog on Annapurna in 1950, the first of the eight-thousanders to be climbed. Unfortunately, they were unable to come to Paris as they were both guiding in Chamonix, where it was high season. However, Maurice Herzog himself made the introductory speech at my first Paris lecture.

In the autumn of 1953, I attended a twenty-year school reunion in Graz. Sadly, many of my old school friends had never returned from the war and of the many teachers I and my fellow pupils had so admired, only four now remained, amongst them Professor Hüttenbrenner, who told me he was proud of my achievements but reminded me, too, that I had never really shown any aptitude for his subject, French. "I still learned enough from you to deliver six sell-out lectures in French at the Salle Pleyel in Paris," I said, which seemed to reassure him somewhat.

1953 had been a good year for me; a year of rich contrasts. I had enjoyed a pleasant mixture of the simple life in the high mountains, spending time with people who were happy, even though they could not read or write, and the vibrant cultural life of Europe. As my ship docked in New York I had no idea that 1954 would also prove to be an eventful year full of unforgettable experiences. This time I had a visa, but my interrogation by the immigration official still took forever. Finally I reached the customs desk, where the duty officer discovered an apple in my hand luggage, wrapped it carefully in a hand towel and took it away to be burned. Free at last, I joined the milling throng of confused travellers and looked around for a porter. There were none to be found. Instead, there were a number of people holding placards – a picket line, I was told, whose aim it was to prevent the porters earning an honest dollar carrying travellers' bags. I was beginning to have my doubts about the much-praised freedom that was said to exist in the United States. However, the balance was redressed somewhat when, on checking into my hotel, I was spared the formality of filling in another questionnaire and was not even required to produce my passport.

My American publisher, E. P. Dutton, had left a file at the hotel reception desk with a list of my engagements and the pleasing news that they had decided to use the English translation and Peter Fleming's introduction for the American edition. *Seven Years in Tibet* was already number one in the American bestseller list and over the following weeks I had a number of appointments to keep. I renewed my acquaintance with Lowell Thomas, who interviewed me on his popular radio programme, and appeared as a guest on numerous well-known television shows. Lowell Thomas had an office in central Manhattan and was able to get me tickets for the Carnegie Hall or Madison Square Garden whenever I wanted them.

I also visited the renowned speakers' agent, Colston Leigh, in his bureau on Fifth Avenue, where I was presented with a draft contract for a lecture trip that looked very tempting indeed. According to the terms of the contract, I would earn an average of three hundred dollars per lecture, but the list of fees also included several payments of five hundred dollars and for one evening at IBM in Edincott alone, the fee was seven hundred dollars. Leigh was to retain half of the money, out of which he would pay all rail costs, including the two night train journey to Miami, while I would be expected to pay for my own accommodation. The numbers seemed attractive and it was only later that I realised that there was a significant drawback to this arrangement; namely, that I would also have to pay for my food and accommodation during the breaks between my lectures, which sometimes ran to several weeks.

For the time being, I rented a room for two months in a modest hotel on Lexington Avenue and set about acquiring a work permit. The list of lectures was enough proof for the immigration official, although the many strange stamps in my passport did give him pause for thought. This was the passport that had been issued by the Austrian Embassy in

New Delhi. It originally gave my place of residence as Lhasa, but this had been crossed out by the passport office in Vaduz and replaced with "Principality of Liechtenstein", which the official had never heard of. Eventually he accepted my return ticket with Swiss Air to Zurich in December as evidence of my intention to leave the USA and stapled the work permit to my passport, together with a note bearing the name of the office where I would have to pay the tax on my earnings before I left for Europe.

My time in the big city was highly entertaining. I gave lectures at women's organisations, where I was introduced to each and every one of the lady members in a formal "receiving line", and was a guest speaker at the Audubon Society, the oldest conservation organisation in America, which numbers around half a million members. In the evenings my speaking engagements generally took me out of town, but if I was free I would sometimes catch a musical on Broadway or go out for a meal. There were noticeable differences between the food here and at home, and things that were still hard to obtain in Europe were available in abundance. My lectures were often rounded off with a sumptuous buffet meal and I would have loved to have sampled one of the famous Maine lobsters but usually had to field so many questions about Tibet and the Dalai Lama, about whom little was known in America, that there was precious little time to eat. If I wanted to eat sea food, I used to go down to Central Station, where they served the best oysters and clam chowder in town, but my favourite haunt was a little delicatessen near the hotel, run by a friendly ex-pat German, who would look on in approval as I perched on a bar stool and ate my fill of the delicious food he served. Pickled pig knuckle and Italian antipasti were always on the menu, but his most popular dish was pastrami, which he cut into thick slices and served on a bread roll with ketchup or relish. A cup of coffee with milk and sugar cost ten cents and a weekend treat of a one pound turkey drumstick cost just one dollar. The proprietor of the deli explained to me that it was cheap because the Americans preferred the white meat. At weekends, I used to buy the *New York Times* and with a whole kilogram of newspaper to keep me occupied, I never experienced that feeling of loneliness and malaise that Sundays in the big city were said to bring.

Back in the winter of 1952/53 I had received a visit from Walter Edwards, a picture editor with the famous *National Geographic* magazine in Washington, D. C., who had written to me with suggestions for another article. I now went to visit him. The National Geographic Society publishing company occupied a huge building that housed six thousand employees. Edwards led me into a conference room where Melville Bell Grosvenor, the son of the founding editor, introduced me to the photojournalists present with the words "This is the man who did our fifty page cover story for the July issue, the one who only had two rolls of film." When Grosvenor then added that the magazine's staff photographers usually received two hundred rolls for each assignment, I tried to explain away my work as a lucky coincidence.

After the meeting we repaired to Walter Edwards' spacious office, where he explained to me that the magazine used a portion of its tax-free income to finance expeditions and specialised in the publication of accurate maps. As we were chatting, Edwards was handed a note, which said that Hurricane Bertha was scheduled to strike at two o' clock that afternoon and advised all employees to leave their offices early to give them time to secure their homes and belongings. Edwards invited me to accompany him. When we arrived at his house his wife had already taken the necessary precautions, but in the event the hurricane passed by the district without causing any damage. *National Geographic* magazine ran my article in July 1955. It was illustrated with forty-eight photos, thirty-seven of which were in colour.

Over the following months, I travelled widely in America on my lecture tour. My last assignment was in Miami. I boarded the Florida Express in the evening and made myself comfortable in my cabin. At first glance it all looked perfect. There was a toilet, a shower, a bed and a friendly conductor. However, the compartment was equipped with air conditioning and it was impossible to open the window, even slightly. I managed to overcome the feeling of claustrophobia and after two sleepless nights, I disembarked on the morning of the third day, relieved that the journey was finally over. Fortunately, I did not have to check in at one of the huge, impersonal hotels, as I had been invited to stay at the home of an Austrian family who lived in Miami. The house was built in the Hispanic style and was located in a pleasant suburb of similar villas. As I walked into the lobby I was greeted by several of my fellow countrymen. Breakfast was served and the long train journey was soon forgotten. My hosts suggested a trip out to the Everglades, a region that has now acquired World Heritage status. The Audubon Society in New York had informed their Miami branch of my visit, so Florida was to become a further highlight of my lecture tour. The work of the Society's researchers in Florida was concentrated on the preservation of the flamingos in the extensive swamplands of the Everglades, which were a special attraction of the region. I was impressed to learn that the Americans had designated areas like the Rocky Mountains as National Parks fifty years before similar laws were passed in Europe. The Yellowstone National Park, which covers an area of almost ten thousand square kilometres, was actually placed under legal protection as long ago as 1872.

ALASKA

My appointments diary allowed me to take a four month break from my lecturing commitments in the summer, during which time I intended to visit Alaska. I had no firm plans, and I suppose that in a way, I was again trying to recapture times past. Whenever I had shown the Tibetans pictures of the Eskimos, they had become quite animated. "They are our brothers," they used to say. In fact, the ancestors of the Eskimos did indeed originate from Asia. They had crossed the Bering Straits to Alaska and travelled right across Canada as far as Greenland.

I bought a car in New York to get me to Alaska: a light green Packard convertible, which the dealer reckoned I ought to be able to sell easily out west for double the price. Following the advice of friends, I took Highway 66, spending nights in motels recommended by the American Automobile Association, which was a pleasant way of breaking the long car journey. I had plenty of time on my hands and made a detour in Arizona to visit the Grand Canyon National Park. The horizontal stratification on the walls of the deep canyon was clearly visible, even to the untrained eye.

I was also interested in visiting a Navajo Indian reservation, as I had been told that, like the Tibetans, the Navajo artists are famous for their fabulous ritualistic sand paintings. The owner of the motel said I would not have far to go to meet the Navajo; they would be coming to the motel that very afternoon. A short while later several cars drew up next to a raised dance platform and disgorged their occupants, who swiftly changed into their ancient tribal costumes and performed a selection of wild Indian dances to the accompaniment of drums and singing. The tribal chief's huge headdress was mightily impressive. There were about a hundred spectators watching the performance, and a man from Kodak, who dispensed information and tips on the best film, aperture settings and exposure times. After half an hour the dancers finished their performance and left for their next show at a motel down the road.

From Arizona I drove to California, where I followed the Pacific Coast

Highway north from Santa Barbara. San Francisco and the Redwood National Park, with its huge trees, are world famous tourist attractions, but I decided against visiting them and instead drove a further thousand kilometres to Crater Lake National Park in the state of Oregon. The renowned vulcanologist Haroun Tazieff had delivered the opening speech at one of my lectures in Paris. At considerable risk to his own life, Tazieff had filmed several large volcanic eruptions and it was he who had advised me to visit Crater Lake on my American trip. As I drove the two hundred kilometres around the almost perfectly circular blue lake, I could understand his enthusiasm. When the volcano erupted during the last ice age, it left a crater ten kilometres in diameter. In the middle of the lake, a new volcanic cone was forming, which clearly demonstrated the awesome power of the natural forces at work here.

The next stop on my trip was over the border in Canada, where I visited the town of Victoria on Vancouver Island. I had been told that here everything was even more British than in Britain and when I met him at Kew Gardens, Bailey had recommended that I visit the beautiful flower gardens on the island. A young married couple from England had acquired a piece of land with a hill on Vancouver Island. There was limestone rock beneath the vegetation and when Victoria became the capital of the province of British Columbia the young couple profited considerably from the construction boom that followed. One day they decided to close the quarry and turn it into an alpine garden. They loved flowers and invested generously in their new hobby, building Japanese style bridges and planting many species of alpine plants. They were particularly proud of their display of blue poppies, whose vivid blooms shone brightly in a shaded corner of the gardens.

I still had about six thousand kilometres to go to my destination. The second half of my journey followed a dusty gravel road that was later to become part of the Pan-American Highway, which stretches from Alaska to Tierra del Fuego. I had been advised not to exceed sixty kilometres per hour on the long, straight sections, but as monotony and loneliness got the better of me, the tachometer slowly crept upwards. I was still only doing seventy when the inevitable happened: the friction of the wheels on the gravel caused the tyres to overheat and the rear tyre burst. The cheap Packard ended up costing me money after all. In

Fairbanks I told my story about Tibet, but the climbers present at my talk were more interested in hearing about the Eiger. Alaska's mountains are an ideal mountaineering venue and I would always advise climbers to try one of the many unclimbed Alaskan peaks rather than going on an expensive Himalayan trip. The glaciers calve straight into the sea and the summits rise to a height of six thousand metres, so the actual height gain is about the same as in the Himalaya. However, it is cheaper to get there, there are no peak fees to pay and fewer problems acclimatising. I decided to give it a shot.

Amongst the audience were two young men, who were interested in my plans. Fred Beckey hailed from Seattle, where he worked for the big aircraft company Boeing, and was spending his holidays here in Fairbanks. Henry Meybohm had been born in Germany, had just finished bringing in the raspberry harvest on his farm and wanted to head up into the mountains. I quickly explained my plans to them. In New York I had found an old edition of *National Geographic* magazine with pictures of the most famous peaks in Alaska. Mount McKinley was the highest, at 6,194 metres, while Mount Hunter (4,442 metres), the third highest summit, was described as "unclimbed". On a subsequent page there was a description of another mountain and, in parentheses, the comment "Mount Deborah – unclimbed". I had torn these two pages out of the magazine and showed them now to the Americans.

That evening it was decided that we should climb as a rope of three. We calculated that we would need four weeks for the trip and I suggested to Fred and Henry that they organise the provisions. In my experience you need about one kilogram of food per person per day on this type of expedition. I told them to buy things they liked, since taking personal food favourites like sauerkraut and salami can make a big difference to the mood of the team. However, when we arrived at Mount Deborah base camp and opened the food bags there was a nasty surprise in store. Every packet bore a label with the words "Contains only …calories." My American friends had somehow managed to buy food with the minimum calorie count and maximum weight, instead of the other way around. Fred said this was the usual custom in America. As a result, we would have to establish at least one extra interim camp to avoid having to carry too heavy loads.

The weather was splendid and after three days we reached the final exposed ridge that led up to the virgin summit of Mount Deborah. We had achieved our first objective but we did not rest on our laurels. There was still the little matter of Mount Hunter.

Alaska is 1.5 million square kilometres in size and flying is the only feasible way to get from one climbing objective to the next. The Alaskans had built six hundred landing strips, large and small, across the state; one of these was at a place called Talkeetna. It was there that we met Don Sheldon, a young bush pilot who had the necessary licence to fly passengers and had equipped two little Piper Cubs with pontoons for landing on water. He would take off on wheels from Talkeetna airstrip and retract them to land on the floats on one of the remote lakes, which were highly prized fishing venues, attracting anglers from all over the world. Sheldon had recently swapped the floats for skis on one of his planes, which was why we had sought him out.

Instead of pitching tents, we were allowed to sleep in the hangar. The weather had turned a little unfriendly but there was plenty in Talkeetna to keep us occupied. The few locals viewed us climbers as something of a curiosity – strange people with a crazy hobby – but they had the typical pioneering spirit, too, and all of them wanted to help. Each of them owned a hut stocked with provisions out in the remote backcountry and they all offered us the use of these cabins, or slabs of salmon to take on our expedition. As the aboriginal inhabitants of the region, the Indians and Eskimos were accorded the privilege of catching as much salmon as they wanted and to this end had built a dreadful contraption on the river bank that looked like a mill wheel. The blades of the wheel were not set at right angles, but were angled towards the water and scooped the fish out of the river onto the bank. The salmon were then picked out, hung up to dry and sold. The fish was the sled dogs' favourite food. We also enjoyed a huge, grilled salmon steak every day and when the time finally came to set off for the mountains, we packed a twelve kilo fish to supplement our expedition provisions.

We took off very early, flew over craggy ridges and remote lakes and landed to the west of Mount Hunter on the Kahiltna Glacier. The sun had softened the surface of the snow and although we unloaded our luggage as quickly as we could, Sheldon still had to use all his skill as a pilot to repeatedly flip the plane from one ski to the other before he could take off again. Since we were near the Polar Circle and it was the end of June, there was no night, so we broke trail when the snow was more frozen and slept when the sun was high in the sky.

In this way, we reached the West Ridge. There were several cornices but the main difference here was the state of the ice. The Alaskan glaciers are faster flowing and form only a thin layer overlying the rock. The ice is treacherous and requires greater care than in the Alps. To our surprise, the steep summit ridge turned out to give really pleasant climbing. I dug out a vertical trench in the rotten snow with my ice axe and worked my way up, chimney-fashion and on the 4th of July, a national day of celebration for my two friends, we stood on the summit of Mount Hunter in the first rays of the rising sun. In the whole of North America there were only two peaks that were higher, Mount McKinley and Mount Foraker, and both seemed almost close enough to touch.

The return trip drew heavily on our resources of strength and patience. We walked for nine hours each day down the moraines of the Kahiltna Glacier, following little streams lined with purple willow herb that simply begged to be photographed. Gradually, the streams grew bigger and at times we had to wade waist-deep through the raging torrent. At last, we reached the tundra and the dense thickets of aspen and alder. Our food supplies were exhausted and by the time we reached the hunting cabin we had been offered in Talkeetna, we were getting rather hungry. The cabin was unlocked and the shelves well stocked with provisions, including a number of unmarked tins that probably contained caribou or reindeer meat. Whatever it was, it tasted delicious to us.

No longer lacking the basic necessities and comforts of life, we decided to take a leisurely rest day. The joins in the walls of the log cabin were sealed with moss and the place reminded me of my favourite book – *Unflinching*, by Edgar Christian, which I had devoured during my time in the prison camp. In 1926, the eighteen-year-old Edgar had been taken on an expedition by two more experienced men, the aim of the trip being to explore a new route through the barren Canadian tundra to Hudson Bay. For Edgar, who had recently left college, it was his wildest dream come true. However, they were forced to take refuge in a log cabin during the exceptionally cold winter. The two older men perished first; Edgar Christian was the last to die. The bodies were discovered two years later, together with Edgar's diary, which was found in a cranny in the fireplace. It gave a vivid account of the eight months of suffering he had endured. It was a moving document of loyalty and courage and has taken its place as one of the outstanding tales of arctic adventure and tragedy. The films that were found were spoiled, which made the images created in the written account all the more precious. During the time he spent alone in that cabin, Edgar became a man and writing became a necessary part of his life, which is one reason why, to this day, *Unflinching* remains such an inspirational book.

Well rested now, we marched happily through the dense vegetation of the tundra. Don Sheldon had flown several reconnaissance trips and knew exactly where we were. His only concern was that we were walking through an area that was the habitat not only of the brown bear but also of the feared grizzly and, rather foolishly in his opinion, had neglected to take a rifle. I did not even have any pepper powder with me, but I do have a story about bears. In the birthplace of my fellow countryman Martin Zeiller, in the Austrian Steiermark, there is a memorial stone that bears the inscription "In the presence of a bear, lie flat on the ground as if dead and hold your breath." Over the years I have received many pieces of advice, several of which are still valid today. For example, "mental preparation is as important as physical fitness" or "travelling means adventure and one should always plan well for adventure." As far as the danger of being attacked by a bear is concerned, it is worth bearing in mind the research conducted by Lynn Rogers, who notes that in the last hundred years forty people have been killed by brown bears and eighty by grizzlies and compares this with the statistic that, over the same period of time in Canada and the USA, no fewer than 374 people have been killed by lightning.

Suddenly we heard the noise of a pump coming from the forest and were approached by one of the last remaining gold panners. He was a former German sailor, who had settled here after the war with his family. We enjoyed their generous hospitality and in answer to our question about the success of his prospecting enterprise, he took down a bowl from the shelf and tipped several gold nuggets onto the table, explaining that things had become much easier since he started using a powerful jet of water with a motorised pump instead of panning the paydirt laboriously by hand. I acquired several larger grains of paydirt as a souvenir before he drove us in his tractor along a narrow, bumpy track back to Talkeetna – a huge relief with our sore feet and heavy rucksacks.

We spent the evening at the home of Don Sheldon, where we finally got to eat another delicious salmon steak. The big salmon we had taken with us is probably still lying, deep frozen, at our base camp on the Kahiltna Glacier. My friends had had enough of the mountains for the time being, so I teamed up with the great wildlife conservationist Georg Schaller, whom I had met by chance in Fairbanks, for an ascent of Mount Drum. The climb went without any hitches and I had now made the first ascents of all of the peaks described as "unclimbed" in the *National Geographic* magazine.

The Alaskan newspapers had been reporting our climbs on their front pages for several weeks and the publicity this generated led to an invitation to visit the scientists working at the Air Force base at Point Barrow on the northernmost tip of the American continent. The area was completely devoid of trees and could best be described as dreary, yet I was nonetheless fascinated by the place, and by the fact that I was now five degrees north of the Polar Circle on the Arctic Ocean. My meeting with the Eskimos was as I had expected. They were delighted with the photos of the Tibetans and the few days I spent with them in their aboriginal homeland were enough to convince me to return. I photographed the laughing Eskimos, particularly the children, marvelled at the Eskimo rolls they performed in their kayaks and bought a finely carved figurine made of walrus ivory as a memento. It was the end of the 1970s before I had the opportunity to make a return visit, by which time oil had been discovered and the Eskimos, like everyone else in America, were buying their spongy bread and tasteless salmon from the supermarket.

Back in Fairbanks, my Packard was still parked on the car dealer's lot. However, there was no chance of selling it here for double the purchase price, as I had been led to believe when I bought it in New York, so instead of accepting five hundred dollars I decided to keep my nice convertible. On the outskirts of Fairbanks I stopped to pick up a young hitch-hiker who was on his way to college in Berkley. We shared the driving, keeping to the 40 miles per hour speed limit and travelling non-stop, day and night, down the gravel road of the Alaska Highway. Tyres intact, we arrived at Spokane, where I put the student on a Greyhound Bus.

My publisher had sent me a list of appointments which, in the interests of book sales, I ought to try to keep. Amongst them was an invitation to appear on a TV show in Seattle. I met up with my old friend Gottfried Schmidt-Ehrenburg and together we set off for Seattle. During the drive we were followed by an old Ford. Suddenly, the driver put a flashing blue light on his roof, overtook us and waved us to the side of the road. "You are under arrest, follow me!" the policeman said.

We parked in the back yard of a large building complex in the next town. Without a word, the uniformed guardian of the law showed us to a metal door with a sign that read "Lift to Jail". It is hard to describe what I was thinking, but taking us straight to prison seemed a little harsh to me and it looked as if I could forget the TV programme now. An elderly, distinguished looking man invited us to take a seat. The American Stars and Stripes flag hung on the wall behind him. The traffic cop gave his report. He explained that our crime was having exceeded the statutory speed limit by eight miles an hour over a six mile stretch of road. The judge asked whether these figures were correct and we confirmed this without hesitation, as we both knew the policeman had seriously underestimated our speed. We were then asked if we were prepared to pay a sixty dollar fine and again answered in the affirmative. When we mentioned that I had to be in Seattle that evening to appear on a TV talk show, the kindly judge bade us farewell with the words "That is the most popular programme round here. I'll be seeing you!"

The advantage of arriving late in Seattle was that there was no time for the make-up artist. However, even without this questionable pleasure, the show was a lively affair and well received. Perhaps I should explain why I mention the make up scenario. It seems that, regardless of the length of time you spend on camera, you always have to report to the make-up room hours before the start of the broadcast. Once seated, you shut your eyes and hold your breath while powder is applied to your face with a soft brush, all the while trying to suppress the thought of how many times the same brush has been used on other people's skin. To hide the bags under your eyes, the make-up artists then tells you to open your eyes and look upwards while she takes an equally well used powder puff and smooths away the wrinkles. The lipstick and comb would hardly pass the hygiene test, either. On subsequent TV appearances I argued that we had managed perfectly well without make-up in Seattle, but my pleas always fell on deaf ears.

When I returned to New York I learned that the agency had arranged a series of autumn lectures at university towns right up as far as the Canadian border. Once again, I loaded the Packard and drove north through the colourful maple forests to Lake Placid, where the Winter Olympics had been held in 1932. I gave the trusty Packard to an ex-pat Austrian friend in Buffalo.

I spent a lovely few days in Vermont and particularly enjoyed my time in Stowe. Lowell Thomas had financed the construction of one of the new ski lodges there and the architecture of the hotel was a testament to his love of the Austrian mountains. Alfred Hitchcock was staying at the lodge with his film team, making one of his thrillers, where, in typical Hitchcock fashion, the body was buried amongst the autumn leaves of the maple forest.

After my Tibet lecture I was invited to the home of the von Trapp family, who were later to become world famous through the film *The Sound of Music*. Baroness von Trapp had arranged a party with an Austrian theme and when I arrived she took me silently by the hand and led me into a wood panelled room, adorned with a simple crucifix, that I assumed must be the family chapel. "This is my family," she said and pointed to the twenty or so people present. A Christian hymn was sung, then we all kneeled and the Baroness praised God for standing by Heinrich Harrer in his time of need and delivering him from danger and hardship during his escape to Tibet. I was deeply moved by her gesture and thanked her profusely. I had never experienced anything quite like this before. Over dinner we swapped experiences.

In Vermont I was also pleased to make the acquaintance of Fritz Wiesner, a German mountaineer who, in my opinion, has thus far not been accorded the respect he deserves in the history of mountaineering. Wiesner was born in Dresden in 1910 and emigrated to America in 1936. In 1939, while we were reconnoitring the Diamir Face of Nanga Parbat, Wiesner was on an expedition to K2 – just over the hill from us, in a manner of speaking. We learned that Wiesner and his Sherpa, Pusang, had been forced to retreat just four hundred metres below the summit. That was twenty years before the first ascent of K2, which is without doubt the most difficult of all the eight thousand metre peaks. Fritz Wiesner now owned a ski factory in Vermont and in subsequent winters I met up with him for a spot of ski touring in the Alps.

While I was away lecturing, a special edition of *Seven Years in Tibet* was released for members of the American Book of the Month Club, whose founders, Mr and Mrs Löw, had arranged a big launch party at their apartment on Park Avenue in New York. In addition to the usual media types, the Löws had also invited several people who maintained close associations with Asia and in particular with Tibet. Amongst those welcomed by name was Pearl S. Buck, who had received the Nobel Prize for Literature in 1938. After greeting her guests, Mrs Löw interrupted the lively conversation to announce that there was plenty to eat and drink but that, regrettably, she now had to abandon her guests for a while as she simply had to watch a television programme about Rogers and Hammerstein, as she had not missed a single episode so far. There were no televisions in Austria in 1953 but the significance of this new medium became clear to me that evening for the first time.

For me personally, the most interesting encounter I had that evening was with Pearl S. Buck. I was naturally acquainted with her book, *The Good Earth*, for which she had been awarded the Nobel Prize before the war. I had devoured it enthusiastically and now I was sitting at a little side table chatting to the famous author in person. Born in West Virginia, she had lived for forty years in China, where she grew up in a typical Christian family of kindred adventurous spirits, who pursued their mission with idealism and devotion. As we exchanged thoughts, it was as if we were in an oasis of calm amidst the noise of all those present. She was outraged by the Chinese Communists' treatment of Tibet and stressed that it was the wretched politicians who bore the guilt and not the Chinese people. She also predicated that I, like she, would soon be regarded by the Chinese authorities as *persona non grata*. She was to be proved right, yet we both regarded their subsequent refusal to grant us entry permits as an honour.

When it was time to leave, Pearl S. Buck asked if I would like to spend Thanksgiving at her country home in Pennsylvania with her and her friends. She said it would be a nice opportunity for me to acquaint myself with this American custom. Harvest festivals have been celebrated by cultures all over the world since time immemorial, but in the USA, Thanksgiving was also a national public holiday.

Pearl S. Buck's country residence, Green Hill Farm, lay in parkland studded with mature trees, with a pond surrounded by weeping willows. The guests all seemed to be amongst the more prosperous members of society. After drinks, we seated ourselves at a long table. The two chefs presented the traditional turkey, which was roasted to a crispy golden brown, and were greeted with a round of applause. The size of the thing astonished me; I had never before seen a turkey quite that size. Full of enthusiasm, I mentioned that it would be a nice idea to surprise my family at Christmas with such a delicious feast, whereupon the lady seated opposite me straightaway said "Don't you dare go and buy one, now; I own the farm that that turkey on the table comes from." We discussed the potential difficulties of me taking delivery of the turkey and, of course, she had the solution: I only had to give her my date of departure and flight number and she would see to it that the parcel arrived on time.

Before I left New York, I paid a visit to the Internal Revenue Service. It was the first time that I had had any dealings with this much-feared institution, but the official who dealt with my file was surprisingly friendly. There was nothing to discuss in any case, really, since my agent had retained the prescribed percentage of my earnings and my expenses would be reimbursed by bank transfer at a later date.

At the airport, I passed through Departures without undue delay and made my way to the Swiss Air desk to check in for the flight to Zürich. They very generously turned a blind eye to my two over-weight suitcases, but there was also the matter of a twenty-five kilogram packet that needed paying for. I had forgotten my evening with Pearl S. Buck and the turkey, but there she was – the turkey. I could not simply abandon it there, as I had done the previous year in Peru when the customs official had demanded nineteen U.S. dollars per kilo for the parcel containing the crocodile skin, so we bartered, and after considerable to-ing and fro-ing, the turkey still ended up costing me more than half a dozen fat geese in Austria. As if that were not enough, I could find no oven in Kitzbühel large enough to accommodate the huge bird. It had to be chopped up into pieces, which finally put paid to my vain attempt to impress my friends. The charming lady benefactor never did find out that her well-meant gift had met with such an ignominious end. A case of "beware of Greeks bearing gifts", perhaps.

In the spring of 1955, I continued my lecture tour of America. Based on my experiences on the previous tour, I decided this time to make the travel arrangements myself. My favourite means of transport was the pan-continental Greyhound Bus. The main New York bus station lay on the other side of the Hudson and was easy and quick to reach by subway from Manhattan. For long journeys you simply boarded the bus in the late evening, reclined the seat and slept the trip away. It was cheap, too – sixty dollars for the three thousand or so miles to San Francisco, for example. You could interrupt the journey as often as you wished. The safety procedures were particularly impressive. At unmanned level crossings, the driver was required by law to stop the bus, turn off the engine and open the doors, so he might better hear the signal of any train that happened to be approaching down the line.

I can still vividly recall my visits to the elite universities in the New England states. I had a room on campus at both Yale and Harvard and spent several days at the renowned Massachusetts Institute of Technology.

I spent the time between lecture trips in New York. It was always nice to see Lowell Thomas and we met frequently. Thomas was a very popular man and was often greeted with a cheery "Hi, Lowell!" on the streets or at a New York Giants baseball game. His popularity had increased since his visit to the Dalai Lama in Lhasa and the publication of his book, *Out of This World*, which had become a big success in America. As a benefactor of the team and a member of the Giants Club, there was always a seat for Lowell and a guest in the otherwise sold-out stadium and when we went to a game together he took the opportunity to explain the rules to me. Baseball, it seemed, was a more complicated version of a game we used to play at school in Austria called "Schlagball". Two other prominent members of the Giants Club were sitting nearby. They were Sam Snead and Joe di Maggio, who was rated as the best baseball player of all time and achieved even greater fame when he married Marilyn Monroe.

Thomas was the President of the New York Explorer's Club and asked me one day if I would be prepared to speak at the Club. I did the talk without slides and spoke about my time in Lhasa, the place where I had first met Lowell Thomas. The only people present were the committee members and after my talk the Secretary asked me if I would accept an honorary membership. The honour was conferred later at the annual dinner in the Great Ballroom of the Waldorf Astoria Hotel in front of two thousand members. Next to me on the podium sat Wernher, Baron von Braun, the German World War II rocket scientist, who entered the United States at the end of the war through the then-secret Operation Paperclip. After our memberships had been conferred, there followed a long night of stimulating conversations, which led in turn to numerous invitations being made.

Von Braun had become a naturalised U.S. citizen and conducted research at the NASA Centre in Huntsville, Alabama. He said I could stay with him when I gave my lecture there. I had previously accepted an offer of accommodation from the President of the Sierra Clubs in San Francisco, Bill Farquhar, so I bought a round trip ticket. In Huntsville, I was shown around the research centre with its rocket towers and was amazed at the lack of security controls. Von Braun recommended that I also visit Willi Luft in San Antonio, New Mexico, where he and several other former members of the German Nanga Parbat Expedition worked at the Institute for High Altitude Physiology.

After a few days in Mexico City, I flew to San Antonio, New Mexico. I was the only passenger on the flight. I had met Willi Luft before in Munich, during the initial research for our Nanga Parbat Expedition. Luft was a remarkable climber. He was the sole survivor of the 1934 Nanga Parbat tragedy and had described in his diary how the other seven climbers and nine Sherpas had perished in an avalanche. He returned the following year, together with Hias Rebitsch and Wiggerl Schmaderer, and found the bodies of his companions. Luft picked me up at the airport. That evening was the first time for ages that I did not have to talk about Tibet; instead, the conversation centred around our mutual friends. "Why did Wiggerl have to die, and what is Hias doing with himself?" Luft wanted to know. He kept talking about American ideals and the favourable working conditions he enjoyed here, but I soon formed the impression that his frequent references to this Utopian situation hid a deep dissatisfaction with his life in the US. Whereas Wernher von Braun become completely assimilated into the culture and was now an American citizen, Luft seemed more the Peter Aufschnaiter type, who kept his emotions to himself and never really expressed his true feelings. I had the feeling that he would enjoy escaping his comfortable, affluent life and the eternal fine, dry weather for a while, so I suggested that he make contact with Don Sheldon and head off to experience the snow and ice of Alaska. We bade each other a fond farewell and he asked me to tell his Munich climbing friends all about him. "Say hello to Bavaria and Hias!" he said as we parted company, his voice hoarse with emotion.

Bill Farquhar had arranged an interesting programme for me in San Francisco. I was supposed to be staying with the family of a well-to-do member of the Sierra Club and had been promised the surprise treat of a room with a balcony and a view of the Golden Gate Bridge. I always found it hard to convince the organisers of these lecture trips that I would actually prefer to stay in a hotel. They meant well, and obviously thought it would be nicer for me to lodge with a family. It saved money, too. But in spite of repeated assurances that I would be left in peace, in reality this never happened. I had to show due consideration and gratitude towards my hosts and after a whole day answering their polite questions I simply wanted to be on my own. After giving a lecture it was nice to be able to soak in the bath, even if it was midnight and I liked not having to appear for breakfast at a set time. If I stayed in a hotel, I could read the morning paper and send the boiled egg back if it was too hard. Nor did I ever feel obliged to write a letter to the hotel management thanking them for their generous hospitality. These are just a few of the reasons why staying in a hotel was infinitely more preferable to a private invitation.

I can still vividly recall the reception at the Sierra Club. Above the door was a sign that read "Here spiders don't web", which meant that members were asked to refrain from conducting business discussions on the premises. A forty-person male voice choir greeted us with a song about the beauty of the Sierra Nevada Mountains. The members were greatly concerned with environmental issues and were instrumental in preserving the giant redwoods. Their local mountain was Mount Whitney, which, at 4,419 metres, was the highest peak in the USA, until Alaska became the forty-ninth, and largest, state in the Union.

After my lecture the President of the Club introduced me to several of his prominent members. It was with great pleasure that I made the acquaintance of the renowned photographer Ansel Adams, whom I visited the following day. His little house was almost completely hidden by flowering shrubs and bushes and I had to duck beneath a mass of entwined tendrils to get through the front door. Adams was ten years older than me and had won a shelf full of awards for his books of American landscape photography. Even today, his books still enjoy international acclaim. I was impressed by the chaotic jumble of maps, documents, old magazines, books and photos in the house. This was the first time I had seen a portfolio of photographs, and Adam's was an astonishing collection of exceptionally powerful images. My own portfolio, a limited edition of ten photographs of the old Tibet, signed and numbered in pencil, was published in America in 1999. The Dalai Lama received the first numbered copy; number two was purchased by the Library of Congress and number three by the Cornell University of Ithaca. The famous Smithsonian Institute in Washington also has one of my portfolios.

I left Adam's plant-festooned house with an autographed copy of one of his books and some equally valuable suggestions from the great artist himself. After visiting Ansel Adams, I tried to encourage the luxuriant foliage around my own house so that one had to bend down to get through the door – with some success, it must be said.

During my stay in New Delhi in 1951, I had spent a lot of time at the home of the Burke family. Jim Burke's contacts had helped me to stretch my fee from *Life* magazine, which enabled me to work undisturbed on the Tibet book right through until the summer of 1952. The Dalai Lama had returned to Lhasa in the meantime and I wanted to do something to make him happy, so on my return to Europe I drove to the Leitz factory in Wetzlar to order a Leica for him, a special edition model with a gold-plated housing and a red leather finish. Leitz also very generously gave me a new camera and my old one went into a display cabinet in the Leica Museum. The camera they made for the Dalai Lama bore the serial number 555.555 and appeared in several magazines. A foreign correspondent from *Life* magazine delivered the valuable Leica to Burke in Delhi, who passed it on to the royal house of Sikkim, from where it found its way to His Holiness. When the Dalai Lama fled to exile in 1959, he was only able to take life's bare necessities with him. The odyssey of the golden Leica suffered an ignominious end.

In November 1964 I read Jim Burke's obituary in *Life* magazine. According to the report, he had fallen to his death while working on a photo shoot. On one of my subsequent trips to the USA, I visited his widow to offer my condolences and learned from her that Jim's fatal accident had occurred near our POW camp at Dehra Dun. He had been commissioned by *Life* to take photographs for a series about the Himalaya and to illustrate the bestseller *Man Eaters of Kumaon* by the legendary big game hunter Jim Corbett. Burke had been working up in the Siwalik Hills and had strayed too close to the edge of a big drop in an attempt to get his shot when he lost his footing on the loose sedimentary rock and fell to his death in front of his Indian companions.

At the end of 1955 I spent some time back in Liechtenstein, where I met frequently with Herbert Tichy, a man with whom I had shared many interests. The previous year, Tichy had made the first ascent of the 8,201 metre Cho Oyu and we were now planning an expedition to western Nepal and the peaks of Api and Nampa. On the way, we hoped to spend some time with the Tibetans who lived in this relatively unexplored region. The expedition came just at the right time for me, as I had not been anywhere near Tibet since I left there. Despite frequent appeals to the Austrian ambassador in Peking to intercede on my behalf, the Chinese authorities would not budge. I was persona non grata in Tibet.

Even getting into Nepal proved difficult enough. Nepal had not yet opened its borders to tourism and only a few countries were granted permission to undertake expeditions there. In the autumn of 1956 we travelled to Kathmandu, where we expected to receive an answer to our request for a permit. When none materialised, Herbert went on his own to the Foreign Ministry to enquire about it. By way of explanation, he was told that the expedition to western Nepal seemed very "fishy" and the fact that Harrer was to accompany him made things "even fishier". I was well known to the Nepalese authorities and since Nepal was having problems with China over the situation in Tibet, they were unwilling to issue me with a permit. Tichy was also told that, since the occupation of Tibet, a group of Khampa freedom fighters had been living in the north of the country, supplied by air drops. I left Nepal and Herbert went on the expedition alone.

Meanwhile, in India, news of the Dalai Lama's impending visit was spreading fast. The Crown Prince of Sikkim, Maharaja Palden Thondup Namgyal, had recently been to Lhasa and, in his capacity as president of the Mahabodhi Society of India, a Buddhist organisation dedicated to spiritual and educational development, had asked the Dalai Lama to attend the celebrations to be held in Delhi to mark the 2,500[th] anniversary of the birth of the Buddha. The family of the Dalai Lama owned a modest apartment in the Jawalakhel area and it was here that I met Norbu, who had already been informed of his famous brother's travel plans. So, after six years, I finally got to see my friend the Dalai Lama again. Unfortunately, our encounters were very brief and fleeting and the many secret police that accompanied him treated me in a rather unfriendly fashion. It was a similar situation to our last meeting, when the Dalai Lama was fleeing the Chinese troops and was unsure whether he should return to Lhasa. Now, too, he had an important decision to make and was obviously torn between the options presented to him. Nehru had told him quite clearly that India could not help him, although there were other Indian politicians making themselves heard, who promised him that they would support Tibet's case for independence. Once again, his brothers and I attempted to persuade him that it would be folly to return to Lhasa. A deeply religious people like the Tibetans would simply find it impossible to come to terms with the Chinese style of Communism. The Chinese made their promises and Chou En-Lai made his views perfectly plain: that in the mountains of his homeland, the Dalai Lama was a tiger; in India, however, he was merely one dog amongst many. For his part, the Dalai Lama resolved to return to Tibet and to try once more for appeasement with the Chinese. His beloved brother, Lobsang Samten, remained in India for health reasons.

A short while later, I set off on another lecture tour. Rupert Hart-Davis had written to inform me that there were several venues in Scotland that had expressed an interest in my story. I travelled first to Copenhagen, where Prince Peter of Greece and Denmark had invited me to attend the opening of a Tibet exhibition at the Museum of Ethnology. Prince Peter had donated all of his Tibetan treasures to the country of Denmark. He had also written a nice foreword to the Danish edition of my book.

I took the ferry over to England and went straight to my publisher's in Soho Square. I wondered why the whole team had assembled for my reception, but the puzzle was soon solved. On the table lay the galley proofs of a supposedly authentic story, originating from Tibet and written by a man purporting to be a Tibetan *lama*. It was bad news for my publishers, where it had caused quite a commotion, as thus far my book had been without competitors. Previews in the press spoke of a sensation. I found a quiet corner and leafed through the proofs. The title was *The Third Eye*, the author Lobsang Rampa, the publisher Secker & Warburg, London. At the end of the book there was statement by the author attesting to the fact that this was a documentary report and that everything contained therein was a true representation of events. I was sure that the publisher had insisted on this postscript because he, too, harboured doubts about the authenticity of the story.

After half an hour I delivered my verdict to Hart-Davis. The author was a fraudster, the book a literary deception and the contents a complete fabrication. Since Lobsang Rampa claimed to have lived in Lhasa at the same time as me, I asked Hart-Davis to telephone his friend Frederic Warburg and request a meeting with Lobsang Rampa to enable me to chat to him in Tibetan about our mutual acquaintances and our time in Lhasa.

That afternoon we received word that the *lama* was meditating at present and could not be disturbed under any circumstances. A few days later another message arrived saying that, regrettably, Lobsang Rampa was now on a ship bound for Canada. In the meantime, the British diplomat and writer, Hugh Richardson had also been racking his brains wondering who the mysterious author of the book might be. In an attempt to determine the validity of Lobsang Rampa's tale, a committed Buddhist by the name of Marco Pallis hired a detective, Clifford Burgess, who slipped into one of the *lama's* seances in the guise of a student. He reported that Lobsang Rampa wore a mighty beard, and was lying in bed stroking two Siamese cats. House cats are seldom seen in Tibet and the men do not wear beards. The detective also found it strange that amongst the *lama's* pupils were several members of the English aristocracy. He finally exposed Lobsang Rampa as Cyril Hoskins, a plumber's son from Devon who had a reputation as a hawker and fortune teller and had never been to Tibet. A car accident in 1947 had precipitated his transformation and caused him to reject the materialist ideals of the West and recall a previous incarnation as a Tibetan monk. Hoskins claimed that he was possessed by the spirit of Lobsang Rampa and had a "third eye" in the middle of his forehead that gave him psychic powers and the wisdom of the East. The dubious case of the lama with the restless spirit made Hoskins's book a bestseller and after the scandal those who still had not bought a copy did just that. *The Third Eye* became a profitable business venture and encouraged Hoskins to pen several more works of mystery and intrigue. I found it astonishing that there were so many people prepared to believe such humbug.

During my lectures I referred to *The Third Eye* as a fraud and invited my audiences to imagine how they might react if I were to have the validity of my expedition reports confirmed by a lawyer. I subsequently received a letter from Rampas' German publisher, Klaus Piper, threatening me with legal action and informing me that the company intended to sue me for a huge sum of money to compensate them for the damage I had caused to their business. Instead of replying in full to Piper's letter, I suggested that we meet in person. I prepared my case well and travelled to Munich, where, with the aid of photographs of Lhasa and more than a hundred errors I had marked in Rampas' book, I was able convince those present at the meeting that although there was much in the text that was correct, as a documentary report the book as a whole was a literary swindle. Since no one raised any objections, it became clear to me that the German publisher also had his doubts about the validity of Rampa's tale. As I was leaving, the senior executive of the company mentioned to me that they would be most interested in publishing one of my books at some stage, and presented me with a copy of the recently published bestseller *The Roots of Heaven* by Romain Gary. Piper Verlag eventually removed the master plumber from their list of authors.

Since then there have been many books that have attempted to exploit people's fascination with Tibet for financial gain. I have now given up trying to expose such questionable works; on the contrary, I now believe that in bringing the plight of the Tibetans to the attention of a wider audience they perform a very useful service.

After this rather distasteful episode, I continued on my way to Scotland. My journey took me through the charming English countryside, with its flocks of sheep and blossoming hedgerows, and across the invisible border. My lecture in Edinburgh was organised by Bartholomew, a renowned family publishing house that had specialised for generations in the publication of atlases and maps. John Bartholomew, the current owner, gave me a copy of the latest edition of *The Times Atlas of the World*, without doubt the most famous and authoritative work of its type in the world. I found the dedication at the front typically British in tone: "To Her Majesty Queen Elizabeth II – The Times Atlas of the World is with the most gracious permission respectfully dedicated by Her Majesty's Cartographer John Bartholomew".

I returned to Edinburgh a few years later during another lecture tour. During my talk, an elderly gentleman slumped forward in his seat and was carried from the lecture theatre. The morning newspapers carried the news of the death of John Bartholomew on their front pages, and noted that he had passed away whilst attending a lecture on geographic matters – a fitting end for a man who had dedicated his entire life to the subject.

ETERNAL ICE AT THE EQUATOR

During a lecture tour of Belgium in the spring of 1957, the organisers, Connaissance du Monde, enquired if I would be prepared to travel to the Belgian Congo for a few months to talk to the Belgian civil servants who were stationed there. It was a welcome proposition, since I had been intrigued by some photographs I had seen of the Ruwenzori Mountains on the border between the former Belgian Congo and Uganda. Although there are two higher mountains in Africa, Mount Kenya and Kilimanjaro, the vegetation on Ruwenzori is unique and although it is on the Equator, the mountain boasts a permanent ice field. In a second hand bookshop, I had discovered, and subsequently devoured, the classic *The Snows of the Nile: an account of the exploration of the peaks of Ruwenzori* by Prince Luigi Amedeo of Savoy, Duke of Abruzzi, written in 1909. I accepted the Belgians' offer and left Europe, bound for Africa.

After arriving in Stanleyville, however, I had to put Ruwenzori on hold for a while. The Belgian civil servants spoiled me terribly and I was accorded all the privileges and opportunities enjoyed by them as a colonial power, in a similar fashion to the British in India. As a European, I was respectfully addressed as "Citoyen" rather than "Sahib", the common form of address in India. We covered large distances by car along dusty roads and whenever we encountered another vehicle we would stop and chat for a while; time was of no importance here. Presently, the holiday season began and many of the Belgians flew home.

My companion was David Groote, a young man who had already made three attempts to climb Ruwenzori. Although David spent a large portion of his free time in a holiday bungalow to the west of the mountain, he had never yet seen the ice-clad summit of Ruwenzori, much less climbed it. He did, however, have the benefit of extensive local knowledge of the area, and I was pleased to have him as my climbing partner. Together, we drove to Mutwanga, where the main administrative office of the Ruwenzori National Park was situated. There were cooks and porters available to climbing and research expeditions and many of the locals who worked for the visitors lived in newly built huts next to the Park Office. There was a list of previous expeditions in the office. There had only been a few, but it was no surprise to find the names of the famous English explorers H. W. Tilman and Eric Shipton amongst them. In the previous half-century, only seven expeditions had reached the summit from the western side. There had been many more successful ascents from the eastern, Ugandan, side but the approach from the west, from the Belgian Congo, was far steeper and required a certain measure of rock climbing ability. Although the Duke of Abruzzi's splendid book was a valuable addition to my growing collection, I needed more up to date reports in order to prepare for our climb, and these I had obtained from the Royal Geographical Society in London. According to these reports, there was much that was still unexplored on the mountain and inevitably my attention was once again drawn to the magical word "unclimbed" that was used to highlight several of the ten summits in the five thousand metre zone.

It was raining as usual as we made our way up through the various vegetation zones, passing wild bananas first, then tree ferns and finally stumbling through tortuous heather. The fairy-tale forest contained many species of lichen, amongst them the long, white beard lichen, and the moss on the tree roots hid the large potholes beneath, into which we often disappeared up to our chests. Every evening, after making about a thousand metres in height, we found shelter in a hut. Since it was forbidden to destroy any of the vegetation in the National Park, even for fuel, our porters were carrying several canisters full of petroleum. The awful smell was a constant companion on the approach march and on arrival at the hut it was always better to wait outside in the rain until the petrol stoves had been lit.

The third hut, known as Kiondo Gîte, was situated at 4,200 metres. We intended to stay here for a while and acclimatise before the final stage. David seemed a little uneasy, recalling a previous attempt. "No visibility, no chance, as usual!" he said.

The meteorologists ascribe the fickle weather conditions in the region to the coming together of damp air streams from the Atlantic and the Indian Oceans. Ruwenzori was the weather kitchen of Africa and of the many interpretations of the mountain's name, "rain maker" is certainly the most appropriate. In spite of the rain, the cold and the mist we made several forays to reconnoitre the route, picking our way laboriously through the thick cover of strawflowers to reach one of the twenty-five or so known lakes, which had been christened "Green", "White", "Blue" or "Black", according to their depth and their surroundings. On the side nearest the mountain, these lakes were hemmed in by steep cliffs; on the valley side were sub-alpine meadows of the kind only found in Africa. The lobelias were up to eight metres in height and looked like gigantic mulleins. Even without binoculars, one could watch the collared sunbirds hovering like hummingbirds as they used their long beaks to extract the nectar from the blue blossoms of the lobelias. The landscape looked like a Hieronymus Bosch painting. Even taller than the lobelias was the giant groundsel, the smaller variety of which is known in Europe as the common groundsel or old-man-in-the-Spring. Their thick stems reached a height of twelve metres and were crowned with green leaves and vibrant yellow flowers.

One afternoon we took another walk to the top of Wasumaweso, the nearest summit to our mountain, from where, according to the reports, one could get the best view of the ice covered peaks of the Ruwenzori massif. Freezing cold, we sat down next to the sign that read "Wasumaweso – 4,462 metres", when a strong wind suddenly blew a hole in the clouds. At first I thought I was seeing things as the icy summits of Ruwenzori appeared briefly, only to vanish again into the mists. Then, as the sky cleared, the "Mountains of the Moon", as the English climbers called them, were revealed in their full glory, bathed in bright sunlight. The glaciers and the fresh covering of snow on the cliffs were like a revelation. The vision seemed to confirm the two-thousand-year-old stories about the ancient Egyptians having drunk water fed by mountain snows and the drawings made by the Greek philosopher and geographer Claudius Ptolemaeus, which depicted the source of the Nile as originating in these Mountains of the Moon.

The British journalist and African explorer, Sir Henry Morton Stanley, had been the first to see the eternal ice at the Equator, on 24th May 1888, but when he published his discovery, there were many who doubted him. Some detractors even suggested that what Stanley claimed to have seen – ice covered mountains in the middle of the hot, arid African continent – might have been attributable to a particularly virulent bout of malaria. Nowadays it seems most appropriate that the highest summit of this myth-enshrouded mountain range bears the name of that audacious English explorer.

My Belgian partner slept the sleep of the just, but although it was raining, I woke him long before daybreak to get a good, early start. I tried to explain to him that it was sensible to set off now, even though the weather was bad and to attempt the climb in the hope that conditions would improve. To wait for fine weather would mean that it would inevitably take a turn for the worse at some point, possibly just as we were making our summit push. David could barely hide his scepticism, but the logic of my argument was confirmed when the sky cleared as we were climbing the steep cliffs. In spite of this, I still marked the route with red tags and cairns every few metres or so to prevent us losing our way if we had to descend in poor visibility. Above the cliffs, we strapped on our crampons and continued without further difficulties to the top of the 5,119 metre Mount Stanley.

I could only guess at the emotions my partner was experiencing as we sat in the sun on the summit. Mount Ruwenzori has character. It has taken time and patience, and above all plenty of rain and mist, to cultivate its vegetation. It is not really that important to get to the top; it is much more interesting and worthwhile to experience the gigantic alpine flora, the lakes and the atmosphere of the magical landscape. I knew one thing for sure: I would be back.

Like my tour of the USA two years previously, my 1957 trip to the Congo had proved to be an ideal combination of lecture work and expedition. My agent had arranged several lectures in German-speaking countries for the autumn of the same year. This time, I combined them with golf, a sport I had first played in America in 1955. Back then, I was still competing in small tennis tournaments in Europe and I had taken my racquet with me to America, clamped in a wooden press secured by four screws to prevent it warping. Unfortunately, I never got to play, as whenever I had the time I could not find a partner, and vice versa. Gradually, I learned to take on fewer lecturing commitments in order to have more free time. I also changed my accommodation arrangements. The towns where I was lecturing all had several golf courses, many of which had hotels attached. Some of the organisers even had apartments in the club houses. Around Chicago and Los Angeles, for example, there were hundreds of golf courses, which meant that I no longer had to spend miserable weekends stuck in the big city on my own. I bought a full set of second hand golf clubs, complete with bag, for fifty dollars and spent some time on the putting greens and driving ranges practising my new-found sport. I had always enjoyed ball sports and after just a short time, I was asked if I would like to play a proper round.

Even today, golf is still my favourite leisure pursuit. I have always found going for a walk boring, but will happily walk ten or more kilometres after that little white ball. My old tennis racquet stayed in its press and now lives at the Harrer Museum in Hüttenberg, along with several more items of abandoned sports equipment.

During my long lecture tour in the autumn of 1957, I was hoping to devote some time to my new sport, but golf was still relatively unknown at home and in Bavaria and Austria there were only a few nine-hole courses. During a car journey from Germany to Vaduz I spotted a sign on the side of the road that read "Golfclub Lindau", so I stopped and asked if I might play a round. There was a tournament about to start and they let me participate. The man in charge asked what my handicap was. I told him I did not have one. "What do you play off, then?" he enquired. "About eighteen," I said. I won my first golf prize at that tournament and was bitten by the golf bug for ever after. Baron Pantz and Prince Alec Hohenlohe had founded a golf club in Kitzbühel, and I became a member. Amongst the first celebrity guests welcomed by the club were the Duke of Windsor and Wallis Simpson.

During my autumn lecture series I found myself in Frankfurt am Main with time to kill before an evening lecture, so I went for a game of golf at the exclusive Niederrat Golf Club. There were only a few people at the club, and the president introduced me to some of them. Although I had by now achieved a certain level of fame through my books, for one of the lady golfers there, I was a complete stranger. My future wife, Carina, had come to the club to play bridge and did not have the slightest idea about the North Face of the Eiger or my adventures in Tibet. She was keen to learn more, however, so I invited her along to my lecture that evening.

Thus began a relationship that has lasted to this day. It was a case of two entirely different worlds colliding: on the one hand, the independent, unconventional life of and explorer and world traveller; on the other, a woman who had thus far spent her life within the secure confines of a well-to-do family.

In June 1958 I entered the Austrian State Golf Championships in Kitzbühel, playing with the second hand clubs I had purchased in the USA. I did not think I had much of a chance against a field that included several former champions and several useful young players, all of whom had a better handicap than me. I did have one advantage, however. I had just returned from a trip to Kenya, so I was not bothered by the unusually hot weather during the competition.

Over the first two days of the tournament, we had to play thirty-six holes. Since I did not have a caddy, this meant dragging my golfing trolley over the hilly nine-hole course eight times in all. Saturday came and I found myself in the semi finals. The most exciting thing was not the fact that, at forty-six, I was the oldest player in the competition, or that I had only been playing the sport for three years. What really pleased the crowd was the fact that I was the only local playing.

I had a caddy for the final on the Sunday, and a big crowd of spectators to motivate me. The fact that I actually won, was probably mostly attributable to my stamina, although the secret of my success may have had something to do with the fact that I declined the cold drinks that were proffered and instead sipped warm lemon tea from my thermos flask. It is a known fact that the heart has to work harder to cope with cold drinks on hot days and that instead of quenching one's thirst, these often have the unwelcome effect of causing further outbreaks of sweating.

After my championship success, I gained a place in the team that was to represent Austria in the inaugural World Amateur Golf

Championship at St Andrews in Scotland that autumn. The team consisted of the President of the Austrian Golf Federation, Hugo Eckelt, Count Smecchia, Alexander Maculan, Hugo Hild and me. The strong sea breeze, the huge greens and the many big bunkers made the course very hard to play, but we each had an experienced older caddy with a little dog that fetched the balls from the impenetrable thorn bushes that flanked the fairways. We placed second to last in a field of twenty-nine teams. In spite of this, or maybe because of it, we appeared in the newspapers every day, since we had both the youngest player, Maculan, and the oldest, Smecchia, in our team. The press were also interested in my story about escaping from the British POW camp. The best player there was the American Jack Nicklaus, who was playing his last tournament as an amateur before going on to achieve worldwide fame as perhaps the best golfer of all time, but the star of the show was the fifty-six-year-old Robert Tyre Jones, whom we all called Bobby. In the summer of 1930, Jones had performed a feat never accomplished before or since - to win in succession all four of the major golf championships in one year. Jones won his Grand Slam with a set of hickory shafted clubs. In return for a promised copy of my Tibet book, Bobby gave me a copy of the plan of the Old Course at St Andrews, inscribed with a personal dedication.

My old friend Hugh Richardson provided ample consolation for our lack of success at St. Andrews. I had visited Hugh the previous year, when I was delivering a lecture in Edinburgh. I had signed far more books than usual at the Edinburgh lecture, as the audience included many former civil servants who had served in India and then retired to Scotland. Hugh was a Scot, too. He had married Hilda, the widow of an army lieutenant who had fallen at Dunkirk. Hugh was born in St Andrews and had recently bought a modest little house there. His civil service pension had not been enough to buy anywhere bigger, he once told me. After India gained independence, many British Foreign Office officials were made redundant. Hugh had received a lump sum payment for seventeen years of service as a government employee. Now his incomparable knowledge of Tibet was no longer required by the British Foreign Office, but his expertise was highly valued by the East Asian Institute at Berkeley University, who employed him as an honorary professor for a tenure of several terms.

At Richardson's request, I delivered a lecture at the Institute and afterwards I spoke to his students. Next day we drove over to Pebble Beach Golf Club to play a few holes and I immediately realised why the course is so famous. On several holes you have to play over deep coastal inlets and if you miss the green your ball bounces on the rocks and flies off into the Pacific Ocean. It is all very exciting and great fun, provided you have enough golf balls and a good sense of humour, and even if you play badly, the wonderful views are more than adequate compensation for losing a few balls.

Hugh was also a member of the "Royal and Ancient Golf Club of St Andrews" and on my first trip to Scotland we played a round on the famous Old Course, after which Hugh took me over to see the former Open Champion and club maker William Auchterlonie, who had a workshop right next to the course. Hugh advised me to order a set of Auchterlonie's "tailor-made" woods at the very least. Auchterlonie played three holes with us, then we went back to his workshop where he rummaged around in a box full of bits of horn and bone until he found the exact piece he was looking for to make the club heads. Three days later I was the proud owner of two bespoke golf clubs, made by hand by the last great master of his trade.

During my years in Lhasa I had formed a close friendship with Thubten Jigme Norbu, the elder brother of the Dalai Lama. Norbu loved playing pranks and teased me mercilessly. He was also one of the highest reincarnations in Tibetan Buddhism. He left Tibet at the same time as me and during his exile has worked devotedly for the Tibetan cause. He stayed with me for a few months in the house in Kitzbühel belonging to my friends, the Rüttimanns, which they only used in winter when they came to ski. During our time there I collected and collated all the details of his life, from his birthplace in Amdo to his flight from Tibet, and wrote his life story on an ancient typewriter. It was published under the title "Tibet is My Country". At the time, the Dalai Lama was still in Lhasa and Norbu warned me repeatedly to leave out certain details so as not to endanger his brother.

News from Tibet was at best patchy, but in the autumn of 1958 several photographs were published of a seemingly contented Dalai

Lama. After taking the preliminary examination at each of the three monastic universities: Drepung, Sera and Ganden, he sat his final examination in the Jokhang in Lhasa, where he was examined on logic, the canon of monastic discipline and the study of metaphysics. His Holiness passed the examinations with honours and was awarded his doctorate by unanimous decision. The famous Indian photographer, Raghubir Singh, had managed to take some photographs that showed the Dalai Lama riding a white yak to pray at the top of Gambo Utse, the mountain above Drepung Monastery. These photographs were deceptive, however, for in reality, the Tibetans' discontent with the Chinese occupation was growing day by day. The streets of Lhasa were barely able to contain the many refugees from the countryside and there was seething unrest amongst the masses. The Dalai Lama was later to describe it as being "As if everyone knew that something of great importance was about to happen." Something important did indeed happen. In March 1959, as Chinese troops crushed an attempted uprising in Tibet, I received a telegram informing me that the Dalai Lama had fled into India.

Sarah Churchill called me from London to tell me that she had been asked by Lord Rothermere to fly to India immediately to cover the story for his newspaper, the *Daily Mail*, and to ask me if I would like to accompany her. Her explanatory remarks about the *Daily Mail* being the biggest selling daily newspaper in the world, with a circulation of two million, were unnecessary. I flew straight to London that same evening. There I met a reporter from *Life*, a publication which, with seven million copies sold per week, was then the biggest magazine in the world. He wanted me to go to India, too. After discussing this with Miss Churchill, the conclusion was reached that *Life* and the *Daily Mail* were not competitors and, full of anticipation, we all caught a flight to Delhi.

The Dalai Lama crossed into India at Tezpur, near Assam, in the Northeast Frontier Area (NEFA). Although this area was forbidden to foreigners, our press credentials got us through all the control points with no difficulties. All of the papers carried the news of the Dalai Lama's flight to India on their front pages, and even Prime Minister

Jawaharlal Pandit Nehru was on his way to Tezpur. My experienced journalist companions had rented the only car available for miles around and although the shock absorbers were broken, we loaded it to the gunwales and bounced along the rutted tracks through the tea plantations, one of which, we learned, was the plantation that supplied the Queen of England with her favourite drink.

The Dalai Lama's arrival was delayed, as His Holiness had fallen ill with dysentery during his long and arduous journey. On 18th April, thousands of Indians and Tibetans gathered to greet the spiritual leader of Tibetan Buddhism, referred to by some as "Lamaism". I went along with Nehru, who told me that he had recently reread my book and found it most informative.

Monks with shawms and huge temple trumpets heralded the Dalai Lama's arrival. A convoy of four Jeeps approached. The lead car was red and had a NEFA registration number. The national flags flew from the bonnet – the Indian spinning wheel and the Tibetan snow lion. It had rained earlier, so the border guards had improvised a red carpet using tent groundsheets. The Secret Service and a troop of Gurkha soldiers formed a human barrier between His Holiness and the faithful worshippers, who threw themselves to the ground in awe as he passed.

When the Dalai Lama caught sight of me, he shouted "Grogs po, grogs po!" – "Friend, friend!" Although barely three years had passed since I had last seen him, the sound of his voice moved me. In 1956 I had tried in vain to dissuade him from returning to Lhasa. I was pleased he had recognised me in the crowd but I did think that his words sounded a little like a cry for help and for the first time, I felt as if the young man might be in need of a fatherly friend. On the other hand, I knew that everything he had had to endure had also made him a mature, enlightened man. He had learned the painful way that life means suffering, yet in the life of a Buddhist, the cessation of suffering is attainable. This is a part of the "The Four Noble Truths", a simple exposition of basic Buddhism, which would be of great comfort to the Dalai Lama during his years of exile.

The Dalai Lama's entourage included many of my old friends and acquaintances from Lhasa. A woman detached herself from the group

Homecoming, Summer 1962. After the New Guinea Expedition my wife Carina came to meet me at the airport in Frankfurt am Main

Leaving for Borneo in 1972. Carina says goodbye to King Leopold and me at the airfield at Frankfurt

With cameraman Herbert Raditschnig and King Leopold on the summit of Kassikassima in Suriname after the first ascent in 1966

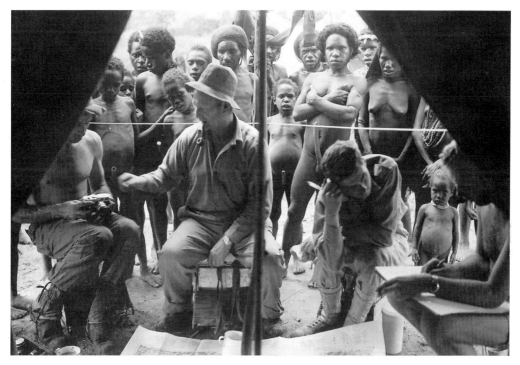

During the 1962 New Guinea Expedition. My Leica arouses great interest

Writing my journal in Suriname, with my new invention, a hammock with an integral rain cover and mosquito net, in the background

My father working on his allotment in Graz

Family visit in Kitzbühel in the mid-1970s. On the right is my mother, next to her my daughter-in-law Barbara with my granddaughter Irene and on the left my wife Carina with granddaughter Birgit

With Carina at the home of Tenzing Norgay and his wife Daku in Darjeeling. We took the Apso puppy that Carina is stroking back to Europe with us.

Family adventures, mid-1980s. Irene and Birgit have pieces of fresh sugar cane and I am holding a bunch of small Indian bananas

Toni Sailer organised an adventure course in the Dachstein Mountains for the winners of the "Jugend forscht" competition

Competing in the 65 km cross country skiing race in Lienz

At the 18th hole on the Seefeld golf course

With the Dalai Lama and Senator
Günther Klinge at Lake Starnberg
in 1990

Herbert Kessler presents me with
the Golden Humboldt Medal in
Brunswick in 1985

March 1995. The Austrian President Thomas Klestil awards me the Fellowship of
the Austrian Academy of Sciences. My friend Fritz Heppner looks on.

With Jetsun Pemala, the sister of the
Dalai Lama, in Dharamsala in 1981

With Rinchen Drolma Taring, one of Tsarong's
three wives, in Dehra Dun in 1990

Drinking millet beer with Hermann Beilhack and Alois Anwander in Sikkim
in 1990

and ran to embrace me with tears in her eyes. It was Dekyila, the wife of Cabinet Minister Surkhang. I had last seen them both ten years ago to the day in Lhasa, when she joined my caravan with her baby daughter and nurse. An over-zealous Secret Service official separated us; rather too energetically, I felt.

Prime Minister Nehru's address was extremely cordial. It was with pleasure that he welcomed the Dalai Lama, his family and entourage to India, he said. This welcome speech came as a great relief to the Dalai Lama, since in 1956, Nehru had refused to let him stay. In the meantime, enough had happened for Nehru to recognise the true face of the Chinese government. Forty years have passed since Nehru spoke those words of friendship and the hospitality extended to the Dalai Lama by India, the largest democracy in the world, continues undiminished.

My task was to sketch in the details of the final few days before the escape. It was not difficult, as the mother of the Dalai Lama gave me all the information I needed. Next to the Holy Mother sat Ngari Rinpoche, the youngest brother of the Dalai Lama, whom I had photographed on the roof of his parents' house in Lhasa as a chubby cheeked young child. He was now thirteen years old and expanded enthusiastically on his mother's account of that exciting night when they had left Lhasa in a sand storm, and their subsequent four week journey of escape over the snowy Himalayan Mountains to India. I received further information from the commanding officer of the Tibetan troops, Kunsangtse Dzasa. He was the younger brother of my former superior at the Tibetan Foreign Office, Surkhang Dzasa.

Sarah Churchill paid three times the standard rate to send a telegram to London. The cost was immaterial, as the *Daily Mail* now held the worldwide rights to the "Story of the Year." *Life* magazine published its own front page story on 4th May, 1959 under the headline "Miraculous Escape", almost eight years to the day since my report, "Flight of the Dalai Lama" had made the front cover.

At the little station in Tezpur, a special train laid on by the Assam Railway Company was ready for departure. On a portable tape recorder, I recorded the affectionate reactions of the many people who had gathered to bid their God-King farewell. The Tibetans offered lucky white *katas* while the Indians shouted "Dalai Lama sinda bad!" – "Long live the Dalai Lama!" My recording ended with the sound of the steam locomotive pulling away. It was my first radio recording and was broadcast in all the German-speaking countries.

The final destination of the special train, after a journey of three thousand kilometres across India, was Dehra Dun of all places. Fifteen years to the day, my own journey of escape had begun at that very place. I had escaped the barbed wire; now, the Dalai Lama was to spend some time behind it, as his place of residence, in the hill station of Mussoorie, situated at two thousand metres, a little way up from Dehra Dun, had been fenced in for security reasons.

The rich industrialist and merchant prince, Ghanshyam Das Birla, had placed his country residence at Mussoorie at the disposal of the Dalai Lama. All the hotels were full of international journalists and all were being watched by the Secret Police. A few days later I met the Holy Mother. She was out for a walk with her eldest daughter, Tsering Drolma, and Rinchen Drolma Taring, who spoke excellent English and was acting as her interpreter. Rinchen Drolma Taring's daughter, Tsering Yangtsom, better known by her school name Betyla, regularly read the news in Tibetan on Indian radio. It was from one of her broadcasts that we learned that many Tibetans had lost their lives after the Dalai Lama left and that the Chagpori School of Medicine had been destroyed.

Soon after meeting the Dalai Lama's mother, I was called to the Birla house to see her son. From the balcony of the house we could see the ice-capped peaks of the Garhwal Himalaya and his homeland of Tibet, barely one hundred kilometres distant. We chatted about inconsequential matters; now was not the time to discuss past mistakes or future plans. The fact that he had escaped with his life and was now in a place of safety was reason enough to be thankful. There are many ways of expressing gratitude in the Tibetan language. Perhaps "gun chog sum" would be the appropriate phrase to use in this instance.

The Dalai Lama spent a troubled year in Mussoorie, while another garrison town, Dharamsala, was being prepared as his place of exile. There was more room at Dharamsala and this has been his home and the seat of the Tibetan government in exile ever since. I visited the

Dalai Lama whenever my travels took me to the region, and it became something of a regular habit to meet him there at least once a year.

Before I returned to Europe, I paid a visit to my old POW camp with Hilmar Pabel, the well-known German photographer. The barracks were now occupied by the families of the Indian soldiers, there was no barbed wire and we strolled across the football pitch to the hut where we had donned our clothes and make up prior to our escape. A retired Gurkha soldier, one of the old prison guards, was conducting sightseeing tours of the camp for the many curious visitors. Pabel took lots of photographs, including one of a small papaya tree laden with large fruit, which I had grown from seed all those years ago.

CARSTENSZ PYRAMID AND
THE FALL IN A NEW GUINEA WATERFALL

In the summer of 1937 – I was training in the Dolomites in preparation for the North Face of the Eiger – I heard for the first time about a Dutch expedition which had just penetrated into the interior of New Guinea, where they had attempted to climb the 5,030 metre Carstensz Pyramid. I already knew that in Africa and South America there were snow- and glacier-covered mountains near the Equator, but I found it difficult to believe that there was anything of the sort on an island in the Pacific. The Dutch had taken measurements on the glacier itself, but the summit of the highest peak in New Guinea, the Carstensz Pyramid, remained unclimbed.

After hearing about the Dutch expedition I was very keen to attempt the Pyramid, but it was in the spring of 1961, when I read that an expedition from New Zealand had also failed to make the first ascent, that I finally made up my mind to go to the Pacific. As a child I had been fascinated by the Papuans and in New Guinea, the second largest island in the world, I would certainly be able to visit the Mountain Papuans, who still live the lives of our remote forefathers in Stone Age times. Without further ado, I drove to The Hague to apply for an expedition permit.

My first port of call was the Austrian Embassy. I had hardly explained my request when the Ambassador pressed a button on his telephone and spoke into the loudspeaker. "Are your children coming swimming with us this afternoon?" he asked. "Can I call by and introduce you to this Austrian chap? You have read his book." On the other end of the line was the Dutch Foreign Minister.

Normally it takes just as much time to organise an expedition as it does to conduct one. Not this time. I was told I had to pay a rescue bond of five thousand guilders and a medical certificate that confirmed I was not suffering from any illnesses, in particular malaria. This was to protect the Mountain Papuans. At the Museum of Tropical Ethnography, I was shown various interesting exhibits and also the

New Zealand expedition report, which talked about the problems they had had with provisions and explained how they had only managed to stay alive by eating roots and leaves. That was not something that worried me unduly.

In October of the same year, I went with the Kitzbühel Golf Club, of which I had recently been elected captain, and my wife Carina, to the exclusive Greenwich Country Club, north of New York, to play a return match. Before my departure from Munich Airport, Lufthansa had arranged a press conference. My plan for the New Guinea expedition seemed to interest the assembled journalists. My aim was to journey to an unexplored part of an island where about two hundred thousand people live, people who go to sleep when night falls, drink water from streams in their cupped hands, have never seen through a pane of glass, and who regard a knife made of bamboo and an axe made of stone as the last word in technical equipment. It was certainly worth a few lines in the newspapers.

From New York I travelled on alone. It was the start of an expedition that was to present me with greater challenges and harsher conditions than any I had ever imagined. The jungle was more impenetrable, the rivers more violent and my encounters with the natives more unpredictable than anywhere else. The laws of nature seemed to have been turned on their heads and underestimating them landed me several times in situations from which I was barely able to escape with my life.

I took a plane from New York and flew to the Hawaiian Islands, where, as a passionate skier, I fulfilled a long-felt desire to ride on the ocean waves. Keeping my balance whilst standing upright on the surfboard was something I managed immediately, but as a redhead I got badly sunburned whilst paddling out on the board and that put an end to what was otherwise a nice sport and a pleasant interlude. I left my Hawaiian paradise to visit another – Tahiti.

In Tahiti I began my immediate preparations for the New Guinea expedition. First, I collected my currency, or rather the currency of the Mountain Papuans. It was not available from any Bureau de Change but on the beaches of Tahiti there was a plentiful supply. I collected

cowrie shells. I left Tahiti a rich man and flew to New Zealand. I wanted to visit Sir Edmund Hillary and also intended to make contact with the Americans in Christchurch. It was shortly before Christmas and during the long hours of daylight, a plane was making supply flights to the American Antarctic research base four thousand kilometres away at McMurdo Sound. I was an honorary member of the New York Explorers' Club, who had given me a letter of recommendation, and it was my intention to sound out the possibility of organising an expedition to Antarctica the following year, with the aim of making the first ascent of the 5,140 m Mount Vinson, the highest peak in Antarctica. Unfortunately, thinking about it was as far as I got, as I was kept busy with other projects. While I was in New Zealand, Hillary and I made a brief excursion to see the 3,764 m Mount Cook.

I spent Christmas in Sydney with my friend Colin Putt. Colin was a well known ocean-going yachtsman and showed me the detailed plans he had drafted to build a catamaran from two dugout canoes. The Indonesian government was propagating the idea of "liberating" the Papuans in Western New Guinea from the Dutch and in the event of a war, it was my intention to sail Colin's boat across the Arafura Sea to Port Darwin in Australia. President Sukarno received support for his neo-colonialist ambitions from the brother of the American President, Edward Kennedy, who made a speech in Jakarta, during which he called for "merdeka", or "independence", for the Papuans.

My time in Sydney was filled with interesting events. While I was there I had to talk about my Eiger and Tibet experiences, too, of course, as was so often the case when I travelled. In New Zealand I had delivered a lecture to the Alpine Club of Christchurch; in Australia it was the Bushwalkers, an organisation similar to the Scouts, who invited me to talk to their club members. I had already been out in the bush with them on some long hikes, where I kept seeing big black mambas, several metres in length, slithering off into the undergrowth as we walked by. My concerns about these venomous snakes were allayed somewhat by the remarks of my companions, who assured me that in Australia it was completely normal to encounter them, an opinion that was confirmed by several other people I met. But I still declined their invitation to go down to the coast with them, since I had read that a man in Perth had been bitten by a sea snake whilst swimming. It must have been a particularly poisonous variety, as the poor man died before help arrived. The Sydney newspapers carried daily front page reports on the condition of a young woman, who had had her leg bitten off by a shark. It was obvious that the old pioneering spirit was still alive in the young men of the Bushwalkers Club, judging by the way they played down such dangers.

All the while, I was being badgered by journalists for interviews. I wondered why I was so well known, until one of them told me that there was hardly a family in Australia that did not own a copy of the Eiger or the Tibet book. It was then that I remembered that, one year after the publication of the English edition of *Seven Years in Tibet*, I had signed a contract with an international publisher's that supplied mainly the Commonwealth nations. A press team drove me down to the south coast sea cliffs to take photographs. It was the most beautiful and rugged rock climbing area I had ever seen. A line of plumb vertical one hundred metre cliffs, sculpted by the wind and the water, offered adventurous routes of all levels of difficulty, while the ocean waves beat against their base.

Before I set off on my expedition I drove to the new capital of Canberra, a boring, test tube city, to pay a courtesy visit to the Austrian ambassador, Otto von Eiselsberg, who was also responsible for New Guinea. Von Eiselsberg was the son of a famous Viennese surgeon. He was pleased to see me and offered to help in any way he could. True to his word, when I sent him a telegram during the expedition requesting fresh supplies of cowrie shells, he did just that. In fact, Eiselsberg forwarded my request to the press, whereupon a Sydney newspaper ran a front page story under the title "Shell out for Harrer". The result was a veritable flood of parcels delivered to the Embassy. However, it must be said that some of the offers came from shell collectors with rare specimens for sale at prices of up to fifty dollars a shell.

I had left Europe without a climbing partner, but in New Zealand I found a volunteer at once in young Phil Temple, who already had some experience of New Guinea. The third member of the team was the Bushwalker and medical student, Russell Kippax. The final member, a young Dutch army officer called Bert Huizenga, joined us in the New Guinea capital Hollandia. I suggested to Bert that he take footwear and clothing suitable for cold days on the mountain, thinking it was only fair that a Dutchman should be one of the team that made the first ascent of The Netherlands's highest peak. I was twice as old as my three companions, so there was no doubt about who was in charge. The only note of caution came from the government, who feared an attack by Indonesia. My young partners were reassured when I opened one of the bags containing the sailing tackle, sail needles, stout thread, rope and so on. I had also packed two climbing ropes, a ten by ten section of plastic sheeting that could be used as either roofing material or as a sail, and the obligatory medical kit and film. On the New Guinea expedition I was still doing my own filming. The four of us were soon packed and ready to go.

For me, familiarising myself with the local language is an important part of the preparations for any expedition. Before leaving home, I would look up the most important expressions and phrases and make a note them on the first few pages of my expedition diary. I always learned the words for the four elements – fire, water, air and earth

– as well as wood, weather terminology, time and numbers. To these I added the words for local foodstuffs – in the case of the Papuans, this was mainly "pataten", or sweet potatoes – and typical local dishes. I was interested only in the colloquial terms, since it was these I would need most. Then there was the obligatory visit to the embassy or consulate of the country in question. Later, when I was in the country, I would usually engage the services of an interpreter familiar with the local dialect and tribal customs, who would stay with the expedition and help with any linguistic or cultural problems that might arise. We did not get very far with my method in New Guinea, however, since there were hundreds of different dialects. In order to address the problem of flying in supplies, I had sought the advice of the FMA in Philadelphia, a well-organised company that specialised in making air drops to remote missionary stations.

We were happy to be leaving Hollandia, since Sukarno's threat to invade New Guinea was hotting up. No fewer than sixty journalists had arrived in the capital and were falling over each other in the two small hotels the Dutch government ran there. The two Missionary Aviation Fellowship pilots had been well briefed on our expedition and there was no need for any further discussion about price or logistics. We knew that the Dani tribe of West Papua, whom we intended to employ as porters to ferry our equipment into the mountains, existed on a diet that consisted almost exclusively of sweet potatoes and a type of green spinach. We had to budget about four kilos of these *pataten* per person per day and since a porter load could not exceed twenty-five kilos this meant that we had to engage a number of additional "*pataten* porters" to carry food for the equipment porters. Nor was it possible to establish food dumps on the approach march to Carstensz, since the daily rain would have made the potatoes rotten and inedible.

Finally, we struck camp and set off, together with more than a hundred Dani porters, male and female. When we arrived at Base Camp we paid off all but ten of the porters and sent them back to their villages. The ten remaining Dani were issued with military surplus clothing, which caused great amusement as usually the only article of clothing the men wear is a penis sheath made of a pumpkin-like fruit. Each of them has his own bespoke model – small, large, straight or bent. The rest of the expedition food was flown in and dropped near Base Camp. I had made sure the rice was double bagged. The inner sack split on impact but the precious rice was contained within the outer bag. All of the essential tasks, and the supply drops in particular, had to be completed during the morning, as midday brought the inevitable heavy rain. This was also responsible for the sharp formations in the limestone rock. To protect our fingers when climbing, I had brought a pair of tough work gloves for each expedition member. We chose the easiest route up the thousand metre cliff, which is standard mountaineering practice on first ascents.

On 13th February 1962, four climbers from four different countries left their national flags, and a note in a yellow cigarette tin, on the summit of the 5,030 metre Carstensz Pyramid, more than three hundred years after the Dutchman Jan Carstensz had first seen it. As a good omen, we also added the new "morning star" flag of West Papua as a symbol of independence, although the United States forced the Netherlands to surrender West New Guinea to Indonesia in 1962, since when a truly free and independent West Papua has remained a dream.

Huizenga had to return to his job as Patrol Officer and Kippax wanted to go back and finish his medical studies, leaving Phil Temple and I to do some more climbing. Together we climbed several smaller peaks in the range, including the second highest peak on the island, the Idenburg Top, all of which were first ascents. We also discovered valleys, glaciers and lakes, which we named in accordance with natural topographical features or local custom – an old principle of mine. The Papuans use the evocative word "dugundugu" to describe ice, a phenomenon they had previously only seen from a distance and which they now greeted with dances of joy.

I knew that the 1936 Dutch expedition had built a series of cairns at the end of the large glacier. We found them covered in moss but in good condition still. Yellow Cymbidium orchids grew on the moraines nearby, the stems of which were used by the Dani men to make little purses in which to carry their cowrie shells, while the women used them to fashion the "uleri" that they wore to cover their pubic region.

Searching for a treasure trove of gold could not have been more exciting than breaking open the Dutch cairns. Inside, we found an old tin box. The papers it contained were badly rust-stained and barely legible, although we could clearly make out the signature of the expedition's geologist Jean Jacques Dozy. Deeper down, we discovered another box, this time made of zinc, which held the expedition's commemorative book. This had remained completely unscathed. I later presented this treasure to the Dutch government, who placed it in the Tropical Museum. As a geographer, I then took precise measurements of the movement of the glacier. Even at first glance, I knew the numbers would be sensational. It transpired that the glacier had actually retreated 452 metres in the twenty-six years since the Dutch expedition. After building new cairns to mark the present position of the snout of the glacier and depositing a note of my observations in a waterproof box, we left the valley contented with our work. Carstensz is an unusual mountain in an unusual region and offers ample scope for future exploration. I also feel sure that the day will come when the Dani will also climb Carstensz Pyramid; not as porters but, like the Sherpas, as mountaineers.

For the second phase of my expedition, I planned to do some research on the ethnography of the Papuans, while the third and final stage would be a north-south traverse of New Guinea, a feat no one had yet accomplished. First of all, however, I visited a salt spring. I had established that, in addition to using cowrie shells as a method of payment, the Papuans also traded in salt, a coveted but very rare commodity. One of the tribal chiefs, in whose region there was a meagre spring that contained salt, had something of a monopoly. The large leaves of the wild banana were soaked in the saline solution and then left to dry in the sun. Once dry, they were burnt and the ash traded as salt.

I enjoyed the peace and tranquillity at the salt spring, and the friendly hospitality of the Papuans. The whole village sat quietly before my tent and admired my equipment. The men carried stone axes over their shoulders made from a unique blue and green stone, a sign of quality and status. For weeks now I had been wondering where they got this unusually hard stone, as the only quarries I knew of that produced slate axes were in the eastern part of New Guinea.

It was while I was at the salt spring that I finally received some information about the mysterious source of the stone axes. I learned from the chief that the remote Wano tribe were the only people who traded in the stone used to make them. He also told me that the Wano were very bad and dangerous people, but that they traded fairly. In the mountains, halfway between two tribal territories, there was a clearing in the jungle. Here they would leave slabs of salt wrapped in leaves and tied with raffia. They would then withdraw to a safe distance and call to the Wano. If the quality of the salt was acceptable to the Wano, they would replace it with stone axe heads. If they were dissatisfied, the haggling would continue, but this was only ever done by shouting, never face to face. The axe heads were rough hewn and would be taken back to the village to be ground and finished. I now had the name of the tribe and the name of the village where the axe heads were made. It was called "Ya-Li-Me", or Jalime, which translates as "source of the stone axes". It was a mystery to me why no previous expedition had ever attempted to locate this place.

One thing I had learned here was that it takes time to implement one's plans, however carefully they are made. Phil Temple had the patience required, and together we started looking for Dani porters who were willing to accompany us to the fearsome Wano tribe. The offer of double wages and the promise to protect them from the Wano did the trick and we set off on the tortuous path to Jalime. In the no-man's land north of Mulia we froze as we crossed the three to four thousand metre ridges and baked in the tropical heat during the numerous river crossings. The mysterious quarry in the Wano territory could only be a few more days away, we reckoned.

Early one afternoon we once more heard the familiar sound of a waterfall ahead. I quickened my pace because I wanted to get there before the others and film it. Suddenly, there it was. Masses of water plunged into the depths in powerful cataracts, hurtling onto rock terraces and sending clouds of spray up to the tops of the trees, continuing its way down, sweeping thunderously through narrow gullies in the rock, and shooting out in a great sheaf of water beyond – a tremendous sight. And dangerous as well, but I noted this only incidentally. At the time

I was interested only in filming it.

First of all I directed my camera towards the porters making their way up by the side of the fall. Then I clambered past them, still keeping very close to the tumultuous mass of water, to film the next group of porters from above as they made their way up. It was then that I discovered an even better vantage point. It was a pile of rubble right on the edge of the falls. Without hesitation I jumped for it. It was at this point that the disaster occurred. The moment I landed on the heap of rubble it slid away from under me and I found myself in the water. Later on Phil told me that the heap had collected on a piece of slate without any firm foundation. To have thrown a stone at it would probably have been enough to set it in motion. And I had jumped on it with all my weight!

At first I was still in possession of all my senses, and I tried desperately to find something to cling to, whilst at the same time bracing myself on the bottom with my feet so that the water could not sweep me away. Today I know that any such attempt was ridiculous: the water rushed against my body with incredible force, and the rocks under my feet had been worn smooth and were very slimy. I hadn't a chance – at least, not here. The water picked me up and swept me on. For a moment, head first, I looked into the depths, and then I closed my eyes. In such situations there is nothing else to be done. Nature takes no notice of any attempts to resist.

When and where I let go of my camera I do not know. From that moment, when I saw the abyss before my eyes, I had no sense of time. Water, gasping for air, a dull blow, more water, more gasping for breath... I can not even remember the order any more. The porters told me later that I brushed against a jutting rock over which the water was shooting, before falling in the next cataract. If I had struck that rock full on I would have been hurled over the fall on to the smooth, almost vertical slab that ended some fifty metres further down. I am under no illusions what that fall would have meant.

Seconds, hours, eternities? I do not know any more. All I can clearly remember is the feeling of absolute helplessness that suddenly gripped me. I tried to protect my head with my arms and instinctively rolled up into the foetal position, which prevented me getting any internal injuries. Although I was only half conscious by this time, I was still thinking clearly. Contrary to what people say, my whole life did not pass before my eyes, but I do remember thinking that this must be how many accomplished mountaineers have met their deaths, in a single stupid slip. I can only imagine how the passengers in an aeroplane must feel in those final few minutes before a crash when they have time to think about dying.

I seemed like a miracle when my helter-skelter rush into the depths suddenly ceased. I could not see anything because blood was pouring down from a head wound into my eyes. I groped around, trying to establish my whereabouts. I had enough sense to realise that I must not try to work my way out of the water at the edge of this natural pool where it led over the next fall, since the cascade plunged down three times as far as before and ended on a slab of rock against which a human body would simply have been smashed to a pulp.

I still could not breathe properly, and I heard myself groaning. In the distance, I thought I could hear the porters shouting something like "Tuan! Tuan!" That brought me my first ray of hope. At least they realised what had happened to me. And Phil – good old Phil – would soon be there, of that I felt sure.

In between clawing at the rocks I desperately kept trying to wipe the blood out of my eyes so that I could at least see. I must have lost a great deal of blood because the whole pool had an ugly reddish tinge. I clung to my rock and waited. Above, below and all around me the waterfall gushed and roared. And then – I do not know how much time passed in between – I heard Phil's voice. He had our medicine chest with him. He bedded me down on the rock as well as he could and administered first aid like an experienced doctor. Not that there was very much he could do for me. He disinfected my head wound, cut away hanging strips of skin and bandaged me up. Only then did he enquire about my general condition, which was very poor. I did not know which way to lie; my whole body hurt. Presently, the effect of shock began to make itself felt. I was groaning and trembling all over. My teeth were chattering, not because I was cold, but because the delayed shock reaction was shaking me to the core. Now and again I felt dark waves of unconsciousness welling up inside me, but I exerted all my will power to remain conscious. I had the feeling that if I lost consciousness I would never wake up again. Phil had sat me up to examine me, but now I asked him to help me to some place where I could lie down and conserve my strength. With his help I crawled along the edge of the pool to the opposite bank. As I dragged myself laboriously along, I realised at every movement that it was not only my head I had injured. I still had difficulty breathing, which indicated broken ribs, and every time I bent my left knee, it felt as though a steel spike was stabbing into it. I could hardly use my right arm at all. I estimated that I had fallen about twenty metres but after their expedition thirty years later, the Eder brothers told me they had measured the drop at twice that height.

I continued to crawl downwards, and Phil helped me as best he could. With touching diligence, the porters removed everything from my path, but every metre of the way was sheer torture. Finally Phil found a place by a little stream which was big enough to pitch a tent. I crouched there in misery and watched him at work. When the tent was up he helped me take off my dripping clothes and bedded me down on our inflatable mattress. I still had the feeling that I was living behind a mist veil. This was partly due to the shock of my fall and partly to the powerful tablets that Phil had given me to ease the pain.

I lay in the tent in a sort of semi-conscious trance. I could hardly move my legs, so Phil pulled my sleeping bag over my feet. Presently, I felt another wave of unconsciousness welling up in me. I had never experienced unconsciousness in my life before, but now the combination of the tablets, the shock and the severe loss of blood were conspiring against me. Grimly I fought against that unpleasant feeling of vertigo and pain. Once again I succeeded, and the wave died away. As I lay there staring at the roof of the tent, my thoughts began to whirr. I thought about Jalime, the "source of the stone axes". I remembered that was where I wanted go; I still did. I had to. Then the idea occurred to me that I might die, that I might lose consciousness and never recover it – just slip over the threshold into death. Then I thought about the missionaries in Mulia. Only a few days ago they had prayed for me. Had their prayers helped? Had they perhaps saved me from an even worse fate? After all, I was still alive, and where there is life there is hope. And then, of course, the question arose in my mind: when did I last pray? A prayer of thankfulness perhaps? Or a prayer in extreme danger? My memories were unclear and faded before I could come up with an answer. Once again I felt a wave of unconsciousness creeping over me, and once again my will to live kept me awake. Just stay awake!

As soon as he had examined me and realised that it would not be possible to transport me, Phil had sent two porters off with a message to the mission in Mulia. Help arrived sooner than we had dared hope. Although Phil had proved to be a wonderful companion, I was still relieved when the young missionary, Scovill, suddenly appeared in the doorway of the tent, out of breath and accompanied by Dr van Rhjin from the medical research station, a full day before we expected them. It was quite amazing that they had managed to cover the distance in such a short time. After all, neither of them was trained for such an ordeal, and it was so hot down there in the Jamu Valley that even the porters, who rarely drank anything, immediately rushed to the stream.

Scovill and Dr van Rhijn had brought a folding stretcher with them and after a thorough examination Dr van Rhjin decided that I should be evacuated at once. My heart and lungs seemed to be in order, and he strapped up my broken ribs there and then.

What then followed, as I experience it again in retrospect, was an absolute nightmare. When the path went uphill, I slipped back on the stretcher until my head touched the knees of the rear stretcher bearer, and when we went downwards, I slid forward so that my feet rested on the shoulders of the foremost bearer. And when we finally reached level ground, the way was hampered by the inevitable fallen tree trunks. The little Papuans had to raise me up over them, but as my injured spine was the lowest part of me, they invariably scraped it against the trunk as they lifted the stretcher over. And if it was not a tree trunk, then it was a rock that had to be negotiated. I lay there helplessly and endured it all, groaning and cursing under my breath.

Just as I thought the pain could not possibly get any worse, the Dani came up with a solution. First they cut a stout pole, from which they suspended the stretcher. Then they wrapped me tightly in the cloth of the stretcher and tied me in so that I could not slip, either forwards or sideways. They then proceeded to carry me as they would a live pig from village to village.

More tablets helped me get through the following hours; or perhaps I was too exhausted to feel the pain so acutely. And the Papuan method of transporting an injured man seemed to be working. The pole, the ropes and my body formed a single unit and I no longer slid around painfully at every jolt. The fact is that our own form of stretcher is not really designed for jungle conditions or steep paths.

Nothing was too much trouble for our porters. The bush telegraph had spread the news of my accident far and wide, and at least a hundred Papuans had arrived to help. There was always one group of them ahead clearing the path with machetes, removing obstacles and building crossings out of tree trunks at a tremendous speed. There were always about twenty of them trotting along with me and willing to render assistance. Now that they had been allowed to do things their way, they were obviously anxious to show the Tuans a thing or two. Every few minutes the bearers changed and new men took over with renewed energy. Whether we were going uphill or down, the chain of porters was always there; everyone was ready to lend a helping hand, everyone did his best to make my situation as easy as possible.

But even the Papuan stretcher method did not work perfectly for long. The ropes began to work loose, my whole body began to sag, and before long my poor ribs were banging against rocks and fallen tree trunks as before. Desperately I clung to the pole with both hands, my arms bound inside the ropes. I could hardly see anything – only the pole and an occasional glimpse of the sky between the tree-tops – as I waited anxiously for the next jolt. When it was late in coming I praised the bearers: "Op, op!" for those who spoke the Mulia dialect, "Pano!" for those who understood only the Bokondini language. Both words mean more or less "Good, good!"

It had been raining steadily since midday and the river was very swollen. Even the Danis were doubtful about attempting a crossing, so Phil organised a human chain and with linked arms they stood across the river to break the force of the current whilst my bearers carried me across below the chain. The river crossing was the worst part for me, and for the first time since my fall into the waterfall I was scared, for now I was not only in danger but absolutely helpless, too. My arms and legs were firmly tied, there were ropes around my whole body and I was attached to a pole. It was a horrible feeling indeed, knowing that at any moment the bearers might panic in the strong current.

But they did not panic; they stuck it out, those brave chaps – although they could see how violently the current was surging against my body and although more than one of them lost his footing. Their faces were hard and determined, and they even marched a good way down stream on the pebbles in the centre of the now much broader riverbed. The water was a great relief for my poor injured back; it made a change from grating against tree trunks and rocks.

No sooner had we crossed the river than it began to grow dark, and now my bearers accelerated their pace to such a tempo that the Tuans, Scovill, van Rhjin and Phil could hardly keep up with them, even without loads. The Dani obviously wanted to reach the nearest village that evening at all costs. When we got there, they just put me down in the pouring rain and left everything else to the Tuans.

Whilst Phil pitched the tent, Scovill and van Rhjin made soup for the four of us. As a special bonus there was a glass of cognac for each of us, from the supply the doctor had brought with him. Soon all was silent, and everyone slept. With the help of the tablets, even I nodded off, but I kept waking up and finally I just lay there listening to the gushing of the nearby stream. At daybreak I was feeling pretty wretched, but I told myself that it would not be long now before we reached Mulia, and this kept my spirits up.

I was trussed up "Dani fashion" once more and when everything was ready we set off. It was our last day and the stretcher-bearers treated me with the utmost caution. I actually think Scovill had read them the riot act last night and told them how much pain I was in. Fortunately there were now only short stretches through the jungle so that at least I did not have to suffer so many tree trunks. However, when we came to the village boundary, I had to be manhandled over fences that were over a metre in height. Finally, early in the afternoon, Mulia lay beneath us bathed in bright sunshine – Mulia, the small mission station we had set off from so hopefully only a few days previously.

In spite of the seriousness of my condition, I could not help seeing the funny side of our entry into the village. I became aware of a strange pushing and shoving going on around my pole. I turned my head to one side as best I could and saw what was causing it. Every man in my escort, which had now grown to around two hundred, wanted to take hold of the pole to show everyone in the village that he had done his share of the carrying, too, whilst the actual bearers now proceeded with almost indescribable enthusiasm, running as if they had only just started the job and clambering over the wall around the airfield at Mulia until Dr van Rhijn was at last able to give the signal for them to lower me gently to the ground. The long ordeal was over.

But I was not out of the woods yet. Now we were in Mulia, the tremendous tension relaxed and my remaining strength started to ebb fast. I was aware that the moment was dangerous and I fought against my weakness. I remembered Hias Noichl. He had smashed his hand on the North Face of the Eiger and had managed a descent which would have been a fine performance for a man with two uninjured hands. But then in the comfortable seat of my car on the way to hospital, he had lost consciousness. Once again I managed to remain conscious, but now, after hours and hours of being patient, I almost panicked because it seemed to take such a long time to release me from the cords that bound me. I felt that I was going to suffocate – right then and there, at the last moment. And when I was finally freed from my mummy-like cocoon, I was quite convinced that I could not have survived another hour in that close constriction.

But I must praise my helpful bearers all the same. After all, they had had to carry me, the pole and the whole stretcher contraption, something like a hundred kilos in all, up hill and down dale, through pathless jungle and across rivers and streams. And they had done it at a speed a European would have found great difficulty in emulating, even with a light pack. Of course, for their childlike temperament, it had been a sort of circus, and a welcome opportunity to show off their strength and skill to the Tuans. The white man with his civilising ways had made their lives monotonous. As born warriors they had once been accustomed to using bows and arrows and spears, either to attack other tribes or to go hunting. And now they had at last been given the opportunity of showing what they were capable of. My accident will undoubtedly remain in their minds as the happiest incident of the whole expedition.

In Mulia I was already beginning to wonder whether it might be possible to organise a second expedition to Ya-Li-Me, since I thought the Danis would probably interpret my accident as a warning sign from the Gods who protect the quarry from interlopers. After all, the flat, elongated stones used for ceremonial and magical purposes in the Long Houses, in which the Papuans hold their orgies, also come from this quarry. Those stones represent a sort of phallic and fertility rite symbol. On the other hand, we certainly succeeded in establishing friendly relations with the Danis, just as we had done on the Carstensz expedition, so perhaps we might be able to count on the "Old Guard" to come with us again after all.

I spent the night in Dr van Rhjin's house in Mulia, where a room had been prepared for Phil and me. There was a good deal of conversation that evening, and a Professor from Leyden gave me another thorough examination. Pulse and blood pressure proved to be normal, my broken ribs were well plastered up and there were more tablets for the pain. For the first time we heard something about a new invasion by Sukarno's troops; the situation was said to be serious. The nurse then gave me an injection to make me sleep and I went off gently.

But it did not last long, and at two o'clock in the morning I was wide awake again. I felt around for pills but there were none within reach, so I had to wake up Phil. The poor man had had a lot to put up with these last few days. In my sleep I was still jolting against tree trunks and groaning out loud.

The next morning I was taken by plane to Hollandia, where I spent the following few weeks in hospital. On the drive into town we stopped at the post office and I was able to send a telegram home. I hoped that it would arrive before the press reported the accident.

The sum total of my injuries came as quite a shock. I had four badly fractured ribs and a broken kneecap. My head wound was stitched, while the various cuts and grazes were left to heal of their own accord. Back in Austria, I was assessed and certified as having a sixty percent disability, whereupon my health insurance company cancelled the contract. The new insurers quoted a premium of five hundred Swiss francs per expedition day. Years later various doctors discovered further injuries that were attributable to my fall and it was only after several operations on my ribcage that I was finally restored to health.

BACK TO THE STONE AGE

There were about forty bored journalists in Hollandia waiting for the imminent Indonesian invasion, so my accident, and my expedition to the stone axe quarry and the Wano tribe, aroused great interest. I began my preparations as soon as I was discharged from hospital. I was still determined to look for the source of the axes, the Ya-Li-Me, since I instinctively knew that I could not allow any hesitation or doubt to creep in after my accident. I was driven by ambition to make haste, as I had no intention of allowing anyone else to profit from my ideas.

The porters no longer wished to accompany me; they were convinced that demons had cast me into the waterfall to prevent me, a stranger, from finding the source of the stone axes. However, Phil came up with the idea of recruiting new porters from another village and presently we set off again, this time with seven Papuans and our baggage reduced to the absolute minimum. For the next few days we retraced our steps, passing through the same villages as before and changing porters when necessary. Two Dani women accompanied us for part of the way and when they saw the pain that my injured knee was causing me, they took pity on me. They picked nettle leaves and rubbed my bad leg with them until the skin was red and inflamed and blisters began to form. My right shoulder was sore, too, so I split one of the Dani battle spears in two and used it as a walking stick. It poured with rain every afternoon and it was only the fierce will to succeed in my search for the quarry that kept me going through all the hardships of the trip. The doctor had recommended that I "take exercise" and the new expedition seemed like as good a way as any of doing just that, although this daily grind was probably a bit too much physiotherapy.

I felt a deep sense of gratitude to be making my way along the same paths I was carried over, half conscious, just a few weeks before. I knew every rock, every swinging liana bridge, every bivouac cave. We took the same path we had used on the first expedition. Everyone was in good spirits and despite their loads the porters soon took up their rhythmic "Wa-wa-wa!" chant. But when we came to my near-nemesis, the waterfall, they suddenly fell silent and hurried past me without pausing. For the Papuans, the evil demons were ever-present; they believed that the trees, the rocks and the waterfall could speak to them and that any act of desecration, any profanity or sacrilege, would be severely punished.

I sat down on the rocks – the same rocks I had lain on half-conscious seven weeks previously – and lost myself in my thoughts. It was raining again, but that was attributable to the local weather conditions here at the Equator, and my soaking wet clothes were nothing compared to the ordeal I had previously suffered at this place. I had no cause for complaint. Nor did I ever consider that I should perhaps start taking things a little easier; instead, I considered what I had done wrong. My biggest mistake had been my failure to equip the expedition members with the correct footwear for the job. Had I been wearing nailed boots like on the Eigerwand, I would never have slipped on the pile of rubble when I jumped over the torrent of water. Analysis complete, I took hold of my spear and hobbled after the porters. The guardian angels had emerged victorious over the evil spirits here after all, I concluded with a smile.

I caught up with the team at the base of a steep cliff, where the Papuans were fashioning a rope ladder from liana vines. We were now entering uncharted territory, and on pathless terrain, in the densest jungle in the world, more impenetrable even than the Amazon or African jungles. I crossed one river by straddling a fallen tree trunk, whilst our Danis, light-footed and elegant as usual, just danced across it.

It was tough going and demanded all our strength and endurance, but we made good progress. We scrambled up to the crest of a ridge, hoping to catch a distant glimpse of Mount Idenburg to the north, but the view was obstructed by enormous, lichen-covered oak trees and rhododendrons. At least there were no more dangerous waterfalls ahead of us, and the caves we came across were dry and suitable for making camps.

Suddenly the Danis stopped, whispered to each other and pointed to a cluster of small, round huts with roofs thatched with reeds. Slowly and cautiously, Phil and I approached the little Wano settlement, announcing our presence with a friendly shout. It was a rather disagreeable feeling, not knowing whether we would be greeted with a shower of arrows, or a cheerful babble of welcome. But as we approached the first of the huts, there wasn't a soul to be seen, and the village looked quite deserted. Then we spotted them: about thirty or forty men crouched together and staring at us silently. I did not feel too happy at the sight of their black painted faces and their forbidding headdresses made of animal skins. The women and children were crouching beside them, just as silent and motionless, but with their faces averted.

Phil gave the men tobacco, whilst I distributed salt and colourful glass beads amongst the women and children. It took several hours before trust was established and we were given permission to pitch our tent. We erected a large tarpaulin between two pandanus trees, thinking it safer to sleep under it rather than in the close confines of the tent, as we had heard of several instances when tents had been collapsed and their helpless occupants clubbed to death by robbers during the night.

The next day dawned fine and after a lengthy period of haggling, we managed to buy a pig from our hosts. Our porters dug a fire pit and started to heat stones for cooking. The pig put up a desperate struggle before being brutally slaughtered with a bow and arrow and hacked into pieces. These were then wrapped in *pataten* leaves and placed in the fire pit. The "hog roast" restored the porters' spirits and after we had all eaten I spoke to the chief of the Wano about my desire to visit Jalime. He instructed several of the Wano to accompany us. They led us through a field of sugar cane to a river we had crossed several times already and stopped at a cluster of boulders. This, they said, was Ya-Li-Me.

To my surprise it did not look much like a quarry, but when I thought about it, the Papuans had never said anything about a quarry; they had only ever referred to this place as "the source of the stone axes". It was certainly a more romantic place than I had imagined. I had suddenly been transported back to the early part of the Stone Age, and a way of life that we Europeans had known some seventy thousand years ago. It was fascinating to watch the naked Wano using fire to split the hard rocks. Whenever they were unable to prise the stones apart, the shaman would speak to the rocks and cast spells upon the fire. The Wano would then pour cold water on the hot stones and smash them with large pebbles from the riverbed to break off long pieces of various sizes. My porters had no use for the larger pieces, but collected several smaller fragments that could be used to make knives. It slowly dawned on me how sensational this discovery was. No European had ever seen this before. It was an unforgettable experience.

Before we left the Wano village, I experienced another event that required tact and diplomacy. I was sitting in the tent writing my diary with the Wano crouching around me and watching me intently, as usual, when suddenly there was an air of excitement. A young boy of about four years of age approached the tent timidly, carrying an armful of freshly washed *pataten*. With animated gestures, the Wano explained that I should take both the sweet potatoes and the little boy as a gift. A decision was expected, but I was unsure what to do, so I strolled over to see the boy's father. I thanked him for his kind offer and showed him the injuries I had sustained. The negotiations were difficult and time-consuming, since I did not wish to offend him with too brusque a refusal. I finally managed to appease him by promising to return and trade with him when my injuries had healed. A new steel axe blade for the father and some sweets for the boy did the job of placating them both.

It was now the middle of May and at the next Mission Station Phil said goodbye. He had proved to be a competent and trusty partner and he was sorely missed on my subsequent undertakings. I returned to Wamena, where I was again examined, this time by a government doctor. He was horrified at the many suppurating sores on my body and my swollen lymph glands. I was covered in festering leech bites and deep thorn scratches. In the surgery, I discovered a five kilo tin with a label that read "Ichthyol Ointment, Seefeld in Tyrol", a cure-all from my home country, which I exchanged for poultices and antibiotics. After a few days in Wamena, I was ready to set off on the third and final stage of my New Guinea expedition – a north-south traverse of the island, ending at the Arafura Sea.

The Dutch geologist Gerard van der Wegen was planning to explore the Baliem Gorge, which lay on my route, and helped me with my preparations. Through his connections with the FMA, we managed to organise supply drops by plane. More importantly, van der Wegen had also managed to recruit ten porters from the Muju tribe. They had been converted to Christianity and some even spoke a little Dutch. To prevent them being taken for enemy interlopers by the other tribes we might meet, they were given shirts and trousers to make them look like Tuans.

Meanwhile, the political situation was intensifying and Gerard was becoming ever more pessimistic about our venture. I was still quite determined to stick to my plan to traverse the island and come out on the south coast and took great care to pack my most treasured possessions, the sacks of sailing tackle. I told Gerard that, as far as I was concerned, he was at liberty to turn back whenever he wanted to. The information we received about the unknown tribe in the Baliem Gorge, whom everyone referred to as the Passema, was not exactly encouraging, but uncertainty always makes for adventure, I reasoned. Shortly before we left, the Dutch administrator in Wamena requested on behalf of the American David Rockefeller that we investigate the disappearance of his son, Michael, when we got to the south coast.

At last we were ready to set off. The first few days along the Baliem River were hard going, but we did manage to recruit some additional porters and there was a plentiful supply of pataten along the way. Soon, however, the well-trodden path came to an end and we entered a region that no European had ever set foot in before. Even the Papuans rarely came here and when they did, it was to steal women or carry out violent acts of revenge. According to the aerial photographs we had obtained, we were now close to Passema territory, but we kept having to make time-consuming detours to negotiate landslips and tributary rivers. We were walking and climbing for eight to ten hours a day, but never made more than about three kilometres a day on the map. At length, we passed by a vertical rock face and reached the crest of a deeply indented ridge, but we were still unable to see the valley of the Passema. The dense oak forest was soaking wet and infested with leeches. They crawled up from the ground and fell on us from the bushes to the side and the branches above, eager for warm blood. Salt and tobacco repelled them; at least that was the theory. If you stood still you attracted more than you could get rid of, so it was better to keep going and flick them off as best you could. In any case, once they were full to bursting and looked like little cocktail sausages they fell off of their own accord.

The forest thinned as we approached an area of terraced *pataten* fields that clung to the steep hillside like the vineyards back home. When reclaiming the land, the natives had used the stones they had cleared to build man-sized containing walls, a tradition that stretched back thousands of years. On one of the walls, two bleached skulls had been placed and at the top of a withered tree the mummified remains of one of the deceased owners kept watch over his field. The porters were scared and fell silent. I must admit I felt a little queasy myself, although I tried not to show it. We had already heard the names of the two local tribal chiefs, Bota and Wahasuma, in the last village we had visited. The villagers had whispered their names, a sign of the respect and awe in which these men were held. The porters' fear seemed justified; there was certainly something eerie in the air. I had been told by the neighbouring tribes that the arrows used by the Passema had barbed tips. Whether or not they also used poison remained unclear. Gerard and I debated whether it might be better to head further up into the mountains in order to avoid the entire Passema territory. Gerard even talked about turning back. Our deliberations soon proved pointless, however, as we crested a ridge and were suddenly confronted by about a hundred armed Papuans. Communication was difficult, since these tribesmen spoke a different dialect. My Dani vocabulary, which I had been learning over the past five months, included the words for the numbers, the four elements, water, fire, earth and air, and the terms for foodstuffs like potatoes and pork, but these were useless in this situation and even the porters were unable to make themselves understood.

It was Gerard's shotgun that solved the language problem. Taking careful aim, he fired two shots into the soft trunk of a nearby pandanus palm. This impressed the Passema greatly and they scattered in alarm. Presently they returned, slowly and cautiously, to inspect the shattered wood, poking their fingers into the many exit holes at the back of the tree and tapping on their penis sheaths with their thumbnails, a sign of surprise and amazement.

Apparently, the bush telegraph had warned the Passema of our arrival, just as it had done with the Wano, but after witnessing Gerard's shot they cleared a path for us as far as their huts. It later transpired that the word "Passema" was a generic term for a large territory with many villages, all of which were ruled by the two tribal chieftains, Wahasuma and Bota. The tribes in New Guinea usually numbered about a hundred souls, but judging by the amount of huts we estimated that the Passema territory was home to more than two thousand Papuans.

We began to pitch the two six by six metre tarpaulins outside one of the larger huts. It was raining heavily and the ground was very muddy. Suddenly the crowd of inquisitive onlookers parted and two men appeared. There was no doubt; they had to be Wahasuma and Bota. It was easy to see that these were the two chiefs, since even without their war paint and feathers they were mightily impressive, particularly Bota, who must have measured at least 1.8 metres in height. His body was covered in scars that bore witness to his courage and daring. Here was a man who, when he led his people into battle, bore the brunt of the enemy's first hail of arrows.

In order to curry favour with the two taciturn chiefs, and to still the hunger of my expedition members, I decided to organise a pig roast. Sweet potatoes were brought and the meat prepared but the peaceful silence could not conceal the feeling of tension that prevailed. I had a special gift for Bota, a shiny new steel axe that I had carried in my luggage since we left Wamena for just such an eventuality. I explained to him that with this axe he could fell a tree in a matter of hours instead of days, but with a dismissive gesture and a look that seemed to say "Why would I want to do it any faster?" He just stuck it in the straw roof of the hut and left it there.

The situation was not becoming any less tense and I now had a decision to make. Once again, my procedure with unknown tribes has proved valuable: to arrive preferably in the late afternoon, to distribute presents at once, and – if at all possible – to organise a display of strength to impress the natives. In case relationships turn sour, it is also important to be ready to leave as early as possible the next morning, before the natives notice that they actually have the upper hand. To attempt to defend yourself by violent means would be just as futile as running away.

By the time morning came, the tarpaulins were packed and we were ready to leave. All we could see of the tribe was a row of spears behind the stone walls. Gerard agreed with me that it was time to push on. This was the point of no return, he said. We could not expect any help and our porters were frightened and wanted to make haste. Together we marched out of the village and headed south. From time to time, one of the natives would appear at the side of the path and indicate the direction we should take. We had no way of knowing if he was trying to lure us into a trap. Perhaps our suspicion was unjustified, but these Stone Age people had a different way of thinking, so I preferred to rely on my instincts.

To add to our difficulties, I also managed to injure myself again crossing a narrow bridge that spanned a raging tributary of the Baliem River. One of the strands of liana snapped under the combined weight of me and my rucksack, my leg plunged down between two branches and I barked my shin on the rough wood. There was no time to treat the wound properly; we had to keep moving on.

On 1st June we reached a clearing in the forest with fields and a few huts, where we had arranged to receive a supply drop. We lit a fire with dry leaves and waited. Presently, the little yellow bird flew in, circled twice and dropped five sacks of rice. This brought the Papuans out of their huts. One glance was enough to establish that all of them, men and women alike, were suffering from yaws, a dermatological infection that is very common in New Guinea. Their attitude towards us seemed anything but friendly. It was difficult to know who was more scared – us of them, or them of us. In any case, they looked too weak to carry loads, so Gerard ordered our ten Muju porters to open up their private bundles and ditch any unnecessary ballast. To our surprise, out came a variety of odds and ends, including glass bottles, hair pomade and the new clothes we had provided them with, which we now insisted they put on in place of the rags they were wearing. To the growing pile of useless junk, we added the heavy jute sacks from the provisions drop and even some of the precious rice, before setting off again, still heavily laden. From a distance, I saw the unfriendly Papuans pounce with delight on the pile we had left behind, but I could not help wondering if they knew what to do with it all, since they had probably never seen such things in their lives before.

We had now left the region of the mountain Papuans and before us lay the No-Man's Land between them and the coastal dwellers. We had been travelling for four weeks and the torrent of the Baliem River had become a calm flow. If I were to describe in detail all the suffering and hardship we had to endure on this final stage of the journey it would beggar belief. We built bridges across the wide tributary rivers and ladders to scale sheer cliff faces. The rice began to ferment, and our rations were meagre. Using the compass to navigate was complicated by having to negotiate the funnel-like craters of several huge dolines, so we counted steps instead and entered the distance we had covered on the map at the end of each tortuous day's march. The ever-present ticks and lice were soon accompanied by more leeches and on one memorable day, the now weakened porters simply sat down and refused to go any further. At first Gerard and I took no notice, but when the Muju continued to refuse to move, Gerard grabbed his shotgun and fired a warning shot over their heads. It was as well that he did, for if they had remained where they were they would have fallen victim to the bloodsucking leeches in no time at all. I recalled instances in the Himalaya when Gurkha soldiers had lost their way and all that was later found were their skeletons. Sometimes you have to be cruel to be kind.

Gerard was fighting a losing battle with his shotgun, particularly on the narrow paths that we had to hack through the dense jungle, where it constantly became entangled in the undergrowth. His repertoire of untranslatable Dutch swearwords was inexhaustible, it seemed. Yet in spite of all the rigours and hardships, there were still moments to savour. In the evenings, when the tarpaulins were pitched, it was nice to get out of our soaking wet clothes, change into dry tracksuits and clamber into our hammocks. In the morning we would have to replace the dry clothes in their protective plastic bags, wring out the wet stuff and wear it again, but we could think about that when the time came.

We were now about two hundred kilometres from the coast. We caught some fish in the river and discovered a rotten sago palm full of maggots in the jungle. In spite of their hunger, the porters refused to fell it, on the grounds that someone, somewhere must own it and to tamper with another person's private property would mean certain death for all of us. We finally agreed to chop down the tree and leave its value in Dutch guilders on the stump. The yellowish-white maggots were as thick as a man's thumb and were grilled over the embers of the fire. It was the first time since Wamena that we could all eat our fill.

Whilst the Muju set about building a balsa wood raft, Gerard and I had time to relax and recover before the next adventure. We had just got used to the stately tempo of the raft, when we hit a set of rapids and lost control. There was a loud crack as we crashed into a huge tree trunk across our course and I caught a glimpse of three of our Mujus being catapulted into the river. They swam back to the raft as fast as they could as there were some very large crocodiles lying in wait amongst the reeds near the river bank. A series of less violent bumps followed and then we straightened up the raft and floated slowly down the meandering river. There was no time to get bored, however, as the coastal tides affected the state of the river and we had to keep a constant eye out for further rapids.

We felt relatively safe now and as the expedition was drawing to a close, I found time to think about some of the things we had experienced. Frayed tempers, cursing and swearing were all part and parcel of expedition life; in fact they helped to release the pent-up tension, since generally each of us had to deal with his problems alone. But success could only be enjoyed if we worked as a team. For my part, I was pleased that the early explorers of New Guinea had left me some important areas of the island to discover, that Dutchmen had been involved both in the ascent of the highest peak and in the north-to-south crossing of the island and that men from the Dani, Wano and Muju tribes had played such an important part in the exploration of West New Guinea, the largest natural history museum in the world. I hoped that one day, perhaps, the Papuans might look back on this expedition and take pride in their achievement.

When we arrived in Agats on the Arafura Sea, the Dutch administrator De Jong arranged for our cuts and sores to be treated and we learned from him that the Indonesian invasion had not yet begun. Before I left Agats I managed to find out more about the mysterious disappearance of Michael Rockefeller and sent the following report to his father, whom I was later to meet in person in New York.

"Asmat, June 25th 1962

The rumours of a wristwatch having been found in a cannibal village are untrue. What is true is that two red canisters, which Michael Rockefeller had used as a kind of life vest, were found washed up on the shore. Whilst up in the mountains, Michael had fearlessly stood his ground amidst a hail of arrows and spears during a tribal battle and had taken some sensational photographs. He had then come down to the coast to collect samples of the famous Asmat art for a museum. Together with his companion, the Dutchman René Wassing, he had built a catamaran using two native dugouts attached by boards and with a protective roof of corrugated iron. To make it easier to manoeuvre the boat, they had fitted it with an outboard motor.

The two of them left Agats in the early morning and visited the villages of Per and Djepen, where they purchased some valuable items. In the afternoon they set sail fully loaded and set course for a series of islands. But Michael Rockefeller never got there. A wave swamped the catamaran, the outboard motor died on them, and they drifted helplessly out to sea. This was at about four o' clock in the afternoon. The two natives who had accompanied Rockefeller and Wassink leapt into the sea and swam to the shore, a distance of about a kilometre. They reached their village at night and raised the alarm. In the meantime, Michael Rockefeller and René Wassing had been carried far out to sea by the current. They spent a terrible night as the waves grew stronger and finally the catamaran capsized. The young men managed to save themselves from drowning by clambering onto the wreck. Their situation would have been nightmarish, even for the most seasoned sea dog, as the seas between Australia and New Guinea are notorious for their huge waves and the difference in tides between ebb and flow often reaches record breaking heights of up to eleven metres. Rockefeller and Wassing clung to the slippery upturned hulls of the two dugouts and in this way they managed to survive the night in extremely perilous circumstances.

By daylight, each had come to a different conclusion as to what was the best thing to do. Wassing felt that their only hope was to stay with the wreck and wait until help arrived. Rockefeller disagreed and decided to attempt to swim the fifteen kilometres to the shore. His decision was not prompted by panic, but reflected the temperament of a young man who found it intolerable simply to wait for something to turn up and preferred instead to act decisively. Against Wassink's urgent dissuasion, he tied two empty petroleum canisters to his waist, pushed off and started his long swim. It was a courageous but ultimately fateful decision. To swim fifteen kilometres in normal sea conditions would require an almost superhuman effort, but in big waves and high tides it was hopeless. Then there was the danger of sharks in the open sea, and, further inshore, the crocodiles of the River Eilanden. Even in the unlikely event that he did manage to reach dry land, there were still the cannibals to contend with. In short, Michael did not stand a chance.

All of the rumours, born of hope, have little to do with the sad truth of the events, that this young explorer paid for his courage with his life. René Wassing was spotted by the rescue planes and was saved. Ultimately, his decision proved to be correct."

I learned that Michael Rockefeller had repeatedly expressed the wish to discover a new waterfall. During our expedition from the source to the mouth of the Baliem River we had seen many waterfalls, the largest of which I dedicated to Michael Rockefeller. Gerard van der Wegen, my trusty companion and now a firm friend, bade me farewell with the promise to send me a copy of his geological report. In addition to their pay, the ten Muju porters each received a bonus of a wristwatch, provisions and tobacco. As expedition leader, it was my duty to see to it that they returned safely to their home village of Tana Mera. The Dutch administrator De Jongh agreed to place my rescue bond at their disposal to pay for the necessary planes and boats to get them home. Each of the Mujus had to confirm the receipt of his pay with a fingerprint on a piece of paper. This document is a valuable reminder for me of a people who can not write and are commonly viewed as "savages". I knew better, since I had got to know them rather better than most over the past few weeks and had experienced their emotions, their fears and their joy. They have different customs and different morals, to be sure, but they are certainly no more "savage" than many a white man.

After six months, my New Guinea expedition was drawing to a close. I thought of the people who had accompanied me, of my friends and climbing partners: the Dutchmen Bert Huizenga and Gerard van der Wegen, the Australian Russell Kippax and the New Zealander Phil Temple. I would be more than happy to have any of them along on future expeditions.

The New Guinea expedition was the toughest I have ever been on, and like any large undertaking, the adventure extends far beyond the actual trip itself. First, there is the excitement of planning the expedition, then the hard work of realising those plans and finally, the fascinating job of sorting through and editing all the photographs and diary entries. The little things that keep you going through all the hardships – like the dream of drinking cold beer instead of swamp water filtered through a sweaty sock or dining on roast potatoes and fried eggs instead of sweet potatoes – are soon forgotten when you return home. Those dreams are replaced by others and unpleasant experiences are left behind. What remains is the joy of these contrasting experiences. During those long months in New Guinea, my theory that nature can neither be fought nor conquered was confirmed once more, as I came face to face with the elemental power of a moving body of water, a force that carries all before it.

I flew first to Sydney, where I sent Carina a lengthy telegram informing her of the successful outcome of the expedition and explaining that I would be landing in Frankfurt on my fiftieth birthday. Before I boarded my flight, the Austrian consul handed me a written request from a *Life* magazine correspondent, who wished to interview me. I proposed that we meet during one of the stop-overs in Singapore, Bangkok or Bombay, or in Frankfurt and boarded the Alitalia 707 flight bound for Bangkok. In Bangkok airport I was just about to buy a mangustin, one of my favourite fruits, when an announcement over the loudspeaker instructed me to proceed to the information desk. The *Life* correspondent had reserved a room for me, so I broke my homeward journey in Bangkok.

The journalist arrived at my hotel early the next morning and showed me a strip of ticker tape with a message from the news agency Reuters: "Alitalia 707, which took off from Bangkok on 6th July, is overdue." A second strip of tape carried the news that the Austrian explorer Heinrich Harrer had been on board the missing aeroplane. I remembered sitting next to a young pilot, who was on his way to Europe for a holiday. He told me he was planning to climb the Matterhorn and asked me if it was dangerous. I told him that with a guide it was no more dangerous than flying.

The flight crew that had taken the plane as far as Bangkok were sitting in the lobby of the hotel. They now knew that the Alitalia 707 had been caught in the monsoon rains during the approach to Bombay and had crashed in the Ghat Mountains. None of the ninety-seven people on board had survived. The reporters all wanted to know why I had not taken my flight. "But for *Life* I wouldn't be alive", I answered.

Carina had spent several anxious hours waiting for news. The German Sunday papers had carried the story of the crash on their front pages and noted that I was on board. In fact, I was the only passenger who had left the flight, but it was only after receiving my telegram from Bangkok that Carina knew this for certain. I caught a Lufthansa flight to Bombay, and flew from there direct to Frankfurt. A crowd of reporters had gathered at the airport, and Carina was there waiting for me. A few weeks later, on 10th August 1962, we were married.

Carina did not give up her career after we were married, and she kept her apartment in Frankfurt. I also kept my home in Liechtenstein. The Liechtenstein-Verlag was financing the building of a house in Kitzbühel where its authors could go to write and we used this as our holiday home. We usually stayed there when I was in Europe, until we built our own house in the Liechtenstein town of Mauren.

Carina and I were often apart for months on end with no news of one another. With the benefit of hindsight, I am glad that I always insisted on maintaining radio silence. It was better that way, both for the folks back home and for me. Having no contact with home meant that I could concentrate fully on the expedition itself and my friends and family did not have to start worrying if there was a breakdown in communications due to technical problems. Far from civilisation, I was timeless and unfettered and felt casual and relaxed. Letters were the only form of contact and even deep in the jungle of New Guinea we received our mail, together with the supply drops.

Life at my side was certainly not always easy for Carina, yet we both agree that our relationship is the most important thing in our lives. This is how she once described it:

"Our marriage began after Heinrich's happy return from New Guinea. I was working in the marketing department of a large chemical company at the time. My husband continued to go off on expeditions, and gradually I, too, began to involve myself in his passion for exploration. From the beginning it was apparent to both of us that it would not be possible for me to participate in his expeditions, which were both difficult and demanding undertakings. In any case, there was plenty to do at home: editing his journals, cataloguing the ethnographical objects he sent back to Europe and, very often, just planning his next trip.

His love of the peoples and cultures of East Asia was not something I found difficult to share, since my father, Fritz Ferdinand Haarhaus, who had lived for eleven years in China, and his cousin, Eduard von der Heydt, had introduced me to the culture of this region when I was a very young girl. Cousin Eduard was a banker in Berlin and for many years the owner of the Monte Verità centre near Ascona. Over the years, his art collection grew steadily and he was in constant contact with art dealers in Paris, London, Hamburg and Cologne. His collection is now housed in the Rietberg Museum in Zurich and the Von der Heydt Museum in Wuppertal, the home town of my father's family. Cousin Eduard made a gift of his collections to these museums, and the Wuppertal gallery latter added several French Impressionist paintings and Modernist works from Germany and France. It was therefore quite natural that I should enthusiastically support my husband's interest in collecting works of art, particularly Tibetan art, and I was always excited when he showed me his latest acquisitions.

My mother's family came from Thuringia, in the eastern part of Germany. Her family owned the Sonneberg toy factory and when we were children we loved to visit the factory and admire the wonderful dolls they made there. My grandfather Oskar Dressel was dearly loved by all the children. An exceptional man, in 1916 he developed Germanin, a drug used in the treatment of African sleeping sickness, whilst working as a chemist at Bayer-Leverkusen. It was a happy childhood, full of love and care.

Heinrich is a hard-working and diligent man and I am happy to support him by taking on some of the more mundane chores of daily life. In spite of our differences, we share the same basic opinions and have developed many mutual interests, like our yearly visit to the Salzburg Festival. We probably do not lead a normal life in the established sense of the term, but our marriage has been a good one, although I have had to learn the hard way what it means to be married to an explorer.

It is not easy to characterise my husband, but Dietmar Polaczek managed it when he wrote 'Heinrich Harrer does not give the impression of being very European. "He's Asian," a Carinthian friend of mine once said, after spending an evening in Harrer's company, "Are you sure he's from Carinthia?" To be honest, I am not really sure at all. His mountaineering and exploratory achievements are full of superlatives, but Harrer himself dismisses this view. "Superlatives soon become boring," he says. He is incredibly at ease with himself, almost like a yogi. He follows the middle way, a superlative achievement in itself, as it were. He accepts the things he does not like, without ignoring them, but neither does he take any pleasure in attacking or criticising them. Perhaps he really is Asian?"

I showed some of the stones I had brought back from Jalime to the Graz geologist, Professor Angerl, whom I had known since my student days. He established that they were silex, or flint stone, of a high degree of hardness. My expedition journal was published in book form in the spring of 1963 under the title *"I Come from the Stone Age"* and was translated into fifteen languages. It documented my experiences on that unforgettable journey into the past.

THE INDIANS OF THE XINGU RIVER

During the 1960s, when more and more Tibetans were seeking political asylum in Europe, Carina and I decided that we would also like to extend our hospitality to a Tibetan national who had been driven from his homeland. In 1964 I travelled to Nepal, and whilst I was staying in New Delhi the opportunity to do just that presented itself. A young man approached me, speaking the dialect of West Tibet, with which I was familiar. He asked me if he might come back to Europe with me and work for me as a cook and housekeeper. We first needed to obtain permission, both from the Tibetan government in exile in Dharamsala and from the Indian Foreign Ministry. It was a lengthy process, but six months later we picked young Tenzing up at Zurich airport and drove him to our home in Liechtenstein.

Tenzing regarded his room with en-suite shower as the height of luxury. He had never experienced such a thing before and his gratitude was effusive. We paid him a monthly wage, and his cooking was heavenly and entirely to our taste. When he prepared Tibetan dishes or curries he always used plenty of spices, which he had brought with him, and his *momos* were juicy and delicious. During the four years that Tenzing stayed with us our kitchen always smelled of the most wonderful spices: ginger, coriander, cardamom, caraway and saffron.

Tenzing found it difficult to understand why well-to-do people like Carina and me should be living in a house with old wooden ceilings and exposed beams. The many antiques lying on the hearth and mantelpiece were also a mystery to him. One day he found a broken ski binding and ski pole basket in a nearby meadow, which he solemnly placed with the other valuable cultural treasures. "You collect old things, don't you?" he said when questioned about this.

Tenzing sometimes had difficulty breathing and the hospital in Innsbruck diagnosed that he was suffering from asthma. Carina made sure that he took his prescribed medication every day, which brought him some relief and made his life a little easier. Tenzing only spoke Tibetan, so Carina learned enough to express simple wishes and instructions and found that this also helped her to understand his odd little ways a little better. As he grew more confident, his initial exaggerated submissiveness gave way to occasional displays of originality and self-will. On one occasion he became almost hysterical when he believed he was being punished by evil spirits. He had found what he thought were traces of blood in his urine and was convinced that the Gods were punishing him, even though he lived a celibate life. The following day all was well again; the scare was explained by the beetroot we had eaten for lunch.

Carina found Tenzing's unpredictability a little unsettling, whereas I had spent half of my life in Asia and found it much easier to get along with him. He told me one day of his childhood in a village high in the hills, where the abbot of the local monastery had regarded him as a kind of oracle. This went some way to explaining his often highly emotional reactions to things; he sometimes reminded me of those clairvoyants who would gasp for breath and then lose consciousness.

Tenzing lived a contented life in our home. Like all of us, he used to enjoy going to the annual fair, where he would usually treat everyone around him to beer and grilled chicken. The following day he would announce that he had spent all of his savings. He once explained proudly that this was the reason why he did not want a wife, to whom he might be held accountable for his actions.

After four years living the bachelor life, Tenzing suddenly announced that he wished to take an extended holiday and visit some Tibetan friends in Switzerland. Carina made sure that he packed his asthma medication, and thereafter we heard no more from him. We later learned that he had found work as a cook in a refugee camp in Switzerland. Six months after he left, we received word from the charity organisation Swiss Aid to Tibetans that Tenzing had suffered an asthma attack and had suffocated. There seems little doubt that the people at the camp had not been aware of the seriousness of his illness and that Tenzing himself had neglected to take his medication on a regular basis. Perhaps he has now been reincarnated as an oracle in that little village in Tibet.

Meanwhile, I was busy with the preparations for my next expedition. I never once considered whether I ought to go; the only question was where to go. With exploration in general, and geographical expeditions in particular, imagination plays an important role in the planning phase. Potential surprises can be factored in and dealt with smoothly as they arise, if you have invested sufficient time and money in the preparations. And in spite of all the detailed research, the thrill of adventure still remains. In order to carry out your plans, the germ of an idea must be accompanied by energy, drive, discipline and optimism and the desire to succeed, tempered by a measure of prudence. Risking one's life is a foolhardy pursuit best left to soldiers of fortune or religious fanatics.

After New Guinea, I was hoping to mount another jungle expedition, this time to the Amazon rain forest, where I hoped to make contact with another ancient tribe. According to several reliable sources, the Xingu Indians of the Brazilian province of Matto Grosso were still living in the Neolithic era. They had first been sighted in 1884 by the German ethnologist Karl von den Steinen during his discovery and exploration of the two thousand kilometre long Xingu River, one of the largest tributaries of the Amazon. The difficulties that von den Steinen had to face are graphically described in his expedition notes. He had neither a map of the course of the Xingu River, nor had he packed sufficient medical supplies. The effect of these missing items becomes all too apparent when one reads the following extract from his expedition report: "Thirty-eight degrees fever today. We continue our march."

I always travelled with a modest amount of equipment in order to remain flexible, so I understood the problem. I also acknowledged the pioneering achievements of these men and was grateful for the research they had conducted. This time I was not to be the first, but I could build upon their experiences and there were certain to be plenty of new things to discover and describe. I had studied the exciting expedition report written by von Karl von den Steinen, together with everything I could find on the ill-fated 1925 Fawcett Expedition, including the book by Peter Fleming, who had travelled to the region to search for clues relating to the mysterious disappearance of Colonel Fawcett and his son. I also visited Professor Schaden, the leading scientist and expert on Indian cultures, at the University of Sao Paulo. He himself had never met the Xingu Indians and was not particularly forthcoming on the subject, so I left without learning anything new. It was the first time that Schaden had been unable to help me. His attitude reminded me of these lines from "Kim", written more than a hundred years ago by my favourite author Rudyard Kipling: "All we Ethnological men are as jealous as jackdaws of one another's discoveries. They're of no interest to anyone but ourselves, of course."

As luck would have it, I was to experience the exact opposite in the very same city. The German Wolfgang Bücherl had been working since 1939 at the Sao Paolo Butantan Institute, a biomedical research centre, or "House of Poisons" as it was commonly known, and he willingly supplied me with information, warnings and advice. More importantly, perhaps, he also provided me with some serum against snake and scorpion venom. Thus far, on all of my trips, I had only rarely encountered snakes. In the dense jungle, the process of hacking a path with a machete is so loud that the timid creatures tend to make themselves scarce when they hear you coming. On one occasion a viper did brush against my bush knife, attracted by the glint of sunlight on the blade. It pays to be cautious, particularly on the newly constructed roads in the foothills of the Himalaya, as the reptiles use the same paths in their search for food for their entire lives, and often cross the roads. Ever since I first heard the deathly sound of a truck tyre running over a snake – it made a noise like a tyre exploding – I have always told the driver to watch out for reptiles on the road.

In the autumn of 1966 my journey began. In order to have more time to devote to my journals, I had asked a fellow Carinthian, Herbert Raditschnig, to accompany me and operate the camera, since once again I had landed an assignment for Hessischer Rundfunk to make a radio programme. I already knew that Herbert was interested in my plans and that he was in good enough shape to cope with the rigours of such a trip. To save having to make a long and arduous approach march to the Xingu, we sought permission to fly in on the old aeroplane that supplied a military post in the region. It was an adventurous flight, like those in the Andes. We sat in metal containers bolted to the fuselage and between us lay a freshly slaughtered ox covered in buzzing black flies.

To protect the tribes of the Xingu region, the 1950's saw the establishment of an Indian reservation, which, in 1961, became the Parque Nacional do Xingu. It was designed to keep out rubber prospectors, missionaries and other speculators. However, increased outside contact facilitated the spread of diseases, which drastically reduced the indigenous population. The mere fact that one could now land a plane at the military station of Posto Leonardo, right in the middle of the reserve, opened the floodgates to further civilising influences, which changed the lives and customs of the Indians forever. For example, in order to collect the splendid coloured feathers of the toucan, the Indians used to entice the birds closer by imitating their calls, whereupon they would shoot them from the tree branches with arrows dipped in a mild poison, pluck a few of the bright red and yellow feathers and set the birds free again. Now the Indians were the proud possessors of rifles, with which the birds could be killed outright from a great distance, and their bows and arrows had become redundant, but they had lost the ability to imitate birdsong and other animal sounds. Bad experiences with the white man had also caused them to become distrustful, and it took a great deal of effort to establish any kind of rapport.

There was much of interest for us to observe and record, like the cultivation and harvest of the region's staple plant, the manioc, or cassava. The women would place the peeled manioc roots on a wooden board and grind them into flour using piranha teeth. The manioc flour would then be washed to remove the toxic prussic acid and baked to produce a delicious flatbread. We also filmed the Indians fishing. They would select a particular plant, grind it to a paste and use the poisonous juice to kill the fish. The poisoned innards of the fish would be removed before it was cooked and eaten. It was obvious that the Indians had posed for photographs for other visitors. They seemed to enjoy doing so, and they expected some form of payment. Unfortunately, they also stole from us. One night, without making a sound, they purloined one of our expedition crates. The following night it was replaced, again silently, but anything that might have been of use to them, such as knives and scissors, had been taken. At least they had left the cameras and lenses.

I still hoped to find tribes in the area that maintained a natural rapport with the water, the trees and the animals, and to find evidence of primitive workshops where these Neolithic tribesmen fashioned their axes. The opportunity to do so presented itself in the person of Hakanei, from the Kalapalo tribe, who was travelling through the area at the behest of his chieftain, Bororó and was charged with inviting all of the tribes of the Xingu to a funeral celebration, or *kwarup*, to be held in honour of the recently deceased tribal chief, Jupala. The celebrations served to ease the passage of the dead man to the "Eternal Hunting Grounds", to heal old feuds and promote peace amongst the various tribes of the region. It was to be a great occasion, during which traditional wrestling contests, or "*huka-huka*", would also be held. Hakanei agreed to take us along.

We set off downriver in Hakanei's dugout canoe, which he steered skilfully through the rapids using a single paddle. During one of the rest stops, Hakanei energetically dissuaded us from taking a swim to wash and cool off, since the river was infested with piranhas. He had a fund of gruesome stories relating to these fish, and showed us an ugly, gnarled scar on his finger caused by a piranha biting him as he was reeling it in. These carnivorous fish can strip a bleeding cadaver in a matter of seconds, leaving nothing but bare bones.

Hakanei chose a sandy river bank as our campsite for the night. In a matter of moments we were being attacked by a swarm of mosquitoes. I protected my face with a net attached to the brim of my hat, while Hakanei's preferred method involved smearing his naked body with the ethereal oil of the red uruku plant. He then followed a faint set of tracks in the sand and in no time at all returned with an armful of turtles' eggs. The cicadas were making a deafening racket, and as the sun went down the frog chorus began. The next morning, we were woken by the screech of the macaws. All in all, it was quite a concert.

The first tribe we visited was the Yawalapiti, whom Hakanei had spoken of with great respect. As the emissary of the Kalapalo, Hakanei was received by the Yawalapiti with due honour. In the middle of a clearing in the jungle, a hand-carved stool had been placed on which he sat, head bowed, until all the tribesmen had gathered. We were here experiencing the authentic tribal ritual that we had been looking for. The muscular men of the Yawalapiti tribe, firm favourites to win the wrestling competition, were a sight to behold.

The rest of the day was spent filming and photographing the traditional way of life of the tribal families. We found the indigenous people here a refreshing change from those we had encountered during our few days at Posto Leonardo. It seemed perfectly natural for one of the women to be breast feeding a small animal, possibly a baby tapir, which she had presumably found wandering about helplessly on the savannah; in fact, I had seen this before in New Guinea, where the Dani women also feed their piglets in this way.

It was the Indian custom that Hakanei enquire about the routine events of his hosts' daily lives on the day of his visit; for example, he asked how the fishing and the manioc harvest had been. The Yawalapiti had to curb their curiosity, even though they all knew the real reason for Hakanei's visit. Pleasantries were exchanged, after which two women, whose beauty and youth had long since faded, brought their honoured guest smoked fish wrapped in sweet-smelling flatbread. The old women's hair was tousled and tangled and their faces deeply wrinkled, but their eyes shone with kindness and good humour.

There are nine tribes scattered across the Xingu Indian Reservation. They have a similar appearance, but differing customs and ways of life, and each has its own tribal chieftain. Hakanei still had to extend his chief's invitation to the Kamayura, and to the Waura, who were the only tribe to have mastered the art of pottery. The Wauru were regarded as high-spirited and were not particularly well liked, but the large round vessels they made were used by all of the Indians to prepare manioc paste. Bororó had sent Hakanei to the Waura as his messenger in the hope that he might take a Waura woman as his wife, who could then teach the Kalapalo how to make these pots. His tribe would then be independent of its arrogant neighbours. Unfortunately for Bororó, Hakanei had already decided to marry a Yawalapiti girl.

By now, Hakanei knew what interested me most, so he suggested I stay with the Kamayura until the *kwarup* festival began, while he went to visit the Waura, and said he would come back for me in three days time. Before he left, he introduced me to one of the shamans, telling him that I was a friend of the Indians. The shaman puffed on a thick cigar, whose green tobacco leaves were held together with a wooden skewer. I was looking forward to having the time to observe the shaman and accompany him during his ritual wanderings.

The shaman disappeared into to a hut roofed with sape grass and emerged with a little monkey and together we walked over to another dwelling built from long wooden poles in the shape of a tent. The caged eagle had recognised its master from afar and flapped its mighty wings with pleasure. Golden eagles are kept as mascots and lucky charms in several Xinguano villages. They are well looked after and fed daily with live animals. The shaman slid one of the wooden struts of the cage to one side and placed the monkey inside. The eagle killed the monkey with one blow from its sharp beak, grasped its prey in its claws and began to feed. When the shaman spoke, however, the eagle stopped tearing at the flesh and appeared to answer him. At length, the shaman went into the hut and the eagle sat on its perch, where it seemed quite happy to let it's master stroke it.

Herbert and I were given a couple of hammocks in which to spend the night. They were woven from plant fibres, dyed in soft, muted colours and decorated with imaginative patterns.

It was very early the next day, the damp morning mist still mixing with the smoke from the huts, when I became aware of a strange humming sound. I followed the sound to the plaza of the village, where a naked Xingu Indian was swinging a bullroarer, or *wuri-wuri*, a piece of carved wood attached to a long string, which he whirled around to create the melodious humming sound that I had heard. If the bullroarer touched the ground he had to start all over again, gradually building up the tempo to produce the high notes. I was told that the *wuri-wuri* could be used to call up thunder and lightning and raise the level of the river to attract more fish.

I thoroughly enjoyed the quiet, peaceful life of the Kamayura Indians. The time was measured only by the rising and setting of the sun and every day was like a river that began and ended nowhere. I was reluctant to leave this tranquil place but when Hakanei returned, as agreed, after three days, it was time for us to move on.

In order to reach the tribal territory of the Kalapalo we had to cross a bewildering number of tributaries of the Xingu River. Luckily, Hakanei knew the way. He had little notion of time and never hurried, and I adjusted my pace accordingly. Monkey brains are considered a real delicacy by the Indians, and Hakanei wanted to kill a monkey to go with the fish we had caught, but when he discovered the tracks of a jaguar, the plan changed. The hunt was seriously hampered by the screeching of the monkeys, which warned the jaguar of the impending danger. Hakanei was disappointed; he had doubtless imagined himself impressing the women at the *kwarup* with a necklace made of jaguar claws.

When we reached the Kalapalo village the first thing I did was pay a courtesy call on Bororó, the proud chief of the tribe. He was very hospitable and showed us to a large hut where we could sleep. One end of our hammocks was fixed to the thick pole in the centre of the hut, the other to the two metre high posts along the semicircular walls. The hut itself was empty, as everyone was busy with the preparations for the *kwarup* ceremony.

The men went out into the woods, where they felled several large trees and cut them into two metre sections; these were then fashioned into the *kwarup* trunks, which represent the deceased person. The trunks were placed upright, side by side, and painted and decorated with feather adornments and articles of clothing while two shamans played rattles made of hard-shelled gourds. Six small loaves of bread were then placed at the foot of each *kwarup* trunk – provisions for the long journey to the hereafter. Each of the deceased tribesmen had several wives, all of whom now crouched on the ground, heads bowed, and loudly bemoaned the death of their men.

All of the tribes had honoured the Kalapalo's invitation – even the unpopular Waura, who had brought two red painted pots along as gifts – and to prevent old tribal rivalries arising, each group had been allocated its own camping area. In the still recent past, little boys had been kidnapped to be trained as warriors and pretty young girls abducted as wives for the tribal chieftains, but there would be ample opportunity to give full expression to any simmering feelings of resentment or hatred that might still have existed during the following day's wrestling bouts. Now, however, it was time to dance. All of the men had daubed their bodies and faces in tribal war paint made from yellow pequi oil and *uruku* paste and each of them wore necklaces fashioned from freshwater mussels or jaguar claws. There were almost two hundred dancers on the village plaza and there was such great confusion that Herbert and I were only able to capture a tiny fragment of the spectacular event on film.

The strange and melancholic strains of the *jakui* flutes could be heard emanating from one of the houses. All of the guest tribes had brought their own *uruá* flute-players. The *uruá* flutes consisted of two bamboo tubes of differing lengths and produced a memorable sound. Clad in their feather headdresses, the dancing men ran across the plaza from east to west, imitating the passage of the sun in the sky, for according to Xinguano beliefs, the earth is a flat disc. As dusk fell, they lit fires of pindaíba logs at the foot of each of the *kwarup* trunks. The Xingu Indians believe that their deceased kinsmen stay awhile in the realm of the living, but now it was time to prepare them for their journey to the land of shadows that lay beyond the Milky Way. On their journey they would have to perform various tests, and would have to slay a jaguar or anaconda to enter the realm of the spirits, a place where all men were equal, where bad deeds were not punished and acts of kindness were not rewarded, and where there was always enough fish and manioc to eat.

The first day of the festival had been a strenuous affair and several of the Indians went down to a nearby lake to wash away the sweat and dust before retiring, exhausted, to their hammocks for the night. The *huka-huka* wrestlers did not want to sleep; they feared that they might dream of defeat. They believe that he who dreams of losing a bout will indeed lose.

Herbert and I found little time to dream, either, but for different reasons. We had heard too many tales of cruelty amongst the Indians and decided as a precautionary measure to take turns keeping watch through the night. We also decided to do without our mosquito nets so that we might be better able to ward off any possible attacks. From time to time, a bird eating spider would fall from the straw roof and land on us with an audible thump. Although I had been reliably informed by the Butantan Institute that their bite was painful but not usually fatal, this information did little to ensure a peaceful night's rest. The howler monkeys in the nearby jungle were also having trouble sleeping, it seemed. The loud, guttural cries sounded disconcertingly human in the dank, dark night, even though we knew better. Throughout the night we also felt the gentle draught of the vampire bats as they flitted past us. But our admiration for their skill at avoiding contact with us had its limits and was tempered by the knowledge that these creatures possess teeth like piranhas and feed on fresh blood. The sleeping victim never feels their bite, but once bitten, he must endure several extremely painful injections in the stomach to prevent him succumbing to rabies. We were pleased when the grey light of dawn finally came.

In the morning I took a bath in the lake to cool off. I had to tread extremely carefully through the shallows, as this was where the well camouflaged stingrays lay. If disturbed, the rays use their venomous tail spines as a form of defence and the resultant wound takes many weeks to heal.

I sometimes ask myself why it is that I voluntarily expose myself to these rather alarming daily encounters. And as if the indigenous wildlife were not enough, when I returned to the windowless straw house, I found a club-wielding Indian waiting for me in the dark.

Fortunately, he must have noticed my interest in ethnological artefacts and had come to trade. The club was made of dark ebony wood and the Indian swung it above his head and challenged me to attack him so that he might demonstrate how it was used. I recalled the story of the disappearance of the Fawcett expedition, and since we were quite alone in the hut I politely declined his suggestion. I finally acquired the club without prior demonstration.

At last, the eagerly awaited wrestling match began. As a former sports teacher, this was the most important event of the whole *kwarup* festival for me. The *huka-huka* was seen as a replacement for the intertribal wars of the past, but Bororó had instructed his wrestlers to treat their opponents fairly. All of the wrestlers remove their necklaces and feather adornments and plaster their hair down with a kind of red paste. Many of them wear strips of cloth tied tightly around their upper arms to accentuate their biceps and, like the dancers, they covered their bodies with *pequi* oil to make them slippery and difficult to hold onto. *Huka-huka* is named after the sound the wrestlers make as they circle around their opponent before the wrestling begins. The hosts confront one invited tribe at a time, beginning with simultaneous matches of various pairs of rivals, including the youngest wrestlers. These are followed by individual matches of recognised champions. Some tribes wrestle standing, others start the contest kneeling on the ground. As a mark of friendship and respect, the winner of each contest always accompanies his opponent back to his tribespeople.

Hakanei won his bout, but the ritual was then interrupted when one of the Waura spectators, in a foolish display of courage, challenged a Kamayura tribesman to wrestle with him, whereupon the Kamayura simply picked him up and threw him to the ground. The spectators reacted with shouts of alarm – the Waura had broken his right arm, which now hung uselessly by his side. Howling with pain, the injured man was taken off to one of the huts, where his cries could still be heard through the thick reed walls. A shaman blew cigar smoke on the injured man's arm but this failed to relieve the pain and the Waura continued to scream, thus refuting the age-old theory that Indians do not know the meaning of pain.

The Kalapalo wrestler, a man by the name of Kaluene, was one of the last to fight. He had prepared well for his performance, but his antics seemed only to inflame the ire of his opponent. His bearing reminded me of Bota of the Passema tribe in New Guinea. He was high spirited and self assured and mercilessly taunted his challenger Kanato, the champion of the Yawalapiti. The crowd encouraged the two wrestlers with frenetic shouts and raised arms but it soon became apparent that Kanato was not in good shape and had little chance of winning. He had put on weight and was soon out of breath. At the end of the match, the Kalapalo were declared as the winners of the team contest, while Kaluene was proclaimed as the individual champion. Hakanei explained that it was no coincidence that the hosts had emerged victorious; at the last *kwarup* two years ago the Kamayura had been the host tribe and had won the match on that occasion.

The women then served bowls of delicious pequi seeds to the wrestlers to restore their energy. This reminded me of an old Chinese custom: when the exhausted warriors returned from battle, the women would place crowns of lychee fruit on their heads, which were believed to act as an aphrodisiac. Sadly, I was only ever presented with garlands of oak leaves or, at best, laurel.

The *huka-huka* spectacle was followed by the young girls of the tribe, who performed a delightful and elegant dance to the music of the flute players, their left hand resting on the shoulder of the man in front. It was an enchanting sight to see these lovely young creatures, with their brown skin, firm breasts and black hair, prancing in a circle. The dance ended as the sun went down. The *kwarup* trunks were then stripped of their ritual adornments and lowered into the waters of the lake.

The celebrations were over, and peace returned to the Kalapalo village, as the shaman continued to swing his bullroarer. The Xinguano Indians had every reason to be contented. Although they required courage and vigour in their daily battle for survival, there was a logical and natural order to their lives. Children were born and grew into healthy adults, fish were caught in the rivers and jaguars hunted on the wide expanse of the savannah. Only the strong survived. I had been privileged to experience one of the last untouched paradises of this world and had witnessed a tribal way of life that has now all but disappeared. It fills me with sadness that, after the establishment of a reservation designed to protect them, many of the aboriginal inhabitants of the Xingu had to pay for the so-called march of progress with their lives.

KING LEOPOLD OF BELGIUM

In the depths of winter, on a January afternoon in 1966, we received an unexpected telephone call from Princess de Réthy, the wife of King Leopold III of Belgium, inviting Carina and me to dinner that evening at their hunting lodge in Hinterriss. King Leopold and I had met fleetingly at the annual golfing invitational held at the American base at Ramstein near Kaiserslautern. In those days there were not many golf courses in Germany, but at the US base at Ramstein you could not only buy golfing equipment, you could even dine out on succulent T-bone steaks, another rarity in post-war Europe.

I was familiar with the enclave of Hinterriss in Tyrol from my climbing trips to the Karwendel Mountains and the splendid autumnal colours of the maple trees were a well known attraction. Now, however, a snow storm was raging, and the poor border guards had to drag themselves out of their warm cabin to check our passports and lift the barrier.

We were greeted at the entrance to the lodge by one of the hunters. The house had been furnished in true hunting style and at dinner we were seated at a rectangular table with a maple top that was so ancient that we had to take great care that our wine glasses did not fall over when setting them down. There was no shortage of interesting conversation topics, as both the King and I were, of course, well acquainted with each other's expeditions. Our host had been a keen amateur social anthropologist for many years and, like me, had travelled in South America. We were pleased to accede to his suggestion to view some of the photographs of his expedition to Brazil.

That evening marked the beginning of a close collaboration with a like-minded companion, a man who, over the years, would become a firm friend. King Leopold was the perfect partner with whom to plan and execute expeditions. We could act independently, since neither of us had any duty to sponsors or patrons, and our interests and abilities complemented each other well. He was the patron of the Prince Leopold Institute of Tropical Medicine in Belgium and specialised in photographing trees and tree roots. I learned that some exotic trees have more than a hundred aerial roots, which are frequently used by the indigenous peoples as drums to send messages to one another. On our expeditions we both looked forward to the evenings, when everything was prepared for the night and we had the time to record our daily observations in our journals at leisure. In some respects, he reminded me of Peter Aufschnaiter, with whom I had established an understanding that went beyond mere words. We conversed in a mixture of German and English. When we were alone I addressed him informally as "Leopold" or "Sire". In the company of others, I used a rather more formal tone, as I had done with the Dalai Lama.

During the following months I visited Leopold several times at Château Argenteuil in Waterloo, where he lived with his family. After dinner we would disappear to his huge studio, where all the documents and artefacts relating to his expeditions were carefully labelled and stored. He would open the flat drawers in the map cabinet, take out some maps spread them out on the map table as we reminisced over past expeditions and made plans for future ones. It was with Leopold that I finally got to watch the film "Masters of the Congo Jungle", which had been made in the Belgian Congo at the end of the 1950's to accompany the book of the same name that he had written. The film portrayed the then unadulterated harmony that existed between man, beast and nature, a harmony that I sought in vain to find during my visit many years later.

We also visited the natural history faculty at the University, where I met two of Leopold's expedition team: Xaver Missone, a leading expert in rodents, and the ichthyologist Jean-Pierre Gosse, who had discovered many new species of fish. It was around this time that we decided to form a charitable organisation for the protection of indigenous tribes threatened with extinction. We called it the Tribal Fund, but unfortunately we had to close the office after a few years due to lack of funds. It is easier to raise financial support for the protection of animals than the protection of humans, it seems.

Château Argenteuil was set amongst extensive parkland and the King had had a set of golf clubs made for him from the roots of the many ancient box trees in the park. A green had also been laid, where we held a putting competition with Leopold's family. From the extensive collection of golf clubs available, I selected a classic old hickory model and when I won our little competition Leopold gave me the putter as a memento of the occasion.

A little while later, we were playing a round of golf at Lake Starnberg. The King was an excellent golfer and I regularly lost to him. On this occasion he was on top form and enjoying himself tremendously. Then, realising what time it was, he urged us to make haste, as his wife was expecting us for lunch at the Four Seasons Hotel with a number of other guests. We arrived late and after we had taken our places at the table the famous chef Walterspiel offered His Majesty the dish of the day, a superbly cooked select cut of wild venison. The King's preference was for something a little more humble, however, and he asked if he might have a plate of sausages and sauerkraut. The wine waiter was similarly disappointed when, instead of the vintage red wine, King Leopold ordered a large Bavarian beer to accompany his meal.

In the autumn of 1966, not long after I had returned from my visit to the Xingu Indians, Leopold and I set off on our first expedition together. Our destination was French Guiana and Suriname, where there was plenty of interest for the whole expedition team, which included a botanist, an ornithologist and an ichthyologist. I was primarily interested in the indigenous Indian tribes and former slaves of the border region between Suriname and French Guiana to the east, while the others hoped to find rare species of fish and plants. I had assumed overall responsibility for the leadership of the expedition, while Leopold's task was to co-ordinate the work of the various scientists.

The team included Xaver Missone, Jean-Pierre Gosse, Herbert Raditschnig and the zoologist Peter Bolwerk. We flew first to Paramaribo, the capital of Suriname, to begin our search for the last Indian tribes and the Maroons, or Bush Negroes, former African slaves who had been forced to work on the sugar plantations before escaping and creating their own independent communities in the jungle, where until recently they maintained a West African culture and remained separate from mainstream society. The slave traders had selected only the fittest and healthiest men and women, mostly from the Ewe and Ashanti tribes, and this might explain why so many of them managed to survive the appalling conditions on the sea voyage from Africa to Suriname. For the Dutch plantation owners, the loss of their African workforce was a serious blow and they paid large rewards for their capture and return. After the Emancipation Proclamation of 1863, the last of these African slaves left their places of work and were replaced by Indian, Javanese and Chinese workers, a move that is reflected in the colourful multi-ethnic society of present day Paramaribo.

The five major Maroon tribes in existence today are the Djuka, Saramaccaner, Matuwari, Paramaccaner, and Quinti and it is the river system that provides their vital line of communication, since travel through the impenetrable jungle is only possible by boat. During our expedition we hired several pirogues equipped with outboard motors, capable of negotiating the many dangerous rapids.

The villages of the Paramaccans and Saramaccans were never located on the river banks, but the presence of a settlement could be determined by the half hidden curtain of palm fronds and the trampled sand on the beach. Our team was anxious to respect the local customs, so we only went ashore after being granted permission to do so by the emissary of the tribal leader, or *granman* as he was known. As expedition leader it fell to me to present the first of our gifts, so I grabbed a couple of bottles of Schnapps and went into the village, where the council of elders was meeting. They spoke *taki-taki*, a type of Creole pidgin said to consist of at least eight different languages. Permission to stay was granted on the strict understanding that we would not disturb the spirits of the earth by digging for oil or gold. The elders also extracted another promise from me: that we would not take any of their money. They were worried that we might be Dutch tax collectors from Paramaribo.

It was important to treat the *granman*, easily identified by the ceremonial staff he carried as a sign of his office, with the utmost respect to avoid causing offence to his fellow tribespeople, whose extreme sensitivity to any kind of injustice or disregard for their freedom was attributable to the years of oppression and inhuman treatment suffered by their ancestors.

We then made our way to the House of the Gods, where some of the alcohol I had brought was duly sacrificed. Only then were we

allowed to land our boats and unload our equipment. The house in which we were accommodated had a richly carved front; next to it, two men were hollowing out a new boat and outside one of the other huts we saw other men carving drums and paddles. The carvings depicted symbols of domesticity or elementary wishes such as fertility.

We had plenty to occupy us over the next few days. Jean-Pierre went fishing, while King Leopold took photographs in the jungle. As a general principle, Leopold only ever took photographs when the sky was overcast. I spent a lot of time with a woman of indeterminate age who owned a collection of carved wooden combs, spoons and clothes pegs that had been given to her as a young woman by her admirers. The Maroons were not well versed in the art of writing but had learned to represent the concepts of love, place and time in their carvings. The old woman must once have been a much coveted beauty. I managed to record her *taki-taki* in my journal in a reasonably accurate fashion. She kept pointing to the symbol of a frog and explained that this creature was regarded as the symbol of love, since the male of the species calls to his mate all night long until morning comes.

313

I was so impressed by the Paramaccans carvings and the sweet smelling red cedar wood they used that I contacted my wife at the earliest opportunity and asked her to measure up the dining alcove and the doors in our house. By the time our expedition was over, the Paramaccans had carved sixty wooden planks and two door frames with the symbols I had chosen.

Suriname is a true paradise for the explorer. The next stage of our trip took us further inland to Palumeu, where we established a base in a government bungalow. It was now late autumn and the weather at the Equator was tropically humid, but the monsoon period was over and we did not have to allow for the weather when making our plans. We travelled down the Maroni River to the Wajana Indian community, where we wished to experience the wasp and ant ceremony for which they were known. The initiation ceremony is a test of courage and endurance for the boys and girls of the tribe, a rite of passage performed as part of the celebrations that mark the youngsters' acceptance into adult society.

A raffia mat in the shape of an animal or fish, a piranha or armadillo for example, is rolled up and filled with as many as two hundred wasps or biting ants, which are arranged in such a way that their stings or pincers protrude on one side. The mat is then pressed against the naked backs and chests of the young acolytes, who have spent the whole of the previous night dancing in a trancelike state. Bundles of dried nuts are tied around the knees of the young boys and girls, which rattle noisily when they move. The youngsters' skin is decorated with colourful toucan feathers and they play a monotonous tune on little bone flutes.

The wasp and ant torture is used in initiation rites and hunting rituals. Before they go hunting, the tribesmen allow themselves to be stung by wasps or bitten by ants in the belief that this will bring them greater success during the hunt. The shapes of the mats represent the spirits that rule the bush, the lords of the jungle and the animals, and the tribesmen believe that when they are stung, a part of these spirits is transferred to their bodies along with the venom.

The village of the Wajana was situated a little higher than the slow

314

flowing Maroni River. The thatched roofed huts had no containing walls and the Indians relaxed in their gently swinging hammocks. For us, this was paradise. Leopold remarked that our families probably imagined that we were hacking our way, sweaty and exhausted, through the thick jungle and suggested staging an appropriate photograph. I borrowed a khaki coloured tropical helmet from one of the porters, clenched a pipe between my teeth, stuck out my chin, wiped the sweat from my brow and struck a suitably manly pose. Two years later I came across the joke image in a large format illustrated book about explorers, where it was captioned as a typical expedition photograph.

Anapeike, the chief of the Wajana, had visited the capital Paramaribo as a guest of the government. He approached me one day with a request. "You told me that you also have a king with you," he said, "So can you ask him to speak with his white colleagues in Paramaribo and arrange for me, as King of the Wajana, to get the bright light, too?"

I did not wish to disappoint him, so I said I would pass his request on, although I knew it was not possible at that time to bring electricity to the deepest jungle. Yet time did not stand still, even here, and just a month later the enterprising Anapeika made a lucrative arrangement with a Club Méditerranée travel guide on a nearby Caribbean island to bring groups of visitors across to the Wajana village in fast boats. The tourists would strip naked, have their bodies painted in the traditional tribal style and dance with the Wajana before returning to their holiday island.

There was plenty for all of the expedition team to observe and record, of course. For example, the Wajana had their own method of catching fish, using the roots of a certain species of liana, called *neku*, which contain a substance called rotenone. This has a numbing effect on the respiratory function of fish. Jean-Pierre strung a net across a stream, the poisonous liana extract was tipped into the water and very soon a variety of aquatic creatures floated to the surface. The Wajana then selected the edible fish, slit them open, removed the poisoned innards and threw them back into the water. It was the same method I had observed the Xingu Indians using. Jean-Pierre's method differed slightly from that of the Wajana. He threw the fish into a plastic expedition barrel filled with formalin solution for later identification at the research institute. He discovered a number of new species, one of which he named *Geophagus harreri*, or "Maroni eartheater". Jean-Pierre also caught two large piranhas for our supper, which he placed carefully to one side. I picked one of them up to look at its sharp, saw like teeth. "Drop it, now!" Jean-Pierre shouted, and proceeded to show me why. He prodded the mouth of the supposedly dead fish with a stick and it bit so hard into the wood that he was able to lift the creature bodily, stick and all.

That evening, as we were enjoying the usual cicada concert and the colourful spectacle of the tropical sunset, some of the children who had been playing on the riverbank brought me a sloth they had found swimming in the river. The cute little animal seemed perfectly tame and wrapped itself around me affectionately as I held it in my arms. Seeing my obvious delight, Peter Bolwerk offered to stuff it for me, but the thought of taking this living creature home as a dead souvenir appalled me, so I took it over to a tree at the edge of the jungle, where I photographed it instead. Then, with a typically languid display of unhurried movement, it slowly made its way back to freedom.

As darkness fell, the air was filled with innumerable fireflies. These glow-worms were much larger and more colourful than their European counterparts and Leopold told me about the Indian women who would string together alternating red and green ones and wear them around their necks as jewellery. To keep the insects alive during the day, they would be kept in hollowed out pieces of sugar cane.

Leopold was still suffering from the effects of a previous back injury and had packed a folding camp bed to sleep on. The rest of us slept in hammocks like the Indians and welcomed the evening breeze that meant we could dispense with our mosquito nets. From time to time we felt a breath of air on our faces as a bat flitted past. Peter assured us that they were not vampire bats, and we slept well that night.

Every day, our gaze had been drawn to the steep profile of a prominent rocky mountain, the sacred Kassikassima. Its size and steepness reminded us of the Dolomites, and it was just crying out to be climbed. Leopold's father, Albert I, had been an excellent climber and his son took after him. I had met King Albert back in the early 1930s in the

Dolomites, before he lost his life in a climbing accident at a crag near Namurs. Our climbing team consisted of us five Europeans, several Saramaccans and five Indians, whose experience on the river and in the bush would prove invaluable.

Herbert and I went ahead to reconnoitre the route while the rest of the team cut a path through the jungle. It transpired that the cliff was composed of weathered porphyry and was quite smooth and featureless, with none of the usual cracks and fissures where pitons might be placed for protection, and we had to use an assortment of slings and etriers to overcome the lower, slabby section of the face. The rock was hot to the touch and we slaked our thirst with gulps of water that we hauled up the route in six litre containers. Finally, a little bruised and scratched by the thorns and the spines of the cacti and wild pineapples, we reached the notch between the twin summits. There was an eagle's eyrie beneath an overhand and a hole in the rock face above. It was later explained to me that this was the window through which one could view the myth-enshrouded city of Eldorado.

The route ahead looked possible, so we abseiled off and left all the carabiners and slings at the notch, intending to return in the morning. Leopold had been watching our struggles with interest and took some convincing to join us the following day. It was a strenuous climb but by three o'clock in the afternoon we were shaking hands on the main summit of the Kassikassima massif and waving happily to our friends down below. The natives even performed a celebratory dance. We unfurled the Suriname flag and spread it out so that the ring of five coloured stars was clearly visible from the air. The stars symbolise the various indigenous groups of Suriname and the exemplary way in which these ethnically diverse peoples have banded together to form a single nation. Although the country is still under-developed, it stands as a glowing example to the fact that a nation's happiness does not depend on wealth alone but on the willingness of the people to treat each other as brothers, regardless of race or colour. The notion of apartheid is an unheard of concept here.

We took photographs of the Oranje and Tumac-Humac ranges to the south – our next objectives – and were back in camp by six o'clock in the evening. Leopold took a well-earned rest while the rest of us cooked dinner. The choice of menu was extensive, since Peter had killed a wild boar, a cockerel and a young caiman, the tail of which is considered a rare delicacy, and our porters contributed two monkeys. Everyone was given a measure of rum mixed with freshly squeezed lime juice and we all drank a toast to the mountain. Leopold had recovered from his ordeal and was beaming with delight at his first ever first ascent. We all agreed that it was an impressive achievement for someone over sixty years of age.

Two days later, back at the bungalow in Paloumeu, we received a congratulatory message from the government and the news that the Suriname flag on the summit of Kassikassima had been photographed from an aeroplane and had already appeared in the newspapers. Leopold now planned to take the boats back to Paramaribo with the two scientists, Jean-Pierre and Xaver, and to set off from there into French Guiana. His plan was to travel from Cayenne up the Oulemari River to its source and meet us there. He informed us that he thought it preferable to collect fish and birds for his institute than to march for days through the mountains – quite rightly so, in my opinion.

In the capital city of Suriname I had learned that deep in the interior of the country there lived a completely unknown Indian tribe, whose members were considered to be dangerous savages. They were known as the Wayarekule, and the fantastic tales we heard of their supposedly superhuman abilities made the idea of visiting them all the more exciting for Hubert and me. They were said to be much taller than us Europeans and were rumoured to use poisoned arrows. According to the stories they would break the neck of anyone they captured and used to cross rivers like pole-vaulters, never getting wet. As the tales grew in the telling, so did their physical size and the size and scope of their weapons.

We were joined by the Dutch geologist, Jaap Graanoogst, who was exploring the region hoping to find fresh bauxite deposits, an important mineral used in the production of aluminium and the biggest source of income for Suriname. With Jaap and the porters, our party now numbered twelve in all. As we said goodbye to Leopold's team my eye was again drawn to the words on the door of our bungalow, which had caught my attention on our arrival: "If you venture into the interior of the country, be nice to the people you meet on the way in, since you will need them on the way out!" I remarked to the custodian of the bungalow that this seemed a rather obvious thing to say, to which he replied that it was intended only as good advice and explained that, on occasion, items of expedition kit had gone missing after the natives had experienced difficulties with some of the expedition members.

Our team was actually too big, since we had to allow three weeks for the trip and there was no possibility of restocking our provisions en route. On the very first day we came across a number of old stone workings by the side of the river. They were no longer used to produce stone axes and other tools but a hundred or more years ago the natives had probably polished their tools here using sand and water. At length, we left the river bank and had to hack a path through the undergrowth with our machetes. We pitched camp early that day out of consideration for the porters and went off to comb the area for more stone workings. To prevent us getting lost we bent a few small tree branches to mark the way back to camp.

We came across several old fire pits and some pieces of wood that had been shaped using stone axes but did not meet any people. The Wajarekule changed their hunting grounds like nomads and were probably on the south side of the Tumac-Humac Mountains, on Brazilian soil. We had moved away from the river now, so dining on fish every evening was no longer possible and we found ourselves having to ration our food supplies. Water was getting scarce, too, and we had to conserve what we had in our field bottles carefully. It was all part and parcel of expedition life, but some of the newcomers found it hard to adapt. The romantic campfires, with flocks of colourful birds and butterflies circling above the water, gradually gave way to the boredom of the arid bush. We had now reached the crest of the mountain chain, at a height of about a thousand metres. The jungle was not especially dense, but it was still untouched, primary rainforest and our view ahead was limited. As I lay in my hammock listening to the almost human shrieks of the howler monkeys piercing the darkness, I kept telling myself that here in the jungle the night ruled over everything; it was not just the Indians who guarded this territory from intruders.

The next morning I checked the porters' loads for unnecessary ballast and discarded several bottles and a pair of rather fashionable town shoes. I let them keep their transistor radios and mirrors, however. Two of the Indians cleared the path of tiresome thorn bushes with their machetes while Jaap used the map, altimeter and compass to determine the direction they should take. The porters' fear of the "wild Wajarekule" diminished as our path led downhill to the first fresh springs of the Ojapok, where we quenched our thirst.

As on previous expeditions, it was the many biting ants, large and small, that I found most troublesome. Only once did anyone find a use for these foul little creatures. When one of the porters gashed his hand whilst carving a paddle, he placed one ant after another in the open wound, waited until they bit into the skin and then tore away the rear part of their bodies, effectively stitching the wound closed with four dead ants.

One night the rains came. It began to thunder, and a tropical cloudburst followed. It took a while for the rain to penetrate the thick canopy of trees and reach us. That was the moment when I had the idea of designing a hammock with an integral mosquito net, a rain cover and clothing bag, a design that was later taken on by a large company that specialised in rainwear. The heavy rain soon turned our path into a quagmire. We helped each other through the worst of the mud but it seemed as if one boot would always become stuck fast in the stuff. I now understood what the pessimists had meant when they warned us that it was just as impossible to cross the mountains in the rainy season as it was during the long dry period.

The streams all flowed in an easterly direction now, which meant that in just a few days we would reach our destination, the main Oulemari River, where we were due to rendezvous with Leopold's group. There were fish and game in abundance here and our tinned provisions were superfluous to requirements, but we found no sign of human habitation. Nor did we encounter any crocodiles or snakes, but I must admit I was not unduly disappointed about that.

As each day passed, the differences between the African and Indians in our group grew ever more apparent. During rest stops the Africans were loud and boisterous, singing and dancing as they went about their camp chores before washing, looking at themselves in the mirror and oiling their hair. The transistor radio would then be tuned to a football match. As I write this I am reminded of Ruud Gullit, the footballer from Suriname, who achieved worldwide fame as a member of the Dutch national team. The Indians, by contrast, were not interested in football; they preferred to hunt. In the morning, the Africans would be keen to get moving and always wanted to cover long distances during the day. They kept looking at their watches, obviously feeling the pull of home. The Indians, on the other hand, had no real concept of time; they simply enjoyed being in their native homeland and the bountiful gifts that nature bestowed on them. One of them speared a huge fish, showed it to us proudly and let it swim free. He did it for fun, for sport. Nature provided these people with everything they needed to sustain life.

Two weeks in the bush seemed to be the ideal length of time for our diverse ethnic group to spend together without everyone getting on each other's nerves. Although we had used up a lot of our provisions, the porter loads were not getting any lighter, since Jaap had found the minerals he was looking for, including several large chunks of valuable red bauxite.

Journal entry from 18th November 1966:

"Yesterday evening it took a long time before we were finally able to relax in our hammocks. Our wet clothing is now hanging from the branches of the nearby trees, steaming in the sun. We were served a meal of white rice and fish presented on large, green rubber plant leaves and accompanied by rum and lime juice. It all looked very appetising and could easily have come from the kitchen of a speciality restaurant. I had to remind myself that this was the staple daily diet of the local people. Atibaya, who had assumed the role of the spokesman for the porters, told us that he was thirty-eight years old and had seven children, three brothers and five sisters, all of whom had children of their own. All of the porters became quite excited when Herbert showed them photographs of his two children, but the Indians were beside themselves with delight when he produced a picture of his wife, whose healthy, suntanned complexion gave her an almost Indian appearance.

As I write this journal, Jaap and the other men are out in the bush somewhere. They have been gone for over an hour. From time to time, fish leap out of the water of the nearby stream and above me I can hear the shrieks of the colourful Arara parrots. This is the romantic Paradise I dreamed of as a young boy."

Next morning, as we were crossing a river, we met up with Leopold and his team. Since there was not enough room in the boats for all of us we decided to pitch camp and swap experiences. The reunion came at the just right time for both groups, and to mark the occasion we stripped a section of bark from one of the trees with a bush knife and carved an inscription in the wood – the word "Reunion", with the names of all the expedition members listed beneath it. Leopold had the most exciting tale to relate, an encounter with a huge snake, an anaconda that he had found coiled up at the entrance to a cave. As the snake languidly began to uncoil and withdraw to the depths of the cave, Peter had shot it through the head. It had taken four men to carry the beast back to the campfire, where Radin, the cook, had removed the skin for the Institute in Brussels. It was only six metres long, but still weighed something over a hundred kilograms and had a girth of sixty centimetres.

We heard several more alarming snake stories on the walk-out. Some Dutch farmers offered us accommodation for the night and during the communal evening meal we listened with interest to the hair-raising stories told by their employees, stories that, had they not been immediately confirmed by the farmers themselves, we would have dismissed out of hand as the product of an overwrought imagination. One of the Wayana Indians, a man by the name of Pirima, told us of an experience he had had just a few days earlier. He had been fishing on the river with his family with a bow and arrow, but the big fish he thought he had killed turned out to be the tail of a huge snake, which wrapped itself around him in an instant and bit hard into his knee before proceeding to crush the life out of him. The snake was as thick as a grown man's thigh, he said. Pirima's wife grabbed an axe and attacked the head of the snake, while his ten year old boy stabbed at it with a long bush knife. The dead anaconda was swept away by the current and eagerly devoured by a shoal of piranhas.

The museum in Paramaribo had a six-and-a-half metre long stuffed snake as one of its exhibits and I also have it on good authority that the American Museum of Natural History in New York once offered a high price for any anaconda measuring over seven metres in length. The anaconda crushes its victim using its powerful muscles, but the smaller bushmaster has a venom that is far deadlier. The bushmaster belongs to the pit viper family and some specimens grow to three metres in length. It is frequently found in the northern regions of South America and in Suriname, it accounts for many of the fatal accidents attributable to snake bites. We heard one story of a worker in a bauxite mine who was bitten through his boot by a bushmaster and died as a result. Two weeks later his brother put the boot on and died, too. In both cases, the doctor established the cause of death as snake venom. One of the bushmaster's fangs had broken off and become lodged in the fabric of the boot and the scratch had been sufficient to kill the original victim's unfortunate brother.

Another story concerned a group of three Saramaccans, who were bitten by a bushmaster whilst employed by the military to cut a path through the jungle to Bloumstein Lake. One of them died on the way to the field hospital, the second received a life-saving injection of snake bite serum and the third died two days later after refusing the injection in favour of the *sneki-koti* prepared by his tribe's medicine man.

In addition to the syringes and serum from the Xingu expedition, I also had a phial of *sneki-koti* from the Saramaccan medicine man in my first aid kit. The *sneki-koti* is an ancient preparation – roughly translated, it means "against snakes" – and every medicine man had his own secret recipe. I purchased mine at considerable expense from one of the most famous medicine men, whose method involved drying and crushing the body of a dead bird at a specific rocky place on the bank of a river where the spirits lived, and adding his own secret mixture of herbs and alcohol. I was solemnly informed that the costly potion was only effective for six months at the most and had to be imbibed before setting foot in the jungle.

In spite of its dubious worth, demand for this potion was high, since there were other venomous snakes in the region in addition to the bushmaster. One of these was the rattlesnake, which has a rattle on its tail tip composed of segments of beadlike scales that it uses to warn intruders of its presence. In the case of one unfortunate Dutch banana plantation owner we heard about, the warning came too late. Late one evening, his dog started to bark and when the farmer went outside to investigate he discovered a huge armadillo. What he failed to notice, however, was the rattlesnake that was stalking it. The snake bit the Dutchman in the leg and he killed it with his bush knife. He then drank a mouthful of the *sneki-koti*, but during the night he became feverish and the following morning he decided to ride his motorcycle to the doctor's. His wife came to the door to wave him off, but as she watched he fell off his bike and died.

My journals contain several pages of notes about Asian snake charmers, who earn their living handling highly venomous snakes like the bushmaster and coral snake in the most casual way imaginable. It all looks very brave, but generally they remove the fangs first. My advice, based on my expedition experiences, is to make sure that you shake out your boots in the morning, since it is not uncommon to find a poisonous scorpion or a small snake that has crawled in there during the night for warmth and shelter. The advice applies to travellers in Europe, too, where on more than one occasion I have been stung by a wasp that was nestling in the warm folds of a carpet slipper. As the leader of an expedition it is important to ensure that all of the members of your team take sensible precautions, and are carrying the appropriate medication, against possible allergic reactions to bites or stings of any kind, for if the required medication is not available, even a wasp or bee sting can lead to a potentially fatal anaphylactic shock.

The expedition was now drawing to a close, and it was time to pay off our helpers. The porters each received forty-five guilders, the cook double that amount. As usual, they confirmed receipt of their pay with a thumb print. Leopold and I spent a few relaxing days on the river and made a brief excursion to the coast, where the Cariben Indians lived. It turned out to be a bit of an anticlimax after the unforgettable experiences of the previous few weeks, as the region had fallen victim to the ravages of tourism. I said goodbye to my friends at the airport. It was now December, so we wished each other a Happy Christmas, too.

I had to stay on in Paramaribo for a while to pack the many ethnological artefacts I had amassed during the trip, including the carved sections of wood for our house, and arrange for their shipment back to Europe. In just a few weeks, the valuable items would arrive in Amsterdam on a fast steamer. I had acquired more than three hundred carved pieces from the Saramaccans and Paramaccans, but had tried in vain to persuade a *granman* to part with his ceremonial staff. A symbol of his absolute power and status, it was made of high quality wood, beautifully carved and worn smooth to the touch. The *granman* had inherited the staff from his father, together with the title of tribal chief, or oracle, which, unlike similar titles in Tibet, was never bestowed anew on the death of the incumbent, but was always a hereditary title. I came across many such staffs of office during my travels. On my visits to the Indian tribes of the high Andes, for example, I noticed that the medicine man, or shaman, always carried a carved stick when he spoke to the mountain gods or attempted to invoke the eruption of a volcano. Ceremonial sceptres have played a part in rituals for at least three thousand years, and even the English army officers in my prison camp at Dehra Dun had carried a swagger stick as a symbol of their authority. There is, of course, a rather more prosaic explanation for this stick carrying. The shaman, or magician, frequently consumes alcohol or other drugs to induce a state of trance and the staff thus provides him with a very useful means of support and helps disguise his intoxicated gait.

I always enjoyed the final phase of an expedition, and the task of supervising the packing and shipment of the various artefacts I had collected. It was a time of rest and relaxation after the rigours of the expedition itself. Over the years I developed a certain skill in deciding on the best place from which to dispatch my finds and the most effective way of organising the whole process when I was unable to be there in person. One must always try to find trustworthy helpers, pay them generously and be prepared to use smaller ports to avoid the tedious delays caused by unnecessary bureaucracy. Unfortunately, one must also take into account the fact that, in certain circumstances, the shipment might never actually arrive in Europe.

During those last few days in New Amsterdam, as the harbour

town of Paramaribo is known, I was reminded of the impressive exploits of the natural historian, artist and adventurer Maria Sibylle Merian, who had also spent time in Suriname. I thought about how difficult it must have been for her as a woman traveller in this country. As a schoolboy, I had often been praised for my detailed drawings of flowers, fruit and birds and had sometimes wondered if it might be possible to pursue my interest in a professional capacity. Then, one day, as I was leafing through an art book, I came across the hand coloured copper engravings from Maria Sibylle Merian's 1705 masterpiece, *Metamorphosis Insectorum Surinamensium* and I knew that I had set my sights too high. Sybille Merian was the gifted daughter of the famous Frankfurt engraver, Matthäus Merian. After hearing about Surinam and its tropical flora and fauna during a stay in Holland, she decided to travel with her youngest daughter, Dorothea, to the Dutch colony. Nowadays it is hard to imagine what her voyage must have been like, on a small sailing ship, in stormy weather and with insufficient food. It took her three months to get to Suriname, where she stayed for two years, collecting and drawing the local plants and native insects. Sybille Merian's book was an instant success and gained worldwide acclaim. The great Swedish botanist, Carl von Linné, described Sybille Merian's work as an immortal achievement, and her image once graced the German five hundred mark note.

MALARIA

In the autumn of 1969, Leopold and I returned to French-Guiana. We had just two months in which to visit an Indian tribe that lived near the source of the Oyapock, as we both wanted to be home again for Christmas. It was to be a pleasant trip, with no great hardships, but towards the end there was an unpleasant turn of events, the consequences of which we were to suffer for some time to come.

We flew in to the capital, Cayenne, where King Leopold was received with due ceremony by the Governor. It was often the case that Leopold's status opened doors that would otherwise have remained closed to me, and on this occasion the Governor invited us to attend a rocket launch at the French Guiana Space Centre in Kourou. We drove west down the coast to Kourou, where we made ourselves comfortable in one of the many new houses that had been built to accommodate the fast growing population. Kourou lies almost on the Equator and is well situated as a launching site for European Space Agency (ESA) missions. I had met the Father of Space Travel, Hermann Oberth, on two occasions at his home near Nuremberg, and had also visited his famous student Wernher von Braun in Huntsville, Alabama. And now I was strolling around one of the facilities that had been established to turn the ideas of these pioneering scientists into reality.

We spent the day making a boat trip to the Isles du Salut, the smallest of which is better known as Devil's Island. It was a notorious French penal colony until 1946, and achieved widespread infamy when it was featured in ex-Devil's Island convict Henri Charrière's bestselling 1970's novel *Papillon*. As we climbed the steep stone steps leading from the landing place to the top of the vertical cliffs, I got a fair idea of the harsh conditions endured by both the convicts and their guards. During our visit we were shown the bell that tolled whenever one of the inmates died. The body was then tossed into the sea, and the sharks did the rest.

That evening, back at Kourou, we dined with the Director of the Kennedy Space Center at Cape Canaveral in Florida. While we were chatting, we could hear the countdown through the loudspeakers in the mess. The tension was growing, and with two hours still to go before lift-off we were shown into the large room where the experts with headphones sat at a row of flickering control screens. Then we went outside, where the whole facility was lit up, bright as day, and floodlights shone on the rocket. Everyone has seen a rocket launch on television, but to experience the bubbling and hissing of the huge engines at close quarters is another thing entirely. My respect for the rocket engineers grew as we counted down the minutes to lift-off.

The rocket, which had been christened "Vesta", after the brightest asteroid in the sky, took off slowly and picked up speed as it traced a graceful arc across the Atlantic. Then, suddenly, it vanished. There was talk of a technical defect and the champagne that had been put on ice remained unopened. Most of the missions ran without a hitch, it must be said, and all were documented in a novel way in the mess. The Kourou space facility had seen a hundred such launches and there were ninety-two champagne corks arranged in a row on a shelf above the bar, along with eight plastic water bottle tops that represented the failed or aborted attempts. The Ariane Space Programme at Kourou is now recognised as the most successful satellite launch programme in history.

Although my own expeditions had all been accomplished without the use of extravagant technological equipment, I was mightily impressed by the commitment and pioneering spirit of the research scientists, without whom the development of space travel as we know it would not have been possible. Even today, I still take note of every new discovery that is made and I am well aware of the fact that those who discover extraordinary new things achieve a kind of immortality. On July 23, 1995, an unusually bright comet was discovered, simultaneously yet independently, by Alan Hale in New Mexico and Thomas Bopp in Arizona. Henceforth, it became known as Hale-Bopp. The two astronomers demonstrated that even without UFOs there were still "miracles" to be discovered out in space.

On a vaguely related note, a little closer to home, I was also impressed by the discovery of the skeleton of a new species of dinosaur by two fossil collectors, Hans-Dieter and Hans Joachim Weiss, in the Altmühltal Nature Park in Bavaria in 1998, the same year that one hundred fossilised dinosaur eggs were found in a sea cliff on the South Korean coast. The violet coloured eggs were estimated by palaeontologists to be one-hundred-million years old and the scientists were hoping to find a fossilised foetus inside one of the eggs that would prove that they came from herbivorous dinosaurs. According to microbiologists, countless microscopic creatures become extinct before they are discovered, so it came as something of a shock for the zoologists when a team of scientists announced the sensational discovery of a strange new species of hairy, six centimetre long deep sea worms. The study of these creatures will doubtless keep the marine biologists busy for some time to come.

In the remote corners of the Earth, new life forms still await discovery, while beneath the ice of the Antarctic there is a mountain range the size of the Alps. Our world still offers limitless scope for adventure and exploration. As human beings, we should observe the natural world, and adapt ourselves to it, but we should never seek to conquer it. We are dependent upon Nature, and it is therefore our duty to preserve our natural heritage and to pass it on to future generations in the same state in which we found it.

Back in Cayenne, we paid a visit to the office of the World Health Organisation, to seek medical advice for our forthcoming trip into the interior of the country. On the walls of the office were several maps decorated with little coloured drawing pins that illustrated the spread of various dangerous diseases. According to the maps, there was no serious risk of infection where the Oyampi Indians lived, at the source of the Oyapock, our intended destination on the border with Brazil. The government had already issued us with our travel permits, but we still had to be examined by a doctor to rule out the possibility of carrying any infections to the local inhabitants, as we had been obliged to do in New Guinea. It was explained to us that the Oyampi, who lived at an altitude of over one thousand metres in the mountains, were far healthier than the coastal Indians.

We hired two Oayana men with a boat to help us on the trip. They had been converted to Christianity by the missionaries, and were thus regarded as "civilised". Before leaving Cayenne, the last outpost of Western culture, we decided to spend the night in a hotel, although "doss house" might be a more apt description of the place. Our double room had bare boards on the floor. It was right at the top of the building, and reached by a steep set of rickety wooden steps.

Over the following few days we paddled gently up the Oyapok in the dugout-canoe, slept in hammocks, wrote our journals and enjoyed the atmosphere of the river. We found several more stone workings near shallow rapids, and the air was full of butterflies. An entomologist had once told me that the best way to photograph the azure blue *Morpho brasiliensis* was to entice it closer with one of the blue metallic ashtrays used by Air France. During our stopover in Martinique I had asked the stewardess if I could have one of the ashtrays. As promised, the ashtray lure did the trick, and I got my shot.

The Oyampi behaved as if they had not noticed our presence; even the children carried on playing by the river. We respected their right to give us a cool reception and refrained from clambering up the notched tree trunk that led to their hut. Compared to the Indians in nearby Suriname, we found the chief of the Oyampi rather arrogant and we thus acted with some restraint when handing out the presents we had brought.

After just two days, we left. We estimated that the return journey would take about five days, but as we were drifting slowly down the river in our dugout, we heard the unmistakable sound of a helicopter, which landed close by. It transpired that the Governor had instructed the pilot to come and look for us, so we paid off the two Oayana boatmen and accepted the helicopter pilot's kind offer of a lift back to Cayenne. We did not know it at the time, but it was a decision that probably saved our lives. We landed in Paris on 20th December and wished each other Merry Christmas again before parting company.

A few days after arriving back in Europe I started suffering from shivering fits and a fever and my pulse rate increased alarmingly. The doctor said there was an outbreak of influenza doing the rounds and gave me a flu injection. When this failed to help, my wife telephoned our friend, Dr. Wechselberger, who had published a book of medical tips for travellers in tropical countries. He sounded the alarm and instructed me to go at once to the hospital in Innsbruck. Carina, who could always be counted on to rise to the occasion in times of crisis, drove me straight there, and I was admitted to the department of the well-known specialist Herbert Braunsteiner. Due to the flu epidemic, there were no rooms immediately available and I had to lie on a trolley in a corridor whilst waiting for a bed, but by then I was semi-conscious and only dimly aware of what was going on around me.

For the next few days I was in a state of delirium. I remember very little of what went on, apart from the many blood tests I had to endure. My veins are not particularly well suited to such things and I recall that there was an awful lot of prodding and probing necessary to obtain the samples. The blood tests showed no definite signs of any specific condition, but my temperature remained dangerously high, so the samples were dispatched to the Institute for Tropical Medicine in Hamburg, and a specialist in tropical diseases from Tübingen sent a courier to Innsbruck with a box of anti-hepatitis serum.

After a fortnight of feverish shivering fits I started to get pains in my spleen and liver, and the cluster of experts around my hospital bed grew larger by the hour. Some of the doctors suggested surgery, whilst others argued for a computer tomography. A big, strong hospital porter lifted me easily onto a trolley – I had lost twelve kilos in weight by then – and wheeled me off for yet another examination. As instructed, I lay there for an hour, completely motionless under the x-ray machine, killing time by thinking dark thoughts and reciting holy mantras and vulgar profanities under my breath.

According to my notes, I lapsed into a coma on 16th January 1970. In my delirium, I imagined that someone had grabbed me by the ankle and was slamming me repeatedly into the wall of an art gallery, with such force that a variety of colourful bodily fluids squirted out and spattered onto the wall like an abstract painting.

The doctors treated me for the full array of tropical diseases, with the exception of *Malaria tropicana* or, to give it its more scientific name, *Plasmodium falciparum,* which in those days was known to the medical profession but was virtually undetectable and not readily treatable. I was given another large dose of penicillin, and on 23rd January, after a further session with the radiographer had failed to reveal the cause of my illness, my scheduled operation was cancelled. On the same day I received a telephone call from Brussels informing me that King Leopold had been very ill since 23rd December and that his condition was now critical. In my weakened state, this news came as a great shock to me; I felt responsible somehow, and refused to talk to anyone for a while. Three days later Carina learned from Princess de Réthy that Leopold had been diagnosed as having contracted *Plasmodium falciparum* and was being treated with a crash course of pure quinine. Finally, my doctors had something concrete to work with.

During the worst days of my illness, some unscrupulous magazine journalists had obtained permission to visit me by pretending to be good friends of mine. As soon as I spotted the photographer I hid under the blankets. Shortly afterwards, Toni Sailer arrived with some of my real friends. They were on the way to the skiing world championships in the Dolomites and brought me a bunch of Christmas roses from the Kaisergebirge. Thus far, I had refused all offers of flowers on the grounds that the smell reminded me of a funeral parlour, but these I accepted with pleasure. When I flung back the bedcovers and my friends caught sight of my withered legs they all dissolved into fits of laughter.

By the end of January I was over the worst, and in early February I received similarly good news from Brussels. During the weeks I was in hospital, Carina had been staying at a hotel nearby, so she was usually able to spend the whole day with me. Every morning two nurses would arrive to make my bed. The job took no time at all, and as a finishing touch they would routinely tuck the sheet and woollen blanket tight under the mattress. I used to struggle like mad to create a bit of breathing space for my legs and usually had to wait until Carina arrived to free me.

After forty-five days of illness my test results finally showed a reasonable number of leucocytes in my blood and Professor Braunsteiner arranged for me to be discharged the following day. I was in high spirits on receiving the news, so I thought I would cheer Carina up a little, too. I placed a Christmas rose between the toes of each foot, pulled the blanket over my head and lay there with my feet sticking out of the bed covers. It was only after I sat up and winked mischievously that she realised the whole thing had been a bad joke.

On the drive home I wondered why my wife was not smoking her usual cigarettes. She told me that since she had not been able to feed her nicotine habit whilst at the hospital, she had decided to give it up altogether. She has never smoked since, so the malaria had one positive effect at least. Leopold spent time convalescing in Biotte on the Cote d'Azur, and when we spoke we soon determined that our bouts of malaria had occurred at exactly the same time. We concluded that we had probably both been infected by the same anopheles mosquito.

From then on, it was only natural that I took a keen interest in any magazine or newspaper articles relating to malaria. I came across a piece in *Time* magazine about a New York man who had died of malaria after a car accident. A US soldier, who had taken drugs whilst serving in Vietnam, had found himself back in New York and short of money to feed his addiction, so he went to sell some blood. At that time it was impossible for doctors to detect the *Plasmodium falciparum* pathogen in blood samples and so the victim of the car crash was given a transfusion of the soldier's blood. He died of malaria shortly afterwards. There had been similar cases in Europe, some of which were caused by malarial mosquitoes that had somehow found their way onto aeroplanes during stopovers in the tropics.

During my next lecture tour I visited the Boehringer biopharmaceutical facility at Biberach, where they were conducting research into anti-malaria drugs. Like the employees, I wore sterile clothing and a plastic cap as I sat at my microscope. What I saw through the lens came as quite a shock. The thought that, only a short time previously, there had been millions of these tiny, sickle shaped malaria pathogens dashing about inside my body filled me with dread. Nonetheless, I found it fascinating to observe these deadly microscopic organisms, and I came away eternally grateful to the doctors for having survived the nasty little beasts. I vowed to continue my strict regime of hard exercise and good food, as I was well aware that I had only survived the malaria because I was in excellent physical shape.

Nowadays, more than thirty years later, the hidden dangers of *Malaria tropicana* are well known and equally well documented. We are better informed of the complications, and the life-threatening consequences, that often accompany this infection, and with hindsight it is easy to understand the confusion and misdiagnoses that occurred in my case. I would strongly advise anyone intending to travel to the tropics to inform themselves of the potential health risks first, to spare them from the pain and misery I endured as a result of my illness, and to be mindful of the fact that, although various quinine preparations have achieved some measure of success in combating *Plasmodium falciparum*, resistant strains of the disease do now exist. It is therefore advisable to consult a doctor who is a specialist in tropical medicine, preferably one who has contacts with the World Health Organisation, who will be in a position to prescribe the correct medication to ward off the disease.

THE WARRIORS OF THE HADENDOA

For the time being, there was no question of me embarking on any new expeditions. Instead, I dedicated 1970 to the pursuit of several other interesting projects. Since 1966, the Raiffeisen banking group had sponsored a worldwide competition for young researchers under the title "Jugend forscht". The winners received a prize of an adventure holiday in the Austrian Alps or a trip of a lifetime to some far-off country, and I had been invited to accompany them. I organised a training course for the youngsters, based in a mountain refuge in the Dachstein Mountains, where I taught them some of the skills needed to survive in the mountain environment, including how to splint an injured leg and the best way of avoiding snow blindness. During the summer, we camped out in the mountains, and we also took a trip to America to visit Wernher von Braun and went paddling on a lake in Canada.

During the summer after my illness I took a group to Iceland and Greenland, but the most unforgettable experience was the three week trip we made to Japan. We were particularly impressed by the high speed "bullet trains" and thoroughly enjoyed the experience of being served free tea by the smiling stewardesses as we watched the tachometer on the wall of our compartment climb to over two hundred kilometres an hour. What was equally impressive was the fact that when the train pulled into the station all the doors were perfectly aligned with the corresponding marks on the platform, and were at platform level, which made boarding the train a far simpler process. I still find it incredible that, thirty years later, when catching a train in Europe, I have to lie in wait for the correct compartment to flash past and then grab my luggage and run, before clambering up a set of steep, awkward steps to board the train.

We also made a trip to Yakushima Island, the most southerly of the Japanese islands. It was a little selfish of me to suggest we go there, I suppose, but I had long been fascinated by the place and the prospect of finding tropical fruit and arctic vegetation on the same small island was too tempting to miss. We followed a succession of well-marked and signposted paths through the thick forest to see the stands of Japanese cedar, or *Cryptomeria japonica*, one of which had a notice that proclaimed it as "The Oldest Tree in the World – 7000 Years." Some of the old, damaged cedars had Shinto shrines built inside their hollow trunks, where one could sit awhile and contemplate. Up in the mountains there were unmanned huts where one could spend the night, but we were all feeling the cold and were happy to descend though the damp mist to the warmer coastal region in the morning. I now have a splendid *Rhododendron yakushimensis* in my garden as a reminder of the many beautiful flowers I saw on that trip.

Of course, we also drove up to see the holy mountain of Fuji-san and visited the Nikko shrine with its famous carved figures of the three monkeys, who "See no evil, Hear no evil, Speak no evil" and whose message is an important part of the Shinto-Buddhist faith. I also enjoyed our trip to the temples of Kobe, where we found an inscription that read: "If you have never seen Kobe, do not say that it is beautiful." We also went to the famous Sorakuen Garden in Kobe, where we selected ten bonsai that were later exhibited at various Raiffeisen banks before ending up at our home, where they slowly perished.

I got a great deal of pleasure from my trips with these youngsters and it was nice to see their hard work being given the public recognition it deserved. Winning the "Jugend forscht" competition sometimes led to them being offered good jobs in large companies and, on more than one occasion, to their work being patented. I derived similar satisfaction from my involvement in the International Schools' annual skiing competition, whose winner's trophy bore my name. We generally opted to hold the event in Seefeld, where we obtained preferential rates for accommodation and ski passes and my former ski instructor Toni Seelos helped with the prize giving ceremony. The International Schools were expensive and were responsible for the education of the offspring of many rich and famous people, so there was no shortage of sponsors; in fact, there were often as many prizes as there were competitors. In later years, I was delighted to see many former winners returning to Seefeld with their children to show them the place where they had once won their "Heinrich Harrer Prize".

336

During this time, I visited New York at every available opportunity to see the latest musicals or visit my friends at The Explorer's Club. Although I was an honorary member of the club, I was not allowed to borrow any of the library books, but it was nice to be able to sit in a comfortable armchair with a pile of books and maps and plan my future trips. The little restaurant at the club was another excellent reason to go there, as every day there was a different exotic dish on the menu. Fortunately, roasted goats' eyes – a highly prized delicacy in North Africa – only featured on the menu once a year. I was also a regular visitor at the Austrian Cultural Institute, where I gave talks. The audience was mainly comprised of emigrant Austrians, but the director of the institute, Hans Waldner, often invited other guests, too.

When I stopped in New York on the way home from my Xingu expedition in 1966, I mentioned to Waldner in passing that I had been giving some thought to my pension provision and was considering selling off my ethnographic collection. I had always been an enthusiastic collector and the pleasure I derived from cataloguing beautiful and interesting objects had always been a motivating factor for the trips I made. As a young man I had collected stamps with a mountain theme and had scoured shops and flea markets for stamps of that type. I was also an avid coin collector. Whenever I visited a new town, I never missed the opportunity of rummaging around in the antique shops and I had made several interesting finds over the years in places as far afield as Calcutta, Scotland, London and New York. My book collection now includes almost everything that has ever been published about Tibet, together with many books on pioneers like Marco Polo, Alexander von Humboldt and the polar explorers. The ethnographic artefacts that I brought back from my expeditions were mainly purchased from the local people, or traded for something of mine that they found useful. I did not always get the items I wanted, often for religious reasons, which I of course respected. The bulk of my collection was made up of the many Tibetan artefacts I had brought back from Lhasa or had acquired over the years during various trips to Nepal and India.

When I bade farewell to my Tibetan friends in 1951, the mother of the Dalai Lama presented me with two beautifully woven rugs, which we still have in our home. Other Tibetans gave me *thangkas* to remember them by, as they knew of my interest in these scroll paintings. It was not possible to purchase religious artefacts such as these in the bazaar. They were generally commissioned directly from the artists, who would often spend years working on a series of scroll paintings for their patrons. When the destruction of the Cultural Revolution began, many pious Tibetans threw their priceless works of art into the rivers; it was said that the Tibetans became poorer and the rivers richer as a result. In 1959, when hundreds of thousands of Tibetans fled to India, many of them tried to save their personal religious icons and in order to smuggle the *thangkas* past the border guards, they would wrap them around their bodies beneath their clothing. Some even chose instead to make arduous treks across the six thousand metre mountain passes, where no Chinese guards were stationed.

After years in exile, many of the Tibetan refugees needed money to pay for their children's education, and they began to offer their treasures for sale. They could only get a pittance for them in Dharamsala, as the Dalai Lama's government in exile was only able to offer a nominal price. This meant that I was able to acquire several items on each of my yearly visits to the refugee camps in India. Word soon got around that I paid a fair price for Tibetan art and treated everything with the greatest of respect. For example, the Tibetans knew that I would never desecrate a statue of Buddha by touching its face, or place a holy book on a chair; this would have been sacrilege, and according to Tibetan belief it was the original owner who would be held accountable for any such desecration.

To begin with I received a certain amount of criticism, but later, when the Dalai Lama had had the opportunity of visiting some of the museums and exhibitions that contained items of Tibetan art, I was praised for my efforts in trying to save at least some of the treasures of Tibet and giving the many visitors the chance to acquaint themselves with this ancient and honourable culture. I have a vision that one day Tibet will again be free, and that collectors around the world, who have learned to love all that the Dalai Lama, his people and the kingdom of snow at the Roof of the World stand for, will return one precious item from their collection to the place from whence it came and to which it rightfully belongs.

When I spoke to Hans Waldner at the Austrian Cultural Institute in New York about disposing of my collection of ethnographic items, he agreed to approach various foundations in New York and elsewhere, whom he thought might have funds available for such a purchase. Shortly after my return to Austria in 1966, I received a call from the Cultural Ministry of the State of Styria, who said they wished to negotiate a price. Waldner had done as promised, and had informed his Foreign Ministry in Vienna of my intentions, and they had forwarded the information to Styria. It marked the beginning of years of to-ing and fro-ing, a tug-of-war that was only finally resolved in 1972.

The mayor of Graz initially enquired whether I would be able to fill all sixteen rooms in Castle Eggenberg with my exhibits. I informed him that my Tibetan collection alone, with over a hundred scroll paintings, bronzes and handwritten books, would fill the space easily, and that this estimate did not include the ethnographic items I had brought back from my other expeditions, or the journals, photos, various pieces of equipment and medals. There followed a series of meetings; the file grew thicker and concerns were raised about the money needed to finance the project after the collection had been purchased. Since it appeared that a lump sum would be difficult to obtain, I suggested that they grant me a senior civil servant's state pension, as this seemed to me to be the best solution for both parties. My suggestion was rejected on the grounds that I was "so tough" that I would be a financial burden for many years to come. Several years passed, and then one day the newspaper articles about the long drawn-out process came to the attention of the Director of the Zurich Museum of Ethnology, Walter Raunig. An Austrian by birth, Raunig asked me if I would be willing to let the collection go to Zurich.

I was unable to give an immediate reply to Raunig's request and approached Professor Rohracher in Vienna for advice. He was immediately of the opinion that, since Switzerland was a friendly neighbour of Austria, he could see no objections to the plan. I therefore compiled a list of the Tibetan exhibits and sent it to the Austrian National Heritage Board, together with a request for an export licence. Since there were no specific Austrian artefacts on my list, my request was immediately approved.

On 13th October 1972 we received a visit from Swiss Minister Gilgen and seven members of the Cantonal Great Council, who wished to view at least part of my collection. They stayed for the day and left without comment. Two galleries specialising in Tibetan art then valued the entire collection, piece by piece, and after the briefest of interludes, I received the news that the Cantonal Government of Zurich had unanimously approved the purchase. So it was that a large part of my Tibetan collection ended up in the Museum of Ethnology at the University of Zurich. The *Neue Züricher Zeitung* dedicated an entire page in its culture section to the acquisition under the title "Lucky break for Switzerland". The Austrian press demanded an explanation, but I was able to demonstrate at the press conference that I had tried for six years without success to negotiate with the Austrian authorities over the sale of my collection.

I used a portion of the money from the sale to purchase further items of Tibetan art during my subsequent trips to India, many of which were later acquired by the museum in Vaduz. We kept quite a few pieces, however, and I was continually adding to my private collection. Towards the end of the 1970s Carina and I had started building a new house in Mauren. From the garage at street level a twenty-five metre long passageway led to the lift. To brighten up the cold concrete walls we hung fifteen Tibetan scroll paintings on each wall of the corridor and near the lift there was an alcove with more ethnographical objects for our guests to look at before they entered the lift. When the Dalai Lama came to Vaduz in 1991 to open my Tibet exhibition, he came to visit us at our new home in Mauren. As is the custom in Tibet, I had drawn several good luck symbols on the road by the house with a piece of white chalk. I then showed him the "gallery" of *thangkas* and the alcove, but he preferred not to use the lift. As we climbed the steep steps that led through the rhododendrons to where our friends were waiting to welcome him, I remarked that I had had to climb many more steps than this when I visited him at the Potala, which made him laugh. When he walked into the living room he picked up one of the prayer mills. He said he had never seen such a beautiful example, even in Lhasa.

After his escape in 1959, the Dalai Lama had given me a little figurine of Tsepame, the "Buddha of Longevity", and on a later occasion he presented me with a specially commissioned *thangka* that depicted the yogi Milarepa. I have kept both of these gifts to this day. Carina has also kept the small effigy of Milarepa that I once gave her.

In 1992, on the occasion of my eightieth birthday, the Dalai Lama opened the Heinrich Harrer Museum in Hüttenberg. He returned to Hüttenberg in 2002 to bless the pilgrims' path opposite the museum and to join me in celebrating my ninetieth birthday. The museum now houses exhibits from all of my many expeditions, some four thousand five hundred in all, together with many documents and books, my comprehensive archive of photographs and a large collection of ethnographical items – a gift from my wife and I to the place where I was born. It is a worthy place for such a collection and my thanks go to Rudolph Schratter, the curator, for looking after the exhibits and for his sterling work in transcribing this book from the original thousand pages of handwritten script.

During my recovery from malaria I had to build my strength up again from scratch. It was a slow process, but soon I was able to take part in the Engadin Ski Marathon, a cross-country ski trip around the Wilder Kaiser and the 60 kilometre Lienz Dolomite Race. During a holiday on Tenerife I also climbed the 3,718 metre Pico de Teide, a tedious and sweaty slog up the pathless mountainside beneath the cable car. The tourists waved at me from the cabin and must have thought I was crazy. They were not far wrong. My great role model Alexander von Humboldt had climbed Teide in 1799. There were no paths then, either, and I was determined to follow suit. All of these activities were getting me fit, to be sure, but after a while I derived little satisfaction from them, it must be said.

A good excuse to organise a small expedition presented itself when I learned that the Austrian company Vöest was in the process of constructing an irrigation dam on the Nile in southern Sudan. I had already visited the Nuba people of Central Sudan once before and had made a TV film about a neighbouring tribe entitled "Beni Sheko, the village without water". It was a documentary about the women of the region, who were obliged to walk long distances every day, often for six hours or more, to fetch water from the nearest oasis. When the film was aired, the TV channel broadcast an appeal for donations to help the tribe. No large sums of money were forthcoming, but several large companies immediately offered to provide water pumps. Unfortunately the companies did not wish to take on the job of transporting and installing the pumps so the project never came to fruition and the women of Beni Sheko did not receive the help they so urgently required.

I had many such experiences over the years and they taught me one thing above all else: that one should never count on charity appeals or government aid programmes to provide the help required. After one of my television broadcasts I was invited by Walter Scheel to visit the Federal Ministry for Economic Co-operation and Development. It was suggested that I might visit some of the developing countries in which the German government had invested and report back on their progress. I left Bonn with a briefcase full of documents pertaining to existing projects. During an expedition to South America I visited a nitrogen manufacturing plant that had been established to provide artificial fertilisers used to increase the soil yield. The concrete building stood on its own in the middle of the savannah and a man told me that the factory had not produced anything for months. Bonn had initiated the project and financed the construction of the plant, but there was a lack of qualified maintenance personnel. The bearings in the machines were worn and damaged and several crucial components had never been lubricated.

A further example of a well-meant, but ultimately inadequate aid measure, was the supply of modern milling equipment designed to grind corn to produce flour. The locals came from miles around, eager to avail themselves of this new facility, which would grind their millet in a fraction of the time it normally took them using the traditional flat stones. The drawback of this new method soon became apparent however. The locals began to exhibit deficiency symptoms and become ill, and at first no one was able to come up with an explanation for this phenomenon. It transpired that the locals were lacking the trace elements, the all-important minerals that were so essential to their physical health, which had previously found their way into the locals' food from the millstones.

In the spring of 1971 I landed in the Sudanese capital Khartoum with my old team from the German TV channel and my friend Fritz Wechselberger. Fritz was a hunter and had an extensive collection of ibex trophies, which he hoped to add to during our trip. It was our intention to cross the Nubian Desert. The Austrian Embassy and an engineer from Vöest obtained vehicles for us and placed a driver and other helpers at our disposal. We practised the drill for getting the Jeep moving again when it became stuck in the sand, using a couple of sheets of metal that had last seen service in the Second World War.

There was no shortage of advice and warnings about the seriousness of the desert crossing and the likelihood of encountering the dangerous Hadendoa tribe. I was well used to such horror stories; had I heeded all the warnings I had been given I would never have embarked upon any of my expeditions or written any books. In my experience there are two reasons why certain tribes remain isolated: either they are described as dangerous by those who live near them so they have a valid excuse never to go there, or someone who has actually been there writes a book about the tribe that portrays them as dangerous, so that the author of the book remains the only person ever to have visited them.

The drive through the desert between the Nile and the Red Sea was a whole new experience for me and my respect for the pioneers who were the first to cross deserts like the Sahara and the Gobi grew with every kilometre of our arduous journey. In spite of the Jeep's four wheel drive and differential lock, we kept getting stuck in the deep, soft sand. When the bolts on the leaf springs broke the driver fixed the suspension using pieces of my climbing rope; other repairs were improvised using pliers and wire or bits of tin. I had to navigate through thickets of thorn bushes using a compass and whenever we reached one of the few oases Fritz would treat the sick and wounded in the meagre shade of a palm tree.

We had to ration the food and water, but the biggest problem was that all the Sudanese were Moslems and the labels on the tins of meat all bore the manufacturer's trademark of a pig's head, even when they contained beef or chicken. I was aware of the fact that Moslems consider pork to be an unclean meat and that when building their houses they often bury a piece of pork under the threshold to ward off evil spirits, so it was no real surprise to me that, despite their obvious hunger, our local guides could not be persuaded to eat any of the tinned meat. We ate ours straight from the tin; there was no need to heat it first – the scorching sun had already done that for us. As a special treat I had brought two whole salamis with me, packed in wood shavings. Imagine my disappointment when, on opening the packet, I discovered that the fat had liquefied and the only solid matter remaining was the skins.

We finally left the difficult terrain of the desert sand dunes behind and reached the Nubian Mountains, where Fritz went off hunting with his team of beaters. There was a road of sorts here, and it led us into a region rich in history. It was here that, during the Sudan Campaign, a British Army relief force suffered a humiliating defeat at the hands of the Hadendoa. Armed only with hand-forged swords, clubs and shields made of hippopotamus leather, but fighting like lions, the fearsome Hadendoa warriors attacked and killed the soldiers, who were camped near the Akaba Pass in the Nubian Mountains. The large cemetery that lies beyond the pass bears bleak testimony to the terrible price the British Army paid that day; it contains the graves of several hundred men.

During the late 1800's the Hadendoa had supported the Sudanese Mahdi, who claimed to be the prophesied messiah of Islam, in his war of liberation against the Egyptian Ottoman government. They earned a reputation as savage warriors, a reputation that has persisted to this day. It was said that one never saw a Hadendoa warrior without a weapon of some sort: a sword, a dagger or a club. They were also highly skilled in the use of the throw-stick, a kind of boomerang, which they mainly used to kill small animals and to herd their camels. Even today the young men of the tribe still practice the art of sword fighting for hours on end, using sticks with protective leather hand grips. During these bouts the fighters are encouraged by their fellow tribesmen, who shout, sing and clap their hands ecstatically. Although this is a part of their tribal life, like the Xingu Indians of the Amazon the whole point of the exercise nowadays is to be the best fighter in the tribe and they would only react aggressively to an outsider if provoked.

All of the men have elaborate frizzy hairstyles and wear carved wooden combs in their hair, each of which has a design that is unique to the artist that made it. The most highly prized combs are made from horn and decorated with silver. They are purely ornamental in nature as their hair is so matted that it is beyond combing.

Not far from the dilapidated old cemetery we came across the first local tribesmen. Judging by their appearance they fully deserved the appellation "wild men". They were Hadendoa, and it thus seemed prudent to avoid taking any photographs, even though I was of the opinion that they could hardly be any more difficult to deal with than the Papuans in New Guinea or the Xingu Indians of the Amazon region. As so often on my expeditions it was a chance encounter that provided the solution.

At a watering hole beyond the cemetery, we ran into a large group of Hadendoa. We received a cold and very unfriendly reception from the men. Their leader's eyes were inflamed and septic. It was obviously that he was suffering from gonorrhoea, so I offered to treat him. I always carried some silver nitrate in my expedition medical kit, which is used in the treatment of gonorrhoea and eye infections. On hearing this he became a little more approachable and I ventured to explain our intentions to him. I told him we wished to spend a little time with his people to get to know their customs and traditions. He agreed in principle and allowed us to photograph him as a good example to the rest of his men. Hour by hour the atmosphere improved, so much so that I asked the leader if he would take us to their kraal. The man's face suddenly grew serious. He told me that we should stay here at the watering hole; he and his men would return the following day and we could take our photographs then.

We managed to trade a few items and acquired a few hand-forged swords, whose value I estimated by the flexibility of the steel, and several heavy leather scabbards. To fight with such a sword for any length of time must require extraordinary strength, I thought. It was far harder to persuade them to part with one of their shields, however. This was understandable: the Nile was a long way away and the hippopotamus that provided the leather for the shields was becoming a rare creature. Eventually one of the Hadendoa agreed to exchange two of the shields for my large hunting knife.

The men wore little pouches strapped to their upper arms, which contained verses from the Koran. These fearsome warriors, who only a hundred years ago would decapitate their enemies and carry the severed heads with them as trophies as they rode around on their camels, became completely different people when one of them suddenly grabbed a musical instrument and started singing. The song told of the glorious history of the Hadendoa tribe. As the men sat and listened to the song, all the tension and pent-up aggression gradually evaporated and an air of melancholy descended on the group.

Since there were no women of the tribe to be seen anywhere, I asked the chief again if we might accompany them to their kraal. Once more he refused. The tents were too far away, and in any case it was too hot and it would soon be dark, he said, trying politely but firmly to dissuade me from my plan. When I persisted, this hitherto friendly man leapt to his feet, clenched his fists and began to shout at me. Alerted by his shouts, the other men drew closer. Their attitude changed abruptly and it was then that my experience told me it would be better to pack up and disappear.

A few days later we came across another group and had the opportunity to take a few photographs in the vicinity of their camp. The black tents were made from rough camel hair felt and were partially fenced in by thorn bushes. But here, too, the reception was far from friendly and a stone was thrown at me as I was trying to get a telephoto shot of one of the women about a hundred metres away. I always carried a wide angle lens with me for just such an eventuality. I changed lenses, pointed the camera at right angles to the subject and succeeded in getting my shot. Later in the trip, when we stopped at an oasis, I used the wide angle lens to get a lovely shot of a woman with a heavy gold nose ring and a row of silver bracelets on her arm.

I believe one should view the Hadendoa's aversion to foreign influences and to tourists with cameras who try to "steal their souls" as something positive. It is this attitude, and their uncontrollable character, that will prevent them from joining the rural exodus to the large cities and becoming dislocated members of the proletariat. The Hadendoa will live in the mountains between the Nile and the Red Sea for many years to come, as proud and free as they have always been.

In the port of Suakin on the Red Sea, we checked into an old hotel in which Lord Kitchener had once lived when he was Governor of Suakin. Next to the entrance to the hotel a street trader sat in the shade of an awning. I noticed he had a set of ibex horns leaning against the wall, which I thought I might buy for Fritz. The trader asked for twenty pounds and I jokingly replied that I would give him a pound for them. The merchant halved his price but I still thought this was too much to pay and went back into the hotel. During dinner that evening the trader brought me the horns in a jute sack. I could now no longer refuse and gave him two pounds. He seemed quite happy with this and left with a smile. Fritz graciously refused my little gift, however, saying that he did not wish to adorn himself with borrowed plumes. The ibex horns finally ended up in the "Haus der Natur" in Salzburg.

Back in Khartoum I said goodbye to my team. I stayed for a few days more to pack my treasures. While I was there I went to an old ironmonger's shop, where I found an old copper drum that had once been beaten by the elite troops of the ruling Mahdi prince when General Horatio Herbert Kitchener came up the Nile to defeat the Mahdist forces at the Battle of Omdurman in 1898. The body of the drum was in good repair, and once I had had the skin replaced it sounded just like it would have done all those years ago. The same Khartoum craftsman also made me a leather rack with which to carry the forty kilo fossilised tree trunk I had brought back from the desert. The drum is now in the museum in Hüttenberg, where the children are allowed to play it, and the two million year old piece of wood is displayed next to the Hadendoa swords and throw-sticks.

IN THE REALM OF THE ANCESTORS

I had visited Borneo, the third largest island in the world after Greenland and New Guinea, once before, in 1968, during a round the world trip. When I first went there I found many ritualistic symbols designed to ward of demons and evil spirits but I did not find what I was really looking for, *hampatongs*, the carved ancestor statues of the aboriginal tribespeople. Practically every book I consulted on the subject contained the fear-inducing word "head-hunter" in the title and gave the distinct impression that the original Bornean tribespeople all lay in wait with blowpipes and poisoned darts, hoping to add another head to their collection. One of the more serious accounts was written by C.A.L.M. Schwaner, a Mannheim doctor who had traversed the island from south to north in 1843, forty years before Karl von den Steinen embarked upon his expedition to the Xingu Indians. Schwaner's courage and exploratory zeal were nothing short of remarkable; he accomplished his journey without sponsorship or media attention and without recourse to any of the medicines commonly available today. Schwaner achieved immortality, as the mountains he crossed now bear his name. Tragically, Schwaner did not survive the vicissitudes of his expedition and died at the age of thirty-four in Batavia, the modern-day city of Jakarta, as a direct result of the illnesses he contracted.

In 1972 I decided to make a second attempt to locate the *hampatongs*. It later transpired that this was to be the last of my ethnographical and scientific expeditions to unexplored regions. This time, unlike my previous undertakings, I did not dismiss the offer of sponsorship to contribute towards the costs of the expedition. I had spoken about this to the President of the Austrian Research Council, Professor Rohracher, who had assured me that financial assistance was frequently granted to expeditions that brought far less back with them in terms of knowledge and materials than I did. My application for funding was immediately approved, and this meant that I was able to bring back many more cultural items than I could otherwise have afforded to do. At several times over the years I had evaluated similar grant applications for other large foundations, such as VW and Thyssen in Germany, and had noted that the amounts requested were generally very modest and often failed to take into account the huge increases in items like porter costs. I could well imagine the expedition members' delight at discovering that they had been awarded more money than they had originally requested as a result of my intervention.

My TV broadcasts had always attracted good viewing figures but it was becoming increasingly difficult to find competent cameramen to accompany such expeditions. Each new applicant for the job was advised to read up on my trips first to get an idea of the hardships he was likely to encounter. For the Borneo trip I had a good man for the job in Günther Hackbarth, a cameraman from the Hessischer Rundfunk, but the same could not be said about the new equipment, which in my opinion was not entirely suitable for such work. The expensive new cameras were heavier and more sensitive and had to be transported in watertight containers. The column of porters often had to wade knee-deep through mud, negotiate tree roots or cross rivers, and the porter with the camera was usually right at the back of the line. It was unreasonable to expect the rest of the porters to stop and wait in the mud or in the middle of a fast-flowing river until the camera was unpacked, and this meant that we were often unable to capture the more difficult, dangerous or exciting passages on film. As always, the safety of the expedition members had to take precedence over everything else.

We set off from Pontianak in western Borneo and travelled by boat eastwards along the Kapuas River. There were plenty of rest houses and "restaurants" along the river, where we could sit outside and enjoy the spicy local cuisine. It was a pleasant a start to the trip, and although we were almost on the Equator we were even spared the usual heavy rain at first. The riverside settlements were built well above the water, which led me to conclude that the Kapuas must swell to a mighty torrent during the rainy season. After a week we left the wide river and the settlements behind, and the serious part of the expedition began.

I had selected four local men to accompany us on this stage of the expedition and had purchased a boat from them for the trip along a small tributary river to the south. We had long since left the northern region of Borneo, the part that belonged to Malaysia, and as a precautionary measure we had obtained visas for Indonesia from the embassy in Vienna before we left. We were now in the province of Kalimantan, which is the Indonesian name for Borneo. The word "Borneo" was totally unknown here and I was reminded of the nomads I had encountered on my escape to Tibet, who referred to their homeland as "Bo" rather than "Tibet". Although there were several political borders marked on the map of Borneo there were hardly any border controls. The long coastline and the easy access by boat to all parts of the island accounted for the multiracial population mix.

The local porters and boatmen proved their worth on the very first day. They wrapped the expedition kit in waterproof plastic sheets and stowed them neatly in the boat, and while two of the men steered the boat, the others cleared a path along the river bank with their machetes. Impassable sections of the river were portaged, a laborious and time-consuming process that required them to unload all the kit and carry it and the boat through the dense jungle to the next navigable section.

We were now heading for the Schwaner Mountains. It was becoming more difficult to make progress – one set of rapids alone took us hours to negotiate – so we began setting up camp in the early afternoons. Although it had not rained yet, it was wet in the jungle and we were all troubled by our old foes, the leeches. We had travelled several hundred kilometres since Pontianak, but it was hard going now and we were having to schedule the odd rest day, when we would pack the exposed film in silica gel, sew on buttons, treat our wounds and attend to numerous other little housekeeping tasks. We had taken plenty of provisions and had rice, dried fish and bamboo shoots to eat. Two of the group were Dayaks, as the aboriginal inhabitants of the Borneo interior were known, but said they knew nothing about the carved ancestor figures I was looking for. Perhaps they were merely unwilling to part with the information.

We finally negotiated the last of the rapids and floated gently downstream on quiet water beneath an overarching canopy of high green trees to reach the first native village. My Dayak companions left the boat and went off bearing gifts to find the village elder and enquire where we might pitch our camp. I had my eye on a little meadow that was shaded by a huge tree, but the porters pointed out the thorny durian husks, which would hurt if they fell on us. The fruit of the durian tree has a lovely taste and is a highly prized delicacy in the tropics, although little known in Europe. It has a pungent onion-like smell when cut, which is why it is sometimes called "heaven and hell fruit". It is forbidden to eat durian in the larger hotels in Asia, as the odour penetrates into the air conditioning system and permeates throughout the rooms.

The village elder indicated that we should set up camp on a fallow rice field a little way from the houses. It is always advisable to camp some distance from a native settlement, as the locals, and particularly the children, are often very inquisitive; in fact, they are just as interested in us as we are in them. Presently, an old man, whom I assumed was the shaman of the village, walked over to one of the huts, in which the bones of his tribal ancestors were kept, and left a few little figures made of rice at the base of one of the posts that supported the house as a ritual food offering to the deceased. I knew then that I was on the right track, as the carved gargoyles and ornamentations on the posts were very similar to the artwork on the *hampatongs* I was looking for.

The altimeter showed that we were already a thousand metres above sea level. During the night heavy rain spattered on our tarpaulins and turned the soft earth into a thick morass. I could well understand how a special type of rice grew here that did not require the usual intensive irrigation. Our native helpers, who all hailed from the warmer Kapuas Valley, grew cold and miserable and expressed the wish to return home, so we paid them off. I even let them keep the boat I had bought from them. When the villagers saw how friendly and generous we were with them we had no difficulties in finding willing replacements.

This, I realised, was the point of no return in our expedition. My plan had always been to look for the *hampatong* statues in the middle of the island; now I had to find the patience and energy I needed to continue my search. We had already covered half of the distance, but I now rejected my original plan to return by the same route and decided instead to press on to the south coast with my new team of porters.

Although we were now in the mountains we kept coming across fields that belonged to tiny villages and were linked by a network of paths. It was very wet underfoot and every day we repeated the same tiresome procedure in a vain attempt to keep our feet dry, leaping over puddles and walking round larger pools of water until we realised that we were going to get wet anyway and that it took far less effort simply to wade straight through the water after the porters.

I asked everyone we met about the statues and where we might find them. The responses I received were very confusing, since different tribes had different names for them. Some called them *hampatongs*, while others appeared to refer to them as *chahans*.

One day we came across a particularly imposing long-house. A man, probably the village elder, insisted we stay overnight in the house when he saw our filthy, dripping wet clothes. The long-house stood on a slope; on the downhill side, a notched tree trunk led up to the family quarters. I noticed that this ladder was decorated with carved sex symbols designed to prevent evil spirits entering the house. There was a corridor running the full length of the house and each family had their own separate living area.

Günther and I were shown into a room where a gaunt old man, dressed only in a leather loincloth, sat tending a small fire on a slate slab. He paid no attention whatsoever to our greeting. He wore a short bush knife at his side and a heavy copper ring in each of his ears, the weight of which had stretched his ear lobes so that they touched his shoulders. A cluster of eight or ten smoke-blackened human skulls, tied together with thin rattan cord, hung from the ceiling and there were two metre-long blowpipes and a bamboo dart quiver on the wall. I nodded discreetly towards these dangerous and macabre objects and asked the cameraman to film them later.

The porters brought tea and biscuits but even this failed to brighten up the grim demeanour of our room-mate. Later that evening, when the porters had received their daily cigarette ration and Günther and I were enjoying a cigarillo, the smell of the tobacco loosened his tongue a little and, as one of our porters translated for me, I learned that his wife had recently died and his sons had disappeared, probably to go and live in the city, he thought.

We slept well, in spite of the bizarre surroundings, and decided in the morning to take a rest day to dry out our kit. With the help of my special vocabulary notes, I managed to ask our room-mate if he would be willing to take us to one of the burial sites in the jungle. This he agreed to do. I learned that the skulls in our room were trophies from kills he had made with his blowpipe decades ago, before the missionaries came and tried to convince the tribes that killing people was a false act of courage. Perhaps it was this that had been weighing on his mind when he saw us. It would certainly explain his initial reticence. We followed him through the thick undergrowth to the burial site, where he unearthed two stone urns. Unfortunately, the ritual offerings had long rotted away and the urns themselves were too heavy for me to carry back.

The next morning all of the families came to bid us farewell. As we were getting ready to leave the old man appeared with his blowpipe and quiver of poison darts. When the rest of the villagers saw that I wanted to trade they rushed into their houses and reappeared with several more blowpipes. I ended up having to employ an additional porter to carry these precious ethnographic artefacts.

A few hours later, after a steep and pathless climb, we crested the pass, the watershed between the South China Sea to the north and the Indian Ocean to the south. I was now in the heart of Borneo. The pass was marked by a solitary pile of moss covered stones that might have been the remnants of the cairn built by Schwaner more than one hundred years ago. If only my old geography professor, Otto Maul, were here with me now, I thought, he would have been absolutely delighted. For the past few weeks we had been walking against the flow of the streams; now we were following the direction of flow. The jungle grew less dense and we soon caught up with the porters, who had stopped and were pointing wordlessly to a human head carved from wood that glowered down at us through the leaves of a large tree. The village was just a hundred or so metres further on and I barely managed to conceal my excitement at finding the *hampatongs* as we went through the usual greeting procedure and asked for permission to set up camp.

While the porters put up the tarpaulins I drank tea and wandered around looking at the many *hampatongs*, large and small, some of which were half-hidden in the undergrowth. I had found what I had been looking for, and the setting could not have been more perfect. I wanted to celebrate but decided instead to hide my interest for the time being. I was determined to acquire one of the carved ancestor statues, but had no idea that during the next few days I would see literally hundreds of them.

The next day I asked the village elder if he knew of any *hampatongs* that might once have belonged to tribespeople who had died and were therefore no longer needed to protect them. He told me that it would only be possible to grant my request to remove one if the shaman, or *dukun* as he was known, agreed. The *dukun* said he required a blood sacrifice, so I bought a chicken and he slit its throat and let the blood drip onto two small *hampatongs*. According to the animistic beliefs of the Dayak, the performance of this ritual meant that they no longer had to fear their ancestors' revenge for taking the statues. Nevertheless, they refused to dig them up; I had to do that myself. I had to shake them violently from side to side to prise them free and whilst doing so I slipped and gashed my hand. I wrapped a handkerchief around the wound to hide it from the villagers, who would almost certainly have attributed my injury to ancestral revenge, and walked happily back to our camp with the carved wooden posts tucked under one arm and the dead chicken under the other.

Two days later we reached a clearing in the jungle. At first I could not believe my eyes: there by the riverbank, at the edge of the jungle, stood row upon row of mighty statues, some fifty or more in all, their carved faces staring at me with fixed expressions – a whole forest of *hampatongs*. Even now, I struggle to describe the emotions I felt at that moment. I felt like I had done on discovering the source of the stone axes in New Guinea; all of the hardships of the journey, the river rapids and the leeches, were forgotten in an instant. I was spellbound.

The village was called Akam. The inhabitants were friendly and brought us ripe papayas. I curbed my feelings, ignored the forest of statues and waited until late afternoon before going for a stroll and photographing about thirty of the large *hampatongs* from various angles. Most of the figures depicted men as they had lived, as fishermen, hunters or warriors; the women cradled infants in their arms and wore loin cloths. I could only guess at the age of the carved posts, but the equatorial rains had almost certainly contributed to the worn facial features on the older examples. Several of the *hampatongs* bore no human likenesses but were carved with the faces of demons, gargoyles and monsters with protruding tongues. At the tip of each stood a vase, in which the ashes of the deceased were kept, and one could tell by these vessels how rich or poor the dead person's tribal relatives had been. A five metre tall post topped with a precious porcelain vase stood next to a smaller, more modest example with a rusty petrol can serving as a receptacle that was partially obscured by the long grass.

That evening I carefully enquired of the village elder whether I might take one of the old carved posts that were lying on the ground rotting. He was horrified at my request and refused point blank. No missionary had ever visited Akam and it seemed as if the old ways were still strictly adhered to. But just two days later there was no further talk of blood sacrifices and ancestral revenge; how many *hampatongs* I could take was merely a question of money. I acquired two large examples, rented a small boat to transport them downriver and two days later, at the missionary station, I paid off the trusty men, who had accompanied us all the way from their homes on the other side of the mountains. The missionaries at that lonely outpost must have thought we had come from another planet.

The Borneo expedition was now over and all the stress and tension evaporated. After resting for a while, we took a boat with an outboard motor down the ever-widening Barito River to the busy port of Bandjarmasin. After the peace and solitude of the interior the contrast could not have been greater. Huge Japanese machines processed high-grade timber that had been extracted on an industrial scale with scant regard for sustainability. A transport company packed our ethnographic treasures without even checking them, something that would have been impossible in Jakarta without the payment of baksheesh. My expedition kit, my collection of over five hundred photographs, the *hampatongs* and blowpipes, were crated and shipped back home the slow, cheap way on a freighter bound for Europe. Two of the man-sized carved figures are now on show at the museum in Hüttenberg.

In an autobiography like this, there is no room for the detailed sketches and detailed lists that scientists find so useful and that help to evaluate the success of an expedition. My own personal observations are all recorded in my expedition journals. Other indispensable items of kit include my pocket altimeter, which also displays barometric pressure, a compass and a large quantity of waterproof bags of different sizes that I use to transport sensitive items. All of the artefacts I collect have to be bagged and clearly labelled with the place they were found and a brief description. The 1972 Borneo expedition produced a rich haul of valuable ethnographic objects and in spite of the fact that the trip was accomplished without any great risks, it still had the feel of a big adventure. As I write this in the spring of 2002, the daily newspapers are reporting on the latest developments in the region, with headlines such as "Thousands Flee Borneo Head-hunters", "Bloody Ethnic Unrest in Borneo" and "Aboriginal Dayaks Slaughter 3,000". The problems appear to stem from the large flow of immigrants into the area. The Indonesian government is pursuing a policy of resettlement, shifting large numbers of people from the densely populated islands of Java and Madura to other regions, in particular to the Kalimantan province of Borneo. The aboriginal people fear the economic superiority of these new arrivals and defend themselves in the traditional way. New tribal leaders have legalised the once forbidden practice of head-hunting and many of the new immigrants, fearing for their lives, have had to be evacuated. There seems to be no easy solution to the problem, since the immigrants are reluctant to leave their homes and the original inhabitants of the region do not want them to stay. Similar problems exist in New Guinea, and I am pleased that I visited both islands in more peaceful times. It seems unlikely that my strange room-mate in the tribal long house would have lived to see peace return to the island of Borneo.

THE LAST FEW HUNDRED

After my two Borneo programmes were broadcast on German television, the journalists asked their usual question: "And where will your next expedition be taking you?" "To the Andamans," I replied. This seemed to unsettle the journalists. "Is that a mountain range, an island or a tribe?" they wanted to know.

The Andamans are a group of several hundred islands in the Gulf of Bengal, about thirteen hundred kilometres south east of Calcutta and two hundred kilometres west of Burma, in the Indian Ocean. They arise from a submerged mountain chain and cover an area of 6,495 square kilometres. The chain of islands disappears briefly into the Indian Ocean before resurfacing to the south as the Nicobar Islands. They were first discovered in the ninth century by Arab merchants and were colonised by the British, who established a penal colony there in the 19th century. The aboriginal inhabitants are pygmy Negritos, a race of people I had already spent some time with during my 1957 Congo trip, when I visited the largest pygmy tribe still in existence in the Ituri Forest. What I was unaware of was the fact that there were pygmies on the Andaman Islands who were still living in the Stone Age.

In 1974 my travel plans started to take shape, and to begin my expedition preparations I first visited the anthropologist and ethnographer Father Martin Gusinde, one of the leading experts on pygmies, at his missionary headquarters in Vienna. From there I travelled to Brussels to see King Leopold, under whose patronage the expedition was to be mounted. As usual, I stayed at the Château Argenteuil near Waterloo. Like me, Leopold had long since recovered from his malaria and we used the opportunity to play our customary round of golf with the captain of the Belgian national team. We filled our days with sport and visits to the best local fish restaurant and the time with my old friend was over all too soon. In the autumn of the same year our little group, which once again included Leopold's colleagues Xaver Missone and Jean-Pierre Gosse, set off for Asia.

We flew first to New Delhi, where we had to obtain permits to visit the Andamans, as at that time the islands were closed to tourists. Leopold and I knew the President of the Indian Golf Union, Subin Malik, and we played a round with him on a course situated in the middle of the city surrounded by the ruins of temples. In the evening we went to dinner at the home of the Maliks, a family of industrialists who owned a splendid house set in large gardens near the city. Mr Malik's daughter was a well-known journalist. We had met the previous year and I had promised her that I would bring her some new varieties of roses for her garden. Since we had flown with Leopold as VIP's there had been no need to fill in the usual landing cards, on which one normally has to confirm that one has not brought any plants into the country, so I was able to present our dinner hosts with rose trees instead of the customary bunch of flowers. We spent a very pleasant evening and left with a promise from Malik to the King that he would inform Prime Minister Indira Gandhi of our wish to visit the Andamans and arrange an audience with her. It was doubtless due to the charm of King Leopold, and his assurance that we would act responsibly in our encounters with the timid inhabitants, that we secured permission to proceed with our Andaman expedition. Happy with this result, we left India in a turboprop plane on 18th November, Andaman-bound.

We had been in the air for a little over two hours when, instead of a chain of islands, a huge river delta appeared below us. It was the mighty Irrawaddy, a river that has its source in the mountains of Tibet. The pilot was landing in Rangoon to refuel – a routine stop for him, but an unpleasant surprise for me. Burma's communist regime maintained close ties with the Chinese government, whose occupying forces still controlled Lhasa. Before refuelling we were obliged to leave the aircraft and were shown to a heavily guarded waiting room for transit passengers. I breathed a sigh of relief when we took off again without having our passports checked.

The pilot flew a loop over our destination and I could see that Saddle Peak, the highest mountain in the Andamans, was covered from sea to summit in deep jungle. The provincial governor, Shri Harmander Singh, was waiting for us on the short landing strip of the capital, Port Blair. Although he was a Sikh, he was not wearing a turban and looked splendid in his European style clothing. He welcomed King

Leopold in an accomplished diplomatic manner and greeted me politely with the words "The Ministry of External Affairs informed me that you were in the party, Mr. Harrer." I was unsure whether he was expressing his pleasure at meeting me or whether he was expecting me to be troublesome. Harmander Singh had succeeded Hugh Richardson in Sikkim, after India had occupied the little kingdom. In the years prior to this, I had often visited him to apply for permission to enter northern Sikkim, a region that borders Tibet, but my request was always refused on the grounds that there were three ministries in Delhi responsible for such matters – the Ministry of Home Affairs, the Ministry of External Affairs and the Ministry of Defence! Here in the Andamans, Mr. Singh was the all-powerful Governor and instead of the usual vehicle registration, the number plate of his limousine bore the emblem of the Ashoka pillar, the symbol of the Republic of India. His official residence lay on a hill with a view of the ocean. The garden, the mature trees and the multi-coloured bougainvillea shrubs still bore the unmistakable stamp of the British, who were the ruling power here until India gained her independence in 1947.

Over the next few days Xaver set traps to catch the rats and squirrels he needed for his scientific research while Jean-Pierre, our ichthyologist, was more interested in the freshwater fish. The rest of us accompanied Leopold on his VIP tour of the local authorities and museums, a task to which he was well accustomed. We also visited a training camp for elephants, where we watched as they manoeuvred tree trunks around and lifted them with their trunks onto flat bed trucks. After their work was done they were freed from their heavy chains and raced against each other – something they obviously enjoyed as much as we did – before consuming mountains of sugar cane. The *mahout*, or elephant driver, then told us a story that proved the truth in the saying "an elephant never forgets". He had once had to separate two bull elephants who were bitter rivals, he said. After fifteen years, the two elephants met again, quite by chance, whereupon the younger animal killed the older one, ramming his tusk into his rival's belly in one last vicious attack as he lay dying on the ground.

After the Indian Rebellion in 1857, the British established a penal colony at Port Blair. We visited the Cellular Jail, in which twenty thousand Indian prisoners had once led a miserable confined existence. We were also shown the gallows and given a graphic explanation of how they worked. All this was in the past, of course, but new problems had replaced the old. More and more Indians from the mainland colonised the islands, and this led to a fundamental conflict of interests between the new arrivals and the original inhabitants. The immigrant Indians regarded the indigenous Negritos as uncultured savages and treated them with a total lack of consideration. Horror stories abounded of black monsters with carnassial teeth and cannibalistic tendencies, stories which portrayed the Negritos as nothing more than dangerous predators, instead of fellow human beings whose existence was to be pitied rather than feared. They were driven from their homelands, and the few hundred that survived from a population that once numbered three thousand fled to the west coast, where they live to this day in total isolation. The largest group of these last surviving pygmy Negritos are known as the Jarawa. Having once observed how their tribal forbears disappeared after interacting with the immigrant Indians, they now instinctively shun all contact with the outside world. A few months before we arrived, the Chief of Police, Bakhtawar Singh, had finally succeeded in making contact with them, after many years and several failed attempts. He advised us to visit the Onge tribe first and in the meantime he would try to find out where the Jarawa were currently living.

The Onge were an aboriginal tribe like the Jarawa, and like the Jarawa their population had been severely decimated. When we visited in 1975 there were just one hundred and twelve of these Negrito pygmies left. They lived in a cluster of simple huts on the island of Little Andaman, which we reached easily by boat. They had built additional huts from bamboo and reeds to accommodate us during our stay, and each of us was free to pursue his own interests. For my documentary, I asked the powerfully built men to build a hut and also filmed them out on the open sea as they steered their catamarans with considerable skill through the breakers. The women wore the tiniest of loincloths to conceal their modesty and were less remarkable for their beauty than for their extraordinarily large backsides. Lordosis and posterior steatopygy made it almost impossible for them to bend over and their dancing consisted solely of slow, ponderous steps. Tiny infants in raffia papooses hung from the women's backs, their little heads lolling to one side, sound asleep.

Their rituals, their jewellery and ornamentation and their mud-and-ash body paint were highly artistic. Tattooing was unknown here, but the Onge, some of whom were gifted artists, painted their bodies in different earth colours or smeared themselves with a thick layer of ochre and scratched decorative symbols in it with their fingertips. The adornments were not only decorative; they also provided a measure of protection from the cold and the insects.

There was a newly established coconut palm plantation near the village, where the Onge worked. An Indian, Patrik Lobo, supervised the proceedings and was constantly having to urge them to get some work done. The Onge, for their part, were constantly asking him "Why?" and "What for?" They could not really see the sense in working when everything they required was freely available in such abundance. In addition to their work in the plantation they went hunting with bow and arrow. They fished, too, and up in the trees one could see the swarms of bees that provided them with a free source of honey.

I was unable to collect any interesting ethnic artefacts, since the Onge's old household items had been replaced by plastic and metal utensils. There was a lovely Nautilus shell full of honey in one of the huts, which I was keen to acquire. The women in the hut shrugged indifferently and pointed to a midden where there were dozens of them lying around. The pile of refuse turned out to be a veritable treasure trove; it was similar to the Kökkenmödinger find in Denmark, whose individual layers gave an indication of the various phases of the indigenous peoples' history.

Our visit to the Onge demonstrated once again how civilisation had marginalised the ancient ways of life and had slowly yet inexorably eradicated the aboriginal inhabitants. The people we met on Little Andaman behaved very differently to the way they were portrayed in the books we had read and the stories we had heard. The interest shown was a one-way process; we were interested in them but the Onge were not the slightest bit interested in us. Their behaviour was apathetic; the men and women spent most of the time lying in their gloomy bamboo huts and even the children seemed indifferent to the presents we gave them. Nor did I find any evidence to suggest that the Onge ever played any games or competitive sports. As I carefully packed the fragile Nautilus shell I felt rather sad and depressed. We were all happy to exchange the damp, cold atmosphere of our bamboo huts for the rooms of the Governor's residence.

Bakhtawar Singh had been observing the Jarawa while we were away and explained that now would be a good time to visit. He had prepared everything meticulously. Strips of red and yellow cloth fluttered from the mast of our boat, and two big bunches of ripe bananas hung beneath. We sailed through the breakers and shot through a gap in the coral reef to the calmer waters of the lagoon beyond. We were now just a kilometre from the shore. We approached the beach slowly and everyone stared in anticipation at the thin strip of sand and the dense jungle beyond for signs of life. We did not really know whether the Jarawa were in the vicinity or whether they were off hunting deep in the jungle. They might even have been watching us, hoping that we would leave presents for them on the beach and then depart, or lying in wait with their poisoned arrows until we drew close enough for a clear shot. Each of us tried to conceal his trepidation, but the tension became almost unbearable. I thought of the Englishman James Cook, who had sailed across the Indian Ocean two hundred years ago and was later killed by the native Hawaiians.

Suddenly, a naked black figure appeared from the green swathe of jungle, ran along the beach and vanished again into the undergrowth. It was followed by a second and then a third Jarawa, both of whom began shouting and waving their arms excitedly. When Bakhtawar returned their calls they jumped around with glee, happy to see their friend again. Bakhtawar advised us to lock all loose items of personal kit in the cabin, since during his first encounter with the Jarawa they had thrown watches, camera lenses and bank notes into the sea and taken only handkerchiefs, hats and foodstuffs.

The water grew shallower, we dropped anchor and the Chief of Police clambered into a rowing boat with our two Indian helpers. Each of them held a coconut above his head and on seeing this sign the

Jarawa raced into the water gesticulating wildly and pulled the boat onto the beach. Bakhtawar stepped out, the Jarawa jumped in and were ferried back to us as we watched from the deck rail. It is difficult to describe the chaotic scenes that followed and at the time I was not sure whether to film it all or simply enjoy the moment. We were quite literally mobbed. The coloured strips of cloth were torn from the mast and soon adorned the Negritos foreheads, arms, waists and legs. An elderly Jarawa discovered the jute sack containing the fruit we had brought. He had obviously never seen ripe oranges before and threw them over his shoulder into the sea. It was a good job that we had stowed our personal possessions in the cabin, I thought.

The Jarawa men and women examined us all as thoroughly as they would a strange object that had been washed up on the beach. They were not particularly gentle with us, either. They tore the buttons from our shirts to get a look at our skin, thrust their hands in our trouser pockets and grabbed us between the legs. When they discovered something unexpected they summoned the others to take a look. They maintained an expression of seriousness and studied fascination throughout; there was seldom any laughter. Since they themselves had no body hair they found the blond hairs on my arms every bit as interesting as the young Dalai Lama had once done, and I was reminded of his remark "Henrig, you are as hairy as a monkey!" Our Belgian friend Xaver had not shaved for a few days and when one of the Jarawa saw the thick stubble on his face he rubbed his cheek against it, causing our friend to smile broadly and reveal a single gold tooth. The Jarawa then grabbed Xaver's jaw, rather brutally I thought, and shouted to his friends, who all came and poked their fingers in his mouth. One of the women took a great interest in Leopold's blue eyes and pulled at the skin on his face to see if she could find any more blue. There was nothing for it but to submit to these examinations with patience and good humour.

The excitement continued on land. The Jawara leapt and danced around on the white sand, stared into our camera lenses and when they saw their reflections tried to wipe the image away with their fingers. The cutest scene of all was when a little girl sneaked up on her beloved Bakhtawar Singh from behind to give him a hug but could not quite make her short arms meet around his ample stomach.

During the general confusion I managed to slip away and take a peek at the communal hut that stood just a few metres away. It was an impressive round construction, at least ten metres in diameter, made of bamboo and reeds. A fire burned in the middle of the hut. I had read somewhere that the Jarawa had discovered fire after a rotten tree stump was struck by lighting and that they had tended it ever since and never let it go out, as they did not know how to make fire themselves. Meat and seafood were cooking slowly over the flame. The Jarawa did not know how to make earthenware pots and instead of axes they used sharp shells lashed to wooden handles. These people were not living in the Stone Age at all; they were actually at a much earlier stage of human development, a period that is sometimes described as the pre-Mesolithic era. Their language is spoken by their tribe only; even the name "Jarawa" is an exonym, ascribed to them by outsiders.

By now Bakhtawar Singh was anxious to leave. He felt responsible for his charges and was acutely aware that the merest cough or sneeze could have terrible consequences for the Jarawa, amongst whom diseases like the common cold were unknown. Two hours of excitement were quite enough for his "children", he said, and added that we might be able to visit them again at a later date, when we might even get to see the bows and arrows that they had this time kept hidden from view.

The Jarawa's curiosity and interest in us had now lessened somewhat, but we still found it difficult to take our leave. The Jarawa filled the rowing boat, so a few of us waited on the beach for it to make a second trip. Some of the women and children went across to the hut, and suddenly the beach was empty. One of the men began to beat on the roots of a huge tree with a stick, a rhythmic drumming like a bush telegraph. I felt a certain sense of unease begin to creep over me and I was happy when I, too, reached the boat. Bakhtawar was still concerned for the welfare of the Jarawa and it required all of his skill, patience and affection to persuade them to leave the boat and return to dry land.

On the Andamans, as on all of my expeditions, I was also interested in the mountains, of course. Although mountaineering per se had not been the main objective of my trips for many years, the opportunity of climbing a high, unclimbed peak was simply too good to miss. I had seen Saddle Peak from the aeroplane as we flew in, but at the time I could never have anticipated that it would turn out to be the toughest ascent I had ever accomplished. I saw it close up for the first time while I was in the village of Diglipur, when the veil of clouds parted briefly and I got a glimpse of the twin peaks with a col between that gave the mountain its name. Saddle Peak is eight hundred metres high and covered in thick jungle. It did not look as if it would present too many problems, and even when I was told that the slopes were the habitat of large, poisonous snakes and huge centipedes, I simply put this down to local horror stories. As a precautionary measure, I engaged the services of three local guides, two policemen and a man who described himself as a "real" mountain guide, each of whom assured me that he knew the mountain well. As a student I had also acquired my mountain guide's diploma, so nothing could go wrong. Or so I thought.

My companions dismissed my suggestion that we take a canister full of water with us on the grounds that there were enough freshwater springs on the route, but I filled my water bottle anyway from one of the little streams we passed. I first began to have my doubts when the two policemen thanked me effusively for giving them the chance to climb the highest mountain on the Andamans for the first time. Oh well, I thought, swallowing my anger and disappointment, at least I still have the "real" mountain guide. Presently we reached the village of Kalipur. I could not believe my ears when my third companion asked one of the villagers the way to Saddle Peak. A little alarmed at all this cluelessness, I took the precaution of adding a tin of corned beef and a slab of cheese to my pack and counted myself lucky that I had at least brought my compass. My companions' "easy little stroll" turned out to be a mammoth undertaking. We trudged for hours up steep slopes covered in thick undergrowth, balanced along huge tree trunks and waded through knee-deep swamps. Eventually we came to a band of slippery rocks topped by a thicket of thorn bushes. I was just in the process of cursing the so-called "route" when I lost my footing and fell. As I came to an abrupt halt on a large rock I knew straightaway that I had bruised several ribs, perhaps even broken a couple. My spectacles and my hat had vanished, too, lost in the bubbling stream.

We had no choice but to press on. Three supposed "experts", and none of them knew the route! In point of fact, there was no route. I decided to take over the lead. Instinctively, I found a faint path but this soon disappeared into even thicker jungle and so we battled on through dense woodland, bogs and yet more thorn bushes until we suddenly found ourselves standing on the main summit of Saddle Peak. The coast was barely discernible, but I knew that somewhere down there near Diglipur our boat lay at anchor. One of the Indians had constantly been asking me for sips of water on the way up, and he had now managed to empty my water bottle. We had shared what little food I had brought. I had been unable to take any photographs during the climb and now, on the summit, there was no point either, since the view was still obscured by trees and bushes. There was nothing on the summit at all: no cross, no trig point, not even a cairn that might have induced us to sit and rest for a while. The only indication that we were on the summit was the fact that the ground sloped away on all sides.

The descent followed the same pattern as the ascent: we crawled, cursed, got thirsty and failed to find a path. The sun was setting and I knew we would have to spend the night on the mountain. I had to find a place to bivouac and suggested that we head east and look for the steep slope we had climbed on our way up. My compass now proved to be a valuable navigation aid. Each of us managed to find a rock to lean against but sleeping was out of the question. It was bitterly cold, so I folded my arms across my chest like the Papuans did, in an attempt to maintain my core body temperature at least. My teeth were chattering and I was damp, cold and sore. I felt dreadful.

We set off again at first light. For five long hours we scrambled through the undergrowth and crawled through thorn bushes to reach a welcome trickle of water in a riverbed. We drank greedily, then I sat on a rock, examined my injuries and took stock. When I rolled up my trousers I was horrified to find dozens of leeches sucking the blood from my legs. I suddenly realised that they were feasting on other parts of my body, too, but I could not do anything about them; even if I had been able to remove them all, there were plenty more in the undergrowth waiting to take their place.

Finally, we reached the coast. The sun was at its zenith and burned down on my head, so I improvised a hat from a knotted handkerchief to provide a little protection. I paid off the three Indians at the first farm we came to and trudged on alone, fortifying myself with coconut milk at every little settlement I came to. At length, I arrived at a larger village, where I experienced one of those spontaneous moments of comedy that often accompanies times of hardship. A well-dressed young man approached me, bowed respectfully and informed me that the children at his school had been waiting to hear my talk since yesterday. I tried to explain that I was in no fit state to deliver a lecture, and pointed to my filthy, tattered clothing. It was no use; the children trotted along behind me waving flags and only then did I realise that they had mistaken me for King Leopold! At first I was unsure what to do. Should I pretend to be the King so as not to disappoint the children? I felt sure that Leopold would understand. After due deliberation, however, I finally decided to tell the truth. My appearance could hardly have been described as regal, anyway; my shirt was torn from collar to hem, I was wearing a knotted handkerchief on my head and I was filthy, sweaty and unshaven. I suggested to the teacher that he bring the children to the boat at Diglipur, where they could meet the real King.

Back at the boat, Jean-Pierre helped me to shower and wash my body down with disinfectant. I had severe swellings in my armpits and at the backs of my knees, which I treated with antibiotics. I also estimated that I had about fifty leech bites; Jean-Pierre then counted them and came up with a hundred and eight. I wondered why on earth I had ever felt obliged to do Saddle Peak in the first place. It was the lowest peak I had ever climbed in my life, and it had turned out to be the most difficult. I had never suffered like that before, but it was entirely my own fault. Poor preparation can turn the easiest looking mountain into a major, and often hazardous, undertaking.

In spite of my unfortunate experience on Saddle Peak we were still pleased with our achievements. Jean-Pierre, with whom I always shared a room when we went on expeditions together, was particularly happy with his results. Next to his bed was a large blue barrel filled with Formalin (the room smelled like a hospital), in which he had preserved his specimens. He was sure he had discovered several new species of fish, which he intended to name after the Negrito tribes.

On the return trip to Port Blair I spent an hour treating one of Leopold's leech bites with a styptic powder; one of the nasty little creatures had injected too much hirudin, an anti-coagulant, into the wound. While I worked to stop the bleeding, we planned the last few days of our trip. We wanted to pay a second visit to the Jarawa and also hoped to visit Sentinel Island, the remotest of all of the Andaman Islands.

Meanwhile, back in Port Blair, the Indian immigrants were experiencing something of a sensation. A young Jarawa boy, who had broken his leg in the jungle, was lying in hospital and long queues had formed to look at him through the window. I was reminded that, fifty years previously, my interest in foreign cultures had started with a similar "anthropological show", when I saw a native Papuan at the circus.

When we anchored for the second time in the bay near the Jarawa village there were several natives on the beach. The first time we had met them they had been friendly and cheerful, and this time, too, they seemed pleased to see us. When we lowered the rowing boat into the water eleven of the Jarawa men swam out to meet us, and the sight of these muscular black men cutting powerfully through the azure blue waters of the lagoon is an image that I will never forget. They boarded the boat, grabbed their presents and dumped them in the rowing boat. On the beach, six women stood with their children and waited anxiously for the men to return, but as soon as we beached the rowing boat, the women turned and walked to the communal hut. Leopold followed them and returned to tell us that they did not wish to be photographed inside the hut. Apparently it was not the camera itself they were worried about; they were frightened of the flashlight. From my experiences with other aboriginal tribes, I knew that one should not show them any photographs on which they might recognise themselves. However, Bakhtawar Singh had shown them several such photographs on his last visit before our arrival. Perhaps it was this that had caused such consternation. Whatever it was that had spooked them, their reaction to us now seemed quite different.

We stood on the beach and the Jarawa unloaded their presents, which were hurriedly carried off to the hut by the women as if they were afraid we would take them back again. One of the other women must have told her man that we had photographed her inside the hut, whereupon he made a great show of shouting at us, ransacking our kit and pelting us with large shells. The situation was becoming serious, and Bakhtawar Singh, who understood the Jarawa better than anyone, implored us to give them anything they wanted. The warning was unnecessary; we would never have attempted to provoke a skirmish anyway. They took everything they could find and their behaviour was so savage that we decided to cut the visit short. During the melee my spectacles were torn from my nose; I nearly lost them forever, but luckily the Jarawa contented themselves with the chain to which they were attached.

There was no stopping them. They shouted and screamed at us, becoming angrier and angrier, and we realised that there was little point in staying any longer as the situation would only get more dangerous. We rowed back to the boat, where we found nine more Jarawa, who refused point blank to return to the beach. We sailed up and down the coast for an hour as they investigated every last nook and cranny on the boat. Finally, we returned to the anchorage and took them ashore in the rowing boat.

We had parted company from the Jarawa twice, once in friendship and once in a tense atmosphere; we had lived practically next door to the Onge; now we were on the way to visit the tribe of mysterious, unapproachable Negritos, who lived to the north. Little was known about these indigenous tribespeople, and they were referred to simply as the "Sentinelese", after the little island on which they lived, North Sentinel Island.

Shri Harmander Singh had prepared our excursion well, as he also wished to avail himself of the opportunity to take a look at the Sentinelese for himself. We approached the island from the east in the early morning, dropped anchor and took to the rescue boat. A soldier in civilian clothing carrying a round metal shield sat next to the King; a machine gun lay hidden at his side. I had never witnessed such precautionary measures as these on any of my previous expeditions, and the tension in the team was palpable.

During the boat trip from Port Blair, Bakhtawar Singh had explained to us that when he had first attempted to make contact with the Sentinelese, one of his people had been shot in the arm with a metal-tipped arrow. The as yet unpublished photographs they had taken during that trip were later to cause a worldwide sensation. I had also been given a shield to hold but I preferred to keep my trigger finger firmly on the camera shutter.

Slowly, very slowly we motored along the coast, keeping a safe distance of about seventy to eighty metres between us and the shore, until we spied the roof of a hut half-hidden in the jungle. At that very moment the boat ran aground on a sand bank, and for a few brief moments we were in a very vulnerable situation. The boatman told us to shift our weight, and a wave helped to get us afloat again. Bakhtawar had also told us that the last time he had been here the Sentinelese had advanced on his group in a military formation, with the leader at the front followed by a row of two, then four, men. We had no way of knowing exactly how many pygmies there were on the island but conservative estimates put their number at around a hundred.

All at once, a man appeared from the green swathe of the bush. Black-skinned and muscular, he strode self-confidently along the white sand, slotted a long arrow into the string of his bow and walked into the water towards us. As the waves began to lap around his knees he stopped, tensioned the bow and took careful aim. Presently, several more Sentinelese came out of the bush, all of them armed with longbows. These Stone Age people were instinctively defending themselves against the outside world with their traditional weapons of battle, refusing all contact with a world that to them was alien and hostile. We had no intention of provoking these brave people and began to withdraw, metre by metre, watching the shore the whole time. As we pulled away we caught sight of more armed men standing amongst the trees, camouflaged by the leaves and ready to defend their freedom to the death.

It was an unforgettable scene. There was no doubt that what we were witnessing was a unique event on this planet of ours: a moving attempt by a group of aboriginal inhabitants to defend their ancient culture. Moving, because these men were actually convinced that their show of strength with bows and arrows had actually prevented us from landing. Naturally they had no idea that many thousands of years had passed between the discovery of their weapons and those that we carried, or that the lid from one of our metal oil drums would have been sufficient to parry their arrows. They had won because we had allowed them to win, and because we had decided to forgo imposing upon them the questionable blessings of our civilisation. For them, to defend their territory was a matter of survival.

As soon as the Sentinelese realised that we had abandoned our plan to land they began to celebrate their victory, shouting and dancing around on the sand, their bows held triumphantly above their heads. They were convinced of their victory; it was better that way, I thought. After all, this was their homeland, a place where they could live, alone and independent. Their mistrust of outsiders was justified; it could not have escaped their notice that many thousands of their kin had been forced to cede their lands to the new arrivals from the mainland. Most of our attempts to protect such tribes from extinction end in failure. Here, the Sentinelese were protecting themselves.

There was a splendid sunset that evening, but there was an air of melancholy, too, as I thought about how much I had grown to love and respect the life of the aboriginal people of the Andaman Islands. It was a great privilege to have been given the gift of such an experience, and an adventure that I will never forget.

THE DARK CONTINENT

In 1977 I returned to Africa once more, twenty years after my first visit. Over the years I had developed a foolproof instinct for when it was time move on, and it would prove its worth this time round, too. I often found myself one step ahead simply because I had chosen the right moment to begin a new project rather than carrying on with something just for the sake of it. There were many places I was the first European to visit, and sometimes the last as well, because they now no longer exist in the same form. I had written books and lived through the golden age of educational television in the seventies, alongside such figures as Bernhard Czimek and Heinz Sielmann, but I retired from broadcasting at the end of the decade when the technology began to become more complicated and threatened to restrict my freedom of movement.

When I was on the Andaman Islands I learned that even exploration has its limits. As my visit to the Jarawa and the Sentinel Islands had taught me, one has to be prepared to forego further discoveries in order to protect the natives, or to avoid subjecting oneself to excessive hardships. I had many such experiences in Africa. Amongst the primitive people there, the transition the continent was undergoing was becoming increasingly apparent. The tribes had retreated either deep into the jungle or into the desert, or else their way of life meant that it was unclear whether they would adapt to our form of civilisation or die out. Africa had become a tourists' paradise, yet their very presence affected the world of the locals whom they were hoping to find largely unchanged. If this gigantic continent was to remain the home of proud and confident nomads, hunters, fishermen and warriors for much longer, people needed to visit it with a willingness to learn.

Africa was a paradise for scientists. There were hundreds of tribes and languages, from Pygmies to the tall Watussi, burning wastes and icy peaks, jungle as well as savannah and the biggest wildlife reserves – it would take more than one lifetime to experience all this variety and describe it. The challenges were enormous, ranging from extremes of climate to the dangers of bilharzia and malaria or the small bloodsucking tsetse fly, and not least the political complications that made exploration so difficult.

In June 1976 I sent a letter applying for permission to mount an expedition to the Minister for Tourism in Kinshasa (formerly Leopoldville) in Zaire, previously the Belgian Congo. I wanted to return once more to Ruwenzori. The equatorial ice and the alpine flora in the middle of Africa had made such an impression on me that I wanted to go back and share this unique beauty with my friends. One month later in Brussels, I received the news that Citoyen Nzeza Makunsi, the Minister, was waiting to receive me in the Jägerwinkel Sanatorium in Bad Wiessee. "Citoyen" was a synonym for "sir" or "sahib", and since the independence of Zaire all citizens were given this title. We had a pleasant dinner, each of us wearing a dark suit, and Citoyen Makunsi promised to ask his representative in the Ruwenzori Wildlife Park to support my expedition. My next visit was to Mercedes-Benz in Stuttgart, where a car and a Unimog off-road vehicle were placed at my disposal, no questions asked; the Unimog was equipped with a winch that could be used to pull it out of swamps. Both of these vehicles were shipped to Kinshasa, and I was able to pick them up from the Mercedes-Benz outlet there. The only condition attached to the use of the vehicles was that I should write an article for the company magazine at some point. It was clearly thanks to my many successful expeditions that I received such privileged treatment. It is well-known that success attracts good fortune, whereas failure brings bad luck in its train.

In 1960 the Belgian colony had become the independent Democratic Republic of Congo. Since my last visit the place-names had changed, and independence had brought self-confidence and pride in being self-sufficient. The change was apparent as soon as we landed. The airport was now called Kinshasa Airport, and the uniformed customs official was tattooed on both cheeks with the marks of his tribe. The taxi driver also bore a deep scar from his hairline to the tip of his nose, and as he drove us past the new fifty-seven thousand seat stadium, he proudly told us that he had a ticket for the boxing match with Muhammad Ali.

I met my expedition team in the hotel: my friend Axel Thorer, and Manfred Passel from Berlin, with his cameraman. It was their job to make sure that my account of the journey became a professional television programme. At the suggestion of the helpful car outlet, we travelled the first two thousand kilometres to Kisangi (formerly Stanleyville) by ship up the Congo rather than on the poorly maintained highway. It would have taken ten days or so either way, but taking the river route avoided damaging the cars. The journey lacked variety, but the cars remained firmly lashed down on deck, and their comfortable seats were often preferred to the small cabin. The deck resembled a colourful market, what with the clucking of the hens and pots and pans rattling about, and even the aromas of smoked fish were the same as those in the bazaar. We negotiated rapids and even came across cliffs. On many occasions we ran aground on sand banks, and the steamer stopped at every town. Fruit could be bought everywhere, and ivory carvings were offered for sale on the sly.

At times it was almost impossible to make out the farther bank of the river, and the Congo became as wide as a lake. The ship moved slowly. On occasion there were big areas covered by water hyacinths that we had to go round; this flower had originally been introduced as a garden plant, but in all the tropical countries it had become a troublesome weed, getting caught up in propellers and offering shelter to mosquito larvae. The only remedy is expensive: using aeroplanes to spray the flowers with weed killers and insecticides.

We were finally in Kisangani, from where we were going to set off on our tour of Ruwenzori. I always looked forward to meeting the friendly mountain-dwellers; whether in the Himalayas, the Andes or the Ruwenzori. In the mountains people are more helpful and hospitable than in towns, where you always have to be on your guard against thieves. We drove in the cars to the airport of the little town of Beni, where we had to leave our vehicles behind, as we were entering a flooded region. We travelled on foot, passing over swaying rope bridges made of lianas, to our base camp at Mutwanga.

I found my name in the guest book – "8th ascent 1957". But nothing remained of the friendly atmosphere of those days. In 1960, Ruwenzori had been declared a national park, arousing the interest of

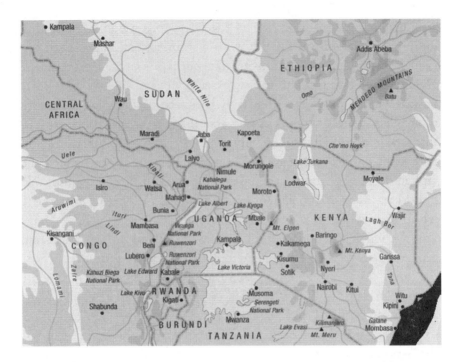

many climbers as well as scientific expeditions composed of botanists and climate researchers. As there was little accommodation available, the park manager had introduced stricter arrangements, and there was an organisation in Mutsanga to ensure that everything ran smoothly with the porters, who were from the Baswanga tribe.

The only one of the porters who had accompanied me twenty years before who was still alive was Joseph Kitambale, now sixty. Kitambale was well-known as the first African to reach the summit of the "rainmaker", so starting a tradition comparable to that of the Sherpas in the Himalayas, though in Ruwenzori it was still in its infancy. Being a porter in the national park had become a well-regarded and sought-after profession; to earn the title of capo, or head porter, it was necessary to undergo lengthy training. This institution marked an important change in the life of the tribes, because now they had rights and duties and were no longer mere porters. Things may not have been completely trouble-free under the new circumstances, but the porters made the Africans feel more confident, as well as having a positive impact on relations with us Europeans.

Joseph Kitambale told me his tale of woe. God was displeased, he said, for on account of the uncertain political conditions, only a few visitors had come to Ruwenzori, and he had not been able to save enough money to make the annual sacrifice in the form of an animal. I asked whether it was possible to make up the omission and so get rid of the displeasure. I was happy to give him the money, but first – so that it would not fall into the wrong hands – I wanted to find out how Kitambale knew that the god was annoyed. The old man shivered and replied that he had been heard singing in the jungle as though drunk. I said I was prepared to pay for the sacrifice, but how were we going to set up the contact?

"We will play the wooden piano for three days, then if God has accepted the sacrifice, he will turn himself into a rainbow, and protect the expedition as well!"

This meant I would experience the traditional Baswanga faith ritual, so for me it was really anything but a sacrifice. But what on earth was the "wooden piano"?

Before we set off, the village blacksmith came to offer us a set of "climbing irons" to deal with the ice. Of course, I had packed my crampons in case of need, but I thought his sample piece was so fine that I ordered it for our museum. As an elder, Kitambale, who had become a national hero, wanted to come at least as far as Ihingero, the sacrificial site. Our capo Wambo did not object, and he also allowed some of the older porters, already established and approved by the government, to employ younger, so-called aspirant porters on the first day to cover the thousand metres of narrow and muddy track. In the small villages some of their relatives brought us beer and passion fruit, because the news had preceded us that we preferred these juicy fruits to all others.

After two more days we reached the boundary of the Ruwenzori National Park, where the icy peaks of the mountain range lie. It was in this uninhabited region that the difficult part of our task began. Hours of rain had turned the narrow path into one long swamp, and thick banks of fog made it hard to see. The ridges we crossed did little to raise our spirits; when you finally got to the top and began to go downhill, you knew that you would have to climb back up again later. Using fixed ropes, we managed to negotiate several escarpments, which at least confirmed that we were going the right way.

At the first hut, at an altitude of 2,138 metres, we found a rubbish bin with a sign saying "Keep Ruwenzori tidy". We used a jam jar suspended from a long wire to draw water from a hole that was barely ten centimetres wide. The water was a rusty brown colour. We hung our soaking clothes on lines that had been stretched right across the room, but they did not dry out until we were making our way back to the warm valley a week later. In the morning we found that two mice had drowned in the coffee water on the petrol stove.

I asked Capo Wambo if the weather would hold, whereupon he took me to a rain tree; its bark was marked with the scars of previous enquiries. With his bush knife he cut a notch in the bark. A pale yellow drop gradually formed. His answer was, "It will not rain for another three hours." If humidity is high and the temperature is right, the tree sweats, and the capo was able to draw on the experience of many generations to interpret the yellow liquid. The weather was not without importance, because ahead of us lay difficult ground and an ascent of more than a thousand metres.

At the half-way point we reached a clearing that afforded a view of the valley. There was a semicircle of little houses improvised from leaves and bamboo twigs, some of which had collapsed; Kitimbale called them temples. We had found the sacrificial site of Ihongero with its "wooden piano" – a simple xylophone consisting of a series of long, thick round pieces of wood held together by pegs. Kitambale took two beaters and began to play. To my ears there wasn't much of a melody, but the rhythm was pleasant, and at that altitude the resonant notes carried a long way.

Kitambale stayed in Ihongero to make contact with the shaman Kasibabu, who was due to arrive at the sacrificial site in five days' time. Kitambale wanted to send his own porters down into the valley with my money to get a goat, a white hen and other offerings such as salt, tobacco, sugarcane and manioc. Although it was quite clear that the offering was not just to the angry god, the Baswanga tribe at the foot of the Ruwenzori was going to get its share too, I raised no objection.

The remainder of us carried on with our march until, several days later, we reached the hut at Kiondo where we had rested up twenty years previously. At four thousand two hundred metres, the same height as the Matterhorn, the air there contained still less oxygen. Our wet clothes froze solid even during the day, and the rainwater we collected in a tent flap formed a layer of ice that had to be removed in the morning. I convinced my friends to come with me to the Wasuwameso to see the incredible view. Only by scrambling and hanging on to roots or foliage was it possible to traverse the 262 metres up from the Kiondo Hut. But they stopped cursing when the Ruwenzori massif, clad in white, could be made out before them. A small trail of powder snow blew across from Savoya to the summit of Mount Stanley, and from Margherite, which showed just how cold it must be up there. Beneath gleamed the cliffs, shining with melt water and various minerals; the differently coloured lakes appeared like jewels.

The cameraman was enthusiastic and thought that he could certainly accompany me as far as the snout of the glacier the next day. But though he began the ascent the following morning together with me and Wambo, who acted as our porter, two hours later his body would serve him no longer. Remarking consolingly that he had climbed as high as Mont Blanc, I went on alone to the hut that stood beneath the way up to the glacier. In 1957 I had been able to spend a dry night there, but the shelter now had no roof; remnants of ash showed that previous expeditions had used the wood for fires. The mountaineers now began their routes from the Kiondo hut, and so the higher hut was no longer maintained. Setting off with plenty of oxygen in our lungs gave us a quicker and easier start, and raised our spirits, except for the cameraman, who kept saying he wished he had come with me the day before, and that he would definitely come next time. Over the years I have come across many examples of people making such extraordinary declarations shortly after giving up – I call it "the miracle of memory failure".

Meanwhile, Kitambale had mended the xylophone and the little drum, and as soon as we returned to Ihongero, he began to beat a tree drum, a long root of a big tree that stretched deep into the earth so that the sound carried a long way. Then he put his hands to his mouth and shouted something into the valley beneath. From far below resounded the answer that Shaman Kasibabu was tired and felt unwell, but he would come shortly. Not long afterwards the magician's attendants appeared with a truculent goat, hens and other offerings, followed somewhat later by Kasibabu himself.

Supported by a long staff, with the sacred knife in a carved wooden sheath hanging round his neck, he sat down, gasping for air. Although not yet fifty, he seemed twice that age, because he had been weakened by the frequent use of drugs to enter into the trance state, as well as by his spiritual contact with the human psyche and the caprice of the gods; the unaccustomed height compounded this. He was a powerful man who had the ability to curse and cure, and the twenty-four tribesmen adopted a reverential posture until he deigned to take notice of us four white men as well. With a cry he stuck the Sacred Knife in the ground, drank from the calabash filled with beer, and instructed his attendants to begin the ceremony.

After offerings had been placed in front of three houses that represented the dwelling-place of various spirits, a young attendant gave a hen to Kasibabu; he passed it from one hand to the other, whispering incomprehensible words into the bird's ear each time. Suddenly he struck off its head and put it on its feet. The hen ran headless past the fire, stopping right in front of the house that was dedicated to the god of life and good fortune. There could not have been a more propitious oracle.

With this, the first part of the ceremony was concluded to the satisfaction of all. Now the god had to accept the goat as well. The shaman's son asked his father for the Sacred Knife and slit the animal's throat with a single cut. The blood was collected in an earthenware pot while the goat's head continued to make anguished sounds. The vessel, half-full, was topped up with water, and passed round the men, who drank up the contents. The meat was divided, and Kasibubu received the liver, spreading the entrails out in front of him on the forest floor, where he predicted the future on the basis of the twists of the intestine. Everything went as desired; the tribe had confirmed its faith through magic ritual and a celebration, and we had had a tremendous experience. Kitambale, the elder, thought it was the "God who knows the whole world". "He is your God and mine as well!"

Down in the valley, families were waiting longingly for their menfolk to return, and in the very first village a pretty young woman gave me freshly fermented banana juice and asked whether her husband had eaten of the sacred goat too. "Of course he did, everyone got some!" I replied. Then when Capo Wamba arrived, she asked him with a snarl whether he knew that anyone who had eaten the meat of the sacred goat had to refrain from all sexual activity for at least twenty-four hours – and he had been away from home for more than a week!

Like all adventures, the experience of the lush alpine vegetation in the rainy mountains came to an end. Just as after my years in Tibet, I find myself unable to describe the beautiful landscape, which is too lovely for words. Even without climbing to the summit, the Mountains of the Moon are still a tremendous experience, and all the effort had been worth it; the memory of that heavenly landscape and the charming natives remains.

I find it rather easier to describe the last evening in the porters' village. The sweet banana beer that the women brought in earthenware vessels contributed to the atmosphere when I paid the men their wages. They were sitting on the grass with their families behind them, gazing proudly at their menfolk. Some signed their sonorous names in a barely legible hand, but most confirmed that they had been paid with a fingerprint. Each of us had placed useful items no longer needed after the cold, wet days up in the mountain on a pile. Kitambale distributed these items, including radios and knives, as he saw fit. I included my light crampons, because I had acquired the climbing irons, heavy but authentic, from the village blacksmith. I managed to barter for a typical black Congolese mask for my collection, plentifully adorned with cowries.

A hollow tree trunk was brought, and a man began to beat the dance rhythm with a stick; it sounded just like the bush telegraph. We Europeans also tried to join in the dancing, but our stiff movements gave more cause for pity and laughter than for admiration. The rhythm and gentle movements of the natives are inimitable. It was the atmosphere, the mixture of beer, fermented manioc and salted meat, of fire and tobacco smoke, that incomparable atmosphere that awakens the wanderlust of seasoned European explorers. Our experiences in the Ruwenzori range had shown us that despite the tractors of the Congo's great copper and gold mines, the old ways of the tribes had not yet disappeared completely.

The Wagenia, a tribe that lived to the south of Kisangani on an island in the middle of the Congo River, also maintained their traditional way of life. They stubbornly refused to concede their age-old privileges, and were considered to be haughty and unapproachable. However, they used a unique fishing technique that I wanted to record on film. When I had visited this region twenty years before, there were tribal feuds, but now the Congo had become independent of its Belgian colonial masters, and economic considerations led the central government to combine all the tribes in a single association, the Co-operative. The chairman was a politician in the capital, to whom a fee had to be paid before negotiations with the Wagenia could even begin. However they are far too proud to let the authorities tell them what to do. With such hard-boiled men as these – after all, they put their lives at risk every day with their daring techniques – it is also a good idea to negotiate the price for a visit in advance. Once the deal has been struck, the watery adventure can begin. Eighteen strong men paddled across the foaming cataracts to the island in a boat fourteen metres long carved from the trunk of a single enormous tree. Only the effort required to hold on stopped us from throwing up.

After an hour-long journey through numerous rapids and whirlpools, we reached the island and the village. Women were washing clothes in an inlet, and scrubbing cooking pots with sand. In the background a forest of stakes, with men clambering about amongst them, could be seen in the midst of the rapids. They had driven five-metre high wooden stakes into cracks in the rocks amongst the raging currents, linking them together with a network of lianas. They had lashed funnel-shaped traps made of bamboo, over a metre wide at the opening, to the stakes, half-submerged. Once a day, in the early morning, they collected the catch. The rest of the time they danced acrobatically through the forest of stakes to carry out repairs. Just how

Expedition to French Guyana, 1969. The joy of adventure is something that accompanied me throughout my life.

Ruwenzori. The tent offered little protection from the damp equatorial climate

The last metres to the summit of the 5,119m Mount Stanley in the Ruwenzori Mountains

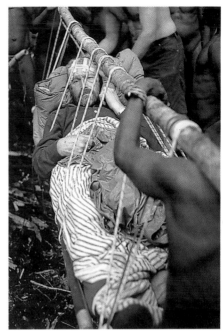

At the source of the stone axes, New Guinea 1962. The stones are heated and broken up into smaller fragments for ease of transport

After my tumble down the water-fall I was carried by the Dani in an improvised stretcher

My Dutch companion Bert Huizenga pays off our Dani porters after our ascent of Carstenz Pyramid. To his right is our interpreter.

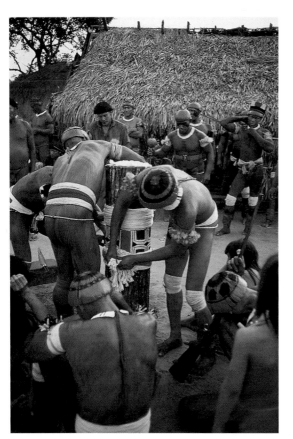

With the Xingu Indians in South America in 1966. The funeral pole, known as a kwarup, is prepared for a ceremony

Huka-huka wrestling. The loser is the first wrestler to touch the ground with any part of his body other than his legs

With Carina and one of the carved ancestor statues that I brought back from my 1972 Borneo expedition

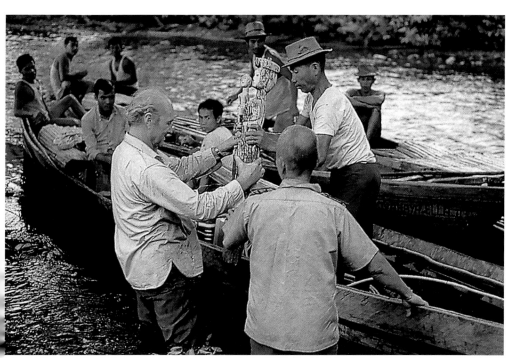

After the village shaman had sacrificed a chicken to his ancestors I was allowed to remove the blood-spattered statue

1975. The Jarawa people of the Andaman Islands were astonished at the sight of us fully clothed Europeans

An Onge man shows off his nautilus shell. The shells were once used as drinking vessels

An aboriginal inhabitant of Sentinel Island strikes a threatening pose with his spear. His tribe shun all contact with the outside world

Filming in East Africa in the late 1960s

Wagenia fish traps in the Congo. The Wagenia walk along the poles like circus tightrope walkers

Many of my trips took me to Africa. With two Ugandan women

A warrior of the Hadendoa tribe, armed with a sword and a shield made of hippopotamus leather. I visited the Hadendoa during a trip to Africa in 1971

The Karamajong in the north east of Uganda drink the blood of animals mixed with milk

A yogi demonstrates how he is able to slow, or even stop, his heartbeat

Washing in the ice cold glacier water of the Ganges in Gangotri is an important ritual for a pilgrim. The photo was taken during my 1974 trip to the sources of the Ganges.

The traditional Nepalese "farewell" gesture, at the foot of Annapurna, Western Nepal

A Tibetan *trashi gomang* cabinet, traditionally used to store religious artefacts

On the golf course in Lhasa at 4000 metres. The thin air means that even complete novices can hit long tee shots!

n 1987 my friend Helmut Kreuzer and I visited the semi-nomadic Sakteng tribe in he north east of Bhutan

With Tuksey Rinpoche, the highest incarnation of Samdenling Monastery, during a visit to Darjeeling in 1994

I returned to Tibet in 1982 and met several old acquaintances

With the Dalai Lama at our holiday home in Hüttenberg on my 80th birthday, July 6th 1992

Tibet 1982. The cliff with the Blue Buddha is all that remains of the eight kilometre pilgrims' path around Lhasa

With the artist Balthus in May 1999. Here I am presenting him with the traditional Tibetan good luck scarf

Helmut Newton came to Hüttenberg in August 1997 to take my photograph for Vanity Fair

With David Thewlis and Brad Pitt, who played the roles of Peter Aufschnaiter and I in the film "Seven Years in Tibet", at our house in Hüttenberg in September 1996

The film director Jean-Jacques Annaud visited us on three occasions. Here, I show him the Heinrich Harrer Museum

At my desk with my wife Carina

dangerous their work was, was shown by the Co-operative's report, which stated that every three or four months a fisherman fell into the water, and only the corpse was recovered, if he was found at all. It was the young men who had the strength to climb down from the stakes to the baskets and reach the nets filled with fish. The old men and boys repaired the baskets in the village when they became damaged.

To signal danger or to communicate with the mainland, the Wagenia drummed on a hollowed-out tree trunk with a slit; the sounds it made were not drowned out by the roar of the rapids. But for the most part they did their best to look after themselves, and rather than summoning a doctor from the big city, they relied on their tribal medicine man. I saw that he had had an array of natural medicines in little bags and vials. He had some especially effective powders for painful injuries, and these were just the same as our narcotics, but derived entirely from plant material – so his skills were not limited to magic and spells.

I asked the elder of the tribe when their right to live on the part of the river with the most fish dated back to. His answer was, "Forever!" and I suppose this meant "as long as anyone can remember." The Wagenia were proud of this ancient privilege, and they were managing successfully to preserve their way of life.

Compared to the Wagenia, things had gone less well for the Ituri, a pygmy tribe to the east of Kisangani. Even here, in the largest unbroken area of jungle in Africa, there was a commissar to tell them how to lead their lives. The felling of hardwood trees had compelled many pygmies, who had previously lived as hunter-gatherers, to leave their territory, and now they farmed the land. They sat by the side of the dusty road and sold their produce. Instead of loincloths made of raffia or tree bark beaten until it was soft, they wore scraps of dyed cotton, and they used plastic bowls and tin pans rather than gourd vessels decorated with ornaments. Twenty years before I had watched in admiration as they built a liana bridge, but when I asked if they could produce another similar work of art for the film, one of them replied that there was no longer any need as there were no crocodiles in the river now, and in any case, they would need to get permission.

All along the seven hundred kilometre long jungle road from

Bunia to Kisangani, we kept meeting pygmies who suddenly stepped out of the forest to beg for a few coins or some liquor. They offered musical instruments, such as harps or drums, for sale cheaply, and were prepared to part with their hunting weapons, such as bow and arrow, and even the short spears they had once used to kill elephants; they would creep right up under the bellies of the thick-skinned animals and boldly stick the spear into them. One pygmy offered us a net he had previously used to catch small deer. His loin cloth was tied on with a belt made of imitation leopard skin, and on the buckle was written, "007, You Only Live Twice".

So that we could at least preserve a few scenes from their former way of life, we set up camp in a clearing, and the cameraman and I went off into the jungle on our own. Crouching down, we made our way along a path that the little forest dwellers could take walking upright as if in a tunnel. We reached a typical old settlement consisting of six huts. A woman hid the face of her baby at her breast while I took photographs; there were tin cans on the ground, and a broken black umbrella and some dirty bottles. The woman's face was decorated with blue tattoos done with plant juice, and in ten minutes flat, two men showed us how one of their round huts made of leaves is built. All this was done in haste, because both we and they were doing things we wanted to do but were not allowed to; we had not applied to the Co-operative for permission to make this visit. We returned in a gloomy mood, and I could see that these cheerful, hospitable people had given up hope, and were having to cope with fears they had never known before.

The Pygmies are in a difficult situation. They know that the jungle is their very own world that gives them shelter, and that no-one else will lay claim to it because of the difficult living conditions. If they give up their freedom and live outside on the road, life seems to be easier, and it offers the many temptations of the modern age. Alcohol, which they use as an escape from their problems, is known to be a great danger. As intelligent people, they are tormented by the conflict between remaining free but "backward", or losing their identity if they become "civilised".

A nervous Commissar was waiting in the camp, and he was clearly relieved that we were back. With him was a uniformed Pygmy who had been appointed as a guard in the Kahuzi-Biega National Park. This was an exception, but represented an ideal way of combining the traditional way of life with the modern age. The official said proudly, "We are helping to promote unity amongst the various peoples of Zaire."

There is still time to hope that these kindly, defenceless jungle dwellers can be prevented from suffering the fate of the Indians on the Trans-Amazon Road, who make up the new proletariat of Brazil. Their songs and the sounds of their instruments could still be saved and nurtured, and the rhythm of their dances and the dialogue the medicine man holds with nature could be preserved. The time is coming for the various Pygmy tribes, just as in many tourist destinations from the Tyrol to Tahiti, when they drive a tractor by day and "dress up" as natives in the evening.

OF MAN AND BEAST

I thought it prudent to make friends with Lusenge Muschensi, one of the game wardens of the Kahuzi-Biega National Park, since he was the man who would take me to visit the gorillas. He drove with us to Bukavu, which had been the stronghold of the white mercenaries during the Congo War, to report to his superiors. Bukavu lies 1,460 metres above Lake Kivu, which is 350 metres deep; its clear water looks ideal for a swim. Apparently it is free of the terrible bloodsucking worms that cause bilharzia, but I make a point of never entering still water, and only swim where a fresh stream flows into the sea and there is a visible current.

Then we went on to the National Park. Visitors are greeted by a sign at the entrance showing a terrifying larger-than-life gorilla – this is supposed to be Kasimir, the legendary male famous for his strength and intelligence. He had been observed years before by Belgian zoologists and ethnologists, but since then he had died; his skeleton, severely damaged, was on display in the small museum run by the park management. His successor Mushamuka had killed him in single combat. The fight had been observed by Pygmies; the first time anyone had seen how gorillas kill. At the beginning of his attack, Mushamuka had bitten the ageing Kasimir on the chest and hips, before taking his lower arm between both fists, breaking it in two, and pounding his rival with the sides of his hands. After the fight Kasimir had crept off into the undergrowth, and his corpse was not found for several days.

We were going to visit Mushamuka and his family. There was no guarantee of finding these shy animals; they lived in the wild, and two Pygmies employed by the park management trailed them at some distance, returning to headquarters every evening to report where the gorilla herd was sleeping. It was always possible that the apes, having been scared off during the night, might be somewhere completely different by morning. Under the guidance of Muschensi, we were hoping to track them down and film them at close quarters. We parked our car under the gorilla sign and clambered into a Jeep that took us to a weather station at an elevation of 2,376 metres. Beneath us, the mist drifted through the wooded valleys. Kazi and Biega, the two peaks the park was named after, rose up to the north and south. From this point onward, we proceeded on foot. In the virgin forest, still completely untouched by human hand, we had to cut our path with a bush knife; we often had to creep on all fours through tunnel-like stretches of shrubs, and then our way would be blocked by fallen tree trunks a metre across that we had to clamber over. When there was a track to be seen it was barely fifty centimetres wide, with two or three metre high undergrowth on either side. Muschensi led us down almost vertical gorges, and we climbed back up the other side by holding on to lianas. After about two hours one of the Pygmies stopped in the damp heat, told us to be silent, and after standing there for a while he turned off sharply to the left for no apparent reason. "He says he can smell the gorillas," whispered Muschensi. "They are not far away now."

We reached a clearing about a hundred and fifty metres across, with waist-high grass and the odd bush. Muschensi put an index finger to his lips in warning. There it was – suddenly there was a movement in the grass. The head of a female appeared twenty metres away. She looked across at us suspiciously, and a few seconds later she had disappeared back into the undergrowth. It was quite obvious that we had disturbed the animal while it was eating.

Believing that we had now reached our goal, we started filming and taking lots of photos; but that was just the beginning. After choosing a different spot and waiting for fifteen minutes, we managed to get almost the entire gorilla family in shot within a fifty square metre area. Nine babies leaped about on trees and bushes, paying us hardly any attention as they stuffed leaves into their mouths. Six young males romped about on the ground like high-spirited boys, or tried to impress us by beating their chests. No fewer than fifteen females were lying on their backs in the grass or collecting food. In all, the herd was thirty-one gorillas strong.

And then came Mushamuka, the giant, whom the natives called "Silverback" on account of the almost white fur on his back. The translation of Mushamuka is "family head". He was thirty years old, and Muschensi estimated his weight at four hundredweight and his height at over two metres. In ten years, according to the warden, he would be defeated in single combat by one of the younger – and still smaller – males; Kasimir had been forty when Mushamuka killed him.

The giant was kneeling about seventeen metres away in the clearing and did not let us out of his sight. Whichever way we moved, his eyes followed. After around an hour he tried to cut off our escape by disappearing into the jungle and taking his place on a platform up above. "If he manages to get into a position where he is looking down on us," Muschensi warned, "then things will get dangerous." So we climbed upwards alongside him, fortunately without losing sight of the other gorillas for a moment, because they followed behind their leader.

We didn't think anything of it when Mushamuka suddenly disappeared, but the men who live with these giant apes know their tricks. Muschensi had been attacked twice before on similar tours, and he knew exactly what to do – lie down completely still without making a sound, just like the younger males in a similar situation. It worked; Mushamuka accepted this gesture of submission, and left us alone.

While the gorillas ate their fill before our eyes, we maintained a distance of fifteen to twenty metres. Perhaps we could have got closer still to the herd, but Muschensi kept us back, even when Mushamuka stopped eating, lay on his back and allowed himself to be groomed by younger males, about the size of a full-grown chimpanzee. Some of them were visibly annoyed by our presence; they rose up to their full height and beat their chests. It is an incredible sound, but somewhat disappointing too, because it sounds nothing like the muffled thudding familiar from Tarzan films; it is more like a high-pitched slapping sound, like someone clapping.

After around two hours we noticed a penetrating smell, and Mushamuka too appeared to become worried. Muschensi advised us to withdraw, explaining that at times of danger or excitement, gorillas release a scent from their armpits that is not particularly pleasant for our noses. It is meant to warn off human beings and other enemies before the apes go into action.

Back in Bukavu, Muschensi told us about the life of his charges.

At eight o'clock in the morning, the gorillas get up and eat for two or three hours, and then they rest until around two. These were the two parts of the day we had managed to film. Then the herd returns to action, and they continue eating until about six. In the evening the younger animals build nests from leaves and small twigs in treetops, bushes and branches, and spend the night in them. On the way to the clearing we had found a number of old shelters, and we thought they were large birds' nests. The mountain gorillas eat about fifty plant species, including young bamboo, but also flowers, tree bark, a variety of seeds, and above all, leaves. The females only bear young every three years, with a gestation of nine months – the same as humans. There has never been a recorded case of twins.

As an ethnographer, I found this visit to the gorillas utterly fascinating, and there could not have been a better time for it, as conditions were peaceful for once. Again and again the region where the three countries Zaire, Uganda and Rwanda met had been plagued by lawless rebels, supposedly fighting for their tribe, who showed utter contempt for human rights. There are even some sad stories to tell in relation to the last few gorillas that still exist in the jungle there. For instance, a zoologist who lived with the animals was murdered by rebels in 1996, and in August 1998 two Swedes and a New Zealander were kidnapped. To this day there is no sign of them. In March 1999, a group of tourists on a safari holiday, led by the French diplomat Anne Peltier, set out to observe the gorillas living in the wilds. Armed men stormed their tents, demanded their money, jewellery and watches, and kidnapped the group. The only one to escape the rebels was the Californian Linda Adams, who faked an asthma attack. The other eight victims, including Britons and Americans, were unable to get away, and died in the national park.

The unassuming Muschensi had enabled us to spend an eventful time with the gorillas, and I paid him well for his services. After the Ruwenzori Range, the Ituri, and the apes, I had had enough of the jungle, and asked Muschensi what to expect from the neighbouring Watussi, a tribe of shepherds. For the first time our gentle companion failed us, refusing to answer. He said the Tutsi, as he called them, were the cause of all the trouble in the region.

The proud, strikingly tall Tutsi were herdsmen who in the 16th century had gained the upper hand over the Pygmies and Bantus, who were agriculturalists, and founded the states of Rwanda and Burundi. They formed the nobility, and dominated the local tribes. Politicians added fuel to the inevitable flames of conflict, with the result that even Muschensi, otherwise so helpful, refused to advise us.

As a physical education teacher, what interested me about the Tutsi was their reputation as excellent high-jumpers. Supposedly, they could jump more than two metres effortlessly. I knew from my student days that the American Harold Osborne held the world record, 2.03 metres. A present to the proud chieftain smoothed the way to a demonstration by the Tutsi, which revealed the reason for their incredible high-jump skills – the rope was indeed placed at a height of two metres, but the jump was made from a stand around thirty centimetres high. Nonetheless, the slender Tutsi jumped to the respectable height of 1.70 metres. I bought some of their long spears, and I managed to acquire the colourfully painted tall drum that they beat in a standing position during the celebration.

After the weeks we had spent deep in the jungle, I appreciated the open landscape of the highlands, and wanted to get to know more about the pastoral nomads. In the middle of March, Manfred, Helmut, Axel and I left the hospitable border region. I had discovered the onward route we would take to the east coast. It was a journey of two thousand kilometres or so, and there ought to be a few sights worth seeing on the way. One complication was that we would have to cross newly independent countries all along the route that were on hostile terms with each other. The price of petrol was two dollars a litre, but we filled our tanks to the brim. We had no difficulties in leaving Zaire, and perhaps it helped that the border officials in Mahagi were not sober.

It started raining, and the surface of the road soon resembled soft soap. There was a succession of branches to be moved out of the way or holes to be filled. We came to a sort of bridge over a narrow gorge; the car got across the slippery planks at walking pace, but the weight of the Unimog made the "bridge" collapse. There was no one to help, but the steel cable at the front of the Unimog was long enough to reach a strong tree, and it pulled itself ever so slowly out of danger.

All this had taken hours, and the no-man's-land between Uganda and Zaire provided our first adventure. The uninhabited strip between the two countries was only fourteen kilometres across, but it was only in the afternoon that we came close to Uganda. In the border post of Goli, it was oppressively quiet. A man in civilian dress told us that it had been over two years since a vehicle from outside had been seen there – which explained the awful condition of the road. Thanks to my knowledge of English and Hindi, we managed to communicate very well. The man was not unfriendly, and a bottle of beer made him even more talkative. The local immigration official was in Kinshasa, he said, and it was not known when he would return. I showed him some colourful brochures intended to encourage people to visit Uganda, that beautiful country that Winston Churchill had called "the pearl of Africa". We just wanted to visit the famous Kabalega Nature Reserve, I explained, and of course the tremendous waterfalls of the Nile. I took the precaution of avoiding the old names of these natural wonders, such as "Murchison Falls", so as to respect local sensibilities. But the man wouldn't budge, and so I resorted to guile, saying that my friend Axel, being a journalist, knew Idi Amin well, and I would write a petition to him in Kampala and wait for the reply here in Goli.

As we started putting up our tents, he began to get uncomfortable. He came back with two civilians and asked if we would give them a beer as well. This we were well able to do, because there was a whole crate of beer hidden in the Unimog. Suddenly, the situation changed. One of them would go with us to the police station in Pakwak, on the Nile. I was so delighted I gave them the whole crate, and shortly thereafter we continued on our way without having our passports stamped; what with the beer, they had forgotten all about coming with us.

In every village there was plenty of ridiculously cheap petrol, and we filled up our drums. Colonel Mu'ammar al-Gaddafi was the last remaining ally of Idi Amin's reign of terror, and sent fuel in abundance to Uganda. When we reached Pakwak, we simply drove past the camp with its barbed wire fence, but the numerous deep holes made for slow progress. A cyclist overtook us and said politely that the commandant would like to talk to us.

We drove back to the camp, and the main gate shut behind us.

I don't know how my three friends were feeling, but my heart was in my mouth. The tall officer, who was clearly from a Nilote tribe, spoke impeccable English, and when I complimented him he proudly explained that he had attended a course in England before independence in 1962. He was not interested in our papers, and must have simply assumed they would be in order. He just said, "Open up the lorry!" When he saw our luggage, he said dryly, "You've got a lot of nice stuff there. How much of it is for me?" I replied that it was all camping equipment such as tents and camp beds; however, I did have a bottle of genuine Scotch whisky in the car for medicinal purposes. Now that our journey was coming to a close, he was welcome to have it. For security reasons, he explained, the lorry had to be searched for weapons. This task was carried out by two soldiers; the search was perfunctory, and the men were polite and courteous. Then the officer wished us a pleasant journey; he took the whisky and went into one of the barracks to order the guard on the bridge over the Nile to allow us to pass.

After we had crossed the Victoria Nile, we reached the famous Kabalega National Park. We took up residence in the enormous lodge; apart from us and a few Scandinavians and Koreans, there were no tourists. Just in case, I fetched another bottle from the box of whisky for "medicinal purposes". We had a little while to breathe more easily and enjoy a more pleasant side to our visit, and it was a good thing we had a rest, because the next adventure would come when we were leaving Uganda. During the evening we sat by the river and watched the hippopotamuses, or "river horses", as I had learned the name meant when I was at school. The behaviour of these animals, three thousand kilos in weight, as they played with their comical young was by no means as clumsy as their appearance might lead you to expect. After the heat of the day had eased off, a group of chubby Ugandan women came and performed rhythmic tribal dances to the accompaniment of drums. Because of the many crocodiles, we did not dare go for a swim in the Nile to cool off.

The next day we took a boat with the three friendly North Koreans to the famous Kabele Falls, a mere two hours away. The tremendous volume of water, which descends a hundred and thirty metres, was impressive. The political situation meant that very few people were able to appreciate this spectacle, which we thought was a shame. As we returned late that afternoon, our boat glided silently down the Nile, its engine turned off. At one point the sky turned dark as a flock of pink flamingos flew over our heads and prepared to land alongside the banks of papyrus. The three North Koreans were guests of the government, and they were on their way to the nearby Ruwenzori; I was able to give them a few tips on the somewhat easier eastern ascent.

As we got ready to leave the next morning, the park warden came and asked us to come with him and take some photos. During the night, ruthless bandits had poisoned an elephant in order to take its valuable ivory tusks. The pachyderm lay in a pool of blood, and I will never forget the look in its eyes as it died. After its sad end had come, the warden cut off its tail to hand in to his superiors. He wanted to use our photos to denounce the crime.

Travelling east towards Kenya, we reached the remote town of Olom, where we were to be the victims of a dreadful experience after our peaceful days in the Kabele reserve. My diary entry reads, "At five o'clock we arrived, and we were immediately surrounded by twelve soldiers armed with rapid-fire weapons. A drunken sergeant pointed his bayonet at the tyre of the Unimog and screamed that if I said another word, he would shoot or slash the tyres.

The only response to these well-rehearsed acts, which were clearly meant to frighten us, was to keep quiet. Though I had had some experience of sticky situations with tribes or in the wild, this was the first time I had been confronted with unpredictable drunken human beings. I explained to an important-looking man in civilian dress that all we wanted to do was go on a trip to Kenya. I had no idea whether he even understood what I said, but he indicated that we were to drive into the large passage through the barbed wire. By now it had got dark, and the gate closed behind us with a screech.

Once again I found myself behind barbed wire. Before we knew what was happening, an army lorry pulled up and shone its headlights at us; at least this meant we had light to put up our tents by. Our camp was right next to the guardhouse, with the latrines behind us. There was nothing further to discuss, and each man was left alone with his thoughts. A rough-and-ready last post was sounded, and the headlights were turned off. Sleep was out of the question, and I kept seeing the red-rimmed eyes of the drunken sergeant; but suddenly a torch lit up and someone was speaking calmly to me in good English. The friendly Ugandan explained that he was a police officer and had been summoned by radio; we would see what happened in the morning, but for the time being we should get a good night's sleep.

The next morning we were already sitting in front of our tent when the trumpeter sounded his off-key reveille. The policeman from the night before told us the next leg of our journey passed through his home territory, which was inhabited by the Karamajong tribe, and we would be able to get plenty of milk there. He told us to carry on our way.

Relieved, we set off, and after two days and several flat tyres we reached Muruto police station, which had a radio link to the head office in Kampala. The authorities there demanded a photo of each of us; as there was no camera in Muruto, we would have to travel to Kenya via Kampala. We were saved from this detour by Manfred, who took a photo of the Ugandans there with the Polaroid camera. This made quite an impression, and seemed to be a novelty in this remote town.

A meeting was convened. The four of us took our places on one side of the table, the political commissar sat at the head of the table, and the police officer, the military representative and a civilian were opposite us. The negotiations went smoothly, and while Manfred continued taking photos I put my wristwatch in between myself and the commissar. For security reasons, a jeep with seven soldiers would go with us as far as the last police station before the border. As we left I gave the watch to the commissar, who was gazing at it expectantly – not my old Rolex, of course, but a similar, cheaper timepiece.

We took our leave of the escort three kilometres before the Kenyan border. They got their pictures too. It was clear from the state of the road that it was a long time since it had been driven on. The unpleasant feeling of having armed soldiers on our backs disappeared as soon as the escort turned round and drove back to Muruto. Sometimes it really isn't wise to take photos, as our experience with the Jarawa on the Andaman Islands had shown, but it could be very useful too, as it turned out to be on this occasion.

With hindsight, I can explain why our journey across Uganda turned out to be such an adventure. Idi Amin's arbitrary and violent regime was resented by neighbouring countries; Kenya closed the border, cutting off Uganda's only access to the open sea. Resistance also began to grow within the country, and that was probably why we met with such contrasting reactions. Within a year of our trip to Uganda, the dictator had fled to Saudi Arabia.

Africa was marked by political instability, and the conflicts we had experienced in such a short period were just the tip of the iceberg. In some central African countries, foreign powers had acquired considerable influence under the pretext of providing development aid. Political indoctrination and arms supplies led to bloody tribal wars. It was also a major problem that the continent had been divided into numerous small states whose borders often ran straight through the middle of tribal grazing lands. How were the proud nomads supposed to understand that, all of a sudden, they were no longer allowed to enter a region that had been part of their tribal territory since time immemorial?

These were the best pastures, ideally with access to water, the precious resource. In order to survive, everyone had to be as hard as his neighbour, who wanted the same thing. The more ruthless chieftains also stole cattle, and this lead in its turn to revenge and retaliation. The situation would escalate, and small feuds turned into full-blown wars. Traditionally, each animal was branded with a tribal symbol, and I found the same symbols carved on mountain peaks and beside rivers; but now they had lost their meaning.

When the Organization for African Unity (OAU) was founded in 1961, it soon chalked up major victories in the fight against colonialism; but warlike disputes between the numerous tribes increased, because the majority of light arms produced throughout the world find their way to Africa. Hundreds of thousands lost their lives. So it was no surprise that I was offered so many spears and bows and arrows – they had become obsolete.

The OAU has now transformed itself into an African Union on the model of the European Union. But then you read in the paper that in Burundi, a country torn by civil war, a coalition of nineteen political parties has formed a government led by a Tutsi, despite the fact that eighty percent of the population are Hutu. The next bloodbath cannot be avoided, because the Hutus, drawn from the great Bantu people, are in the majority there, and their rebels will get arms, and eventually they will choose one of their number as president. As long as there are dictators and disunity amongst the tribes, the African Union remains a pipe dream.

I have been able to observe this continent, which is three times the size of Europe, on many journeys and at different times – from the colonial period to the creation of over fifty independent states – but without truly understanding it. The problems are simply too complex. But it is important to remember the positive side too. Nelson Mandela's efforts brought apartheid to an end, and he received the Nobel Peace Prize for his work. In 1986, Wole Soyinka became the first African to receive the Nobel Prize for Literature, and in 2001 Kofi Annan, known across the world as General Secretary of the United Nations, was awarded the Nobel Peace Prize.

In January 2002 the city of Goma was devastated by the eruption of the volcano Nyiragonga, bringing yet more suffering to the troubled Congo Basin region. I do not know if the people I met in 1977 and the mountain gorillas I photographed survived. This is yet further proof that man can do nothing to prevent natural disasters.

It only remains to describe my visits to some of the Nilote tribes, including the Karamajong, whose friendly ways the police officer had described to us. The Karamajong are semi-nomadic, and live in a small, remote area in the northeast of Uganda that can only be reached on foot. That may well be why they remained largely untouched by Idi Amin's reign of terror. From time to time they had to hand in their weapons, and they lost cattle to plundering soldiers, but they had held on to their pride. When the government ordained that all Ugandans should wear shirt and trousers, the Karamajong marched to the police stations to protest, naked underneath their cloths knotted over one shoulder.

Our first contact with the Karamajong came about because of a fire. To the right and left of the road that leads through the undulating savannah, trees, bushes and grass were burning. At first we thought the fire was for land clearance, but in fact it had been set by hunters. Warriors with bow and arrow, some of them armed with spears, waited for animals fleeing before the flames in order to bring them down. It was a gruesome sight, not at all like a proper hunt. We were the only ones who thought it was a shame that this method destroyed useful wood, burned seeds and carbonised plants down to their roots.

We followed the men through a rocky valley to a stone platform that stuck up out of the light brown earth next to the thorny hedge that ran round the village, resembling a raised market square. They stopped there, and children ran up; a few old women made their way cautiously out of their huts. When I showed an interest in their hunting weapons, they immediately began an impressive display of their quality. I suggested a contest with them, and so it was arranged. I managed to keep up with their spear throwing, but when it came to archery I had no chance. Only the slim but powerful Karamajong could stretch these stiff bows. As a gesture of friendship after the friendly competition, the men took their intricately crafted snuff-holders, made of horn, leather and wood, out of their ochre shawls. Most of them were made from the horns of goats, cattle or gazelles, with the pinch of snuff ready inside. This snuff was a mixture of grated bark, tobacco and spices. But tobacco does not have to be taken as snuff; the Karamajong are heavy smokers too, shaping the coarse-cut tobacco into little balls with crystal salt and then burning them in hand-made pipes made out of black tree-roots.

I couldn't believe my eyes when a man sat down on the ledge, rummaged in his cloth bag, and lit a fire using a fire-stick. He took off one of his sandals, placed a little wooden stick on the sole, and bored a small hole, putting another stick in the indentation and turning it back and forth at lightning speed between his hands. After just a few seconds, a thin trail of smoke started rising out of the hole and he piled dried grass on top and kept turning the stick. Shortly thereafter a little flickering flame appeared. A fire had been created out of thin air.

I took a box of matches out of my pocket and gave it to him. He thanked me with a knowing "Ah!" – and stuffed this modern acquisition in his bag. Of course, he did not know that we too would not light an expensive Cuban cigar with a match; but he clearly did not want his precious smoke to be contaminated by the smell of sulphur. Then he showed me his fingers, bent with rheumatism, and told me that the medicine man had prescribed him tobacco for the pain. It was just like what happened with some Indian tribes in South America, where the magicians inhale the drug tobacco with a short tube in order to be able to discourse with gods and spirits.

The Karamajong lived in kraals surrounded by a strong thorn fence to protect them against predators and uninvited guests. Several large earthenware pots dangled on a stick, using the evaporation method to chill water. During journeys in hot countries, cool drinking water can be obtained on the same principle by hanging a piece of waterproof canvas in front of the radiator of a car. Decorated urns, related to the Karamajong's ancestor cult, stood on plinths between the huts. These vases were taboo, and I could find out nothing more about them. In one of the huts I found a short arrow with a small metal tip. A man adorned with a fat lip peg explained to me that it was used to bleed cattle. Like the Masai and the Turkana, the Karamajong are blood-drinkers. They do this because of a semi-religious tradition, but also because the blood contains the proteins that are lacking in the rest of their diet. They mix the blood with milk to create a really nutritious, even tastier pink drink.

We asked the chieftain to show us how a cow was bled. It took quite some time for the men to gather in a semicircle on their little stools, called "kom-tok-tok". Women were not allowed to participate, and they vanished into the huts. A cow was fetched, and two men grabbed it by the horns while a third held on to its tail. A forth man tied a rope round its neck until the arteries showed. The man placed the short metal-tipped arrow in the bow, stepped back three metres, stretched the bow, took aim and released the shot. He struck the cow's carotid artery and the arrow fell to the ground. The stream of blood was collected in a gourd bowl; after two litres or so had collected, forming a foamy head, they released the noose and the cow was allowed to return to the pasture. Because the tribe possessed enough cattle for their needs, the animal that had been bled had plenty of time to recover. The bowl of blood was filled to the brim with fresh milk and passed round. The boys got their share too, for they would one day become strong, brave warriors.

Finally, they started to play board games, a popular pursuit amongst many African tribes. They fetched a big board with twenty-four small indentations carved into its surface and began playing Kalaha with pebbles and semi-precious stones. Our visit to the Karamajong had opened with a sporting competition, and a few days later it came to a harmonious close with an entertaining board game. I generally lose such games on purpose, for "tactical reasons" but when it came to Kalaha, I was beaten fairly and squarely.

In Nairobi, our exciting expedition came to an end. It had been a success because everything was carefully planned, from our departure to the return journey. I am reluctant to call it an expedition, because unlike my other projects, we made no new geographical discoveries, and the most important lesson we learned was that in Africa, just like in Asia, you had to have plenty of time and patience.

We returned out vehicles to the Mercedes-Benz outlet. My friend from Kitzbühel, Karl Kahr, made sure we had no trouble getting our visas; he was the head of the Kenya office of UNESCO, so his links with the authorities were excellent. We were able to stay at his residence on the Indian Ocean until our departure, and I played a round of golf with Axel on an old course that had been created in the time of the English. The "greens" were made of black tar, and it was rather unpleasant playing in that heat. Shortly afterwards my faithful companions flew back to Europe, and I picked up Carina and our two granddaughters Irene and Birgit from the airport; we had invited the girls to go on a trip with us.

FAMILY ADVENTURES

In the summer of 1977 we travelled with our grandchildren to Lake Turkana in the north west of Kenya. My son Peter had married young; his daughters Birgit and Irene were born in 1964 and 1968, and he and his wife Barbara had moved into a house near Zurich. Peter worked as a special effects cameraman for Swiss television; it was said that he could faithfully reconstruct the sinking of the "Titanic" is his bathtub. When the girls were old enough to accompany us on bigger trips, Carina and I started taking them with us. I welcomed their inquisitiveness and their many questions; children have a different perspective on things to us adults. Obviously it is neither possible nor desirable to take a child on a difficult expedition but the thought of taking a woman along had occurred to me back in 1957 when I first met and fell in love with Carina. Her demeanour and her obvious physical fitness made me wonder whether a female expedition member might open up areas of experience and knowledge that were inaccessible to me as a man. My friends Lotte and Hans Hass are actually one of the few married couples I know who have successfully undertaken expeditions together. Carina knew her limitations, however. She very cleverly declined my suggestion and all of my expeditions were therefore organised without any female participants. However, as I reached the stage of my life when I was no longer willing to accept quite as many hardships it was nice to be able to travel together and a trip to Kenya was the first of several we took with our grandchildren. We always tried to divide our time between things that were purely fun, like swimming in the sea, and activities that would benefit the children's education. There was an element of selfishness in the trip to Kenya, I must admit, as I was keen to visit Michael Wood, the founder and boss of the Flying Doctors, a charitable aid organisation that I had been supporting with my modest membership fees for several years. Michael reserved a twin-engined Piper Cub for us and arranged our accommodation in lodges.

We landed on a dusty airstrip on the west side of the two hundred and fifty kilometre long Lake Turkana, which the Hungarian adventurer and big game hunter Count Samuel Teleki had discovered in 1888. In his expedition report, Teleki writes laconically that during his arduous trip he lost exactly 36 kilos and 200 grams in weight. When the aircraft doors were opened we stepped out into a wide plain devoid of vegetation and a breeze so hot it took our breath away. Irene and Birgit immediately went and sat in the shade beneath the wings, where the temperature was still forty degrees, and waited for the Jeep to arrive and pick us up. After the pilot had secured the plane we were driven to the air-conditioned comfort of our lodge.

During the next few days we spent the cool hours of early morning and evening making little excursions into the surrounding countryside. Our first visit was to a large kraal where the Turkana lived, a tribe that enjoyed the reputation of being proud and fierce warriors. The friendly chief offered me a beautifully carved stool, called an "ekit scholon", a name that little Birgit found highly amusing. She was also fascinated by the circular scar around the chief's belly button and asked what it meant. Happy to provide an explanation, the Turkana told her that his medicine man had made the cut to alleviate his chronic stomach pains; the wound had then been rubbed repeatedly with soot and the juice of certain herbs to prevent it from healing too quickly. It sounded like a painful procedure. The decorative tattoos on his face and body had been created in the same way, the chief explained.

One of the best experiences we had came during a trip by Jeep across the desert to a missionary station near the Sudanese border. We were just a few degrees north of the Equator and the scorching sun was almost at its zenith when all at once we saw a shimmering heat haze ahead – a *fata morgana*. The trees of the oasis we were heading for appeared to be floating upside down above the hot sand. Confused by this mirage, we stopped the Jeep. I had never seen this natural spectacle before but I explained to the children that the term *fata morgana* was derived from the Italian and described the type of optical phenomenon we were now seeing. Originally attributed in myth and legend to the Arthurian sorcerer Morgan le Fay, the apparition can actually be explained in simple scientific terms, although this is of little comfort to the thirsty desert traveller who sees it, since the water he so craves is in fact much further away than it appears.

After several more kilometres of driving we reached the remote oasis that had seemed so close as a mirage. Michael Wood had radioed in ahead of our arrival and we were greeted in a most kindly fashion by two of the sisters. It was an oasis in the truest sense of the term: cool water was drawn from a deep well, there was milk, and the children ignored the tame wild animals and played instead with the many little kittens that ran around. Next to the altar in the main building was a bookcase that contained, amongst other things, my Tibet story. Nomads from the surrounding region sat in the shade of a large umbrella tree and waited for the sisters to treat their various ailments. When I saw how lacking they were in essential medical supplies I promised to have a consignment of pharmaceutical items sent in by the Flying Doctors.

After the phenomenon of the *fata morgana* I wanted to show my family another wonder of nature – the Omo River delta on the north shore of Lake Turkana. The delta is a geographic and geopolitical anomaly. However one approaches it – on foot, by boat or plane – one never quite knows which country one is in; it could be Kenya, Ethiopia or the Sudan. The Omo rises in the mountains of Ethiopia and flows into Lake Turkana, the northern tip of which lies within Kenya. Five kilometres north west of the river estuary is a triangle of land where Ethiopia, Kenya and the Sudan all meet, and since the course of the Omo is constantly changing, just for once it is the political boundaries that remain consistent rather than the natural ones.

Lake Turkana covers an area of about seven thousand square metres and has a total length of three hundred and eighty kilometres. The River Omo has created dams in the lake that extend more than twenty kilometres beyond the inflow point. These dams have in turn created further deltas up to five kilometres in width. The fact that the Omo does not flow *into* the lake but *onto* it is a natural phenomenon that has puzzled East African geographers and cartographers since time immemorial but can be explained by the interaction of chemistry and physics. The Omo brings fresh water down from the mountains to the north and carries sand and stones with it. These sediments can clearly be seen from the air as a dark yellow or brown stain in the water. Lake Turkana contains a salty, alkaline solution that has a soapy feel and a specific gravity greater than the water of the Omo. The "light" river thus literally floats on the "heavy" lake and the sedimentary deposits form dams, some of which are several metres wide and covered in lush grass. From its point of entry into Lake Turkana to its "mouth", which is actually deep into the lake, the Omo is really not a river at all, but a natural canal.

We had an impressive view of the deltas as we flew north over the lake in the little twin-engined Piper and could clearly see the yellow waters of the river staining the green-grey surface of the lake like liquid marble. Noticing a few dark shapes on the furthest tip of the delta, we asked the pilot to fly low so we could investigate. There on the green swathe of grass was a shepherd tending his goats. I wondered if he knew which country he was in.

The River Omo is hugely important to the region; not only does it support the lives of the nomads; it also feeds Lake Turkana and prevents it from evaporating. We visited Richard Erskine Leakey at his research station on the eastern shore of the lake, where we were able to see the meticulous precision that defines the work of the palaeontologist. Leakey's parents had discovered primitive stone tools and bones in the Olduvai Gorge in Tanzania, an area commonly known as "The Cradle of Mankind". Young Mr Leakey had made further discoveries on the Omo and Lake Turkana and was now the Director of the National Museum of Kenya. As a parting gift Leakey presented me with a copy of a one and a half million year old human skull, which is now on display in the Heinrich Harrer Museum. Since our visit archaeologists in Ethiopia and northern Kenya have unearthed objects up to four million years old, and scientists are now convinced that Africa was indeed the birthplace of mankind.

Our time in Kenya was drawing to an end; we had just one more night at the Oasis Lodge on the eastern shore of Lake Turkana. Some of the Samburu warriors at the oasis offered us large agates and amethysts, which we purchased for a pittance. It is an odd quirk of Nature that these gemstones are found amongst the dreary volcanic wasteland of the lava beds, where the Samburu collect them and then wait for tourists like us to come along and pay just a few pence for a stone as big as a fist.

On the way back to Nairobi we also encountered the El Molo tribe, the smallest ethnic group in Kenya. After meeting the tall, slim Samburu warriors who, like the *Lung Gompa* trance runners of Tibet, are capable of covering huge distances on foot in the shortest time imaginable, the appearance of the El Molo provided a shocking contrast. It is thought that these aboriginal people will be the next race to vanish from our Earth. When Count Teleki first discovered them they numbered more than five hundred. Now there are fewer than three hundred remaining.

The El Molo suffer from a mysterious disease, yet all attempts to alleviate their suffering through the use of medicines or the improvement of their drinking water have so far failed to help. The word "elmolo" is Maasi for "people who make their living from other than cattle"; some of their neighbours refer to them as "the poor people". Both descriptions are accurate. The El Molo are the only tribe in the region that have always made their living from fishing alone, catching their prey with harpoons and nets. Whether it is this unbalanced diet and the high fluorine content of the water that are responsible for the disease that affects them is still a matter for speculation.

An elderly man, obviously crippled, approached the shore of the lake on a raft made of four doum palm trunks. Two young women helped him to drag the raft up onto the beach. One of his legs was badly swollen and distorted, the result of elephantiasis, while the other was withered and as thin as a walking stick. I had been here once before, in 1968, but this old El Molo man was the only one whom I still recognised from the photographs I had taken. All of the others had since died, I learned.

I found it deeply distressing to learn that that the El Molo make money out of their poverty and disease by charging tourists who wish to see how they live an "entry fee", sanctioned by the local commissar. The chief, a young man whose split lips also bore testimony to the disease from which his tribe suffered, was responsible for taking the money, and only then was one allowed contact with the El Molo. The tribespeople had come up with several different ways of making money. For a few coins, the young girls of the tribe would unbutton their blouses; for a little more, they would strip completely and jump into the lake. It was sad to see these once proud people performing in such a way for the white man's camera and a handful of small change.

In the low, straw thatched huts, the old men and women of the tribe waited to die. Some of them were blind and existed on scraps of food brought to them by their relatives. As we were passing one of the huts, a bony hand stretched out, begging for alms. No words were spoken; we all knew that theirs was a fight for survival.

Back in Nairobi we thanked the Flying Doctors, and Michael Wood in particular, for their help before leaving for home. At the airport in Frankfurt we said goodbye to Irene and Birgit and caught a flight to Zurich. We had thoroughly enjoyed the time we had spent with our grandchildren, and had spoilt them terribly. It was little wonder that their parting words to us were "Now we've got to go back to stupid school!"

But Kenya was not to be the last place we visited as a family. Over the years we took our grandchildren to the Caribbean, Hong Kong, Bali and Thailand, and on one memorable occasion we even visited the Dalai Lama in Dharamsala.

We stayed in Dharamsala during our family tour of Asia in 1978 and visited the school for Tibetan refugee children that had been established by Tsering Drolma. Tsering Drolma had died in 1964 and the school was now being run by her younger sister, Jetsun Pemala. The children all lined up obediently before us and gave a little recital before gathering round our little granddaughter. They were very excited by her appearance and wanted to know how she had come by such a fair complexion and such beautiful blond hair. It was just like the scene from the film *Seven Years in Tibet*, where the young Dalai Lama strokes Brad Pitt's head and exclaims in amazement "Golden hair!"

Our audience with the Dalai Lama had been arranged well in advance and we were greeted at the gate by Ngari Rinpoche, who hurried us through the Indian security checks and ushered us into a room where the God King was waiting. In reply to my reverential greeting "Your Holiness", the Dalai Lama answered with "Guten Tag". He remembered the photograph I had shown him in Lhasa of my son Peter and smiled affectionately at the children. After handing him the traditional *kata*, Irene, Peter's eldest daughter, forgot her initial shyness and, using both hands as instructed, and as befits the Tibetan custom, she presented him with the gift we had brought. Whilst in Vienna I had asked the Hotel Sacher to pack one of their famous chocolate cakes in a wooden box and when I explained this to the Dalai Lama he immediately instructed the children to open the parcel so that everyone could have a taste of this Austrian delicacy.

When I unpacked the cake there was great amusement as everyone saw what had happened to it. The thin wooden lid had stuck fast to the icing. The chocolate had melted during the journey and had spread across the whole of the inside of the box. In the cooler climate of Dharamsala, the whole mess had then solidified again and what was left inside looked most unlike the beautiful, round Sachertorte I had so admired in Vienna. It was delicious nonetheless, and an attentive servant brought a bowl and a kettle of warm water to wash our sticky fingers in.

We took our leave with the traditional Tibetan phrase "ga-le chu". The Dalai Lama pressed his hands together and replied "ga-le pheb" – "go in peace".

THE MANY SOURCES OF THE GANGES

The city of Hardwar lies just a few kilometres east of the former prison camp of Dehra Dun. This city is one of the most important pilgrimage sites of Hinduism, and during the days of the Khumbamela festival, millions of pilgrims make their way there. The crowds throng down the steps of the great terraces to the Ganges to cleanse their bodies and souls. In particularly dangerous spots, a succession of chains have been cemented into the ghats for people to hold on to so that they are not carried away by the tremendous current. Despite this, accidents occur all the time, and when we came to stay at the house of the governor Harmandar Singh during the Andaman expedition, he and his wife were in a subdued mood. Their athletic young daughter had gone on a pilgrimage to Hardwar, and she thought she was strong enough to take the waters without holding on to one of the chains. The merciless current carried her away, and she disappeared into the stream before the eyes of her parents.

Hardwar is a large town on the right bank of the Ganges with a bazaar a kilometre long. Those who wish to withdraw to meditate can cross the river on a great swaying rope bridge leading to the peace and quiet of Rishikesh on the left bank. I remember that the manager of the Beatles sent the singers to learn transcendental meditation in Hardwar when their fans began to lose interest in them. They were photographed there with yogis and sadhus, providing material for fresh headlines. One of the four, George Harrison, was so fascinated by the way of life that he kept it up until his death in November 2001.

That is how it is for me too; I am fascinated by the entire subcontinent, which has developed from an oppressed colony into the largest republic in the world during a period of slightly more than half a century. Though the monstrous caste system has been abolished, it is still the well-fed Brahmans who bathe at the best spots along the holy rivers – they can be recognised by the decorative thread they wear across their chest as a token of their status – and it is the sadhus and the yogis that receive pilgrims in search of their counsel. The beggars and the sick sit in a row along the edge of the road, and people carefully change their notes into small coins so that everyone gets something. The sixteen annas in a rupee will no longer buy you anything in a shop, but these coins still circulate here in considerable numbers in the form of alms.

One other thing I love has remained unchanged – the smell of the bazaar, the smoke of the open wood fires mixed with the scent of the parathas sizzling in iron pans. These have a number of regional names in German, and now we call them hamburgers. The best thing about the Indian ones is that they do not contain any meat; they are made of potatoes, peas, beans, onions and garlic. Then there is the curry powder, which itself contains at least a dozen spices such as cardamom, ginger, mint, pepper, chilli and above all turmeric; the turmeric root is a cheaper substitute for the flavour, smell and colour of saffron. If these steaming parathas are served with "vegetable curry" on the firm, evergreen leaves of the sal tree, not even my wife can resist. She has even got used to the tea that is sold at open fires along the road. Fresh tea leaves are used each time; they are boiled with milk and unrefined sugar, so there is no need to worry about drinking the tea, though it is a good idea to use your own cup. These parathas always make me think of my childhood, because the flavour of my mother's vegetarian parathas – made of potatoes, pulses and mushrooms – could not be told apart from that of meat ones, if indeed they were not better.

It must be because of my genes that I have reached such a ripe old age, but diet, sport and maintaining a healthy weight will have played their part too. So it will not come as a surprise to learn that whenever I visited Hardwar, I was always sure to visit the university, where Ayurveda is taught, a body of Indian wisdom over two thousand years old about how to extend life. It recommends plant-based medicines, but bone ash and minerals are also used. On this occasion, in June 1974, as I made my way across the botanical garden to the lecture hall where I was due to speak to the students about my time in Tibet and the two-thousand-year-tradition of Tibetan medicine, a large pan full of fragments of ichthyol shale, the raw material from which rock oil is derived, simmered over a flame.

During an expedition to Ladakh I had seen Tibetans in the narrow

Indus gorge using an old shotgun to shoot at the overhang of a cliff in order to break off the oil-bearing stone, which they would sell in India. Years before, I bought a little out-of-print almanac of Ayurveda medicine from an itinerant doctor, and it referred to this product as "shilajit". According to the almanac, if drunk with milk it can relieve headaches, dizziness, irregular bowel movements, haemorrhoids and wet dreams, as well as a number of other ailments. In New Guinea, I had experienced for myself the effectiveness of ichthyol salve in treating inflammation and wounds.

The ancient knowledge of these medicinal systems has found more and more adherents. The first natural medicine clinic was recently opened in the Hospital of the Teutonic Order in Friesach, the local hospital of the place where I was born. The clinic practises complementary holistic medicine, and its techniques can usefully be applied to psychological illnesses and the diseases of Western civilisation. I remember the time I asked the Dalai Lama about Tibetan medicine; he smiled and said, "You go for a check-up, and there is nothing the matter with you. But if something still isn't quite right, that's where we Tibetans come in." The clinic's herb garden includes some of the plants that are used in the two-thousand-year-old tradition of Tibetan medicine.

I asked the head of the clinic, Georg Lexer, whether the trance runners I had seen in Tibet used herbal extracts as stimulants. He thought that on the contrary, Peter Aufschnaiter and I were an example of how a person who is fit can produce anaesthetic or protective substances from the body; these chemicals are known as endorphins. Recent studies of athletes showed that this was possible. In spite of their athletic performances, the blood tests of the experimental subjects showed near normal results. This was probably also the scientific explanation for the miracles of the yogis on the Ganges. It made it easier for me to understand why I had managed to fight off unconsciousness after my fall in New Guinea in spite of all that pain; I had obviously produced my own anaesthetic, because no artificial anaesthetic was available.

On my journey in June 1974, I was able to see my escape route once more. From Hardwar I travelled through the sal tree forests of the foothills of the Himalayas to Deoprayag, where the two largest sources of the Ganges come together. Deoprayag is the last chance to stock up with provisions at the bazaar before heading off into the mountains, because the prices here are still reasonable. Further on, they increase in proportion with distance and altitude. I followed the course of the Bhagirathi, the more westerly source, in a low, overcrowded bus that barely passed beneath the overhangs along the road where it was built into the rock. Passengers were not allowed to sit on the roof as they generally do in India. The journey was risky, because there are frequent vertical drops of several hundred metres down to the river and there is no safety barrier along the road. This was the same route I had covered on foot during my escape. At one point an enormous landslide had blocked the way and a huge lake had formed. Because the Himalayas are a young mountain chain that is still growing, earthquakes and landslides are not uncommon. The pilgrims and I had to continue on foot, up hill and down dale and without a proper path to follow.

Several days later I reached Harsil, where I had a close look at the forester's lodge from the balcony of which I had leaped in 1943. I wanted to retrace my steps and take a look by daylight at the route I had taken on that failed escape attempt, and then again when I succeeded in 1944, by night with a heavy rucksack. I passed through a shady, tall cedar wood to the romantic pilgrimage site of Gangotri, where the pilgrims bathed in the bitterly cold glacier water at an altitude of four thousand metres; a few old or fat ones who had been carried up the mountain in a basket on a man's back, or in a litter, struggled with the thin mountain air. It was considered a privilege to die in Gangotri, be cremated there and end up in the Ganges as ash. The temple is dedicated to the three most important gods in Hinduism: Brahma, Vishnu and Shiva.

Brahmarishi was a yogi who lived in Gangotri, and had so many interests that he can only be described as an unusual character. I had met him in New Delhi at the annual banquet in the Himalaya Club, where he told the story of his first solo ascent of a six-thousand-metre peak. He lived in a cave, and let me stay in the hut in front of it. As a yogi he was able to adopt up to a hundred different yoga positions, and he had published articles about the meaning of yoga and its philosophy.

He was more than willing to take me to the various meditation sites; different ones are used depending on the time of day and the season. I photographed him at the edge of the giant waterfall, where the atomised spray of the water formed a rainbow over his head like a halo. The place he was able to concentrate best was a slab of stone polished by the water flows of the monsoon rains.

In two days he and I climbed the twenty-four kilometres to Gaumukh, or "cow-mouth", where the murky water of the sacred river flows out of the snout of the glacier. We were far above the tree line, and my friend had brought along a bundle of juniper wood to be on the safe side. Warmed by the fire, I managed to record his stories in my diary. Every day he did a seven-hour breathing exercise in the course of which he blocked his throat with his tongue. He also told me about a yogi friend of his who could make himself unconscious. He had himself sewn into a damp yak skin and drifted in the Ganges until he was found days later somewhere along the bank and released without coming to any harm. There was no doubting this unlikely story; I was in need of something to help me sleep, as the altitude of five thousand metres had given me a headache.

I stayed a few more days in Gangotri, eating vegetarian food, as was the norm here, and collecting herbs with Brahmarishi that he gave to the Ayurveda University. I too was able to offer him something he had not come across before, the valuable and rare Tibetan medicine yar-tsa gun-bu, extracted from mycorrhizae, a symbiosis of "summer plant and winter worm".

I had now seen the western source of the Ganges several times, and I wanted to explore the eastern source, the Alaknanda. The road through the narrow gorges to the sacred site of Badrinath was just as dangerous as the route to Gangotri. Once again I gave the bus driver several times the fare, and I was allowed to sit at the front, perched between two other benefactors. After you have got through the journey, you make an offering to the god Vishnu, who is especially venerated here. The short but dangerous bus journey is more popular than the long trek on foot over dusty or boggy roads. This victory of irrationality over common sense is typical of our fast-paced times.

I covered the last fifteen kilometres before Badrinath on foot in order to record the tight chain of pilgrims on film. It took me all day to get there, but I was able to interact with the pilgrims as one amongst many people united by a common purpose; every tea stall provided an opportunity to offer people a cup of tea and ask them questions. For over two thousand years Badrinath has been one of the most popular pilgrimage sites for Hindus, and every year several hundred thousand of them come to purify themselves in the hot springs. Accommodation is available in hostels, whose corrugated tin roofs keep off the downpours of the monsoon, but I avoided these as far as possible because of the bed bugs. One can also find shelter in the so-called ashrams, those cradles of reflection where gurus learn the meaning of Buddhist asceticism.

I gave the head of one ashram a copy of the translation of my book on Tibet into Gujerati, his mother tongue; he told me that Badrinath had become a commercially oriented place, and even some of the gurus performed to earn money. If an Indian pursues the path of yoga, this is for religious reasons, but unfortunately there are some charlatans who put on shows as fakirs and earn money by burying their heads in the earth for hours on end. Some of the yogis travel about in the world in great luxury. On this subject, my friend in Gangottri once said that the pious go on pilgrimages to their teachers and masters, and the mountain never comes to the Prophet.

The head of the ashram also told me the tale of Advoot Swami Pramanand, who lived in a hermitage, and said I should definitely pay him a visit. The previous autumn, Advoot Swami had sat down to meditate in the temple of Vishnu, and had not moved a muscle even when the temple attendant Rawal came to shut up the building for the winter. Rawal did not know what to do, because he had to get to his house in Joshimath as soon as he could to spend the coming winter there. After he had waited a long time, the Swami finally said in a quiet voice, "Do your duty, and I will do mine." When the temple was opened up again after the long icy months, Advoot was still sitting meditating in the same position as in the autumn. He had withdrawn deep inside himself, and so the cold had been unable to harm him.

I had some extraordinary experiences amongst the holy men at the sources of the Ganges. They are in full control of their bodies, heat and cold are irrelevant, and Advoot said he was always content and that he could live as long as he wished. He was also convinced that all that was required to attain perfection when reincarnated, and so keep the body free of all sickness, was willpower, stamina and training.

I do not believe this is true for us Westerners. There are many people who can successfully learn how to imitate the gymnastic aspects of yoga, but I doubt we can ever attain the same spiritual experiences. We are not Asians, and we have a different mentality; we live by the clock. The spirit of these people, and their ancient traditions, will always remain fundamentally beyond our understanding. Donning a yellow robe, shaving your head and learning a lot of yoga positions cannot help.

I had to screw up my courage, but I got into the murky forty-degree water, and bathed shoulder to shoulder with the other pilgrims. I did not do it so much to wash my body or cleanse my spirit, but simply because I was freezing. After all, I was at an altitude of three thousand five hundred metres, and flakes of snow were mingling with the raindrops. After this rather profane act in the sacred waters, I had something up my sleeve. Just above Badrinath, there was a post of the border police whose job it was to guard the so called "Inner Line", which stretched all along the two thousand kilometres of the Himalayas about two hundred kilometres from the international borders; foreigners were not allowed to go beyond it. I was already familiar with this rule from Sikkim and Nepal, but I knew of a way round it. At night, you have to creep past the guardhouse while the policemen are asleep; or during the hours of daylight, you pack your rucksack and camera in a tent bag and walk through with the Indians while the guards play cards, carrying the bag on your head.

And so I spent two days walking up the valley, which grew ever steeper, up to the village of Manu. It was not far to the border with Chinese-occupied Tibet, but I could not risk going up to the pass to look across at nearby Tsaparang, which I had passed through more than thirty years previously with Peter Aufschnaiter as we made our escape. I made do with the view of the source of the Alaknanda, which flows from the glacier of Satopanth, the mountain rising steeply up to the west.

This 7,075 metre peak was first climbed in 1947 by Swiss

mountaineers, amongst them Alfred Sutter. When Switzerland accepted two thousand Tibetan refugees in 1960, Sutter found jobs in his firm for several families and he invited me to come to Münchwilen as an interpreter. We were talking about Satopanth when I mentioned that a woman, Anneliese Lohner, had been in the party. He smiled and pointed to the gentle person sitting at the table, and said, "She's sitting right there!" Anneliese Sutter became a good friend of ours.

I resisted the temptation to cross the glacier to the west and see Gangotri one more time, because on the return journey I was planning to make a detour to the famous "Valley of Flowers" that had been discovered more or less by accident by the famous mountaineer and poet Frank Smythe in 1931 after his conquest of Kamet, the 7,756 metre peak. To him as a poet, this discovery meant more than just an altitude record. I well remember how Smythe's death in Darjeeling was received in Lhasa. Years later, my wife gave me a copy of his limited edition on the "Valley of Flowers" as a present. Inside the sleeve is a pocket containing seeds of the blue poppy.

In Govindghat, I met up as arranged with Maurice Leonard, the botanist from Brussels. We were not the only ones on the trail, which had been carefully laid with stone slabs for the rainy season. In the 15th century, the founder of the Sikh religion had lived as a hermit in Hemkund, and many pilgrims went there. The old and sick were carried in baskets on the backs of sturdy men. It should be pointed out that this is their profession, and they exercise it of their own free will; for this reason, it is wrong to feel sorry for them, and if they were forbidden from doing so, many families would go hungry.

In the Bhyundar Valley we encountered a few more settlements. Women were harvesting millet, and the children begged. The cedar forest, with its long hanging fronds of lichen, was like something out of a fairytale. After ascending a thousand metres, the path to the Valley of Flowers splits off from the path to Hemkund, the most sacred site of the Sikh faith in the Himalayas. Accompanied by a forest ranger, we started collecting samples of all the different flowers found in the valley and photographing them, more than a thousand varieties. The landscape of flowery meadows with icy peaks in the background was far more beautiful than we had expected – and for my friend the botany professor, it was like nature's own collection of alpine flora. Working with his young female assistant, he carefully placed several specimens of each plant in a herbarium; later the plants would be transferred twice more to a new book with dry blotting paper in order to preserve the natural colours. After carrying out this fiddly work with clammy fingers in the prevailing cold, the two scientists needed to warm up, and I envied the professor his warm assistant in the cold tent.

It was the beginning of September, and we saw the first flocks of sheep coming down from the pass over the fields of snow. We asked how much one sheep would cost, because it was weeks since we had eaten any meat. Our request fell on deaf ears, however, since no living creature is ever killed around the source of the Ganges. The gods reside there, amidst nature in its purest and calmest form, and I could well understand why so many people came here on pilgrimages. I took my leave of the botanists, gladly taking the horse that was offered me for the steep ascent to Hemkund. For long stretches, though, I had to get off and walk, because the rocks were slippery and it seemed too dangerous to ride on the great steep snow fields. What was more, the simple wooden saddles made for hard sitting if you were not used to them. Finally, 1,061 stone steps took me the last part of the way to Hemkund on foot.

Every adherent of the Sikh religion who is able to endure the hardships of the journey makes at least one pilgrimage to Hemkund during his lifetime to visit the little temple where the Tenth Guru, the master and teacher Govind Singh, lived and taught at the end of the seventeenth century. The Sikhs' ritual begins with immersion in the "Golden Sea", whose waters, which come from the glaciers, are icy cold. Even in the water, they keep with them the five insignia they are obliged to wear at all times: kara, the steel armband; kesh, the hair; kangha, the comb; kacha, the white underwear; and kirpan, the dagger.

I went to the warden of the temple complex to make the required donation, in return for which I was given a piece of holy pastry with a very sweet flavour. I was somewhat surprised when he asked me for one more rupee after I had donated the hundred rupees, but he explained the reason to me straight away. Above all, it was a good omen and presaged wealth; and on the other hand, it meant you could always say you had given more than a hundred rupees. It was planned to use the money to build a thick stone wall to protect against avalanches.

According to legend, when Govind Singh lived there, there was a battle between good and evil. Through the prayers of the master, good won out, and as a reward the god Brahma made all the flowers rain down from heaven. The warden emphasised that the Brahma lotus would only flower here in Hemkund. It was here that I found my version of the "blue flower" of Romantic poetry – *Meconopsis aculeata*. At that altitude, over four thousand metres, it bloomed more vigorously and impressively than in other parts of the Himalayas; unfortunately, in my garden at home it bears flowers of every other colour, but not the blue of Hemkund.

The religious faith of the Sikhs had made a strong impression on me, together with the way the delicate flowers contrasted with the chasms and vertical rock faces of the Himalayas, and it was only when I was alone with my torch in my little tent that I managed to describe it all in my diary. Back in the great Ganges valley, I took my chances once again in one of the buses, although only a few days previously one carrying fifty pilgrims had plummeted down a ravine. The cause was not known, because it was impossible to search for the dead in the precipitous Alaknanda Gorge. Thereafter, for a short while at least, a policeman checked to make sure the permitted number of passengers was not exceeded.

Before the road was built, it took the pilgrims at least thirty days to reach Badrinath, and very few of them had the money to pay to be carried there. The most pleasant and also the most expensive way to reach the temple was to take a "dandy". Four men would carry a palanquin on the shoulders with poles; as they walked in step, they would quietly sing a tune to keep their rhythm up. These trips were organised by shrewd managers, and the exorbitant price had to be paid in advance. The season was short, and each dandy was able to make just two round trips. Apparently it was a regular occurrence for clients to fall down a cliff half way there – or be thrown off – and drown in the holy Ganges many hundred metres below. It was the British who put a stop to this dreadful profiteering. When the new road was built, the number of pilgrims going to Badrinath and Gangotri increased tenfold, and now it was over-filled buses that plummeted from the unmade road into the ravines, rather than the victims of the dandys, or people freezing or starving to death.

It was just one year after my visit to the sources of the Ganges that I succumbed once more to the "lure of the East". King Leopold asked me to lead an expedition in the spring of 1975 to the little-known valley of the River Pindar, one of the tributaries of the Ganges. He himself would not be going, but two well-known specialists, for rodents and fish, would – Xaver Missone and Jean-Pierre Gosse – as well as Pierre Devillers, who was an ornithologist and wanted to collect birds for the Institute. On a previous occasion I had turned down the chance to lead an expedition to West Africa which was to include eight different participants; I did not think it would be possible to do justice to so many different specialties. In the Pindar Valley I would only have three experts to look after, which I thought would be just about manageable.

To prepare for the expedition, I flew to India two weeks in advance. One area of traditional medicine I did not yet know anything about was Unani, which is practised by Muslims. I paid a visit to the research centre in Delhi where Unani was taught, as well as the associated hospital and the place where the medicines were produced. Tons of the raw materials lay ready in the warehouse – cumin, aniseed, fennel, linseed, amber, ginger and rose petals. Valuable ingredients such as saffron, gems, gold and silver were kept behind locked doors. As well as medicine, shampoo and various aphrodisiacs were made there, and all of it from natural ingredients – unlike in the West, the manager said. In one room there was an official who was responsible for poisons such as aconite root or opium. He told us that the most expensive medicines, made especially for richer patients, had to glitter with gold dust as well as smelling and tasting pleasant.

There were over two thousand substances recorded in the office, and one of the most expensive at that time was musk, which can no longer be traded today because of the protected status of the small musk deer in the Himalayas. The most expensive of all, made from shark cartilage, was imported from Singapore, and dried lizards from the Arabian Desert, toads from Ceylon, and antlers were not much cheaper. Perhaps to put an end to my curious questions, the official opened up a barrel that came from Canada. The stench took my breath away, and it was only after he had shut the container that I asked him to explain what it was. The barrel contained the dried bladders of a "river dog", i.e. a beaver, an animal that uses the secretion of its scent gland – known as castoreum – for marking. This substance has beneficial effects, and is prescribed for cramp, but I cannot imagine having any pain severe enough to require treatment with such foul-smelling stuff. It is even harder to understand the fact that it is used as a fixative in the perfume industry.

By now the three scientists had landed in Delhi. When I saw them unloading all their instruments and containers, I decided to employ Tibetans as porters, which would be considerably easier in Dehra Dun, where I was known. In this way I managed to avoid the business of haggling with local porters, who often go on strike in the mountains in the middle of a journey, refusing to go any further unless their daily wage is doubled. I soon got six Tibetans together, and one of them could cook, so I immediately bought a set of aluminium dikshi, six pots that fit one inside the other that take up hardly any space and are very light. We took the bus to Hardwar, a two-hour journey, and celebrated the successful start to our expedition. I had managed to get permission to visit the Pindar Valley from the regional commissioner; all we had to do was take a lieutenant of the Indian Army as a liaison officer, and provide for his needs.

A week later, we came to the village of Lata, which seemed to be an ideal place for the scientists to work. The inhabitants, the Garhwals, crowded around us, and the village chief smelled money. Room was found for our camp in an uncultivated field by a stream. The owner would not be able to plant crops once we left because of the approach of summer, so I had to pay him in cash to make up for the millet harvest he would be missing out on.

Lata is three hundred metres above the River Pindar, and the view of the highest seven thousand metre peaks on Earth is concealed by the dark forests of deodar cedar. Everyone was happy here except for Jean-

Pierre, who had to make his way several times a day down the steep path to the river so he could go fishing. I was able to record my ethnographic observations in Lata. The little temple of the black goddess Kali lay in the shadow of a single old cedar; she wears a chain of human skulls. The Garhwal who had come with me moved a stone slab aside, and there was a terrible smell, because in the hole underneath were the entrails of a goat and a few coins that had been left as an offering. The man told us that then, in April, the offerings were more modest, but in October oxen were slaughtered as well – in complete contrast to the customs of the pilgrimage sites. Kali would drink the blood of two buffalo straight off, thirty litres or so, but if you poured a bottle of water down the hole it would not soak in. I could not understand why it was that these black magic rituals had been chosen to protect such a lovely landscape.

The ornithologist had erected a fine, barely visible net along the river up the hillside, and birds flying to the water became hopelessly entangled in it. During the evenings, Xaver prepared the rodents on a stone slab, and Pierre prepared his birds; I suppose someone has to do these things in the cause of science. But it was not long before about thirty women came to our camp and set fire to the net, because we were polluting their precious water. Further upstream they dug a channel to divert the watercourse. Within two hours the revolt had come to an end, but the women were right. When the villagers realised we intended to move our camp to an altitude of four thousand metres they brought colourful hand-woven materials, and even tried to sell us the enormous gold nose-rings the women wore. Two of the men offered to show us the way up to their mountain pastures. Not far from the village we came upon the blacksmith's hut; because working metal and shoeing horses was considered to be an inferior occupation, it made the smith into an outlaw and he could not live in the village. He kept a fire burning under an awning, and used a goatskin bellows to make the charcoal glow. A large stone served as the anvil, on which he shaped the horseshoes.

The higher we went, the thinner the air became, and the Belgian professors were having trouble breathing. Up there, there was no lush vegetation, the rhododendrons were not yet in flower, and primroses were the only sign of spring's approach. The wooden hut the shepherds used in summer had collapsed under the weight of the snow, but the porters had brought some wood with them from the cedar forest, so we huddled together round the warmth of the fire. The Indian liaison officer, who had never seen snow before, was the one who suffered most from the cold. Most of the traps had disappeared in Lata, but Xaver set those that remained. The jackdaws were too clever to fly into the ornithologist's net, and Jean-Pierre had not even come with us, preferring instead to stay in the valley with the fishes. The expedition, with its various focuses, was breaking up, and I was the only one to make the climb up to the top of the pass, where I was richly rewarded for my efforts. Before me lay the Pindar Glacier, and above it the mighty twin peaks of Nanda Devi, 7,816 metres in height. In the mythology of the Hindu religion, the entire landscape surrounding the sources of the Ganges is regarded as the home of the gods, and Devi is venerated as a heavenly being; rivers and mountains bear her name.

As I sat in the warm rays of the morning sun, I reflected on the history of mountaineering. Wherever I went amongst the lonely places of the world, whether in New Guinea, the Ruwenzori or the Himalayas, I kept coming across the names of English explorers such as Shipton, Tilman, Odell, Wollaston and Smythe. They described their tremendous adventures in the regions that were still "blank on the map" with typical British understatement. In the summer of 1936, Bill Tilman and Noel Odell succeeded in climbing Nanda Devi. They were so pleased when they got to the top that they completely forgot to shake hands. Odell, the geologist, measured a temperature of twenty degrees Fahrenheit (minus seven degrees Celsius), and Tilman said that it filled him with sadness that the mountain had had to yield to man and the proud head of the goddess was now bowed. Tilman and Odell achieved a new altitude record that was only beaten by 275 metres fourteen years later when Annapurna was climbed. Twelve years before, Odell had climbed to heights of over eight thousand metres. He was a member of the elite group that attained tragic fame in 1924 through the deaths of Mallory and Irvine during the British Mount Everest Expedition.

There are several books about the tragedy, but I was lucky enough to hear Noel Odell himself speak. In January 1975 Carina and I received an invitation from Ashoka Sarin, the president of the Indian Himalaya Club, to attend the premiere in Bombay of a Mount Everest film. We saw Noel Odell at the press conference. Slim and fit, the old man stood on the stage, refusing both chair and water, and told the story of the tragic days he had lived through more than fifty years before. On 8th July 1924 Odell had taken a photo of George Mallory and Andrew Irvine before they left the final camp at the North Col to make their attempt on the peak – little did he know that it would be the last photograph taken before their tragic end. With his incredible long-term memory, he described how he had made geological notes at an altitude of eight thousand metres and even discovered fossils; but then the weather had suddenly turned, cloaking the climbers in mist. The audience held its breath as he described how he forced down dry oats mixed with jam, with no water, at that altitude – until he gave up waiting; but still he hoped that Mallory and Irvine had managed to get to the summit.

Odell lived to see the conquest of all fourteen eight thousand metre peaks, as well as the successful ascent of the North Face by a Chinese expedition thirty-six years after his own attempt. This team included the Tibetan Pangthog-la, whom I met during my visit to Tibet in 1982. We spoke in her language, and she smiled when I expressed my admiration for her achievement as a Tibetan woman in reaching the summit. She was obviously under Chinese influence, and though she confirmed that most of the seventeen climbers were Tibetans, she continually emphasised that it was the Chinese who led the group. As we were not alone, I did not want to press her any further. However, I did point out that the Tibetans of today are not content simply to walk round their holy mountains like their forebears, but now also climb to the top. This is not really surprising, because after all Tenzing Norgay was born in Tibet. In fact all the Sherpas come from Tibet; when they originally arrived as immigrants in Nepal, they were called "sharpa" – the people who come from the east. As Nepali citizens they became the famous tigers of the Himalayas, indispensable on expeditions as porters, and now also as climbing partners.

To complete the story it should be mentioned that the remains of

Mallory were discovered by a search party in 1999 at eight thousand metres, but they found no trace of Irvine. There was nothing to indicate whether the pair had fallen after climbing to the summit of Everest. Edmund Hillary is supposed to have said that an ascent only counts as successful if you come home again afterwards. When it comes to first ascents there may be something in this, but ascents such as the North Face of the Eiger are counted as completed if the bodies of the climbers are found on their way down.

I had organised a little expedition to the north of Nepal with my friend and cameraman Herbert Raditschnig. In a book by the Englishman Captain Geoffrey Bruce I had read that it was his dearest wish to have a chance to see what he thought was the most impressive mountain scenery in the world, the spot where the two eight thousand metre peaks, Dhaulagiri and Annapurna, face each other, with only the gorge of the Kali Gandhaki River separating them. Bruce was a doctor who lived in Nepal, and part of his job was to assess the physical fitness of Gurkha mercenaries when they were being recruited. Back then, Englishmen were not allowed to leave the Kathmandu Valley, and Bruce respected this rule. Because of his considerable experience with the native porters he was included in the first Mount Everest expedition in 1922, which planned to make the ascent from the northern, Tibetan side. However, he had no experience as a climber, which makes it all the more remarkable that he achieved a new altitude record of 27,300 feet (8,320 metres) with George Finch. It is even more surprising when you see that most of the participants in the old expedition photos were pipe smokers.

The wiry Captain Bruce might have found an example of the brazenness needed to fulfil his wish in the doctor Henry Oldfield, a man who ignored all the rules. The name of Oldfield means a lot to me, because when Peter Aufschnaiter and I spent nearly a year in Kyirong in 1945, we were convinced we were the first Europeans to come to the area, but in fact ninety years before Oldfield, a gifted artist, had brought beautiful sketches of Kyirong and its gigantic mountain landscape back with him to Europe, and these works have made an important contribution to the exploration of the region.

Because of our heavy expedition luggage, Herbert and I began our journey in Bombay by train. Each of us had reserved a row of seats, and we spread out our sleeping bags and made ourselves at home. The journey to the terminus of Raxaul on the Nepali border took three whole days and two nights. The time passed quickly, and during the long stops in the stations we ate railway food, and bought one detective novel after another in the station bookshops. At that time, Ian Fleming was especially popular.

We spent the nights in the new Treetop Hotels, which promised you would get to see a rhino and a wild elephant. You paid your money, and the animal was tied to a tree. As dawn broke we waited in vain for the promised event with our flash and telephoto lens, and instead of the roar of the king of the jungle the tape recorded the pitiful bleating of a goat straining at a rope.

I told the Foreign Office in Kathmandu that when I had been in the Sultanate of Brunei the previous year I had visited a Chinese trader in the bazaar to look for local produce. As usual, we were having a friendly cup of tea when I saw the horn of an Indian rhino sticking up out of a dish. I knew the horn was used as an aphrodisiac and was very expensive, but also that because of the rarity of these animals, it was forbidden to trade in it. After a little while I enquired innocently about the quality and the price. When the Chinese merchant noticed my interest, he told me that he had more in his storeroom. Over the next cup of tea, this time fortified with colourless rice alcohol, he revealed his source. The bodyguard of the wealthy Sultan of Brunei was made up of Gurkha mercenaries under the command of British officers from Nepal, and it was they who brought the precious stimulant in their kit bags. Each Gurkha receives a few rounds of live ammunition for use on duty, and he has to account for them to his commanding officer. Because large sums can be earned by selling rhino horns, the officers may be involved too. On one occasion the press revealed that the princess of a Himalayan state had been carrying a suitcase containing rhino horn in her diplomatic luggage; it was impounded in Hong Kong.

My story was put on record in the Nepali Foreign Office, but I did not receive consent to take the northern route round the Annapurna massif via Muktinath. Instead I was issued with a general trekking pass that was valid up to three thousand three hundred metres. I found some cheerful Tibetan refugees to accompany us on the trip as cooks and porters.

In order to have the expedition blessed we took a taxi to the suburb of Bodnath, where there was quite a surprise in store. In the newly built monastery of Samtenling I was greeted cheerfully by the old monks, who came from Kyirong and had escaped from the Chinese in good time. They had taken the two most valuable divine statues with them, one of which is now with the Dalai Lama in Dharamsala, and the other in the Tibetan museum in New Delhi. They had even managed to take one of the enormous copper kettles that are found in every Tibetan monastery. It was full of dents, because they had simply dropped it down the three hundred metre sheer drop to the Nepali border. The Chinese had completely destroyed the venerable monastery of Samtenling, which shows how right the monks were to do as they did.

The monks surrounded me and shouted to the monastery, "Norbu, your father has come!" A man about twenty years old came out, with a dirty apron covering his robes. He had a somewhat lighter skin than most Tibetans, and it was true that the stubble on his shaven head had a reddish sheen. Rinpoche, who was normally rather reserved, told me it was no use denying he was my son, and the thing that really proved it, he said, was not that Norbu's age fit perfectly, but that he was the only one of the monks who spoke good English. Although I had no clear memory of any amorous adventure, Tibet is well-known for its miracles.

We had been marching eastward towards the Annapurna massif for days, and later on we caught a glimpse of the peak of Dhaulagiri in the west as well. But when we finally reached the spot where the two giants face one another, the view was nowhere near as impressive as Bruce had imagined. We entered a deep gorge several kilometres long, and all that we saw were a few hermitages built into the rocks by the monks. We were coming to the region where the Lamaitic Buddhism of the Tibetans is more common than Hinduism, the dominant religion of Nepal.

On New Year's Day we reached Tatopani, which literally means "hot water". We rested for a day, swimming for hours in the clear water of the thermal springs. Males and females bathed together. My language skills made for easy communication, and there was plenty to listen to and laugh about. In the evening large quantities of millet beer were served, accompanied by the typical music of the Nepalis, which is dominated by the sound of drums and shawms. When it grew cold the men put on white jackets that I thought were loden, but in fact they were made of raw nettle fibres.

In Tatopani we encountered the first police checks, and on the advice of the spokesman of our porters we turned off the main caravan route and called on a local official in Baglung. The town was surrounded by rice terraces, which were dry in winter, and behind it lay the mountains, covered with snow and ice. The official's name was Bahadur Bantaba, which indicated that he had high status within the hierarchy of Nepal. I asked whether he was able to give me permission to move freely within his district. He reacted calmly, simply saying we would have to wait and see, and left me with a question to think about: "Do you want something from me, or do I want something from you?" He instructed one of the servants, who stood with their heads bowed, to make tea, and asked another to show the porters to their quarters.

I forgot my European mentality, and the rest of the day passed in lively conversation and the familiar wholesome food that you shovel into your mouth using four fingers. I explained that during my years in Lhasa I had learned how to eat with four fingers from Kaisher Bahadur, the Ambassador of Nepal. I continued to namedrop, mentioning the Dalai Lama and the Foreign Minister, and the next morning I met Bantaba Bahadur once more on the terrace of his house. I passed him my binoculars so he could see the mountains better and write their names down in his diary. He pointed to the tall bushes at the edge of the fields, and said one profitable source of income was the hand-made paper the natives made out of the tough bark of the February daphne, or paradise plant. Then he sat down at a very old typewriter and typed a letter in Devanagari script. The most important thing was the printed letterhead and the two official stamps, he said. After reading out the text, he said to those present that friendly people who had come so

429

far to see his country should be treated sympathetically and helpfully rather than in the usual way. Once he had explained the main points in the letter, he sent everyone else outside. I took my leave of Bahadur and thanked him by taking the binoculars from my neck and giving them to him with both hands, as was customary here.

It was pouring with rain when we reached Tukuche, the largest settlement we had seen since we left the Kathmandu valley. A monk in Baglung had told me exactly where to find the most important holy sites, but he kept repeating that it would be almost impossible to get that far north now that it was winter, because of all the snow. We found lodging in a caravanserai, and met a man from Mustang, six days' journey further to the north. He described how I could find the route to the cave of the holy Padmesabhava, Ching Shi Rang, and also explained that the Tibetans did not know the town where we were as Tukuche but as "Drug-Che", because here barley from the south was exchanged in equal volume, measure for measure, with salt from the north. During the winter, when he had sufficient time available, he went with his pack animals a week further in the direction of Kathmandu, where he could get twice as much barley or rice as here in Drug-Che.

The next day dawned cold but clear and we could see the two eight-thousanders away to the south. As we passed a couple of small huts, an elderly man wearing warm khaki clothing came out to meet us. I addressed him in Tibetan, as there was no doubt in my mind that he was one of the Khampa warriors from East Tibet, who had been living here on the border with Tibet and fighting a guerrilla war against the Chinese army for the past twenty years. At one time they had been aided in their struggle by the USA, but American sponsorship for their cause was subsequently discontinued, and the Khampas were disarmed by the Nepalese government in the 1970s. In spite of this, I was well aware of the possible dangers of an encounter with them and knew that, for that very reason, it was forbidden to visit this region.

The two eldest brothers of the Dalai Lama, Gyalo Thundrub and Thubten Jigme Norbu, had approached the CIA for help in 1956 but had not informed the Dalai Lama for fear that their actions might compromise him. Tibetan freedom fighters were sent to top secret CIA training camps in the USA, parachuted into northern Nepal and supplied with weapons and ammunition. From there, the resistance mounted a number of cross-border raids on Chinese army convoys on the old caravan route from Lhasa to West Tibet. The campaign, which was known as the "Chu-chi kang drug" – "Four rivers, six snowy mountains", was so successful that all traffic on the route was brought to a halt.

After their betrayal by the CIA, the proud Khampas were forced to lead an undignified existence. Stripped of their weapons, even their old hunting rifles and two-edged swords, and bitterly disappointed that America had abandoned them in their hour of need to avoid souring US trade relations with China, they now felt unwanted. They had done their duty, but they had lost their homeland, and had found nowhere to replace it.

Inside the hut, a butter-lamp flickered on a little altar near the window. There was no glass in the window, and the paper that served as a replacement could not keep the howling wind from blowing the flame. From my camera bag I extracted a more recent photograph of the Dalai Lama, as the picture on the altar showed him as a child. The elderly man pressed the portrait to his forehead in the ritual manner of the devout Tibetan Buddhist, and set it down next to the lamp. He told me that he had been in the rearguard group that had protected the Dalai Lama from the advancing Chinese soldiers during his flight from Lhasa. I could detect a note of sadness and resignation in the proud old Khampa's words.

Herbert and I were much moved by the fate of the brave East Tibetans, but there were many new discoveries to film and record; very few Europeans were familiar with this interesting area.

The letter of introduction had been a help to us, but I knew that we would come to one last police station at three thousand three hundred metres. We passed the building at dawn, keeping to the hillside behind it, and two days later we arrived at Muktinath, which the Tibetans call Chu-mig Gyatso.

A naked yogi ignored us, continuing with his exercises in the bitter cold. To the south we saw the great pyramid of Dhaulagiri, and presently came to the source of the Krishna, which flows into the Kali further south and is then called Krishna Kala Gandhaki. In summer, the source produces a great deal of water, and is divided into a hundred and eight springs. Now, at the end of January, not many of them were flowing, because when there is a frost most of the springs freeze up. During the summer months, when the water is bubbling out of all of them, many pilgrims carry out their ritual ablutions in the holy water. Now there was just one sadhu sitting there wrapped in a military coat. With his bare feet drawn up beneath him he prayed to the god Tsingpoche; there was a small temple dedicated to him nearby. He murmured quietly to himself, and there was no other sound. The sun shone through the bare poplars, and a few birds bathed in the puddles left behind by the thawing snow. It was a peaceful, holy place. The only jarring note was that everything seemed to be neglected, and the building for pilgrims to spend the night in had collapsed. Another sadhu had now arrived, and covered himself with a blanket. He too was barefoot. After they had both finished praying, we accompanied them to a solitary house where they called out to a woman who had the key to the "fire". This was the holy site that has made Muktinath famous, the temple where fire comes out of the water, the earth and the rock. The woman wore a long moth-eaten sheepskin cloak, and her greasy black hair, which was woven into numerous plaits, hung right down her back. Muttering, she went ahead of us towards a house further up the mountain. She opened the door with an enormous key. So this was the famous temple where thousands of pilgrims from Tibet, Nepal and India come! The room was gloomy, with just a ray of light coming down from a skylight. In the middle was the altar, and on top of it were images of Chenresi, the god of mercy, and the dark, demonic god Demdring. Beneath the altar were three holes in the earth. The central one was the size of a football, and it was covered by two flat stones. The woman strained to push them aside as the sadhus looked on, making no effort to help her. When I looked into the hole I saw a bluish flame, and there was a smell of petrol. To the right of the flame water dripped out of a little spring – that was the "fire from the water". In the hole to the left, pale flames flickered out of the earth – the "fire from the earth". When I peered into another hole to the right, I could not at first see a flame at all. Only when I stuck my head further in did

I detect a small flicker in a crack in the rock – it must be the "fire from the stone". Obviously, this was a natural gas discharge, and somehow it had caught fire and become a sacred flame.

The woman hurried us; she obviously wanted to go home. We set up the camera, and Herbert started filming. The woman kept getting in shot to relieve her anger at the disturbance. I shoved a few rupees into her hand, but the money had no effect on her. She put it somewhere underneath her ragged sheepskin coat and carried on complaining. Whole bundles of valuable jewellery that had been left as offerings by pious pilgrims hung above the altar, and a number of old scroll pictures decorated the wall. It had been worth the trouble, and an hour later the impatient doorkeeper was able to close up the Fire Temple once more.

We did not want to go back the way we had come, and we decided to go via the 5,417 metre high Thorung Pass to the north of the Annapurna massif. Only two of the porters were prepared to come with us, and insisted on double wages. We took it in turn to lead the way through the thick snow, and after three exhausting, cold days we crossed the pass and reached the village of Manangbhot. The inhabitants used ice from the nearby glacier to chill their butter, and every year they put on a large harvest festival that attracted many visitors. It was only years later when this route was opened up that stricter rules were introduced, because tourists froze to death, and expensive rescue missions with helicopters had to be mounted to save their lives.

As we were marching along the warm Marsyandi Valley, we came to a police station that monitored access to the forbidden zone. A military "Halt!" forced us to stop. Where had we come from and where was our permit? I argued that our papers had never been checked, and the officer ought to be content that we were now leaving the forbidden zone. Five weeks later, after a forced march and a further police check, Herbert and I reached Kathmandu.

I did not go to Amarnath until 1996. I had been to Ladakh many times, and during my travels I had seen a signpost to Amarnath in Srinagar, but it was only when I was enjoying an extended stay on one of the houseboats in Srinagar that I had the opportunity to visit this last "Nath".

It was mid-August, a few days before the full moon, and Pahalgam was crammed with pilgrims getting ready for the trek to Amarnath. From this point, the only way to get there was on foot, via an ancient pilgrim route. The weather was fine, and about a hundred thousand pilgrims had assembled, intending to make the fifty kilometre trek to the holy site in four days.

On the first day I joined the stream of people, and made my way along the Lidder River to a campsite. It was not yet that cold, and it was possible to spend the night outdoors. There was plenty of wood, and the many fires made the surrounding mountains into a romantic place for my bivouac. Added to this was the sound of cooks crying their wares – steaming chapattis and spicy curry. My pilgrimage could not have had a more dreamlike beginning.

The second day took me through woods and meadows to a deep blue lake, with glacier-clad mountains above. This place was called Wawjan and the scenery was just incredible, such as one can only find in the Himalayas. I managed to make myself comfortable for the night in my sleeping bag, perched on a rack held together by coconut fibres behind the hearth where I had had my meal of chapattis and tea, and drifted off to the sound of monotonous religious chants. At dawn I was woken by a loud cry from the owner; a cold gust of wind from the mountains had ripped off the roof, which was made of woven bamboo. Some of the pilgrims had long since set off, so I hurriedly grabbed my things and followed them. I protected myself from the cold wind with the yellow eiderdown jacket I had been given by Tenzing. Most of the Indians were walking with their heads bowed, and had wrapped themselves in blankets. The shelter of the forest was behind us now, and the route snaked its way through the open landscape up to the four thousand six hundred metre high Mahagunas Pass. There were more and more pilgrims sitting by the side of the road; they were obviously having trouble with the lack of oxygen in the air. They wore light clothing, and many of them did not even have shoes. A few men were carrying a lifeless body on an improvised stretcher.

The wind had moderated, but it had started raining. At the top of the pass the rain turned to snow, and the path was barely recognisable. Women sat helplessly weeping next to their dying fathers, and the thought that thousands more pilgrims were yet to arrive made a catastrophe seem all too likely. It was at least eight hundred metres down from the pass to the meadows. Though it continued raining, at least it was warmer here, and there was plenty of food.

On the fourth and final day there were only six kilometres still to go, but the closer I got to the famous cave, the thicker the crowds became. The police tried to maintain order, but there were just too many people. As an unbeliever I gave up, and I only got the vaguest impression from the mouth of the cave that there is a stalagmite inside, formed by drips from the roof freezing into a phallus-shaped lingam made of ice. There was nothing the police could do, but the sadhus stopped the women who hoped to be blessed with children if they touched the ice phallus from doing so. Their ecstasy would have made the icy cave into a hellish inferno. In return for their forbearance, priests granted the devout pilgrims the blessing of Shivalinga after the laborious journey they had undertaken.

I had experienced the trinity of Badri, Kera and Amar, held in such high honour by the Indians, and now I went back to my own world. The reports of the Indian authorities in their 1996 yearbook strike a sober and factual tone: "239 of the pilgrims did not return from the snowstorm." Their long march to the god of the ice had ended, it seemed, in longed-for nirvana.

THE OTHER "ROOF OF THE WORLD"

In north eastern India there is a region whose tribal dialects belong to the Tibeto-Burmese family of languages, and whose inhabitants, the Naga, have facial characteristics that are Mongoloid in appearance. The Naga were once feared as head-hunters, a practice that was only outlawed in 1991. In 1962 the region of Nagaland became a state of the Indian Union, but it was to be a further thirteen years before the Indian government finally reached an accord with the Naga, whose aim was to gain complete independence from India. Such was the state of affairs when I visited the area in 1975 with the aim of investigating the Naga's relationship with the Tibetan people.

Obtaining an official entry permit was out of the question, so I decided to take a more circuitous route. Posing as a harmless geographer and tourist, I travelled first to the province of Manipur, which lay immediately to the south of Nagaland, with the intention of making my way north to visit the Katcha Naga who lived up in the mountains. With the help of four strong men from the Kuki tribe, an ethnic group that also exhibits Mongoloid characteristics, I built a raft from long bamboo poles and set off, to all appearances aimlessly, on my journey north.

We had a sack of rice with us on the raft, but we had no plates or cooking pots and I had only packed a mug and spoon, as usual. However, in the evening I was shown an ideal solution to the problem. The Kuki cut about ten medium sized pieces of green bamboo, filled them with rice and water, sealed the ends with a leaf and propped them up in the embers of the cooking fire. After about half an hour, as the bamboo tubes began to burn, they were removed from the fire and split in half with a bush knife to reveal the cooked rolls of rice. I rummaged around in my duffel bag and found some salt and hot chilli powder to spice the rice up a little, the Kuki added some freshly picked bamboo shoots and we all ate our fill.

As we headed into steeper territory in the foothills of the mountains, progress with the raft became impossible. The four Kuki were growing more and more nervous now that we were in Naga territory and stayed awake all night by the fire, listening for the telltale noise of branches snapping in the jungle that they believed would signal the approach of the head-hunters. Next morning, they refused point blank to go any further without guns. I could see the fear in their eyes and I must admit I had butterflies in my stomach, too, and only gave the outward impression of being calm so as not to make my companions any more nervous than they already were. By now I had resigned myself to the fact that I was not going to be able to make contact with the Katcha Naga, at least not on this occasion, but the return trip and my porters' pay day restored the harmony somewhat and I consoled myself with the thought that the expedition, whilst not particularly successful, had nevertheless been an interesting adventure.

In 1978, after the success of my regular television broadcasts, I was invited to submit an entry to UNESCO in Paris for the Kalinga Prize for the Popularisation of Science, an annual award with a prize of two thousand pounds. Each of the four jurors received a parcel of my books, while I used the whole thing as an excuse to pay a return visit to eastern India, where the ancient culture of Kalinga, a region mentioned by Pliny some two thousand years ago, has its roots. I had my acceptance speech well prepared, but when the German UNESCO representative was explaining to the jury why he had nominated me for the award, his Austrian counterpart chipped in with the observation that Heinrich Harrer was not German at all; he was Austrian. The prize went to Heimar von Ditfurth.

During a series of subsequent events I met some of the famous members of UNICEF, the United Nations Children's Fund, amongst them Liv Ullmann and Astrid Lindgren, who had recently received the coveted Peace Prize of the German Book Trade. Lindgren came to Munich to present the prizes to the winners of the worldwide "Jugend forscht" competition, where she impressed both the children and the press with her simple elegance, her charm and her modesty. Her lovingly written children's books have achieved world record sales in translation, far surpassing the successes of many contemporary travel and adventure stories. Astrid Lindgren died at the end of January 2002, and one day after her death she was nominated for the 2002 Nobel Prize for Literature.

The lure of faraway places continued to exert its pull on me and I found myself leafing through brochures offering scientific and adventure trips. In the autumn of 1979 I came across an offer that really caught my attention: "Pamir – the Roof of the World" it read, "On paths that no person has ever trodden." The price was reasonable, and included visas, return flights via Moscow to Tajikistan and hotel accommodation. I called my friend Alois Anwander, who agreed enthusiastically to my plan, and booked the trip. When I decided to go on this trip I had an ulterior motive: in 1971 a book was published in Moscow about an archaeological dig on the Oxus, the river that forms the border between Afghanistan and Tajikistan. What I found particularly interesting was the description of a ruined monastery and a statue of Buddha that had been unearthed during the dig.

Alois and I met our little group of like-minded adventurers at Zurich airport, where we were greeted by our "expert" travel guide, a pretty young woman. She was obviously quite shocked to see me; in fact she was speechless for a while. For the first time ever, I had no responsibilities; I was not the expedition leader, I was just a tourist like all the others, and I listened attentively to our travel guide's instructions. We were flying to Dushanbe, the capital of Tajikistan, and I had in my pocket a letter of introduction from Leopold Guggenberger, the Mayor of Klagenfurt, Dushanbe's twin town in Austria. First of all, however, I relaxed and let our travel company rep do all the organising, since it was her job to see us all safely into the mountains.

At the start of our trek we came across caravans of peasant farmers taking agricultural products to town. We admired their colourful headgear and we each managed to acquire a hat of our own. Presently we reached the village of Mukh, where the villagers were busy bringing in the potato harvest from the extensive terraced plots on the hillside. The sandy soil and dry climate up here in the hill country seemed to provide the ideal conditions for a good crop, as there were already more than twenty sacks full of light red potatoes standing in a line on the field and women with babies on their backs were sorting and bagging more of them. Several men were standing around waiting to tie the sacks, weigh them and load them for transport. The children interrupted their games and watched inquisitively as we pulled all manner of interesting things out of our rucksacks and began to set up camp, and one of the young boys helped me to pitch my tent. A local man then fetched firewood and water and brought some hot coals to light the campfire with.

The next day I found the peasant farmers to be very friendly and hospitable. They lit the two communal ovens that stood outside near our camp. It was like a scene from a picture book: the white smoke rose against the dark, bare cliffs and wafted up towards the snow covered peaks of the mountains beyond. A few hours later we were given freshly baked flatbreads, which were so large we had to hold them with both hands. They were nice and crusty and tasted delicious. As the sun went down we were invited into one of the houses for supper. I took a few photographs of the family and admired the many beautiful coloured fabrics that these people spent their winters weaving.

In the morning all the villagers came to see us off. A little further along the trail we came across some yurts belonging to Mongols. I photographed the scarecrows they had placed in the fields to protect their crops and a place of sacrifice at the edge of the field, decorated with symbols to ward off demons and evil spirits and adorned with a set of goat horns. We walked on through alpine pastures, gaining height steadily, to reach the crest of a ridge, where we were treated to a marvellous view of the Pamir summits, all of which were unclimbed, before continuing, uphill and down dale, to reach our campsite for the night.

Next morning I asked our nice travel guide what the actual objective of the trip was – a particularly shapely peak, perhaps, or a visit to a mountain tribe? – and added that I could have gone hiking back home where the air was not so thin. I was rather irritable, I must admit, and ended up telling her that this was the first, the last and the only time I would be travelling with her organisation.

I had read somewhere that nine-tenths of the country of Tajikistan consists of mountains, a statistic that appeared to be confirmed by the view we had of mountains, valleys and more mountains. One of the valleys led to the foot of Peak Communism which, at 7,495 metres, was the highest mountain in the Soviet Union. Alois and I decided to leave the group and go off on our own, with no porters, carrying just a tent, our sleeping bags and some food. We promised to be back in Dushanbe in time to catch the return flight home and after we left I felt a little guilty that I had parted company with our guide on rather a sour note.

We wandered along the sunny side of the valley, passing a vegetable garden fenced with thorn bushes that was half covered with a thriving crop of dill and a cave in the cliff behind that had obviously been lived in until quite recently. Further down the valley stood a little house, where a woman was rinsing dishes in the clear water of a small stream. Two children were playing in the water and our arrival seemed neither to surprise them nor worry them unduly. The woman pointed to the door of the house and told us to ask if we needed anything.

The man who came out to greet us was tall and blond and built like an athlete. He asked if we would like some "chai", then asked again using the German word "Tee". We stayed for three days. Nikolai had studied technology in Tomsk but he and his girlfriend had tired of the big city life and after much searching they had finally found the haven they had wanted in this remote valley. They had adopted the two young boys, aged five and seven, in the last village and Nikolai had obtained permission from the local authorities – a three-day walk away – to educate the children at home. They lived in the cave near the vegetable garden during the winter months when their little house became too cold. It looked more like a garden shed than a house, really, built of birch wood and with a flat roof, but the inside, though cramped, was very homely. Next to the stove, Nikolai had built a wooden draining board on which six beakers stood drying, and there was shelving and storage space along one of the walls. I counted more than forty books – cheap editions of Russian classics, mainly, and a Russian-German dictionary, which we found very helpful. There was a small map of the area on the wall next to the shelves.

There were no tables or chairs; we sat cross legged on a raised wooden platform, which Alois, with his big, muscled legs found a little too cramped. The conversation was limited and consisted largely of a mixture of gestures and odd words I had looked up in the dictionary. The menu never varied from a daily stew, but I noticed that our host family all chewed bunches of fresh dill, which probably contributed to their healthy appearance.

Eating so much roughage really stimulated our digestion and meant that Alois and I had to make several rather hurried trips to the "toilet", which was anything but remote. In fact, you could see from a hundred metres away whether it was occupied or not. The arrangement consisted of a large tree branch spanning the river, with a big drop to the water below. Great care and a good head for heights were required as you balanced precariously above the abyss with feet astride a convenient fork in the branch, and it was crucial not to rush things. I had experienced something similar once before on the Dolomite Haute Route, but that Tajikistan tree trunk toilet was certainly the most exciting I had ever come across.

There was a little waterfall in the stream near the house, where we washed and showered. I took several photos of the children as they romped round in the water. Nikolai gave me the address of the nearest post office where I should send the photographs and told me that he intended to make the long walk into town one last time before winter set in. I was not really able to offer Nikolai much sound advice about his decision to leave his conservative upbringing behind him, since my opinions were those of an older generation. As a young man during the war I had also dreamed that one day I might build myself a little cedar wood house in the forests of South Tibet, with a fresh mountain stream flowing through the garden.

Back in Dushanbe, Alois rejoined the group while I checked into a scruffy hotel, in which I was the only guest. To accompany the evening meal, there was a surprise bottle of Erlauer red wine; not the famous "Bull's Blood" but a nice drop nonetheless, from the friendly comrades in Hungary. The main street of Dushanbe was lined with department stores but the only things for sale were those that had just been delivered. By contrast, the market hall was full of ripe, sweet grapes and huge quantities of fragrant herbs, but the meat and bread stalls were only occasionally open, it seemed. There were mountains of potatoes and tomatoes piled high on the ground in front of the market, too. I had already bought some apples on the "Avenue" after standing for ages in a queue to get my "ration".

A day trip by bus took me over hills and down valleys to Rogun, where a new dam was being constructed which, at 335 metres high, was said to be the largest of its kind in the world. Photography was forbidden, but it was a very impressive construction project nonetheless, and I managed to take a few shots of the seventy kilometre long reservoir from the top of the dam wall.

It was with mixed feelings that I went to visit the rather less impressive government buildings in Dushanbe, where the Mayor also resided. Since I could not speak neither the local language or Russian, I was directed to the office of a man who spoke a little German and fluent English. He was a university professor from Leningrad, and after he had read my letter of introduction he offered his help. I asked if I might be allowed to visit the site of the archaeological dig on the Afghani border to the south. He had read my Tibet book and saw through my ruse immediately, realising that what I really wanted to see were the ruins of the old Buddhist monastery and the statue of Buddha that had been found there. Gravely, he advised me against inflaming the tense situation that existed between the Moslem and non-Moslem factions in the south by insisting on visiting the statue, a symbol of the region's Buddhist past.

The friendly professor did have an alternative idea, however, which would spare me the long journey south and actually turned out to be more than adequate compensation for not seeing the statue. After a lengthy telephone conversation in Russian he turned to me and said "Go to the university. On the south side of the campus you will find an old two-storey building. On the first floor there are two doors. Knock three times on the left hand door, then on the door to the right, then again on the left. The woman I have just been speaking to will open the door for you."

It all sounded very strange, but it was soon to get even spookier. I took the bus to the university and walked around looking for the old building. It felt like I was being watched and I walked purposefully without turning round. In fact, no one was following me at all, but

I still had a strange feeling in the pit of my stomach as I opened the creaking door to the building. The rickety wooden staircase creaked even louder and there was no banister to take any of my weight as I mounted the worn steps to the first floor. When I got there the whole place was in total silence. With beating heart, I knocked as I had been instructed, whereupon a large door opened and an elderly woman in a white lab coat bade me enter. As I heard the key turn in the lock behind me I breathed a sign of relief, even though I was now a fellow conspirator and accomplice, and a trapped one at that.

The high room was filled with objects and in the middle of the room, protected by dust sheets, I could just make out the long fingers of a huge hand in the dim light that filtered through the window. We picked our way carefully between the objects to a table littered with antique pieces. A tea kettle stood on an iron stove next to a very old wireless set like the one I used to have in Lhasa. The lady scientist who had opened the door for me was simply dressed and had her white hair tied back in a bun. She lived here like a hermit, surrounded by antiques and the remains of an eighth century clay Buddha, which she treated with the pious reverence normally reserved for those who have taken a nun's vows. Her school German was good enough to explain to me the provenance of this significant find. The Tajiks had inhabited and cultivated this desolate land since pre-Christian times, and its proximity to the Silk Road had meant that not only rare goods but also new religions like Islam and Buddhism had reached the country, particularly the south, where monasteries and other sacred Buddhist edifices had been constructed. These were destroyed by the Arabs in the eighth century. The history books record the senseless destruction wrought by these barbaric, uncivilised hordes. On a later visit to the ruins of Angkor in Cambodia, I found to my horror that most of the thousand-year-old, hand carved sandstone busts of Buddha were missing. The *Süddeutsche Zeitung* wrote that Angkor, designated as a World Heritage Site by UNESCO, had for many years been nothing more than a "quarry for the art trade".

During the 1960s archaeologists from Dushanbe began digging on the site of the Buddhist monastery of Ajina-Tepe, where they unearthed the remains of various sacred buildings, including stupas and cloisters with well-preserved wall paintings. What excited the archaeologists most, however, was the discovery of a very large reclining Buddha statue measuring twelve metres in length, which was carefully and patiently removed from its grave. Specialists in the conservation and restoration of ancient artefacts were called in from the Hermitage Museum in Leningrad, amongst them my benefactor, the friendly professor. Since the important find consisted of air dried clay, the statue had to be handled with the utmost care and fingertip sensitivity that characterises the work of the archaeologist as it was laid bare and made ready for transport.

And now they lay here before me, the precious fragments of the thousand-year-old Buddha. Using a thin stick the woman carefully moved the cotton sheet from the long hand and explained that the fragile appendage was held together with straws and thin pieces of dowel. As I took some close-up shots I thought about the artist who had shaped the elegant fingers, and the skill of the woman who had restored them.

When she spoke, her face shone with the soft smile of the Buddha; his teachings had brightened her soul. It was quite obviously a pleasure for her to share all her pent-up knowledge with an interested spectator. She rummaged around in a pile of handwritten documents and handed me an old photograph of her as a young archaeologist with her colleagues at the Ajina-Tepe dig. When I left, she shut the creaking door firmly behind me. She remained with her Buddha, while the memories of my encounter with her remain with me to this day.

On the last evening of the trip, the group met up at the hotel to swap experiences and thank our travel guide. Since 1991 Tajikistan has been an independent nation, and in 1998 Peak Communism was renamed Peak Ismail Samani, after a powerful Tajikistan dynasty. In March 2001, news agencies reported that the Taliban militia in Afghanistan had used explosives to destroy the two famous monumental Buddha statues that had been cut into the mountainside of the Bamiyan province between the second and fifth centuries. This time the order to destroy a World Heritage Site came from a supposedly civilised government in Kabul. What must that lady archaeologist have thought as she listened to the news on the old wireless just a few hundred kilometres away in a dimly lit room in Dushanbe? With the terrorist attacks of September 11th 2001 in New York and Washington, the fanatical followers of Islam finally went one step too far. As the world eventually grasped the idea that we are all living in a global village, the great powers of the East and West, united in opposition, sent troops to Dushanbe to put an end to the horrors that were being perpetrated. One of the few pieces of good news to emerge was the fact that the wrecked Bamiyan Buddha statues are to be rebuilt.

RETURN TO TIBET

At the beginning of December 1981 Carina and I flew to New York once more. We wanted to catch a few of the new Broadway musicals and had also arranged to meet up with our friends, Syd and Jean Shiff, to watch the turning on of the Christmas tree lights at the Rockefeller Center. Sidney Shiff was the proprietor of an exclusive publishing company called the Limited Edition, which published classic books in limited numbers for member subscribers. To my delight, he had recently included *Seven Years in Tibet* and *The White Spider* in his list of selected titles, both of which were published in beautiful leather bound editions. He had also designed my Tibet book to resemble an ancient Tibetan manuscript.

Instead of the customary winter overcoat, Syd was in the habit of wearing a long, elegant cashmere scarf. He knew New York like the back of his hand and his excellent connections enabled us to bypass the lengthy queues for the Matisse exhibition we wished to visit. He was also something of a gourmet and knew where to go to find the best risotto in town, which was one of my favourite dishes. He somehow managed to get a table, even though the restaurant was fully booked. As a token of our gratitude, we invited Jean and Syd out to dinner one evening at the Explorer's Club, where we all ordered the exotic "dish of the day".

As I was leaving the club, I stopped to look at the notice board in the lobby and discovered a special members-only offer on a trip to Tibet. I added my name to the list, and in mid-March we were off. I was anxiously hoping that I would be allowed into the country, as the list of participants also included several old acquaintances like Sherpa Tenzing and Blanche Olschak, a highly regarded Tibetologist and one time fellow student. I had no trouble with immigration in either Hong Kong or Peking, and even in Chengdu, where we boarded an ancient Russian plane for the final leg to Tibet, they only checked the number of passengers against their list. As always, I kept a diary of the trip:

447

Monday, 29th March 1982

I am sitting in an aircraft bound for Lhasa. As I gaze out over the ice-clad peaks and the broad expanse of the Tibetan Plateau, I think about frostbitten feet and temperatures of minus forty degrees. This time, almost forty years later, I am in a warm, comfortable aircraft. We will be landing in Lhasa in two hours. Back then, it took us two years.

We are flying over the rivers of the Yangtsekiang, Mekong, Irrawaddy and Salween, all of which have their sources in the high country of Tibet. The landscape appears largely unchanged, but then I spot a ruined monastery. This is the harsh reality of which I had heard, but which I did not wish to believe.

As we fly over the Brahmaputra, which carries hardly any water in spring, I can make out the first villages. Surely one should now see prayer flags flapping in the wind and smell the smoke of yak-dung fires, I think as I get off the plane. But instead there are Chinese officials waiting for us in their plain and simple uniforms. Then, amidst this military monotony, I spot a face: shy, friendly, familiar, Tibetan. It is Thundrub Drolma, now forty-five, the wife of my old friend Wangdu Sholkhang.

Hesitantly, we move towards each other. Softly, I ask the reserved Tibetan woman if I might still call her Drolma-la as in the old days or if I have to address her now as Mrs Sholkhang. `No, no, to you I am still the Drolma you knew before', she says quickly, but I feel it is no longer the same as before. While we are conversing in Tibetan, our courier, a so-called National Guide from Peking, comes up and snaps at me that if I need anything I should ask him. But I barely hear him; I just look at Drolma. I am looking for the graceful movements, the cheerfulness and the carefree ease that had once been the typical features of young Tibetan women; but all I see is seriousness and resignation."

Drolma's grandfather was the great Tsarong II, a progressive man who knew full well that Tibet would have to change and adapt to the wider world and had worked with the 13th Dalai Lama Tupden Gyatso to open up the country's borders to the West. For him, the old hero of

Chaksam, there was no future under the Chinese occupation and on the morning of 14th May 1959, the day he was to have faced a great People's Court on the steps of the Potala Palace, to be humiliated by his own servants, he was found dead on his mattress in his prison cell. He had taken his own life by swallowing some diamond splinters which – as he had once told me – he always carried in a little cloth bag secreted about his person. Death spared him the worst humiliation and injustice, a public trial by a People's Court.

After the ritual exchange of the traditional white good-luck *katas* we boarded a bus for the bumpy three-hour drive to Lhasa. On arrival we were taken to the official government guest house, where we were to be accommodated for the entire duration of our stay.

Late in the afternoon on my very first day in Lhasa, a handsome Tibetan approached me and said "Don't you recognise me, Henrig-la?" I stammered a little and remarked that, after all, thirty years had passed and he would have to help jog my memory. "But you saved my life; don't you remember that?" he replied. Of course, now I remembered. He was Surkhang Jigme, the son of Surkhang Dzasa, Tibet's former secular Foreign Minister, and the first person Aufschnaiter and I had worked for after our arrival in Lhasa. And now, several decades later, this son stood before me, as large as life. He had spent years in prisons and concentration camps, but the political thaw, and his knowledge of English, had recently enabled him to make a living as a liaison officer for mountaineering and trekking expeditions. Two years after our happy reunion, I heard that Jigme had been killed on his motorcycle in a head-on collision with a truck.

Everywhere we went we were watched, spied on, followed and filmed; every photograph we took had to be paid for, every rule was strictly enforced. On one occasion I came across a notice that read: "Taking photographs here is prohibited free of charge", which provided a little light relief. Tourists had been expelled from the country simply for giving away photographs of the Dalai Lama or, in the case of one Swiss lady, for having a copy of my book with her. I was recognised by several of the old monks, and when I chatted to them, young people would stop and stare, astonished to hear a stranger speaking their Lhasa dialect. I finally got my own personal National Guide, as the group I was travelling with had its own fixed itinerary, whereas I wished to visit the places where I had worked as an employee of the Tibetan government.

We visited the dam that Aufschnaiter and I had built in the spring of 1948. I sat on a wall with my Chinese guide and tried to engage him in an objective discussion about the differences between then and now. The extent to which he had been influenced by his political schooling became apparent from the following exchange. He wanted to know how many soldiers and officials had been stationed in Lhasa during the old Chiang Kai-shek regime. "Just an envoy, his secretary and a wireless operator," I replied. After a several minutes of silence, he said "Well, in that case, the Tibetans are better off now than they were back then!" I took a number of photographs and promised to send him copies. We did not become friends exactly, but he did at least try to accommodate my requests. "Call me Pau," he said, "That is my name."

It was quite difficult to locate the bungalow I had once occupied in the grounds of the Tsarong family residence, as what had once been a large area of gardens was now a collection of small, cheap houses. However, over the years, journalists and friends of mine visiting Lhasa had obviously enquired about the place, and we found an old man who knew the way. He led us down a series of dirty back alleys, leant a heavy old ladder against a high stone wall and promptly vanished. Without hesitating, I clambered up onto the flat roof and took some photographs, first of the Tsarong house and then of my bungalow. As my Chinese guide climbed up to join me, a soldier emerged from the big house, gesticulating furiously. Somewhat intimidated by this, I said to Pau that it might be better if we left, but he waved away my suggestion and told me I should just ignore the man. It appeared that political officials wielded more power here than the military, just as they did in Africa. In any case, I had the shots I wanted. The gardens were now badly overgrown, but I told Pau that when I lived there I had planted flowers and little fruit trees, and had even built an ornamental fountain, the first of its kind in Tibet. Back then, it had caused something of a sensation. In common with all the other lovely old houses of the Tibetan nobility, the Tsarong residence and the bungalow were now occupied by Chinese army officers. The vase of flowers that had once stood in the big window of my bungalow, where I used to sit and draw my maps, was gone, as was my desire to see any more things that might spoil the fond memories I had of the place.

This sad state of affairs continued when we visited the private apartments of the Dalai Lama at the Potala Palace. Everything was just as it had been. The yellow painted tubular steel bed still stood against one wall, and the calendar showed the date of his last day in the Potala. It was hard to imagine the king of a country that was almost the size of Europe living in more modest surroundings. In 1950 he had waved goodbye to me from the terrace with the golden roofs that commemorated his deceased ancestors; now, I looked down from the terrace onto a sea of hideous corrugated iron barracks and newly built government buildings. I took a photograph from here of the ruins of the Medical School on the Chagpori, as it was now forbidden for tourists to set foot on the hill. A year later the Chinese replaced the ruins with a huge television mast. The building that once stood beneath the terrace of the Potala and contained a hundred thousand wooden printing blocks, used to make the three hundred volumes of the Buddhist Holy Scriptures, had been replaced by sleazy bars and gambling dens, a red-light district built to entertain the soldiers of the Chinese army of occupation. I kept asking myself if this really was the Lhasa, the Tibet, that had once been my second home?

I rejoined my group and we took a trip to visit the still intact Kumbum Stupa in Gyantse and the town of Shigatse, but to my despair the sixteen monasteries representing different sects and schools of Buddhism in Tibet had disappeared, and the great Shigatse Fortress had also been razed to the ground – two further shocking examples of the way in which the Cultural Revolution attempted to force its political dogma on the people of Tibet. At the end of the film *Seven Years in Tibet* the director Jean-Jacques Annaud makes the observation that "One million Tibetans have died as a result of the Chinese occupation of Tibet. Six thousand monasteries were destroyed."

On the last day before we left I again visited the great Lhaden Tsuglakhang, or Jokhang Temple, the spiritual and physical heart of Lhasa and the holiest shrine in Tibetan Buddhism. Mr Pau again accompanied me and in keeping with tradition we walked clockwise around the Barkhor, the protective ring around this holy of holies. Only the uniformed Chinese walked the other way, against the flow of pilgrims. Many of the older women recognised me and tried to sell me various Tibetan artefacts. Most of the items on sale were profane souvenirs, amongst them a beer jug inlaid with gold and silver threads. Pau watched the scene with detached interest but could not understand a word. I wanted to buy the jug for my museum, and to do the poor old woman a favour, and asked him if this was allowed. "Of course you can buy it," he said, "but you must know that it will probably be confiscated when you leave the country." I noted that Pau's ingrained cynicism and political convictions had returned during my week away with the group in Shigatse.

The ancient willow tree that stood in front of the Jokhang had withered and died. Once the only tree in Lhasa, the willow was lovingly referred to by devout Tibetans as "the hair of Buddha" and in spring, when the first new leaves appeared, this was taken as a sign that the long, cold winter was at last over. Before the main gate, nomads prostrated themselves in prayer on the smooth, polished stones in a centuries-old ritual, while in the main hall of the temple, a queue of pilgrims waited their turn to touch their foreheads to the seventh century statue of Jowo Shakyamuni Buddha. All this could be viewed by the tourist, at a cost of one hundred *yuan*.

It was with a good deal of trepidation that I had faced Drolma, the wife of my old friend Wangdu, at Lhasa airport, and posed the question that was so important to me: "Is Wangdu in Lhasa and is there any chance I might meet him?" Some thirty years had passed since I had last seen my friend. Two young and carefree lads had turned into middle-aged men, and much had happened in the meantime. I must admit I was rather apprehensive at the prospect of seeing him again.

The reunion necessitated a great deal of tedious bureaucracy. I had to apply in writing to the Lhasa branch of the Luxingshe, the Chinese Tourist Authority, giving the reason for my request. Initially I received no reply. As the days passed and the date of my departure approached I inquired whether my application had at least been examined. "Yes," I was informed, "You may visit Thubten Nyima, as he is now known, on Saturday evening at 19.00 hours." In a Russian Jeep, complete with chauffeur, I was driven down to the Kyitchu, on whose bank Thubten Nyima now lived. I was looking forward to our encounter with a mixture of pleasure and nervousness. I felt as if I were setting out on some adventure, the outcome of which was far from certain.

The Jeep pulled up and I got out. Everywhere was in darkness. Then I recognised a figure at the entrance to the house – it was Wangdu. He approached and we embraced wordlessly. Then, arm in arm, we went into his house and sat down. Unfortunately we were not alone; in addition to Drolma, the driver had also taken a seat at a table next to us.

After the first few silent and emotionally charged minutes we burst out laughing at the discovery that we both needed glasses for reading. This broke the ice, and I asked him if we were still friends. He said we were, and offered me butter-tea. We talked of the old days, and I reminded him of the 6,000 metre Mindrutsari, Lhasa's local mountain, which we had climbed together. While we were chatting, Wangdu lit one cigarette after another, and his only son, a lively boy of eleven, kept coming in to refill our cups with tea. I carefully broached the subject of politics, and Wangdu told me that everyone was better off now. I refrained from probing too deeply, but I knew full well that his ideas had been heavily influenced by the Chinese, who had appointed him as the first Tibetan party member of the Tibet Autonomous Region. The Cultural Revolution of the 1960s and 1970s, and the destruction that had been wrought by the Chinese People's Liberation Army, had been a terrible time for him and he did not like being reminded of it. He tried to explain to me that change was inevitable. "Of course," I agreed, "But change should come from within the country and not as a result of hostile external influences." Wangdu clearly believed what he wanted to believe, and regarded anyone who thought differently as an opponent. I changed the subject and suggested to him that we might realise a long-cherished dream of ours from the old days – to make a journey on foot as far as the unexplored bend of the Brahmaputra. Wangdu replied that this was out of the question, since we would require permission from his superiors in Peking and he did not know anyone there. Wangdu had been freed from the patrician rule of a benign Tibetan hierarchy, but as far as I could see his life had not changed for the better, as now he was subjected to the totalitarian rule of a foreign occupying power, to which he was obliged to subordinate himself.

My time with Wangdu passed in a flash, and my driver was getting restless. I glanced down at my empty teacup, which had not been replenished in accordance with the ancient Tibetan custom that the cup of a friend is left full on parting to speed the visitor's safe return, and said goodbye. I hoped that, in spite of our political differences, we might still remain friends. A few years later, his exiled brother informed me of his death.

Early next morning, the bus arrived to take us back to the airport. We drove straight past the Norbulingka and Drepung Monastery, and did not even stop at Kyentsa Lupding, the "Place of Welcome and Farewell". Of course there were no tents there any more, no cushions lying on the ground, and no tea being served. There was no one there to place a white good-luck scarf around our necks, to ensure the Gods protected us and brought us back again in good health. As we rattled along the bank of the mighty Yamdrok Yumtso, my mind went back to those weeks in Lhasa before the Chinese troops came marching in, and the severe earthquake that had been interpreted by the Tibetans as a bad omen. Yet not a single temple had been destroyed, and not even the skyscraper-like Potala had developed a single crack in its walls. It was left to human hands, guided by political hatred and fanaticism, to destroy almost all of Tibet's sacred buildings. Yet the ice-covered peaks that surround The Roof of the World remain unchanged and inviolate. No political system can ever destroy the "Throne of the Gods", and in the cold moonlit nights one can still hear the cry of the wild geese and cranes as they pass over Lhasa. Their wing-beat sounds like "Lha gye lo" – "The Gods will prevail".

The Chinese have now built a 37 metre victory monument in front of the Potala Palace to commemorate the "peaceful liberation" of Tibet.

IN THE LAND OF THE THUNDER DRAGON

In 1982, my mother died. Since my father's death twelve years before she had travelled a great deal in order to spend time with each of her four children. She flew on her own to Newfoundland at a ripe old age to visit my youngest sister Ruth, who was married to Bill Vetter, a computer expert at the university there, and had four children. She took the train to Mannheim to visit my brother Joseph ("Pepperl" in the Austrian dialect), twelve years my junior, who ran a structural engineering office. In 1972 we went to Mannheim together to attend his cremation; Pepperl had died in a car crash due to the negligence of another driver. My sister Lydia lived in Vienna; she had lost her husband in Stalingrad, and had to bring up her two children on her own.

In our house in Mauren my mother had her own room, where the French windows leading to the garden with its many rhododendrons were always open. When I passed in the morning on my way to the swimming pool I could hear her praying. Then she would sing in her rough and ready way: "The best time of all is the spring, when the heart is cheered by everything."

When we picked mother up at the station, she stepped lightly out of the carriage, and behind her helpful men passed out bags full of things. Her face flushed and red, she said the conversation during the long journey happened to have turned to me, and she introduced me – "This is my son!" Once she had arrived at our home, she took her home-made sauerkraut out of the bags, seasoned with juniper berries from the Zirbitzkogel, apples, a bottle of raspberry juice and a jar of blackcurrant jelly. She must have thought it was difficult to get enough to eat in the Liechtenstein countryside, because she had also brought salad and pumpkin seed oil. Then she took the bag of plants wrapped in damp newspaper and hurried off to the garden to plant them. On one occasion she brought an offshoot of the evergreen box tree in the house where I was born, and this sapling grew into a small arbour vitae that today grows in my garden in Knappenberg. She did not return from the garden till late in the evening, and she had gathered seven different ingredients for the salad in the meadow; I remember these included eyebright, buckthorn and sorrel. Her comment was, "Now God in heaven has opened up his herbarium".

Mother never stayed long, because she missed her friends from church, and she thought there was work to be done in the garden of the family home as well. She was always gentle and kindly, and I can only remember one occasion when she lost her composure, when I suggested to her that she should sell the family house in Hüttenberg and spend the money on her beloved journeys. Her answer was, "That house saved the lives of several families during two world wars – I would never part with it!" Many of my acquaintances said I was very similar to my mother, and I certainly inherited her love of travel.

Not for the first time, we had given her a suitcase for her return journey, but when she visited us in April 1982, once again all she had with her was bags. She showed me a magazine she had read during the journey that contained pictures of the garden show on the island of Mainau, which she would have liked to see. But it was not to be; her heart gave out and the ambulance took her to the nearby Feldkirch Hospital where we visited her the following day in intensive care. She recognised the flowers she had asked her grandchildren to bring, but she was no longer able to express her joy. She died on 8th May 1982 at the age of ninety-three. We buried her in Graz next to her husband. The grave was subsequently moved, and the headstone now stands in the little cemetery in Hüttenberg, where her parents and sisters had a cross as well.

After my seventieth birthday I began to scale down my research trips. I had constructed my life organically, step by step, and now it was time to simplify it again at the same pace. Just as the Dalai Lama once said to me, you cannot leap from the ground floor to the tenth floor, and equally, if you jumped ten floors down you would break every bone on your body. My regular television appearances were winding down. The trips I now went on no longer demanded that much physical effort, and were not really expeditions at all.

I had always wanted to get to know the Kingdom of Bhutan better;

with its marvellous architecture, ice-covered mountains, monasteries and people, it offered many opportunities. In 1982 and subsequent years, I made a number of journeys to the "Land of the Dragon", until finally the single newspaper published in the capital Thimpu wrote that I knew Bhutan better than the natives. Despite this, I was never captivated by Bhutan in the same way as other countries, whose customs and manners fascinated me and filled the pages of my diary. Everything is always well-organised in Bhutan, the accommodation is clean, and the porters never go on strike, even on remote trekking routes. On the other hand they are expensive and have to be paid in advance; backpackers who propose to cater for their own needs are not issued with visas. This may be a logical way for the little kingdom to protect its cultural and natural patrimony, but the visitor is hemmed in every step of the way by rules and regulations that leave him no freedom, and the country's lush charm loses something of its friendliness. But tourists have only themselves to blame for this situation if they make their way inconsiderately through the rows of monks deep in prayer to satisfy their selfish curiosity with tape recorders and flash guns. They would never go up to the altar in St Stephen's Cathedral in Vienna during a mass to take a close-up shot of the monstrance. During seven visits to Bhutan I was able to take photos of all the major shrines and temples, and when I later wanted to show this beauty to my friends, it was very disappointing when we were not allowed in.

In the spring of 1983 I travelled to Bhutan to see the great Thangka Festival in Paro and record it on film. I read in the newspaper that Michael de Bakey had carried out a successful heart operation on King Leopold in Houston. Back in Liechtenstein at the beginning of September, I received an invitation from d'Argenteuil, and though my diary was full of appointments, my concern for the King, and a kind of sixth sense, made me drop everything and travel straight to Belgium. As always, we studied maps, looked at photographs and revisited old memories. Leopold seemed to have recovered, so I did not even ask how the operation had gone. As on many other occasions, he gave me a little bag of walnuts. During a journey in the Lower Ardennes many years before he had been given a walnut tree with an unusual feature:

the nuts were "paper walnuts" with thin shells that could be cracked just by being pressed in the hand, and they were almost twice the size of the walnuts in Austria. It was a day of great togetherness, and I went back home having set my mind at rest.

Less than two weeks later Jean-Pierre Gosse phoned us from Brussels to say that King Leopold had succumbed to his heart trouble during the night. It was 25th September 1983. I was very grateful that I had followed my instinct and seen my friend one last time.

In the autumn Carina and I were planning another trip to Bhutan, and this time we had invited our family doctor and friend Hermann Beilhack to come with us. According to Far Eastern custom, you should spoil your "uncle doctor" as long as you are well. We landed at the military airport of Bagdogra, which had been built by the Allies during the Second World War so they could fly direct to China over the Himalayas and support Chiang Kai-shek against the Japanese. President Franklin Delano Roosevelt had sent a mission to Lhasa in 1942 under Ilya Tolstoy to ask the Tibetan government for permission to fly over Tibet to China. The Tibetans gave consent for aid items only, but not weapons. As a present Tolstoy brought the seven-year-old Dalai Lama a Patek Philippe watch showing the date and the phases of the moon. As ever, His Holiness wanted to see what lay within. Other watches had been successfully mended, but the works of this one were too complicated, and only the Swiss manufacturers were able to fix it. I later met Ilya Tolstoy in New York, and he gave me some of his photos of Lhasa.

When travelling from Bagdogra to Darjeeling, it is best to reserve seats on the narrow gauge railway in good time rather than taking a taxi. The locomotive has to be restocked with wood and water several times during the journey, and it crosses the road at least fifty times. Sometimes the driver also has to stop because there is an elephant standing on the tracks. Half of the journey is through extensive tea plantations, and when the train has reached two thousand feet you pass the first Lamaitic monastery, Ghoom, dominated by the backdrop of Kangchenjunga.

I once spent the night with Senator Günther Klinge in the great

Mount Everest Hotel in Darjeeling during the New Year, after he had presented a Tibetan medical centre with pill-making machines. We sat in the unheated dining room in a privileged position in front of the open hearth, where we were burned in front and frozen at the back. To celebrate, my friend ordered the best bottle of French red with the usual request for it to be served at "room temperature". The waiter did as he was asked, but at a temperature of eight degrees at most, we were not able to appreciate the expensive wine.

Since then I have preferred to stay at the smaller Windermere Hotel. It is an institution, as old as its owner Mrs. Thondrub, who had celebrated her ninetieth birthday shortly before our arrival. Without asking, each guest gets a hot water bottle in their bed – the rooms are unheated – and a chamber pot to save going all the way to the lavatory on the chilly landing. It is a hotel in the old English style, and you have to arrive for dinner on time. The guest book contains the names and drawings of the famous visitors who used to come to the cool hill station to escape the summer heat of India.

The only way to get to Sikkim was in old jeeps, a journey along narrow, winding valley roads at an altitude of nearly two thousand metres. At first the route passes through the steeply rising tea plantations, then through deciduous woods, now with trees planted along the edge of the road to produce quinine, which is essential for combating malaria. Women sit by the side of the road separating the bark from the wood with powerful blows of their fists. Our papers were checked at the big modern suspension bridge over the river Tista, and this took long enough for us to have a cup of tea and buy ripe papayas several pounds in weight. Further upstream, we were again kept waiting because of military convoys travelling in the opposite direction. In 1975, Indian troops had marched into Sikkim and abolished the monarchy, declaring the country the twenty-second state of the Indian Union.

The royal family in Gangtok invited us to call on them, and Coocoola and Carina met for the first time. We also met Coocoola's adult sons. The crown prince came first in the archery competition in the palace park; his was the third generation I had come across, because I had also known Coocoola's father. On the other side of the valley we visited Rumthek, the largest monastery of Sikkim, where we were

given special permission to see the golden stupa of Karmapa Rinpoche
– who had already passed away – with its abundant votive offerings.

For me, all this brought back nostalgic memories of the past. My
friends, who had no point of comparison, seemed content, but my
intention had been to show them the people and the landscape I
had described so enthusiastically, and now it did not have the same
charm. Ugly great hotels had been built in Gangtok, the streets were
overflowing with buses and military vehicles, and my old friends in
Sikkim had no time, because they were "very busy".

When we left Gangtok we saw that many of the changes introduced
by the Indians and Nepalese since the annexation of Sikkim to the
Indian Union in 1975 had had beneficial effects. The road was fringed
on both sides with plantings of cardamom, a native plant, and the dark
pods of the expensive spice could be made out on the reed-like stalks.
Cardamom belongs to the ginger family, and it is used in Austrian
Christmas baking because of its hot, spicy flavour, as well as being
indispensable for making *Lebkuchen*. In English this cake is called
gingerbread, and we call it "pepper bread". Suddenly, we had to stop,
and were only able to continue at walking pace, because for hundreds
of metres half the road was covered by mountains of ginger root. The
farmers on the steep slopes of the Tista Valley specialised in "authentic
ginger", and now the Indian wholesalers came to collect the spicy roots
in trucks. On the world market ginger is used not just as a medicine and
in baking, but also in the form of crystallised ginger and ginger ale.

Sikkim was behind us, and now we travelled through the tea gardens
of Assam to the Bhutan border station at Phuntsoling. Indians and
Bhutanese thronged beneath an enormous triumphal arch, crossing the
border unchecked, but tourists have to wait until every document has
been examined; the tour guide deals with this while the visitors have
a cup of tea. The first place we went was the post office, because there
is a unique range of stamps. Only after a few kilometres could you tell
you were in a Buddhist country, with stupas and temples. The symbol
of the dragon could be seen everywhere, including on the yellow flag
of Bhutan. The national religion, Drukpa Kagyupa, is one of the many
Buddhist schools; the word "druk", dragon, is the basis of the country's
name, Druk Yul. So we were in the "Land of the Thunder Dragon", the

last remaining Buddhist kingdom in the Himalayas.

Our journey by minibus to the capital Thimpu took all day, and the altitude of two and a half thousand metres was a blessing after the heat of India. In the city centre you can have a sandwich or a Black Forest gateau in the Swiss Coffee Shop – the pastry chef learned his trade at the Salzburg School of Cookery. Sunday was market day, and large quantities of fruit and vegetables were for sale. But it is best not to linger by the meat stall, because all the flies are enough to turn anyone into a vegetarian. A typical figure carried a heavy box on his back, gradually revealing its contents. He unwound numerous silk and brocade cloths, like layers of clothing, until gradually a *trashi gomang* appeared – roughly translated, a fortune box with many doors. These were raised up on hinges, one on each of the four sides, revealing colourful images of gods and votive offerings; then the man opened more little doors with his nimble fingers, finally using a little hook to gain access to the centre, where his personal divinity, made of bronze, resided. The crowd watched in fascination, touching the box with their foreheads and placing money in front of it. There are only a few such shrines in the entire country, and all of them are well known. I have seen twenty of them, sometimes having to walk all day to meet the owner, if he was working in the fields, since the *trashi* would normally only be shown on certain festival days.

You should visit Bhutan at least twice, once in the spring when the cherry trees are in blossom, and a second time in autumn. In the spring you can see the fruit blossom in the orchards, and there is the famous festival in Paro, but the smoke of dung fires in the fields means the air is less clear than in the autumn. Over the years, I have seen many hot springs, and noted their position on a map. This map shows the fault line in the Himalayas where tectonic shifts make the surface of the Earth open up. In Bhutan monks told me to wash with soap before entering one of the basins. Sometimes there is a larger pool for horses and pack animals beneath the one for people, where the wounds on their backs can be washed. To build up their reserves, they get buckets and buckets of the hot, salty spring water mixed with barley flour.

In the first years after Bhutan was opened up to tourism, a road from east to west was built, but you still had to go the four hundred kilometres back to your starting point. This was particularly difficult during the monsoon when the frequent landslides might mean the journey took longer than planned. Today things are much easier, because there is a good road from Dzong Trashigang direct to the Indian airport Gauhati. This saves time, so that it is possible to visit somewhere like Chorten Cora in the north, the most beautiful of all the stupas of Bhutan. You leave the main road in Dogsum, taking a winding route to the northeast. I always hasten to show my friends the chain bridge at the beginning, which I discovered years before. It is probably the last remaining bridge built by Thangdong Gyalpo, and is still in use today five hundred years later. It remains a mystery how he managed to weld the links of the chain in such a way that the iron did not rust.

The Cora Stupa is in open country, and we had a picnic in a meadow in front of it next to the raging glacier stream, surrounded by colourful cosmos, the most common flower of Bhutan. Prayer mills are turned by little streams, and a bell chimes at each revolution. A jet of water disappeared into a low hut where a man sat at a lathe – the only practitioner of his trade I had seen in the Himalayas. The birch tea bowls are easy to make, but on the floor there are gourd-like growths from deciduous trees, and they seldom remain whole when turned on the lathe. A single bowl with rich veining can bring in a tidy profit. In Lhasa, high-ranking monks or members of the nobility used to wrap valuable bowls up in silk cloths, and to protect them during journeys they were placed in finely worked metal holders.

A little way north of Cora, a reserve for the last hundred black-necked cranes has been established; when a power plant was built in Yamdrok Yumso, it got too noisy for them there. These migratory birds come twice a year, and ornithologists keep track of them by putting rings on their legs. A team of helpers has to endure weeks in the hide under the leadership of an experienced ornithologist, because black-necked cranes are incredibly shy birds. In Bhutan, the only opportunity to track them is in winter, and when the team finally manage to net a crane, it gets a spot of dye on its left wing and a coloured ring engraved with a number on its right foot. Later, observers can follow its route with binoculars.

It had started raining, and our two thousand metre descent turned into an adventure. We had to keep getting out in the mud to push the car – but that was better than staying inside as it slid about. Late that evening, we reached our lodgings in Trashigang, and this in itself amounted to a stroke of luck.

We had asked a Bhutanese student to come with us and explain various things. He now came to convey the request of his director for me to speak at the Jesuit-run school. The first Bhutanese college in Kanglung is run on the lines of an English boarding school, and this gave me the chance to answer some of my questions about the language. I generally managed to get by very well with the Tibetan I had learned in Lhasa, but sometimes people told me they only spoke Dzongkha, and not Tibetan. The language teacher told me that the government had attempted to make Dzongkha the national language, but the sacred books were written exclusively in Tibetan. He thanked me in passing for the Tibetan typewriter I had designed, saying it was indispensable.

Although there had always been close relations between Lhasa and Thimpu, there was also a certain rivalry. After the Chinese invasion of Tibet, the differences were particularly emphasised in order to prevent the occupation of Bhutan. The four thousand Tibetans who had fled to the Land of the Dragon had to adopt Bhutanese nationality, or else leave the country once more.

The people of Bhutan live at peace in ideal harmony with nature, and all their basic needs can be provided for within their own country. No one ever suffers from hunger or cold. The only reason Bhutan is considered one of the poorest countries in the world is that the standard of living is measured according to cash transactions. But in Bhutan, barter with local products continues to be the main form of exchange. Nor does the country need to struggle to discover its identity; the unique architecture of the fortresses and monasteries is proof enough of a culture stretching back over millennia. When you leave a Bhutanese village with its monks and farmers, you take with you the lesson that enjoyment of life and making do with what you have are enough to prevent pessimism. So the people of Bhutan are rich, even though the statistics of our Western world place them at the bottom of the economic ladder.

In the autumn of 1988 I was accompanied once again by Ernst Skardarassy, the owner of an exclusive skiing hotel in the Arlberg; even before the war, I had joined him in downhill races such as the Kandahar Race in St Anton. He was one year older than me, always followed his own regular rhythm, and was never the first or the last to arrive at the end of the day. His nephew Franz Moosbrugger had come, too, together with his friend Gert Rainer. We were a harmonious group, and we were also joined by Alois Anwander and the Staempflis, a Swiss couple. In terms of stamina, too, we seemed to be well-matched. However, an altitude of five thousand metres acts as a magical boundary for those who are in the Himalayas for the first time, added to which there is the effect of the unfamiliar food, having to sleep in a cramped tent, and the sudden changes in the weather.

We had already been trekking for a few days, and I had advised my friends more than once to wear sunglasses and a hat even if it was cloudy, and told them to check their pulse from time to time. We had a long way to go, via the Khar Dungla. We camped in the lee of an enormous stone block beneath the pass, at an altitude of four thousand nine hundred metres. During the night it snowed, and it took some time the following morning to pack up the wet tents. On Monday 3rd October we began our ascent; we were slightly late setting off. The ledges and the scree were covered by snow, but we all reached the 5,040 metre high pass with the first rays of sunshine. We rested a little further down, where there was no snow, among azaleas, gentian and edelweiss; they were still flowering abundantly. There was nothing to hint at the misfortune that was about to befall us, except perhaps when Franz said he had taken two sleeping tablets during the night. He went at the same pace as everyone else, and when we camped on the River Pochu that evening he blew up his Uncle Ernst's air mattress just as on the previous days.

On the morning of 4 October, Franz was in a very bad way. He could barely speak, and his legs gave way beneath him. We tried to put him on our single yak to take him to Tarena, a lower-lying camp. My first thoughts were of sunstroke and altitude sickness, and I gave him some medicine. It was only then that Rainer told me Franz had just recovered from a mild case of flu or a chill. Rather than having physical reserves to call on, he had come in a weakened state, thinking he would be able to manage. Unfortunately, that was not the case. He was getting worse and worse, and we had to do something. Two of our Bhutanese porters set off to fetch a doctor who was following the same route in a group ahead of us. One of the men would carry straight on to the military post in Lhedi to summon a helicopter.

During the night, Ernst and I took turns to watch over Franz's bed. Around midnight I sat him up a little and gave him some corn soup to drink, praising him and stroking his hair. Alois joined me, and we straightened the crooked mattress. His lips were dry, his breathing heavy, and his eyes mostly stayed shut. There was a moment when I gave him something to drink, and he opened his eyes and smiled.

Not wanting to do nothing, I did something completely stupid. I wanted to know what had happened to the helicopter, and the following morning I set off towards the military post. I kept imagining I could hear the sound of a helicopter, but unfortunately it existed only in my worried imagination. It was Wednesday the sixth of October. After several hours' arduous climbing through thick forest, I reached open country. The crops had been harvested, and the only person I saw at the farm was a monk at prayer; the farmers had already gone down the valley. I headed back to Franz and Ernst, but to cap it all, I lost my way. The weather was bad, it had rained all night, and with the boulders and the mud, I made slow progress. As I struggled onwards, I said to myself, "Well, Heinrich, these are the last miles you will ever walk in the thin air of the Himalayas. You're not ever doing it again!" This gave me the strength to get back to the camp at Tarena.

I could see from Ernst's face what had happened; we embraced and sat for hours next to our dead friend. Around two in the morning, one of the two Bhutanese returned, speaking of "bad luck"; he had not been able to find the doctor, and the bad weather meant the helicopter could not take off.

On the morning of 7 October the weather had improved sufficiently to allow the Indian Air Force helicopter to take off. It landed at around eleven o'clock, and Franz's body was wrapped in two sleeping bags and placed on board. Ernst and Gert went too, and eventually the helicopter took us all to Thimpu. After the third flight on the following day, we were all together again. A simple wooden coffin stood in an open tent in the park beneath our hotel, surrounded by six red-robed monks who lit butter lamps and said prayers. I was moved, and thanked them for their pious gesture. I felt that this was a way of putting ecumenical ideas into practice without a lot of discussion. For Ernst, the formalities involved in transporting the dead body to Europe now began. Thanks to the support of the Austrian Embassy in New Delhi, Gert and Ernst were able to fly home with the coffin.

During my long life, I have seen a great deal of misfortune, often with fatal consequences. Hermann Buhl and Fritz Kasparek were climbing partners of mine, and both fell to their deaths when snow cornices collapsed. In March 1936 Franz Kulterer died before my very eyes when he fell over a rock during a downhill race on the Hochreichart, and his elder brother Ludwig subsequently fell to his death on Montasch in the Julian Alps. The Italian downhill skier Sertorelli died right next to me when he ran into a tree on the Kreuzeck in Garmisch-Partenkirchen – no-one had heard of safety helmets then. But nothing has ever touched me so much as the death of Franz Moosbrugger, and my thoughts often return to that night in the Himalayas when I sat at his deathbed together with his uncle Ernst.

To complete an expedition successfully, there are a few prerequisites. The most important thing is one's mental attitude, the illusion – in the spirit of Alfred Wegener – that you are trying to do something that on the face of it seems impossible. Nonetheless you pursue it, just as he pursued his theory of continental drift. Naturally, a cheerful spirit is essential to keep things on an even keel. As leader of the expedition, you have to keep your optimism constantly alive, constantly creating the illusion of a positive situation so that the team does not lose heart, which can lead to accidents. An inexperienced team-mate relies on the leader's experience and is taken in by the leader's confident manner. My great role model, the geographer Alfred Wegener, possessed these qualities in full measure, and described the process in plain words. Wegener's accounts made scientific adventure accessible to anyone who reads travel books.

In 1953 I met the French polar explorer Paul-Émile Victor, and he described the course of Alfred Wegener's final Greenland expedition to me; twenty years later, Victor had stood, his heart racing, in exactly the very spot in the ice where Wegener's research station had once been. As leader of the expedition, in 1933 Wegener had made preparations for his three colleagues to spend the winter in the "Eismitte" station; together with the twenty-one-year-old Eskimo Rasmus Villumsen, he brought them the food supplies they would need. They celebrated his fiftieth birthday together, and after just one day of rest, Wegener set off once more with his faithful Eskimo companion at a temperature of minus fifty degrees. A final photo was taken of the brave men wrapped in furs before they set off on the four hundred kilometre route back to the station on the west coast. They never arrived.

LADAKH – LITTLE TIBET

On 27 October 1986 the Dalai Lama was invited to attend the World Day of Prayer for Peace in Assisi, Italy, together with the heads and representatives of all the world's great religions. It was surely no coincidence that he was seated next to Pope John Paul II during the proceedings.

In 1988, I accompanied the Dalai Lama when he came to Germany for a series of lectures and meetings with politicians in Bonn and Cologne. We visited the house where the former German Chancellor Konrad Adenauer had lived, and were shown around by his son. During his visit, the Dalai Lama specifically requested that he be allowed to visit one of the local monasteries, so we drove in convoy to the thousand-year-old Benedictine Abbey of Maria Laach. He was particularly interested in the cells where the monks lived in seclusion. In Buddhist Tibet there are similar monastic retreats and several devout monks who choose to live the solitary life of a hermit for three or more years – and in some cases for a lifetime – hidden away in remote caves with their entrances walled up and only a novice monk to bring them essential food and water, which is passed through a small gap in the stonework. Even this gap has a curtain across it to prevent daylight falling on the skin of the hermit. After visiting the monks' cells, we wandered through the extensive gardens of the monastery. The Dalai Lama admired the orchid house, and I bought a rare red genista.

Between 1976 and 1991, I was a frequent visitor to Ladakh, or "Little Tibet", as it is often called. Back in 1944, Peter Aufschnaiter and I had travelled through the eastern part of the region during our escape, but in later years it became more and more difficult to obtain permission to enter the area. After the Chinese occupation of Tibet, Ladakh remained closed to tourists, and it was only in 1974 that the Indian government again started issuing entry permits on an individual, case by case basis. Previously, they had been unwilling to do so because of the frequent border clashes that occurred along the military road in the north of Ladakh, which formed the contentious "Line of Control" between India and Pakistan. When the entry restrictions were finally relaxed, my long quest for my lost homeland of Tibet, which had taken me to so many different parts of the world, finally came to an end. Although I have always found the culture of Bhutan to be rather alien, by contrast Ladakh was a place that I really took to my heart, and I visited the classic tourist attractions on many occasions. As I write this in 2002, this "classic tour" is sadly no longer possible, due to the recurrent unrest in the region.

The tour begins in Srinagar, the capital of the Indian state of Jammu & Kashmir, the territory to which Ladakh now belongs. I stayed at the Nedous Hotel, from where Sven Hedin set out on his famous 1904 expedition. There is rarely any need to travel on foot in Ladakh, but the aspirant explorer does need to be prepared to accept with grim stoicism the risks inherent in the bus journeys over the mountain passes on the dusty, serpentine roads with their alarming lack of guard rails. In former times, the only way to reach the capital city of Leh was via the Soji-La, which, although only three thousand metres high, is often covered in snow until well into June and is therefore impassable until the military clear the road, which they now do regularly in order to keep the pass open for the ever-growing tourist industry.

It was certainly no hardship to spend some time on one of the houseboats on Wular Lake whilst waiting for the pass to be cleared. In May the surface of the lake is covered with blossoming water lilies and servants flit between the houseboats serving chilled drinks and the aromatic, highly spiced dishes that are typical of the Kashmir region. From Wular Lake, one can easily make a quick excursion to the hill station of Gulmarg for a view of Nanga Parbat, or play a round of golf on a course where the grass is kept short by a flock of sheep. I would, however, warn the unwary tourist against purchasing any of the musk deer glands that are offered for sale here, since they are in fact just stinking lumps of offal skilfully sewn into goat's skin, and are not the genuine article at all.

A gondola waits to take you across to the lake shore; you lie on cushions while traders offer you carpets and wooden carvings, and other typical products of the region. Great caution is required, particularly when purchasing saffron, which is cultivated in huge fields. Saffron is expensive wherever one buys it and the traders often dye similarly shaped leaves yellow and offer them as the real thing. I know from personal experience that many of the local merchants are not to be trusted. On one occasion, a trader specialising in Tibetan artefacts moored his boat next to ours and offered us some "ancient" and "rare" Tibetan scroll paintings for sale. Since I have often found a genuinely rare example for my collection amongst a bundle of *thangkas* I asked him to show me what he had. Without exception they were all new or poor copies of originals, which I refused to buy. As he was rolling them up again he turned to me and said "You are wrong, sahib – even Heinrich Harrer buys from me!"

I also recall a similar occasion, when a woman acquaintance of mine was keen to purchase a mask from one of these traders, who assured her that this very rare piece had already been reserved for Heinrich Harrer. After extensive haggling, she acquired the mask and presented it to me for my museum. It transpired that the mask was a fake, cleverly disguised with black boot polish to look like an original. It also pays to be cautious when buying bronzes; new pieces are sometimes "aged" by submerging them for a while in cesspits or drains, and even so-called experts have on occasion been fooled by the seemingly authentic "patina" that the bronze acquires.

Once across the Soji-La, another few days journey through the Muslim region brings you to Mulbe and the eight metre high statue of the Bodhisattva Maitreya, the "Buddha of the Future", carved from the solid rock of a cliff, which is emblematic of the predominance of Tibetan Buddhism, or Lamaism, in this region. The monasteries, the clear, clean air, the indescribably beautiful colours of the landscape and the happy, contented people are all reminiscent of Tibet. Even the ice-covered six and seven thousand metre peaks are here – the mountains of the Western Himalaya, the throne room of the Gods – and, to the north, three of the great eight-thousanders of the Karakorum keep watch over Little Tibet. Within Ladakh there are more than a hundred monasteries, fully occupied by monks and nuns and equipped with whole libraries of books, ancient masks and costumes for the famous dances and mystery plays that are performed here. On the Fatu-La, a

4,100 metre high mountain pass on the Srinagar-Leh highway, the five-coloured flags flutter in the breeze next to the windhorse, and carry the prayers to the Gods. Blue represents the sky and white the clouds, red stands for fire, green for water and yellow for the earth. A cairn of rocks hides rare stones and fossils found by the devout pilgrims on their way across the pass to Lamayuru Monastery, a Tibetan Buddhist *gompa* surrounded by fields of green barley that could easily have served as a model for the mythical Shangri-La.

When I visited, the friendly abbot had tea and biscuits served. He knew that the owner, Drigung Rinpoche, was a friend of mine from my time in Lhasa. Beneath the monastery, the many threshing machines bore testimony to the extent of the agricultural benefice of this tenth century monastery. I once met a monk at Lamayuru, who showed me sixteen pages of a little music book, in which the waves of the musical tones were illustrated with beautiful vignettes. The booklet must have been more than a hundred years old; there were drawings on both sides of the paper and the pages still bore fatty stains from the fingers of the monks, who would drink butter tea between reciting their litanies. I gave one of the pages to the Austrian conductor Karl Böhm for his eightieth birthday.

The road from Lamayura drops down to the Indus in a series of more than sixty hairpin bends; on one of them, the turning circle is so tight that the driver has to bring the bus to a stop with the offside front wheel right on the edge of the thousand metre drop, reverse a short way and then wrench the steering wheel round using all his strength (the buses do not have servo-assisted steering) to make it round the bend. This is usually done to rapturous applause from the relieved passengers, all of whom are well aware of the stories of accidents caused by brake failure on this stretch of road. To save petrol the drivers like to turn the engine off and coast downhill in neutral, but whenever I travelled this route as the leader of a group, I used to sit right up front next to the driver and try to insist that he used his gears to brake on the downhill stretches. Whether or not he actually did this seemed to depend on how much baksheesh he was offered.

A good bridge carries the road across the Indus, which is a wide river at this point, to the town of Khalsi, where there are the oldest and largest walnut trees I have ever seen. It was pleasantly warm here when I passed through and the apricot trees were laden with yellow fruit. The apricot oil is sold in filthy old beer bottles and is said to be particularly good for sensitive skin. Sixty kilometres upriver you come to a narrow rope bridge; this is where the bus stops. I recommend wearing a pair of tough gloves when crossing the bridge, as the ropes are rough. It is certainly worth the effort, for just a short walk away on the opposite bank of the river lies the monastery of Alchi. With its large collection of well preserved frescoes and other early Buddhist works of art, Alchi Monastery should be on the itinerary of any visitor to Ladakh.

The city of Leh lies at a similar altitude to Lhasa and after several visits it has become something of a meeting place for old friends of mine. On one of my early trips to Leh, I gave copies of my book about Ladakh to the Rani and to Baku Rinpoche, the first elected people's representative in the Delhi parliament. The young Drugpa Rinpoche was keen to learn French, so on a subsequent visit I took some tapes for him, together with a pair of spectacles with a built-in hearing aid that his teacher, Tuse Rinpoche, had requested. My friend Karma has a tailor's shop next to the great temple and over the years it had become something of a tradition that my travel companions purchase one of his made-to-measure Tibetan coats. Karma's wife also makes delicious *momos*, while Karma himself is something of an expert in rare scroll paintings and bronzes and is more than a match for the devious Kashmiri traders.

Whenever there were any keen golfers in my group, I always took them to the officers' mess in Leh, as the General in command was also the president of the Leh Golf Club. The eighteen-hole course is entirely devoid of vegetation but the caddies are very obliging and place your ball on a little mat on the sand, and when you reach the "green", which is actually hard packed sand mixed with black motor oil, they mark out the putting line for you, too. Golfers of average ability are always delighted to discover that the thin air means they can hit tee shots of more than three hundred metres, and I once took a world-famous pro golfer to Leh, who promised he would pay for the whole trip just for the opportunity of establishing a new world distance record on the high altitude course!

The continued unrest in Indian Kashmir, in the western part of Ladakh on the long border with Pakistan, eventually induced the military to construct a new highway in the east of the region. The fertile Kulu Valley can be now reached from Delhi by road or by air, and contains many kilometres of orchards that provide the whole of India with a supply of delicious apples and other fruit. Before checking into your hotel in Manali it is worth stopping in Naggar to visit the little slate-built museum dedicated to the life and work of the Russian philosopher and artist Nicholas Roerich, who lived a secluded life here until his death in 1947. When I first visited, the key to the museum was kept by the same old lady housekeeper who had looked after Roerich until he died. I had also visited the Nicholas Roerich Museum in New York on one of my trips there, and was just as impressed as the Tibetan visitors were by the colours, the atmosphere and the luminescence of the tempera paintings of Tibetan monasteries, stupas and mountains that hung there. The elderly lady at the museum in Naggar explained the significance of the paintings in simple terms, but it was obvious from her reverential tone that, even twenty years after his death, her admiration for the great man was still every bit as deep as it had been when famous contemporaries like Einstein and Shaw had suggested he be nominated for the Nobel Peace Prize.

Manali has developed into a large town, and has a ghetto inhabited by Tibetan refugees, where Dr Trachi Tsering has her practice. She was studying medicine in Lhasa during my time there, and has managed to save many valuable medical books, prescriptions and instruments. The Dalai Lama pays an annual visit to the hot springs in Manali, and a gifted artist runs a school here that teaches *thangka* painting. A very large and very old Gingko Biloba tree has been left standing amongst all the new buildings as a sacred Buddhist relic, and its history is recorded on a plaque.

From Manali it is a fifty kilometre bus journey along the new military road to the top of the 4,000 metre Rotang Pass. The road leads through meadows carpeted with rare varieties of primroses, and higher up there is such a proliferation of wulfenia, a plant only seldom found in the Alps, that you can not place one foot in front of the other without crushing some of the delicate flowers. The famous Himalayan

Blue Poppy can also be seen here amongst the rocks and cliffs. Tents provided the only accommodation on this stretch, to the consternation of my wife, who had never been on an expedition before, let alone spent a bitterly cold night under canvas. She only really felt comfortable when she was sitting in the bus again the following day. The unique colours of the arid landscape and the thought of our destination ahead provided ample compensation for the tedious bus journey over several further high passes, amongst them the 5,000 metre Bara Lacha-la, and everyone felt much better when we finally arrived at the upper reaches of the Indus and saw the first villages and monasteries of Ladakh. An evening face wash in icy cold water also helped to restore the mood of the party.

This long bus journey over the mountain passes has the advantage of allowing your body time to acclimatise. The problems caused by the lack of oxygen and the dry air at altitude can be offset by drinking plenty of liquids and acclimatising slowly. Ladakh lies at an average height of four thousand metres, and climbing the steps up to the monasteries will be found to be much easier if one has first heeded this advice. At the start of the Trans Himalayan Highway there is a sign with a picture of the Tibetan snow lion and an inscription that reads "Highest Road in the World. Here you can talk to God." I am told that the northern province of Nubra is also worth a visit; unfortunately I never managed to get there, since the Nuba Mountains lie within one of the last "Restricted Areas".

By far the best new development for tourists has been the construction of the landing strip at Leh, which makes non-stop flights to and from Delhi possible and means the visitor can utilise his time better and spend more of it in Ladakh. A visit to the tiny kingdom of Zanskar is always worthwhile, but it should be noted that access is difficult and the journey involves some demanding trekking. The best route starts just beyond the Rotang Pass, heads west and after three days arrives at Phugdal Monastery. Hundreds of years ago, a hermit lived in a cave here until it became a site of pilgrimage, but what attracts the Tibetologists is a memorial plaque that commemorates the fact that it was here, in the middle of the 19th century, that the Hungarian philologist Sandor Körösi Csoma began translating the

"Tibetan Bible". Csoma originally travelled to the north of India on a quest to trace the origin of his forbears, the Magyar, before falling prey to the charms of the Tibetans and publishing his *Tibetan Grammar and Dictionary*. To this day, he remains an inspirational figure for young students of Tibet everywhere.

The Tibetan Holy Scriptures comprise three hundred volumes and are printed in Narthang, to the south of Shigatse and in Kham, near Derge. To transport the printed sheets of paper alone would require a convoy of twenty yaks; if the wooden book covers that contain all three hundred pages of each volume were to be included, the number of pack animals would have to be doubled. The printing blocks are produced by monks in a painstaking process that involves carving the letters in mirror image onto smooth wooden blocks; in effect, the sacred writings are actually more wood carvings than books. In Narthang, where I observed the process, there are several buildings that are stacked to the eaves with more than a hundred thousand printing blocks. Of incomparably greater value than the printed volumes are the books that were commissioned by well-to-do families and hand written by several monks over a period of many years, with each holy name highlighted with yellow saffron dye.

For me, this world of wonder that is the Western Himalaya was like a journey into the past, and a reunion with the Tibet of old that I had missed so terribly when I visited Lhasa in 1982. The Indian government has shown great tolerance in creating in Ladakh a safe refuge for Tibetan culture; it is a place where the people are deeply influenced by the landscape and by the teachings of Buddha. The Ladakhis still have oracles to whom they turn for advice in times of trouble; superstitions and miracles are still completely natural things for them. The world is huge, its diversity inexhaustible, and the differences between cultures often unfathomable, yet for all our differences, there is a common thread that runs through all cultural classes and is found everywhere – it is the desire of humanity to protect itself against evil, to banish danger, to ensure that strength and health prevail, and to propagate our species. Only an arrogant and intolerant fanatic and obsessive pragmatist would ever seek to change that.

ENCOUNTERS

During one of my visits to New York I had made the acquaintance of an agent whose business it was to find the money, actors and directors needed to make big budget movies and to bring them all together in one place. In the summer of 1986 the agent went to Vaduz, Liechtenstein and acquired the movie option for my book *Seven Years in Tibet*. Various screenplays were considered, and there was talk of getting Robert Redford or Kevin Costner to play the lead role. The option was renewed year after year and in the meantime I began archiving my expedition photographs – there were more than one hundred thousand in all – at the Heinrich Harrer Museum. In 1994 I received a telephone call from the New York agent. He sounded excited. Tristar Pictures had succeeded in getting Brad Pitt to play me in the film, and Jean-Jacques Annaud had agreed to direct it.

To familiarise myself with the work of this young actor, I watched *A River Runs Through It*, directed by Robert Redford, in which Brad Pitt plays the lead. I already knew of Jean-Jacques Annaud, and greatly admired the French director's work. His film *The Bear* had been very well received in my home country. After almost a decade of to-ing and fro-ing the contracts were finally exchanged and on 28th September 1995 Annaud visited us for the first time. We got on well from the start and enjoyed a mutual respect that exists to this day. We met the screenplay writer, a pretty and cheerful American by the name of Becky Johnston, at the Banff Mountain Film Festival, where Lutz Maurer's documentary of my life, part of the ORF's *Land der Berge* series, won a special award.

Filming on location in Tibet and the Himalaya was prevented by the Chinese, but Annaud came up with the idea of moving the whole production to the Argentinean Andes, where similar conditions to Tibet could be found. It proved to be the ideal location, and when the Tibetan film extras arrived they had tears in their eyes – it was, they said, just like being in Tibet. My services were not really required as the crew was accompanied by Trethong, a former Minister of the

Tibetan Government in exile, who brought his expert knowledge of Tibetan costumes and ceremonies to the production. I knew Trethong well from my time in Tibet: during my first Christmas in Lhasa I had arranged a party for my friends at his late father's house. Jetsun Pemala, the sister of the Dalai Lama, played the role of her own mother, the Great Mother Gyayum Chenmo. Production costs were high, but there was enough money in the budget to fly in a herd of yaks to provide an additional touch of authenticity.

On 6th September 1996 the leading actors came to Austria with Annaud. Most of the film was already in the can, but Brad Pitt needed to brush up on his ice-skating skills and several members of the cast and crew also wanted to visit my museum in Hüttenberg. Because of Brad Pitt's huge popularity the visit had to be kept a closely guarded secret. It was a beautiful autumn day, and Annaud had a little video camera with him to record the event. I still have some of the stills of Brad Pitt and me standing on the balcony of our holiday home, surrounded by a sea of red geraniums.

Work on the film was now at an advanced stage and although I was not directly involved in the actual production, I still had one or two concerns that I wished to voice. I told Arnaud that it was fine by me if the scriptwriters wished to include a little love interest in the portrayal of my character – it would have been useless to protest, in any case, since Hollywood is a law unto itself – but that the role of Aufschnaiter, who had been dead for twenty years, ought to be played with a dignity that befitted the man's nobility of character. For me, David Thewlis' physical appearance and, above all, his calm, measured manner made him ideally suited to the role. My second request was that the film should be dedicated to the cause of the Tibetans, and should treat the Dalai Lama with the reverence and respect he so richly deserved.

We dined that evening at a cosy little inn tucked away in the hills near Hüttengerg and after a few glasses of beer Brad Pitt turned to me and said: "Heinrich, please don't believe everything you read about me in the newspapers!"

The visit of the film team had been a very pleasant and harmonious interlude, and we parted company with the promise of meeting up again at the premiere of the film in Hollywood. Annaud was really enthusiastic about John Williams' film score. Carina and I were just as pleased that everything seemed to be going so well.

At the beginning of 1997 I received an invitation to deliver the keynote lecture at the 25th anniversary celebrations of the Swedish Explorers' Club, to be held in Stockholm in February. It was a great honour. Carina and I waited in the foyer of the lecture theatre with the President of the club for the Swedish King and Queen to arrive, and after a brief exchange of pleasantries we went into the main hall, where I delivered my slide lecture to a packed house. After my closing remarks, His Majesty leapt athletically onto the stage in a spontaneous gesture and thanked me for my presentation. Later that evening at the gala dinner, Carina sat with Queen Sylvia while I dined at an adjacent table with Carl Gustav, the King of Sweden.

The King and I had plenty to chat about. He told me that he had twice taken part in the world-famous Wasa Ski Race and had completed the gruelling ninety kilometre course on both occasions. It was a notable achievement, since many competitors are forced to withdraw from the race by the stewards at the checkpoints if their progress is deemed to be too slow. The King was particularly interested in hearing about the kind of food I took with me on my expeditions to cold climates. His father, Gustav V, had been an archaeologist specialising in Celtic research, and had often worked in Carinthia. There was actually a man in my neighbourhood who had assisted him on his digs and had been given a Swedish medal, which he wore with pride. Talk naturally turned to Sven Hedin, whose bequest to the Stockholm Museum of Ethnography formed the largest and most important collection in the building. I visited the museum the day after my lecture and was greeted by the director, who presented me with a folder containing copies of the twenty three letters I had exchanged with the legendary explorer. I was allowed to view his original drawings, and to sit at his writing desk, the same desk I had photographed him at back in 1952. All in all, it was a very happy start to the year – one encounter with a king, and another with Tibetan culture.

It was not to last. Things took a rapid turn for the worse when the press, in anticipation of the imminent film premiere, it seemed, suddenly decided to publish the fact that, almost sixty years previously,

I had applied for membership of the Nazi Party, and had subsequently joined the SS. The story originated in Austria but within a few days the news had spread to Germany and across the Atlantic to America. In no time at all, the whole of Hollywood knew about it. I was baffled by this sudden interest, the more so since the facts of the matter had been common knowledge since my return from Tibet in 1952 – I had never made any attempt to hide them. I must admit that I was at a loss to explain why I had suddenly become an international celebrity – an overnight sensation, as it were – but it did make me wonder whether it really was all about me, or whether someone, somewhere wanted to damage the film and thus harm the Tibetan cause. Who was behind it all?

By the summer of 1998 my wife and I had got to know the correspondents of all the newspapers and magazines in the world, or so it seemed to us at the time. The journalists' expressions of gratitude and respect filled twenty-two pages of our guest book, but unfortunately their kind words only rarely matched those that subsequently appeared in print.

One day we received a telephone call from the magazine *Vanity Fair*, enquiring when it would be convenient for Helmut Newton to come and take my photograph. I must have hesitated a little, as the voice on the phone then commented that I would surely have no objection to being photographed by the most famous celebrity photographer of all time. Somewhat reluctantly, I told them I would be happy to oblige. Newton called me from Monte Carlo to fix a date for the shoot and asked me to reserve two rooms for him at the nearest five star hotel to our house in Hüttenberg. I told him I could only offer him a choice of countryside inns and he replied that that would make a pleasant change. The news that the great Helmut Newton was visiting the Harrers spread like wildfire, and friends and strangers alike turned up with books of photographs that they wanted signed.

Newton thought that the everyday clothes I was wearing were too conservative for his photographs and we finally agreed on a long loden overcoat with the collar turned up. His pretty young Monegasque assistant seemed to spend the whole time just handing him cameras and lenses. The shoot lasted two whole days. I spent hours standing around outside in dismal weather, striking poses that were completely at odds with my true character. Newton seemed happy with the results, however, and before he left he wrote a note in our guest book: "Heinrich, you are a wonderful model. Thank you for your patience. Yours, Helmut Newton. Hüttenberg, 6.8.1997." It finally transpired that Newton did the same thing with his camera that his journalist colleagues had done with their pencil and paper: they presented an image of a person that bore little resemblance to the real me.

When the press started publishing their articles, my wife and I had to decide whether we should remain silent or speak out and give our side of the story. After lengthy consultations with our lawyer in Vaduz, and with the English agent who handled the worldwide rights to my books, we opted for complete openness – after all, I had nothing to hide. At the time we had no idea that the smear campaign would turn out to be so vicious, or so lengthy.

The mistakes I made as a young man during a period of dictatorship are something I have now come to terms with. They are in the past. Even in democracies, politicians, idealists and opportunists make errors of judgement, and the latter generally come off best. In 1938, when I made my own mistakes, I was no longer a child, but although I had reached the age of consent I still lacked experience of the adult world. I was on the cusp of adulthood, at an age where one ought to be allowed to make mistakes, the better to learn from them. For my own piece of mind, it has been crucial for me to examine whether I acted culpably, and to consider the way I lived my life and conducted myself afterwards and to this day. As it says in the Bible, the wisest book in the world, "Ye shall know them by their fruits." In other words, you can tell what people are by what they do.

Fortunately, there were some brighter moments amongst all the doom and gloom. On 30th June 1997 I had the opportunity of meeting Simon Wiesenthal in Vienna. We talked for an hour and he gave me a signed copy of his book, which had been published to coincide with his eightieth birthday. I tried to explain to him the distress that had been caused to my wife and I by the articles that had recently appeared in the newspapers. "Look," he said, "We have a house on the edge of town, and when we go out into the garden to relax in the evenings there are bodyguards behind all the hedges, men whose job it is to protect us. We've got used to them now, and I just view them as part of the furniture." One of his secretaries took some photographs and I gave him copies of the most recent reports about my membership of the Nazi Party and the SS. Before I left, Wiesenthal promised to talk to his representative in Hollywood that very afternoon. However, even after this meeting there was no discernible improvement in the situation. The media, and in particularly the media in Hollywood, continued to represent me as a Nazi.

During this difficult time, it was a great comfort for me to have the opportunity to see the Dalai Lama again. He was on a tour of several European cities, and was due to visit the University of Trieste-Gorizia to receive an Honorary Degree in International and Diplomatic Sciences. The Tibetologist Enrico Fasano, who had previously visited the Heinrich Harrer Museum, had also asked me to deliver a lecture at the university. When the Dalai Lama had the stiff academic mortar board with its curious little tassel placed on his shaven head, he could not hide a grin of amusement – I must admit it really did look a little like fancy dress. Before giving his acceptance speech, he removed the unaccustomed scholarly garb and appeared once more as the world was used to seeing him – in his monk's robes and with his right shoulder bared.

That evening, Carina and I were invited to a private audience with the Dalai Lama in his hotel suite, where I presented him with a copy of my latest book of photographs, *Lost Lhasa*. He leafed through it, studying the old photographs closely, and his voice was hoarse with emotion as he turned to me and said: "Henrig, what a happy people we were, in a happy and free country." He was aware of my personal worries, as several journalists had already quizzed him about me, but his words of encouragement were spontaneous. "All you have to do is speak the truth," he said, "and emphasise the fact that you were in Tibet during those terrible Nazi times. In our struggle for freedom, the truth is the only weapon we possess."

In the Dalai Lama the Tibetans have a remarkable ambassador, a man with charisma and charm, who travels the world preaching religious tolerance and freedom. Due to his many commitments, we see less of each other these days, but when we do it is always a heart-warming experience. We often joke, and we use a vocabulary that is, perhaps, a little unusual when speaking to a God King. He calls me "Old Man" and I usually counter with the remark that he, too, is going bald. On one such occasion, I consoled him with the comment that "You can't have both, hair and brain," whereupon he laughed uproariously, as only he can, and with a mischievous glint in his eye told me: "You still have a head full of nonsense, Henrig!" By a pleasing coincidence, His Holiness and I share the same birthday, the 6th of July. I once asked him whether this was fate, divine providence, luck or coincidence. "All of these!" he replied with a smile.

Early in 1998, I received an invitation to go to Rome that June to receive the International Fregene Prize for Literature. The President of the jury, Marina Palletta, told me that previous recipients of the prize included Tennessee Williams, Vitorio Gassmann, Arthur Schlesinger and Henry Kissinger and that the award itself consisted of a beautiful statuette made by Angelo Canevari. To mark the twentieth anniversary of the literature prize, there were two awards made that year – the other went to the Norwegian author Jostein Gaarder for his bestseller "Sophie's World." We stayed in the seaside resort of Fregene and were driven from there to the Capitol in Rome, where the award ceremony was held. I was quite touched that the Austrian Ambassador to Italy, Günter Bierbaum, had also made the effort to attend. After the buffet supper I looked amongst the many statues of famous Romans for the bust of Cato the Younger, but failed to find it. During the last few months I had received many letters of support, several of which had quoted the words of Cato: "It is a terrible thing when we must answer to a generation that has not lived through the same events that we have." These words come from a tribune of the people some two thousand years ago, but it is sentiment that was echoed by Goethe in his '*Maximen und Reflexionen*': "An old man loses one of the most important rights of man: he is no longer judged by his peers."

It was a terrible time for Carina and me, and in the midst of it all were the celebrations held in Grindelwald in July 1998 to mark the sixtieth anniversary of the first ascent of the North Face of the Eiger, to which we were, of course, invited. A commemorative plaque was unveiled at the Eigerwand Station, and I do not think I have ever seen as many photographers and television cameras in my life as I did then. Anderl Heckmair was as calm and relaxed as ever, and took the whole media circus in his stride, whereas I could feel the tension in the air, and knew the real reason for all this interest: the swastika pennant in the rucksack and the text in the first Eiger book that had been written under my name. The Grindelwald mountain guides were less interested, but the press wished to speak to me about little else.

After our first ascent of the Eigerwand in 1938 souvenir hunters had helped themselves to all of the equipment we had left behind, including the often-mentioned rucksack. The Grindelwald guides told me that it had surfaced at the fortieth anniversary celebrations, where it was offered for sale, but at a price they were unwilling to pay. It was subsequently acquired by the museum of the Swiss Alpine Club in Berne. Now, sixty years after our climb, it was on display at the museum in Grindelwald. I recognised it immediately; in fact, I had inked my name on it and this was still clearly visible. Seeing my old rucksack again brought the memories flooding back of those dramatic days in the summer of 1938.

The keen climber will generally have two rucksacks: a large-capacity one, capable of holding forty litres or more of kit and used to carry all the gear he requires to be completely self-sufficient in the mountains, and a second, smaller one with no external pockets, a stripped-down version used for climbing. Before I set off for the Eiger my mother put a whole loaf of bread in my big rucksack and at the last minute brought me two thick slices of bread and butter and some apples, which I hurriedly stuffed into my climbing sack. I lashed both rucksacks to the pillion of my motorcycle with a spare forty metre climbing rope. My mother knew I was going to be away in the mountains for a while, although she had no idea where I was going or what I planned to do, and wished me well. "Go with God," she said as I left. She kept her true feelings well hidden.

On the first day of the Eigerwand climb, two weeks after I had said goodbye to my mother, I ate the bread and butter at the "Swallow's Nest" bivouac. At the third bivouac, at the upper edge of the "Spider", a point from which retreat was unthinkable, I jettisoned all my unnecessary kit, including the loaf, and clipped my climbing sack into the belay. I then slipped my feet inside the sack and spent the night trying to keep my frozen toes warm. That little rucksack saved my toes from frostbite. On our return to Grindelwald I gave all my equipment away, including my empty climbing sack, which I signed with my name. In 2001, the Grindelwald museum also discovered my old motorcycle, which had been found in a sorry state of repair in Hasliberg.

In 1998 a revised and expanded edition of *The White Spider* was published. The same year, almost half a century after it was originally published, *Seven Years in Tibet* made it into the New York Times' bestseller list again, its sales buoyed by the release of the film. I also received a letter from the President of the Alpine Club, Sir Chris Bonington, whom I had met during a conference of expedition leaders in Darjeeling, inviting me to come to London to give the after dinner speech at their AGM and club dinner. The opportunity to address the members of the oldest climbing club in the world meant a lot to me, and I was aware that in so doing I was carrying on the venerable tradition of fostering links with British climbers begun by Peter Aufschnaiter and the German Himalaya Foundation in the 1930's.

The event was held in the Great Hall of Saint Bartholomew's Hospital. I had brought along my old friend from the Liechtenstein publishing house, Hans Heinrich Count Coudenhove, who was well acquainted with the social etiquette of the British establishment. At the start of the proceedings, everyone stood, raised their glass and the President proposed a toast – "The Queen!" This was followed by the formal greetings and the usual agenda of an Annual General Meeting.

Since only the two hundred members of the club were present I spoke without a microphone, and for about an hour. Afterwards I had a very interesting chat to some of the members, including George Band, who had made the first ascent of Kangchenjunga in 1955. He was surprised to hear that the King of Sikkim had refused me permission to climb the mountain in 1951 and confirmed that he had indeed stopped short of the actual summit in accordance with the wishes of the local

Buddhists, for whom the mountain is sacred, as they regard it as the dwelling place of their god. I gave George a copy of the photograph of the precious death mask I had taken at Puntsoling Monastery, with the throne of the god, Kangchenjunga, in the background. The evening at the Alpine Club was a unique event, and was made all the more unforgettable for me by a remark made by Chris Bonington, who told me that he had never before witnessed any speaker being given a standing ovation by the club. For me, being accepted as an honorary member of the Alpine Club was equalled only by the honour of receiving of my Golden Humboldt Medal in Germany.

Around the same time I received another pleasant piece of news from the province of Carinthia, my place of birth. A new grammar school had been founded on the site of the ancient Canons Regular of St Augustine in the historic prince-bishopric of Gurk, and the school had decided to name their library after me. I presented the school with a large map of the world, on which I had marked my toughest expeditions, together with copies of the limited editions of *The White Spider* and *Seven Years in Tibet*, several handwritten Tibetan prayer books and a two-thousand-five-hundred-year-old Singhalese-Sanskrit text written on palm leaves. In 1993 I had also been named as a Fellow of the Austrian Academy of Sciences. To be honoured in such a way by the country of my birth meant a great deal to me, particularly in these difficult times. Other members of the Academy included Walter Thirring, whose father Hans I had met in Kitzbühel in 1952, and the internationally renowned neurologist and psychiatrist Victor Emil Frankl, the founder of logotherapy. Professor Frankl was a cultured man, whose work was the epitome of scientific rigour and moral authority, and he shared with me a deep and abiding love of the mountains. His death in the autumn of 1997 was a great loss for Austrian medical science.

In view of the wave of criticism that threatened to engulf me during this period of my life, I was heartened to receive offers to lecture in Garmisch and at the University of Munich. Several thousand people turned up to hear me speak and I was once again reminded of how the age of my audiences had changed over the years. Most of those attending the lectures were now several generations younger than me.

A further reminder of times past came in the shape of a letter I received from one Thomas H. Taylor. Mr Taylor wrote that although he had been only five years old at the time he could still clearly recall the day his father, Major Taylor, then the deputy commanding officer of the POW camp at Dehra Dun, had arrived home with the news that "some Germans" had escaped and had told he and his mother that they should stay indoors and should on no account attempt to challenge the escaped prisoners if they encountered them. Mr Taylor and his parents left India in 1947 and on Christmas Day 1953 – he was fourteen years old by then – he received a copy of my book, which he thoroughly enjoyed. To my delight, both Taylor and Shiff subsequently informed me that they would be pleased to join me for my ninetieth birthday celebrations in 2002.

In March 1999 I received a letter from Sidney Shiff in New York informing me that the elderly painter Balthus had expressed a wish to make my acquaintance. Syd had already published one book about Balthus and was working on his illustration of "Cosi fan tutte". He had sent Balthus the Limited Edition version of *Seven Years in Tibet* as a gift, and this had prompted the artist to request a meeting with me.

We were happy to agree to the meeting, since we knew how difficult it was to gain admittance to the great artist's refuge in the mountains. After a lengthy telephone conversation with Setzuko, his Japanese wife, the month of May saw us driving through the Gruyere Valley, an area of Switzerland untouched by tourism, en route for the little farming village of Rossinière, where Balthus lived. The Grand Chalet was situated right in the middle of the village. It was well named: certainly neither Carina nor I had ever seen a grander looking chalet! It was easy to imagine Goethe staying here during his tour of Switzerland in 1797, in the days when it was a famous hotel, and stabling his horses overnight in the old coach house, which Balthus had made into a studio in 1977. We admired the Baroque façade made from carved and painted wood – 113 windows in all, we later learned – and the beautiful cat that looked down on us from one of the window ledges. Written across the whole façade between the floors was the inscription: "May God bestow His

blessing on the owner of this place and on all those who come after..."
Since 1977 the owners had been Count Balthazar Klossowski de Rola
and Countess Setzuko and they had indeed been richly blessed.

A man of Chinese appearance helped us unload what little luggage
we had with us. Setzuko, the lady of the house, then approached with
tiny steps and introduced us to the helpful Dr. Liu. We were then shown
into the salon, where Balthus was sitting on an old sofa waiting for us,
and extended his hand in greeting. The old artist radiated serenity and
wisdom and both Carina and I were deeply moved by the occasion.
He asked me to sit next to him on the sofa, to his left, where he could
hear me better. The arrangement meant that Balthus himself sat centre
stage, commanding the attention of everyone in the room. Without
further ado, he directed the conversation to my relationship with the
Dalai Lama and the time I had spent in Lhasa, when Tibet had still
been a feudal state. There was a wonderful atmosphere in the room,
and everything seemed to happen in slow motion. Dr. Liu served tea
and omelettes, and Setzuko lit a cigarette for Balthus and placed it
between his fingers. There was no haste, no noise.

They spoke German, English and French. We agreed on English,
but Balthus would occasionally ask for the odd sentence to be translated
into French, the *lingua franca* at the Grand Chalet. After tea, we were
invited to rest awhile before meeting again for dinner and were shown
up a steep, creaking staircase to Room 22. It was the only room that
still bore a number, a throwback to the days when the Grand Chalet
was a hotel. Our room was beautifully decorated and furnished in the
English style, with a high bed and an old-fashioned bathtub mounted
on three Baroque-style feet. I looked out of one of the little windows
and saw the old coach house surrounded by tall trees. A willow was
displaying its first yellow-green leaves; it reminded me of the solitary
tree in Lhasa, the one the Tibetans called "the hair of Buddha." It was
a pleasure and a privilege to be guests in Balthus' house.

Later that evening, when we went down to the salon before dinner,
Balthus was wearing a beautiful, loose fitting robe that reminded me
of the clothing worn by a Zen priest. I presented him with a Tibetan
good luck scarf that had been blessed by the Dalai Lama and he asked
me to explain the symbols that were woven into the fabric. Setzuko

then requested that I repeat the *kata* ritual with her. She was wearing a sumptuous evening kimono and the grace with which she accepted the proffered *kata* reminded me of one of Tsarong's daughters in Lhasa. Once again, the conversation turned to my time in Tibet. Balthus wanted to know all about my friendship with the Dalai Lama and I tried to explain how important that relationship was to me. We both agreed, however, that the most important thing in our lives was the congenial relationship we had with our wives, Setzuko and Carina. We also spoke about reincarnation, and Balthus told me that he wished to be born again as a cat. As we talked Mitsou, one of Balthus' splendid Persian cats, rubbed against his leg and the old artist gently stroked its silky-soft coat.

Dr. Lui announced that dinner was served, and helped Balthus to get up. As we went into the dining room, Balthus stopped, pointed to a bronze sculpture and told us that it had been given to him by his friend Giacometti. Dinner was a pleasant and friendly affair. Dr. Liu served green asparagus in a delicious sauce, followed by a rice dish with fresh vegetables and salad. Setzuko helped her husband unobtrusively and passed him a glass of red wine as the conversation continued unabated. The crowning glory of the meal was the dessert: a *bombe glacée* in the shape of a snow covered mountain, presented to me as a special surprise by Bathus' Asian chef. Over a carafe of red wine, our hosts asked me many pertinent questions, all of which I was happy to answer. It was obvious that Balthus was thoroughly enjoying the fact that, for once, it was he who was asking the questions.

Both Carina and I thoroughly enjoyed the long evening, and with so much to mull over we found it hard to get to sleep. We lay awake for a while, counting our blessings and thinking about how fortunate we were that the life we led afforded us the opportunity to meet people like Balthus.

In the morning we were given a guided tour of the Grand Chalet. We ended up in the room with the open fire, to which Balthus would retreat when he wanted a little peace and quiet. There was a large, flat bed covered in soft cushions and blankets in front of the window, and Setzuko told us about the time she had found her husband lying there motionless with his eyes tightly shut. She had spoken softly to him but still he had not moved. After a while, he had squinted at her through half opened eyes, blinked at the light and said "I heard you, but I could not answer. I was talking to God. Everything was very bright. I was blinded by His light."

We knew from books and interviews that Balthus only allowed his closest friends to enter his studio, so we had not even mentioned it. Shortly before our departure, however, Setzuko told us that Balthus was waiting for us in his studio and asked us to follow her. We went out of the Grand Chalet, crossed a narrow little lane and entered the large coach house. Balthus was sitting in a battered old armchair and asked me to take a seat on a chair next to him. Before us was a large easel with a painting of a landscape. Other unfinished works stood on easels around the studio. For several minutes we did not speak. It was not an awkward silence; we were simply in awe of the place, this high altar of the great artist. After while, I broke the silence with the comment that the atmosphere in the studio was like a temple. Balthus softly replied that an Irish priest had once told him that this was where he would like to pray.

Balthus had a tape recorder next to his chair and he told me that he liked to listen to Mozart while he worked. We agreed that everyone needed a role model, that every artist, every scientist and every explorer simply built upon the achievements of their predecessors, and I asked Balthus who had been his main artistic influences. He told me that as a young man he had practised by copying works by Piero della Francesca, Cèzanne and Poussin.

The diffuse light that radiated through the north-facing window softened Balthus' striking features. I took one last photograph, and then it was time to say goodbye. Setzuko and Carina had already left the studio. Balthus held both of my hands in his still powerful grip and we looked at each other wordlessly for a moment. Perhaps we understood each other so well because, despite our differing backgrounds and the different paths we had taken, we were both old men who had fulfilled their childhood dreams. "Come back soon," he said, and I walked slowly to the door of the studio. As I turned to take one last look, he raised his hand in a last farewell gesture.

Setzuko and Carina were waiting for me under the big lime tree in the courtyard. We said our goodbyes and wished them both good health. We were never to see them both again. On Sunday, 18th February 2001, Balthus fell asleep for the last time. The old artist had chosen to be conveyed to his last resting place in the traditional hearse of the poor rural peasant, and on 24th February his coffin was carried to the cemetery in a humble horse-drawn cart.

HOMECOMING

During my travels I have climbed mountains on every continent, visited the sources of all of the world's great rivers and explored the three largest islands on our Earth. I have experienced life in both the Palaeolithic and Neolithic eras, an achievement that is now unlikely to be repeated. After treading these remote and distant paths, I finally returned to my birthplace of Hüttenberg where, like the victorious marathon runners of old, I enjoy the recognition and respect my achievements have brought. I was made an honorary citizen of the district of Hüttenberg, where custom dictates that, instead of the olive branch of Ancient Greece, I should receive a lifetime's supply of firewood and fresh water. When you have seen the peasant farmers of the Himalaya carrying drums of foul-smelling petroleum up to their hill farms to power their stoves and witnessed how the women of Africa walk for many hours to fetch water from the nearest oasis, you know that such gifts are to be appreciated.

I left home at an early age, conscious of the fact that my desire to live the life of the adventurer and explorer meant I could not stay in my little village. Like the Chinese proverb says, every great journey begins with one small step, and for me leaving home was that first step. Andre Gide once said, "Man can not discover new oceans unless he has the courage to lose sight of the shore." The higher you climb, the harder it gets; with every metre the view becomes more extensive, yet even from the summit of an eight thousand metre mountain you can only see a tiny fraction of this world of ours. It was this realisation, I believe, that took me from being a passionate extreme mountaineer to a passionate explorer and led me out into a bigger, wider world. My life has been enriched by these adventures; they were born of a desire to explore and a thirst for knowledge and they took me to some of the remotest regions on the planet. It was often the case that even before I had achieved my objective, the idea for a new one had already begun to form in my mind. At no stage did I rest on my laurels, content with what I had already achieved.

The cup is now full, and I no longer feel the need to push myself on arduous expeditions in order to experience new things. Instead, I would like to pass on the sum total of my experiences to others. I am in no way at odds with my decision to retire, as it were, from exploration and expeditions; my physical strength is waning and no longer allows me to realise ambitious plans. Although my short term memory is also failing, my long term memory is still good, and this, together with my journals, has been of great help in compiling this autobiography. During my expeditions, the lack of distractions created the ideal conditions for me to observe what went on around me and record my observations. Even today, I do not find it difficult to recall in detail events that occurred long ago, and this makes it easier for me to describe my earlier expeditions than my later experiences. In life, as in climbing, I have often needed the shoulders of my friends for support. As young boys, we used to steal cherries from a neighbour's garden; one of us would cup his hands and the other would clamber up and stand on his shoulders in order to reach the first branches of the cherry tree. Many years later, when working on this book, I was grateful for the help and support of our good friends, the Paulinis.

I have already written about my most serious illnesses, so all that remains is to mention the many and various insect bites, injuries and broken bones – some twenty in all – that I have suffered over the years as an inevitable consequence of my close encounters with the immutable forces of nature.

I have spent more than a tenth of my life at altitudes of between four and six thousand metres, using butter or bacon fat to protect my skin from the sun – precisely the wrong thing to do, I am told. The Graz dermatologist Helmut Kerl, who treats me several times a year, once remarked that never in the course of his long professional life had he seen skin more damaged by the sun than mine. The ancient Persians used to say that the best thing you can bring back home with you from a trip is a healthy skin, something I never quite managed to achieve – mine had to be rescued by a dermatologist. Nor did I ever use sunglasses to protect my eyes, although I once traded a sewing kit for a Tibetan nomad's sunshade made from the hair of a yak's tail, which did provide some relief.

On two occasions, when visiting King Leopold, I had the pleasure of meeting the famous heart surgeon Michael de Bakey, who told me that the secret to a healthy life was to refrain from smoking and watch your weight. I have always followed this principle and with the benefit of hindsight I can now say that, despite all the injuries, I have been fortunate enough to remain fit and healthy. I still begin each day with the same set of exercises I have done for the past twenty-five years: leg-raises to strengthen my stomach muscles, twenty squats in front of the open window, followed by twenty arm curls with a one kilo dumbbell in each hand and a set of twenty-second isometric arm raises with each arm. As a keen golfer, I also find exercises and stretches to practice my swing very useful, and often incorporate them into my morning routine. After every exercise, I shake out and relax my muscles. All in all, my regime comprises about a hundred individual movements and takes around eight minutes to complete. To finish the workout I put my socks on by standing on one leg, taking great care nowadays to avoid losing my balance and falling onto dangerous objects like red-hot metal radiators. "Brain food" is also important – fish and vitamins that stimulate the mind and the nervous system. Although I eat plenty of fresh fruit and vegetables, I also take additional vitamin supplements. Since I feel healthy, I believe in their beneficial effect.

As with any physical activity, one should never overdo this morning exercise regime; it should be done for a purpose and it should be fun – that way, a successful outcome is guaranteed. Success comes to those who recognise their limits and apply their skills appropriately, and in critical situations those who survive are those who still have reserves of strength to call upon. On difficult expeditions, it is Nature alone who decides whether one will achieve one's objectives and return safe and sound.

When I signed up for Sport Studies in addition to Geography at the University of Graz in 1933, the world of sports was a very different one. Nowadays, it has all become big business, and the prize monies at stake are huge. Athletes, managers and trainers all have their price and are traded like consumer goods, and when a particular city or country is named as the host for a large sporting event, political and economic factors often take precedence over sporting ones. In spite of the deployment of specialists in drugs and doping, and the random tests that are conducted, some unscrupulous athletes still manage to slip through the net, and it is not unusual to hear of medals being revoked or to see once shapely women appearing at competitions with distinctively masculine-looking muscles.

The public's love of sport fills the stadiums and provides the television companies with huge viewing figures. This popularity is nothing new; four hundred years before Christ, the Ancient Greeks were already staging pentathlons and running events, the winners of which received an olive branch and exemption from paying taxes for the duration of the lives. In Roman times the people demanded *panem et circenses* – literally "bread and circuses", a satirical phrase coined by Juvenal to describe the distribution of free food and the violent gladiatorial contests held in the Coliseum that the government used to pacify its citizens. I watch television broadcasts of sporting events with great interest and admire the courage of the skiers who hurtle down those steep mountainsides at speeds of a hundred and forty kilometres an hour and the unbelievable performances of the gymnasts on their apparatus. Although I once competed to a high standard myself, and have the scars to prove it, I find it better to refrain from making nostalgic observations or comparisons.

One of the more pleasing developments in sport has been the increased popularity of mass-participation events, which are held all over the world in both summer and winter and attract millions of competitors, who have trained assiduously for the chance to run a marathon in Rome or New York and feel part of one big sporting community. I have taken part in many such events, including the Kitzbühel Ski Marathon and the Wasa Ski Race in Sweden, and have fond memories of them all.

Peak physical performance is by no means the zenith of one's life, however; that point is only attained when ambition and restlessness give way to patience and thoughtfulness. At the high point of my active life there were still areas of the world that were blank on the map; those were the golden years of geographical field research. I have experienced many countries during transitional phases of their history when it was easier to obtain ethnological artefacts and build collections. Yet even today, when every river and every mountain is documented on NASA's maps, the people in the huts, their souls and their rituals can never be captured by a satellite image; those things remain for the explorer to discover.

These days, having come to terms with my decision to abstain from extended trips and expeditions, I enjoy my life in a different way. I no longer feel the need to travel to foreign places, since the sun, the moon and the clouds are the same for everyone. I believe that it is our duty to look after this planet of ours, in the knowledge that the animals and plants, mountains and oceans require our protection. I do not wish to spend my last years in eternal spring on a South Sea island; I would rather spend them here at our home in Carinthia, where the seasonal changes dictate the rhythm of life and I am surrounded by the mementos of my adventures.

When I sit at my writing desk, wherever I look I see objects that bring me pleasure. The desk itself is three hundred years old and once stood in an English monastery; it is made from solid oak and measures two and a half metres in length, but is just seventy centimetres deep, as the monks only ever worked one to a desk to avoid distractions. My dictionaries and reference works are arranged to each side, with heavy bronze statues serving as bookends – one of an eagle, my favourite creature during the ambitious years of my youth, and one of an odd-looking owl, the symbol of my first publisher, Ullstein, and the symbol of wisdom since time immemorial. The rest of the clutter on my writing desk is, with the best will in the world, indescribable, and the bare wooden floor of my study is piled high with books and manuscripts. There is order in the chaos, however, and it is only by not tidying up that I can find what I am looking for at a moment's notice.

The window ledge is as broad as my desk and on it I keep only those things that have been my lifetime companions: amulets and talismans; a magical carved ivory Bantu figurine that I brought back from the Congo; a set of cross-hairs with medicinal properties from the God-King's private physician; and, of course, the little statue of Tsepame, the Buddha of Long Life, that was given to me forty years ago by my friend the Dalai Lama. Then there are the fossils and rare crystals, and a small stone from the summit of Mount Everest that a friend of mine once gave me. None of these sentimental objects on my window ledge are very tall, so I have an undisturbed view of the nearby Karawankan Mountains and the Julian Alps.

I am often asked which of the phases of my life was the most interesting and most joyful. Whenever I think about this, I always come back to Tibet. It was a feudal system, within which the monks and a few powerful aristocrats ruled as if in an oligarchy; there was no talk of democracy. Yet everyone was happy and contented; even the beggars had a pleasant life. The land of Tibet was economically independent, and this sometimes led to arrogant proclamations, yet by modern standards it was a poor country with only a tiny gross national product. The Tibetan people's unity and self-determination stemmed not from economic wealth but from their unshakeable beliefs and the certainty of reincarnation. Huge numbers of nomads and peasants would stream into Lhasa for the great religious festivals, where they would admire the splendour of the ruling elite with no hint of envy.

The most significant encounter of my life, and the one that was to have the greatest influence on me, was without doubt my meeting with the 14th Dalai Lama. After escaping from prison camp I made my way to the "forbidden city" of Lhasa where, despite the fact that I was a complete unknown, I became a friend and tutor to the young God-King. It is a friendship that has lasted my entire life. Over the years my pupil has become the teacher, preaching tolerance and sympathy to the whole world. In 1989 he received the Nobel Peace Prize for his peaceful struggle for the liberation of Tibet. As I write this, I read in the newspapers that according to a representative poll the Dalai Lama is considered to be the wisest living person. He came to Austria in the autumn of 2006 to teach at the Graz Kalachakra for World Peace, and was awarded the Human Rights Prize at the University of Graz.

Yet there is no single experience that has shaped my life, and each of my adventures was, at the time, the best. The two-thousand-year-old culture of the Tibetans means just as much to me as the hospitality extended in the kraal of an African tribe, the dismissive attitude of the Stone Age Papuans or the pride of the Nilotes of the Upper Nile; it is their culture and it deserves our respect. My attitude towards foreign cultures was always characterised by my desire to take the differences between us seriously. Violence has always been an alien concept to me, and not once in my life have I ever resorted to it. On expeditions, I never carried a weapon, nor did I ever fire a shot.

People sometimes ask me which books I would take with me if I were going to a remote island. I must admit that my choice of "desert island literature" has changed considerably over the years. At this stage of my long life, my selection would have to include the *Bible*, with Cervantes' *Don Quixote* providing a little light relief and alternative food for thought. I would also take Ovid's *Metamorphosis*, which lies on my bedside table, for the simple reason that it contains one of the most beautiful love stories ever written. In it, Zeus offers to grant Philemon and Baucis any wish they might have. Carina and I agree that we would ask the Gods for the same thing – to spend the rest of our lives together. I thank Carina for her unstinting support during my work on this book.

I would also pack my copy of *Kim*, by my favourite author Rudyard Kipling, as it is a story about ordinary people and is set in a part of the world that I remember with great affection. My copy is as old as I am and although it is 414 pages long and includes eight engravings, it weighs only two hundred grams. It is printed on silk paper with gilt edging and bound in morocco leather, is only one centimetre in thickness and can be slipped easily into a coat pocket. An exemplary book, it was first published in paperback in 1908 and is still regarded as one of the great classics of world literature. The previous owner of my copy had obviously treated it with great care, but it is now dog-eared and full of my own notes and annotations, which is another bad habit of mine.

Now that the work on my autobiography is almost complete, I should perhaps take a little time to reflect on the results of the experiences I have had. A few years ago I attempted to defend myself and protest against the untruths that the newspapers had written about me. I am now in my ninetieth year, and whilst I can not say that I have become immune to such criticism, it no longer distresses me.

It is a great source of joy and contentment for me when young people send me essays they have written and ask me for my opinion on them, or when they follow my tracks to the furthest corners of the Earth and send me postcards to thank me for showing them the way. While making a television documentary in Lhasa, an Austrian film team was once asked by a Tibetan "Is Heinrich Harrer still alive?" That question was reward enough for me.

When I look back on my long life, I do so with gratitude. I was fortunate enough to be able to return to the place where I was born; like everyone else, the ties that bind me to my homeland are strong. The people of the Dani tribe in Papua New Guinea prefer to remain in the barren mountains and refuse to move to the more fertile land of the coastal region, while the Dajaks of Borneo reacted aggressively when attempts were made to relocate them to an island in the South Pacific. In the spring of 2002, after the eruption of Nyiragonga, the Hutu and Tutsi, who had always lived close to this active volcano, returned to the devastated town of Goma while the ash-filled rain was still falling. It was a typical reaction. Several years ago, during a trip to Washington, I went to the cinema to watch the film "E.T. – the Extra Terrestrial." The cute little space creature's words "I want to go home" were very moving and might equally be applied to the Dalai Lama, to the exiled Tibetans and to all the people in the world who are unable to live in their homeland.

I have returned home. My house is built on the ancient rocks that lie beneath our small ore-mining community, where the rainwater seeps away slowly. The little springs provide only a meagre supply of drinking water, but the flow is as consistent and reliable as the people of the village where I was born.

The course of my life has been like the course of a river. It began as a modest trickle, and was joined by many more small rivulets to form a stream that cascaded down the steep mountainside to the river. As the river gathered pace and power, sharp-edged chunks of rock were formed into smooth boulders and here, like the river, my life progressed more easily. At the last set of rapids, salmon and trout swam upstream, battling against the flow, before the river left the mountains and ran into an estuary on the wide plains below. Here the clear waters of the tributary were finally absorbed by the greater body of the water, and the river lost its identity. At this point, the force of the water was no longer great enough to shift whole boulders, but the absence of dams allowed the great river to meander down, slowly and inexorably, through pleasant groves, where fish leapt and colourful birds twittered as they fed their young in the safe nesting places of the trees that lined the banks.

After a while, the river reached the first large town. Here, it had new problems to contend with, but on its long journey through the continent, the river had learned to cope with many things. Finally, the great river flowed into the sea, where it had room to expand. The surface of the water evaporated in the heat of the sun, and clouds were formed. Water fell as rain and snow on the mountains; the circle was complete.

For the first time in my life, I can no longer plan ahead as I once used to do. Instead, I have learned to enjoy each day as a gift and I await the inevitable with a feeling of calm and trust.

CHRONOLOGY OF IMPORTANT EXPEDITIONS AND TRIPS

1938	First ascent of the North Face of the Eiger
1939	Nanga Parbat Diamir Face Reconnaissance Expedition
1944-51	Tibet
1953	Andes and Amazon. First ascent of Ausangate
1954-55	Alaska. First ascents of Mount Hunter, Mount Deborah and Mount Drum
1957	Congo, Ruwenzori
1962	New Guinea. First north-south traverse of the island; 31 first ascents in the Carstenz Range; discovery of Jalime, the source of the stone axes
1964	Nepal
1966	Amazon, the Xingu Indians, Suriname
1968	World trip.
1969	French Guyana
1970	Greenland
1971	Sudan
1972	Borneo, north-south traverse
1973	Nepal
1974	Manipur, India, Ladakh, Nepal
1975	Andaman Islands
1976	Ladakh
1977	Zaire, Ruwenzori, Uganda and Kenya
1978	Sikkim
1979	Sikkim, Ladakh, India
1980	Sikkim and Bhutan
1981	Nepal
1982	Tibet, Bhutan
1983	Bhutan
1985	Bhutan
1986	Bhutan
1988	Bhutan
1991	Ladakh
1996	Bhutan

INDEX